The Early Days of Sociolinguistics

Memories and Reflections

Reprint

SIL International
Publications in Language Use and Education 5

Publications in Language Use and Education is a serial publication of SIL International. The series began as a venue for works covering a broad range of topics in sociolinguistics and has been expanded to include a broad range of topics in education, including mother tongue literacy multilingual education, and informal education. While most volumes are authored by members of SIL, suitable works by others will also form part of the series.

Volume Editor
Bonnie Brown

Series Editor
M. Paul Lewis

Associate Editor
Gloria E. Kindell

Production Staff
Laurie Nelson, Production Manager
Margaret González, Compositor
Hazel Shorey, Graphic Arts
Barbara Alber, Graphic Arts (Reprint)

The Early Days of Sociolinguistics

Memories and Reflections

Reprint

Christina Bratt Paulston and G. Richard Tucker
Editors

SIL International
Dallas, Texas

© 2010 by SIL International
Library of Congress Catalog No: 2010927135
ISBN: 978-1-55671-253-1
ISSN: 1545-0074

Printed in the United States of America
All Rights Reserved

No part of this publication may be reproduced, stored in a retrieval system, or transmitted in any form or by any means—electronic, mechanical, photocopy, recording, or otherwise—without the express permission of the Summer Institute of Linguistics, with the exception of brief excerpts in journal articles or reviews.

This book appeared in 1997 as volume 2 in the Publications in Sociolinguistics series.

Copies of this and other publications of the Summer Institute of Linguistics may be obtained from

International Academic Bookstore
SIL International
7500 W. Camp Wisdom Road
Dallas, TX 75236-5699

Voice: 972-708-7404
Fax: 972-708-7363
E-mail: academic_books@sil.org
Internet: http://www.ethnologue.com

To Charles E. Ferguson whose scholarship and
friendship over the years have inspired so many of us

Contents

Abbreviations xi

Prologue

Introduction 3
   Christina Bratt Paulston

A Brief History of American Sociolinguistics 11
   Roger W. Shuy

Pioneers

Development of Sociolinguistics in India 35
   E. Annamalai

Sociolinguistics: A Personal View 43
   Basil Bernstein

Reminiscences: Beginnings of Sociolinguistics 53
   William Bright

The Development of Sociolinguistics 61
   Susan Ervin-Tripp

History of Sociolinguistics 77
   Interview with Charles Ferguson

Bloomington, Summer 1964: The Birth of American
Sociolinguistics 87
   Joshua A. Fishman

Memories 97
   Paul Friedrich

Origins and Milestones 101
    Allen Day Grimshaw

Some Comments on the Origin and Development of
Sociolinguistics 113
    John Gumperz

History and Development of Sociolinguistics 121
    Dell Hymes

The [R]Evolution of Sociolinguistics 131
    Björn H. Jernudd

Sociolinguistics: Birth of a Revolution 139
    Rolf Kjolseth

Sociolinguistic Patterns 147
    William Labov

Personal Views on the Beginnings of Sociolinguistics ... 151
    Wallace E. Lambert

Early Developments in Sociolinguistics 159
    Stanley Lieberson

Another Time 171
    John Macnamara

Contribution to the History of Sociolinguistics: Origins and
Development of the Rouen School 177
    J. B. Marcellesi

On Safari with Sociolinguistics 189
    Carol Myers-Scotton

Sociolinguistics: Some Other Traditions 201
    Jiří V. Neustupný

A Note on Holism 211
    Kenneth L. Pike

Notes on the Development of Sociolinguistics 213
    Edgar Polomé

Beginnings of Sociolinguistics in the Philippines 217
    Bonifacio P. Sibayan

From Sociolinguistics to the Anthropology of Language .. 225
    Andrée Tabouret-Keller

Contents

Journal Editors

Reflections about (or Prompted by) *International Journal of the Sociology of Language (IJSL)* 237
   Joshua A. Fishman

Language in Society 243
   Dell Hymes

Language as a Social Phenomenon: A Perspective on the Emergence of Sociolinguistics. 247
   Humphrey Tonkin

Early Institutional Supporters for the New Field

Center for Applied Linguistics: Interview with Ralph C. Troike 255
   Christina Bratt Paulston

Center for International Education, U.S. Department of Education: The Evolution of Sociolinguistics 263
   Dick Thompson

Ford Foundation: Personal Reflection 271
   Mel Fox

International Centre for Research on Bilingualism: The Sociolinguistics of Language Contact. 273
   William Francis Mackey

Summer Institute of Linguistics: What Does SIL Have to do with Sociolinguistics? 279
   Gloria E. Kindell

The Ethnologue, Language Surveys, and Sociolinguistics 285
   Barbara F. Grimes

Remembrances

In Memoriam: Einar Haugen 297
   Christina Bratt Paulston

Heinz Kloss and the Study of Language in Society 301
   William F. Mackey and Grant D. McConnell

Uriel Weinreich (1926–1967): A Sociolinguistic Appreciation 307
   Joshua A. Fishman

Epilogue

The Development of Sociolinguistics as a Field of Study:
Concluding Observations 317
   G. Richard Tucker

References 325

Abbreviations

AA	American Anthropologist
AAA	American Anthropological Association
ACLS	American Council of Learned Societies
AILA	Association Internationale de Linguistique Appliquée
CAL	Center for Applied Linguistics
CASBS	Center for Advanced Study in the Behavioral Sciences
CIIL	Central Institute of Indian Languages
CIRAL	Centre International de Recherche en Aménagement Linguistique
CIRB	Centre International de Recherche sur le Bilinguisme
CNRS	Centre National de la Recherche Scientifique
COS	Committee on Sociolinguistics
EC	European Community
FLAS	Foreign Language and Area Studies
FNSP	Fondation Nationale des Sciences Politique
FRG	Federal Republic of Germany
FSI	Foreign Service Institute
GAO	General Accounting Office
GRECO	Sociolinguistic Covariance Research Group
HEW	Health, Education, and Welfare
ICRB	International Center for Research on Bilingualism
ICS	Institute of Comparative Research
IJAL	International Journal of American Linguistics
IJSL	International Journal of the Sociology of Language
IRAL	International Review of Applied Linguistics in Language Teaching
ISA	International Sociological Association

IURCAFL	Indiana University Research Center in Anthropology, Folklore, and Linguistics
LAD	Language Acquisition Device
LBRL	Language Behavior Research Laboratory
LPDN	Language Problems of Developing Nations
LPLP	Language Problems and Language Planning
LSA	Linguistic Society of America
LSI	Linguistic Survey of India
NDEA	National Defense Education Act
NEH	National Endowment for the Humanities
NIE	National Institutes of Education
NIH	National Institutes of Health
NOL	Notes on Linguistics
NSF	National Science Foundation
PCLS	Philippine Center for Language Studies
PUF	Publication of the University of France
RCS	Research Committee on Sociolinguistics
SELAF	Société d'Études Linguistiques et Anthropologiques de France
SIL	Summer Institute of Linguistics
SLOPE	Second Language Oral Proficiency Evaluation
SRT	Sentence Repetition Test
SSRC	Social Science Research Council
TESOL	Teachers of English to Speakers of Other Languages
TG	Transformational Grammar
UCLA	University of California at Los Angeles
UTA	University of Texas at Arlington
YIVO	Yiddish Scientific Institute

Prologue

Introduction

Christina Bratt Paulston

Christina Bratt Paulston is professor of linguistics, director of the English Language Institute, and former chair (1974–1989) of the Department of Linguistics, University of Pittsburgh. She has lectured and done fieldwork around the world in such places as Azerbaijan, India, Peru, Tanzania, and Spain, among others. She has published in the fields of language teaching, teacher training, language planning, bilingual education, and sociolinguistics. She was President of International TESOL in 1976 and trustee of the Center for Applied Linguistics from 1976 to 1981.

Almost from the earliest written records, we have evidence of the study of language. We have bilingual clay tablets in cuneiform, from the Sumerian empire some four thousand years ago. The prophet Daniel studied to become a bilingual scribe at the court of Nebuchadnezzar over two thousand years ago. The Greeks and Romans prized the study of rhetoric as the fundamental relation between thought and language and the knowledge of it as the sign of a cultured man. The Chomskyan revolution in linguistics is often cited as an archetype of Kuhnian scientific revolutions. Most often these endeavors in the study of language are basically descriptive, whether prescriptively so or not.

It is fair to say also that in the beginning much of sociolinguistic work was an attempt at better description. Were a man to stand on a street corner and utter all and only the grammatical sentences of English, he would likely be institutionalized, Dell Hymes has remarked and so posited the notion of communicative competence—as a counter concept to Chomsky's linguistic competence—where appropriateness of language use cannot be divorced from mere linguistic form. In this book, we attempt to document and recount the beginnings of sociolinguistics as a new endeavor in the age-old study of language and to do so in the very own words of the participants who helped form it.

We speak throughout of sociolinguistics. In the beginning, there were two labels—sociolinguistics and the sociology of language—for the same phenomenon, the intersection and interaction of language and society, and these two phrases were used interchangeably (e.g., Kjolseth 1972) as we do here.[1] Eventually a distinction came to be made (e.g., Bright's *International Encyclopedia of Linguistics* (1992) with its two separate entries) where the major issues are differences in data, concepts, methods and questions (Grimshaw 1987:10). As an oversimplification, one might say that while sociolinguistics is mainly concerned with an increased and wider description of language (and undertaken primarily by linguists and anthropologists), the sociology of language is concerned with explanation and prediction of language phenomena in society at the group level (and done mainly by social scientists as well as by a few linguists). But in the inception no difference was made nor do we intend any here.

Our intent has not been a history of linguistic thought but rather an account of the genesis of sociolinguistics, of a new angle in the study of language; for a differing design, see Lepschy's "Introduction" to his *History of Linguistics* (1994) or Murray's Chapter 1 "The Sociological Study of Science" (1983) or, in a later version, "Theory Groups in Science" (1994).[2] But like Lepschy, we have been interested in "a view from within" (1994:vii) and so have borrowed an approach from oral history to document the major scholars' own view of what led to the rise of this new field of study; they provide here a multifaceted view of the development of sociolinguistics. We make no attempt at assessment or analysis of ideas, and all the weaknesses of oral history are of course also present here, individual perception and distortion of facts, but the book undeniably presents the view of the major participants as they in hindsight experienced it.

Our first task was to identify these major participants. We contacted five scholars, William Bright, Susan Ervin-Tripp, Joshua Fishman, John Gumperz, and Dell Hymes (actually Einar Haugen as well but in his own judgment, he was then too old to participate, requiescat in pace), told them of our project, and asked for judgment and advice. With their encouragement, we then compiled a list of key individuals. Our criteria for inclusion were loose but rather exclusive. They had to be scholars of the very first generation of

---

[1]This is not quite correct, see Polomé (this volume). The expression "Sociologie du Langage" had been used in Europe much earlier than the time frame, roughly late fifties—sixties and spilling into the early seventies, covered in this volume, but nevertheless Professor Polomé seems to intend no distinction either.

[2]See also Ervin-Tripp 1974; Koerner 1991; or Ammon, Dittmar, and Mattheier, eds. 1987:379–469.

Introduction

sociolinguists who themselves had never heard the word in their own training, less read anything under that rubric; they had to have taken part in the creation of the field. They also had to have had a lasting influence on its development, as evidenced by their own publications, in anthologies and in the reference lists of present day publications and journals. We tried to make sure that we had representatives from the various disciplines which have contributed to sociolinguistics: primarily anthropology, linguistics, sociology, and social psychology.

We were concerned that most of the scholars were Americans and looked diligently for other participants. Certainly the Russians developed their own field of sociology of language which, if Švejcer and Nikol'skij's "first textbook on sociolinguistics in Soviet linguistic literature (1986:vii)" is representative, is almost exclusively—and not surprisingly—about multilingualism, language planning, and standard languages; even so, half of their discussion and bibliography refer to American sources. Rarely are Russian sources cited in western literature—even in the entry "Language and Society from a Marxist Point of View" in *Sociolinguistics: An International Handbook of the Science of Language and Society* (Marcellesi and Elimam 1987:443) there are *no* Russian entries besides Lenin and Stalin, probably a matter of access to the language rather than lack of scholarly compatibility, but the fact remains: the only major initial school of thought on language and society besides the U.S.A. is not influential in present day work. We therefore did not attempt to contact any Russians.

We were not overly concerned about gender representation but could not help but notice the appalling dearth of women in the early days of sociolinguistics. We would like to at least note that today that dearth is rectified, and indeed, women primarily have contributed their own brand of subspecialization, language and gender studies, which were lacking in the early days.

We have also tried to include some representatives of major organizations like the Center for Applied Linguistics, the Ford Foundation, the Summer Institute of Linguistics, and the U.S. Department of Education. Some were influential through their own scholarly work, others served to encourage and support such work. One does not have to be cynical to note that the massive availability of funding was a major contributing factor for the flourishing of sociolinguistics in the U.S.A.

Given our selection, we contacted the participants with an invitation and a list of questions which we suggested they might want to consider if germane. These were the questions:

1. Please try to identify for us a critical milestone—a conference, a publication, an event (of your own or of someone else's)—that marks for you the beginning of "modern sociolinguistics." What was important about this milestone? Did you sense at the time that this was a "landmark" event, or has it only been in retrospect that this particular activity has grown in importance?

2. Please characterize for us the intellectual, social, and economic "climate" of the times. What was it about the period that made the launching of this field possible/necessary/desirable?

3. What were the major intellectual concerns and questions which motivated the early work in this area? What disciplines would you say contributed to the formation of this area? In what ways? What was it about this field that attracted your, and others', interest?

4. In terms of your own early research in the area, did you consider it to be interdisciplinary? Did you engage in joint research with colleagues from other fields? Did you attempt to formally train yourself in a discipline other than that in which you received your doctorate?

5. Would you characterize the early work as being "problem driven" or "theory driven?"

6. If you had to identify one or a small group of individuals with whom you associate the launching of this field, who would that be? Who were the "major players" in the early days? How did they see their work in relation to other scholars in collateral fields? Tell us a bit about the "communication networks" that were prevalent then.

7. Tell us a bit about your own work. How do you see *your* research/writing as having contributed to the shaping of the field? Is there one contribution (article, book, talk, etc.) in particular of your own that stands out in your mind as the "critical" contribution that you made to the shaping of the field? If you were to go back and "revisit" that work today, how would you evaluate it?

8. When did you first give a course in this area? At what institution were you teaching? How did the course get proposed/approved/selected by students in the years when the area as such was little known? Was there any interdepartmental interest in the course? Were there any other faculty members on the campus that shared your interest?

Introduction

9. Tell us a little bit about the expectation and aspirations of those who were working in this "new domain" in the 1960s and 1970s. What was it that you/they hoped to accomplish? Was that goal, in fact, realized? How is the field different today from the way it was in the early days?...in terms of theoretical underpinnings?...in terms of research approaches?...in terms of the "mix" of scholars working in the area?...in terms of the motivating questions?

10. When did you regularly start to attend meetings/seminars/colloquia in order to maximize interaction with other colleagues who had sociolinguistic interests?...were these on your own campus?...elsewhere?...do you remember who the "key" individuals were in convening these meetings?

11. If you had to identify the single most important publication that helped to provide definition and visibility for the field, what would that be?...what do you believe are the most important outlets for scholarly communication in the field today?

12. Do the same questions still motivate work in this field today?...or have the questions and the research paradigms shifted?...in what ways?

13. From your own perspective, was this field largely of (North) American impetus and origin? If not, who were some of the key international players?

14. Were there any funding agencies/foundation or government people that you remember as being particularly central to the launching of this field? ...who/which? Are these same agencies central to the field today? Is there more (or less) support available today for work in this area?

15. Is there any consensus (or perhaps mythology) about who specifically was awarded the first doctorate in the field called "sociolinguistics?"

16. What do you see as the prognosis for this field? Is it as vibrant and vital today as it was a quarter of a century ago? What do you see as the most pressing issues for the field? What do you see as the likely future "practical" concerns for the field?...the likely "theoretical" concerns?

There are a few glaring omissions of writers in the final table of contents. Besides only a few refusals, there were a few promises and procrastinations. The most obvious omission is that of William Labov whose name is to many synonymous with sociolinguistics. Labov has, however, from the very beginning argued against the need of a special field such as sociolinguistics:

> In the past few years, there has been considerable programmatical discussion of *sociolinguistics* at various meetings and symposia. If this term refers to the use of data from the speech community to solve problems of linguistic theory, then I would agree that it applies to the research described here. But *sociolinguistics* is more frequently used to suggest a new interdisciplinary field—the comprehensive description of the relation of language and society. This seems to me an unfortunate notion, foreshadowing a long series of purely descriptive studies with little bearing on the central theoretical problems of linguistics or of sociology. (Labov 1966:v)

He was invited to participate but, because of other pressing engagements, declined the invitation.

Another glaring omission is that of M. A. K. Halliday who has from the very beginning argued for the need of sociolinguistics as a more efficient kind of linguistics, in an approach reminiscent of Labov's:

> We shall not come to understand the nature of language if we pursue only the kinds of questions about language that are formulated by linguists. For linguists, language is object—linguistics is defined, as Saussure and his contemporaries so often felt the need to affirm, by the fact that it has language as its object of study; whereas for others, language is an instrument, a means of illuminating questions about something else. This is a valid and important distinction. But it is a distinction of goals, not one of scope. In the walled gardens in which the disciplines have been sheltered since the early years of this century, each has claimed the right to determine not only what questions it is asking but also what it will take into account in answering them; and in linguistics, this leads to the construction of elegant self-contained systems that are of only limited application to any real issues—since the objects themselves have no such boundary walls. We have to take account of the questions that are raised by others; not simply out of a sense of the social accountability of the discipline (though that would be reason enough), but also out of sheer self-interest—we shall better understand language as an object if we interpret it in the light of the findings and seekings of those

Introduction

> for whom language is an instrument, a means towards inquiries of a quite different kind. (Halliday 1978:3)

But Halliday parts company with Labov in that his ultimate concern is not linguistics but language and the human condition: "Put in more prosaic terms, this means that my interest in linguistic questions is ultimately in an 'applied' one, a concern with language in relation to the process and experience of education" (Halliday 1978:5).

It is an important and complementary perspective to the development of sociolinguistics and one the reader should consider. We very much regret not having been able to include a chapter by Halliday.

The organization of the book is very simple. The first chapter by Roger Shuy, reprinted with kind permissions, simply lays out by events the early happenings and some of the key performers and so serves as a framework for the individual texts to follow. The contributions are ordered alphabetically rather than thematically or typologically. They have been edited for coherence of mechanics but otherwise left as written; we found it added interest to include the authors' uniqueness as part of the presentations. We only hope you enjoy reading them as much as we have.

A Brief History of American Sociolinguistics[1]

1949–1989

Roger W. Shuy

> Roger Shuy is retired Distinguished Professor of Linguistics at Georgetown University, where over the years he taught, headed the sociolinguistics program, and chaired the department since 1968.

There comes a time in the development of any discipline when participants in that field begin to ask the question "Where did we come from?" This is a very human question, one that is asked by small children of their parents. And it is one that deserves an answer. Recently, several scholars of sociolinguistics have, for the first time, become aware of the lack of published information about how sociolinguistics came to be. Most universities now offer courses in this subject. Papers on sociolinguistics are given at academic meetings with great regularity. In fact, entire conferences on sociolinguistics have been held for over two decades now. Journals specializing in various aspects of sociolinguistics exist and flourish. Specialists in sociolinguistics are receiving advanced degrees. Job descriptions specify sociolinguistic expertise and knowledge. In a recent article, "Toward a History of Modern Sociolinguistics," Koerner laments the fact that linguists lack a historical perspective in their own field of study (Koerner 1988). He searched, as I had (Shuy 1988), for some mention of the history of sociolinguistic study in various textbooks, collections of articles, and research publications of this field.

---

[1]This article appeared originally in *Historiographia Linguistica 17*, 1(2):183-209, 1990 and is reprinted by permission of John Benjamins.

Few such books even mention the antecedents of the field, and those that even mention the development of sociolinguistics are very brief (Wolfram and Fasold 1972:26–32). I believe that Koerner is right when he observes that a scientific field reaches some level of maturity when it begins to be aware of its history. McCauley (1988) provides a useful summary of sociolinguistic variables that have been studied but laments that the broad descriptive goals of this field have proven too vast and time consuming.

Linguistic ancestry. It is appropriate for modern-day linguists to regularly reexamine the works of leaders of our field upon whose shoulders we continue to stand (despite our apparent need to claim originality for our own recent breakthroughs and revolutions). Koerner traces much of our current sociolinguistic thought through Saussure by way of William Dwight Whitney (1827–1894), citing the following crucial passage:

> Speech is not a personal possession but a social: it belongs, not to the individual, but to the member of society. No item of existing language is the work of an individual; for what we may severally choose to say is not language until it is accepted and employed by our fellows. The whole development of speech, though initiated by the acts of individuals, is wrought out by the community. (Whitney 1867:404)

Koerner goes on to show that there is an intellectual passing along of this concept from Whitney to Saussure to Meillet to Martinet to Weinreich to Labov. There is much to be said for the validity of Koerner's suggestion. On the other hand, it must also be noted that there is seldom a simple strand of development of a truth or a concept. The great psychologist, Carl Gustav Jung, spoke of the development of a collective unconscious, an almost simultaneous awareness of something in many disparate settings at the same period of time. A perusal of the works of the giants of linguistics in the past century reveals a similar awareness. Bloomfield, for example, devoted an entire chapter to Speech Communities (Bloomfield 1933:42–56). Much of the more modern work in social dialect, gender differences and age-grading, for example, can be linked to Bloomfield's earlier observations. There are those, including Paul Kiparsky, who claim that Labov's variable rule actually can be traced back to Pāṅini (Kiparsky 1979). But, as Koerner points out, most texts and collections on sociolinguistics skip over historical antecedents, noting only such generalities as "sociolinguistics has been established as a distinct discipline for some years" (Pride and Holmes 1972:7).

Labov, as one might expect, does not overlook the thinking of those who preceded modern times, devoting several pages to the topic, "Some Earlier

Studies of Language in Its Social Context" (Labov 1966). He cites the lecture notes of Antoine Meillet in 1905 in which Meillet expressed unwillingness to accept the historical laws discovered in the 19th century and observed that there must be variables as yet undiscovered, continual, even rapid, variation:

> ...but from the fact that language is a social institution, it follows that linguistics is a social science, and the only variable to which we can turn to account for linguistic change is social change, of which linguistic variations are only consequences. We must determine which social structure corresponds to a given linguistic structure and how, in a general manner, changes in social structure are translated into changes in linguistic structure. (Labov 1966:15)

Meillet's words seem strangely modern, yet neither he nor his colleagues seem to have followed up on the idea that social and linguistic phenomena are interrelated. The reason for this is obvious when we examine the theoretical development of the period in which he worked. In the nineteenth century, language change, etymology, and language origins dominated the thinking of linguists. By the twentieth century the major interest became the structure of language. The idea of cultural relativity emerged strongly in the work of anthropologists, turning away from what Edward Sapir referred to as "the revolutionary prejudice" of previous concerns about language (Sapir 1921). This relativism in the view of language and culture was accompanied in linguistics proper by a turn towards structuralism, led by Saussure and others. As Labov points out, little was accomplished until the field had developed a more explicit theory of phonological structure, the development of tape recorders, spectrograms, sampling procedures, and even more recently, computers that were equipped to process large quantities of data (Labov 1966). However right Meillet was in his assessment, the technological and social contexts were simply not yet appropriate for the development of his ideas.

Meanwhile, as structuralism developed with Bloomfield, Sapir, Bloch, Hockett, Pike, and others, the focus of linguistics turned inward to the basic outline of languages in general rather than upon variation within those languages. There was nothing essentially wrong with such a direction, for linguistics probably needed to develop in this manner.

Anthropological ancestry. There are some who say that sociolinguistics is actually a modern version of what used to be called anthropological linguistics. There is something to be said in favor of such a position since, in a broad sense at least, sociolinguists extend the description and analysis of language to include aspects of the culture in which it is used. In that sense, sociolinguistics constitutes something of a return to anthropology, in which many believe it had its origins. The classic four-pronged definition of anthropology—cultural anthropology, physical anthropology, archeology, and linguistics—however, focuses on the larger analysis of human behavior, its patterns and principles while modern sociolinguistics examines in depth more minute aspects of language in social context.

An early indication of the future development of sociolinguistics can be seen in *Horizons of Anthropology* edited by Sol Tax in 1964, in which Hymes noted that the salient trait of linguistics in the first half of the twentieth century, from the viewpoint of anthropology, "has been its quest for autonomy." He predicted, however, that in the second half of this century "the salient trait will be the quest for integration, and the noted accomplishments will concern the engaging of linguistic structures in social contexts—in short, in the analysis of function" (Hymes 1964b:92).

American anthropology has always recognized language as a branch of its domain, probably because of the importance it has placed on American Indian studies. In the nineteenth century, the association of linguistics and anthropology was called by many names, such as "ethnological philology" and "linguistic ethnology." In the twentieth century this intersection of interests became known as "ethnolinguistics," "metalinguistics," and "anthropological linguistics." In the sixties Hymes proposed the term "linguistic anthropology," defining it broadly as the study of language in an anthropological context. Hymes noted that fields like anthropology and linguistics overlap in practice, but do not coincide. Anthropology uses linguistics to shed light on its proper task, coordinating knowledge about language from the viewpoint of humanity. The proper task of linguistics, on the other hand, is to coordinate knowledge about language from the viewpoint of language.

Courses called "Language and Culture" had been offered, for example, as early as 1955 at Harvard (by Hymes in the Department of Social Relations), at the University of California at Berkeley, and at the University of Pennsylvania. Hymes reports that such courses became increasingly sociolinguistic over time but that they depended increasingly upon prerequisite courses in descriptive linguistics. This was important, as Hymes notes, because:

> One wanted an introduction to linguistic description that recognized the need to specify social position and context for the data; and that recognized in phonetics the manifestation of a plurality of functions (identificational, expressive, directive, metalinguistic), as well as the processes of change. In fact to consider descriptive linguistics from a social point of view is to reconsider it, and to begin to envisage a somewhat distinctive content and mode of presentation. (Hymes 1966)

In this same report, Hymes goes on to point out that the more traditional minimal training of social scientists in only descriptive linguistics, though essential, was not sufficient for the kinds of research they were increasingly attempting to carry out. Social scientists need to know how to control linguistic forms, to be sure, but also to control social valuations of language varieties, of their use with regard to persons, channels, topics, and settings. In effect, the social scientist needs to apply the results of a sociolinguistic description.

Other glimmerings of the development of sociolinguistic sensitivity from within the tradition of anthropology could also be seen at other universities in the sixties, such as Cornell, Indiana, Michigan, Tulane, and Berkeley, to name only a few. At the same time, anthropologists and sociologists began to mention the obverse problem, that of making linguistics acquainted with sociolinguistic methodology.

Sociological ancestry. The anthropological origins of sociolinguistics were not the only progenitor. As early as April of 1966, sociologists had organized a session on sociolinguistics as part of the Ohio Valley Sociological Society's annual meeting. Hymes reports that one of the most prominent questions asked at that meeting was, "Where can a sociologist go to study sociolinguistics?" (1966). To address this question more deeply, a follow-up meeting was held in Los Angeles three months later. To emphasize the fact that disciplinary developments do not require the trappings of an academic society annual meeting, this meeting was held in the home of William Bright. A number of scholars who would become the leaders in this emerging field happened to be in Los Angeles that summer and were invited, including Charles A. Ferguson, Joshua A. Fishman, Harold Garfinkel, Erving Goffman, John Gumperz, Dell Hymes, William Labov, Harvey Sacks, Edgar Polomé, Leonard Savitz, and Emmanuel Shegloff. The sociologists present shared their experiences in teaching sociolinguistics at their universities. Savitz stressed the need for training in linguistics for sociolinguists. Fishman supported this notion and added that sociologists were interested in linguistic variables but not necessarily in linguistics, while linguists seemed interested in broad contextualization but not necessarily in sociology. It might be noted that this distinction of concerns appears to be current to this day (Hymes 1966).

In sociology, comparative studies programs began to develop in the early sixties, and many sociology students were sent to foreign countries. They were made aware of the need for language competence but not the need for linguistics. That is, these students wanted to learn the language of the people they were studying, but they apparently did not see language as a source of sociological data.

Most of the early courses in sociolinguistics taught by sociologists were called "Sociology of Language." Joshua Fishman first taught a course by that name in 1956 at the University of Pennsylvania. Subsequently, he continued to teach that course at Yeshiva, primarily to psychology majors. Fishman's approach reflected his own special interests in this area: language maintenance, language displacement, and the social context of language planning.

In 1965 Joyce O. Hertzler's book, *The Sociology of Language*, was published. A sociologist himself, Hertzler noted:

> Among the social scientists, the chief contributors to language study have been anthropologists and psychologists. The anthropologists have been concerned with language as a cardinal aspect of culture, language origins and development, the analysis of primitive languages and the reciprocal relationships of these languages with primitive mental and social life. [...] The general, social educational and abnormal psychologists have been concerned with the stages of speech development in human beings, especially the speech development of children, the relationship of speech and abnormal psychological states, the strategic significance of language in personality development and in the socialization of the individual, and its relationship to the processes of thought. (Hertzler 1965:4–5)

Hertzler's own evaluation of the state of affairs with respect to the contributions of the sociological literature to that point was that they were "superficial, unsystematic, or confined only to certain limited or special aspects of language in society." He noted further that work to date had "merely skirted the edges of a sociology of language" (1965:5). Hertzler then went on to map the areas of future work in this area, including language as a social phenomenon, a social institution, a sociocultural index, social control, a differentiator, and as an indicator of change. Hertzler also sounded a warning, one that turned out to be a common lament of sociologists, anthropologists, and linguists alike; that it is difficult for one field to know enough about the other disciplines to avoid criticism when venturing into new territory:

> It might be considered poor business for a sociologist to seem to be poaching upon linguistic territory. The writer is not, and makes no pretense of being, an accomplished student of formal linguistics. (Hertzler 1965:5)

Other sociologists interested in language were also pursuing their own special research concerns in the sixties. Although there was no course called the sociology of language at UCLA at that time, Harold Garfinkel reported that this subject entered into all of his teaching. In the same department, Harvey Sacks was teaching the analysis of conversation to sociology and anthropology majors. It appears that individual sociologists pursued their own language topics in sociology departments but without labels that might identify them as linguistic. Erving Goffman's research interest, for example, in the sixties, was in lying in public and on small social behaviors in public order. He saw linguistics as essential to the description of the structure and organization of small pieces of behavior. Most linguistically oriented sociologists, however, were at odds with the larger departmental requirements. If a sociology major were to invest the time and effort to become well enough grounded in linguistics to replicate the work of a Goffman, a Garfinkel, or a Sacks, they ran the serious risk of sacrificing other aspects of sociological knowledge required by that field. Naturally, the same thing could be said of anthropologists and, conversely, of linguists.

The cross-disciplinary dilemma. In order for the field of sociolinguistics to fully benefit from the combined disciplines upon which it was based, something had to give in the traditional academic structure. The ethnographic insights of anthropologists, the social theory and methods of sociology and the basic information of linguistics had to be merged more comfortably. To this point, they obviously were not. Anthropology students were getting a taste of linguistics, but not enough to do the type of work visualized by Hymes. Sociology departments were even less willing to stretch their traditional curricula to accommodate enough linguistics to further the seminal work of Sacks, Garfinkel, Fishman, and Goffman.

At the same time, there seems to have been considerably less concern on the part of linguists concerning the need for their students to be trained in anthropology and sociology. By 1966 Ferguson had taught a course called "Sociolinguistics" at two LSA Institutes and at Georgetown University. His students had a background in linguistics but not in sociology. Likewise, Edgar Polomé reports that by then he had taught a course called sociolinguistics at the University of Texas, but almost exclusively to linguists. Labov argued that the sheer amount of linguistic training needed to bring about a change in the character of basic linguistic research and theory was so great that he preferred to train only those committed to linguistics. This thought was supported by Gumperz who also argued for a serious commitment to sociolinguistic analysis, not just an interest in it. Thus the mid sixties revealed great ferment and coming together of social scientists to try to determine how to cooperate across traditional disciplinary lines. There was both agreement and disagreement.

The agreement centered on the growing need for a kind of cross-cultural research that cut across disciplinary territories. Some saw the world as becoming reintegrated as one society, growing smaller in a sense, while at the same time there was a reestablishment of the plurality of societies and languages within societies. Both trends required a shift in focus and theory by sociologists, anthropologists, and linguists.

In American society, it was the time of increased problems with racial segregation, poverty, education, and social structures. The problems were clear enough and these three disciplines had some of the tools needed to address them, but not apart from each other. But these fields faced the traditional problems that academics always face. Social scientists did not want to give up anything to get linguistics. Nor did linguists want to give up anything to get social science. Each wanted to keep its own field, goals, and theory-building foremost while enjoying the most minimal fruits of the other.

We have already noted some of the origins of sociolinguistic thought in the giants of linguistics who preceded us, Saussure, Meillet, and Bloomfield in particular. In England, the Firthian heritage of linguistics created a strong tradition for a sociolinguistic perspective, most recently in the work of Michael Halliday. In fact, in 1966 Basil Bernstein wrote a memorandum called "Culture and Linguistics," which encouraged the development of the field of sociolinguistics in England. One of the recommendations of Hymes to the Social Science Research Council (1966) was to develop a handful of training centers or "laboratories" for training in aspects of sociolinguistics, including London, New York, and Washington, D.C. One can assume that Hymes recommended London largely because the theoretical tradition of linguistics was oriented to a more functional rather than formal approach.

American linguistics in the mid-sixties had clearly taken a more formalist bent. The period of structuralist, descriptive grammars, in particular, was now waning. Since much of what the modern sociolinguists such as Hymes, Gumperz, Labov, and Ferguson had envisaged depended first on rich description, the advent of a modern sociolinguistics seemed out of time with the rapidly developing dominant linguistic theory. A major thread of continuity for a sociolinguistic tradition was found, however, in regional dialectology, in which language variability had been celebrated for many years.

Linguistic geography. Linguistic geography, at least in western countries, is said to have its origins in late nineteenth century Germany, when Georg Wenker mailed out forty sentences to thousands of village schoolmasters.

These sentences contained words which were known to vary locally in pronunciation. With whatever semi-phonetic skills they could muster, these schoolmasters dutifully responded, creating a data base which still exists in Marburg and is now being computerized. The point here, however, is that the focus of Wenker's effort was on the rich variation that characterizes the German language.

From Wenker's study, dialectologists learned at least one very important principle—that the postal questionnaire method permits a vast quantity of language data to be gathered in a relatively short period of time. At issue, however, was, and continues to be, the degree of accuracy achievable, especially in matters of pronunciation, from the written impressions of non-linguists. In 1896 the linguistic survey of France addressed this problem directly. A French atlas was devised and directed by Jules Guilliéron, who determined that it would be possible to achieve more consistent and accurate representations of the actual speech of informants if a single field worker with good phonetic skills would interview subjects and transcribe their speech phonetically. So he sent Edmond Edmont out on his bicycle to various French communities. In a period of four years, Edmont completed the 200-item questionnaire with 700 informants and the *Atlas Linguistique de la France* was published between 1902 and 1910.

Since the French atlas, linguistic geography projects were conducted in many parts of Europe, in Italy, Switzerland, Spain, Holland, and Denmark, in particular. Such work has also been carried out in Australia, South America, Africa, and Asia. Of particular interest is the work in the United States and in England. Harold Orton and colleagues carried out a field survey of English dialects between 1950 and 1961 in 313 communities, using some 1300 questions or topics such as housekeeping, farming, animals, and social activities. In 1977 the *Linguistic Atlas of England* was published. Likewise in Wales, Alan Thomas directed a postal survey with 500 questions. Like the Wenker study, spellings were intended to reflect regional pronunciations. *The Linguistic Geography of Wales* was published in 1973.

The American atlas project, under the initial direction of Hans Kurath, began in 1931. The original idea was to produce a dialect dictionary. Concerned scholars, including George Kittredge and James Russell Lowell, gathered in Cambridge, Massachusetts, in 1889 and formed the American Dialect Society. After thirty years, although the society had not come close to publishing a dialect dictionary, it had collected over 26,000 interesting dialect words and phrases in its publication, *Dialect Notes*.[2] By 1929 the interests of many American dialectologists had turned away from a dialect

---

[2]The title of this journal was later changed to *Publications of the American Dialect Society* and remains the same today.

dictionary to that of a linguistic atlas. With the assistance of the American Council of Learned Societies, a plan for such an atlas was published and Kurath was appointed its director. The plan was to produce a set of "work sheets" containing over seven hundred items arranged roughly according to topics. This unique approach formulated the informants' answers but did not specify the questions, leaving that to the ingenuity of the fieldworker.

The single most active student of language variation in this country was Raven I. McDavid, Jr., whose monumental efforts both as a fieldworker and analyst are widely recognized. Almost singlehandedly McDavid kept language variation alive after the *Linguistic Atlas of New England* was published. At that point in time, the major concerns of most linguists, even those who had participated previously in the Atlas project, turned to the dominant theme of the time, structuralism. The necessary ingredient for any long term project such as a linguistic atlas is that of producing students who will continue the work. But students trained to be linguistic geographers began to find other areas of concern. McDavid produced a few followers who continued the work, such as Lee A. Pederson, who is now completing the *Linguistic Atlas of the Gulf States*, but others who were trained in this area, such as Gumperz, Labov, and Shuy, turned to sociolinguistics.

Linguistic Atlas research in the United States continues on a somewhat regular but slow pace today, aided by computerization of data and by the hard work of a few talented scholars. Many scholars question the value of the methods by which the data were elicited, the accuracy of pre-tape-recorded phonetic transcriptions, the biases of sampling, the focus only on lexicon and pronunciation, and the omission of analytical procedures, such as discourse analysis and pragmatic meaning, that developed after the atlas procedure was unchangeably determined. One serious danger of any long-range project such as this is, of course, that the field of knowledge will develop after the methods and procedures are set. Consistence and compatibility were critical features of the U.S. atlas approach. Later changes were difficult, if not impossible. Whatever criticisms one may wish to make of the era of linguistic geography, however, one has to admit that this period kept variability studies alive, even in the midst of more dominating concerns of the field. It also produced a rich data base of language use which, whatever value judgments one may place on it, provided later scholars with evidence to be considered. We benefit greatly from our predecessors in linguistics, however much more we may think we have learned since they produced us.

In linguistic geography, there were many early features of modern sociolinguistics. The American Atlas traditionally attempted to get informants of three general social classes in more urban communities, but it was McDavid who made the clearest connection between social factors and pronunciation variables. In his classic article, "Postvocalic /-r/ in South Carolina: A Social Analysis" (1948), he noted that in communities where postvocalic /-r/ occurs with constriction, three variables decrease it: the more urban, younger, better educated speakers use less constriction. Such sensitivity to social influences of variation were not common, however, until the sixties, when language variation studies in America entered a kind of renaissance.

As new interest in minorities developed, the country, under President Kennedy's leadership, began viewing its citizens in a new way. Those who are products of later societies might not realize the tremendous impact such ideas had on linguistics at that time. As it often happens, a specific set of events framed the staging ground for a number of changes within our field, some related, but others more serendipitous. One of these events was the annual Linguistic Institute at Indiana University in 1964. The major proponents of structuralism and generative grammar were matched against each other in a series of week-long lectures, first by Chomsky, then by Pike. It was an unusually well-attended institute that summer and, along with the Linguistic Society of America summer meeting, it provided one of the most exciting programs in the history of the field. One reason that the Institute was so well attended has already been mentioned—the arm-to-arm combat for theoretical leadership in the field. But there were other reasons as well.

In May of 1964, a month or so before the LSA Institute, the UCLA Center for Research in Language and Linguistics sponsored a conference on "Sociolinguistics" at Lake Arrowhead, California. The edited papers of this conference appeared under the title, *Sociolinguistics* (Bright 1966). To give an idea of the recency of the term "sociolinguistics," it should be noted that the 1961 *Third Edition of Webster's New International Dictionary* does not list this word at all, although the term had appeared as early as 1952 in an article by Haver C. Currie in the *Southern Speech Journal*. At the time of the Lake Arrowhead conference, a number of scholars had been investigating the relationship between language and society, including Henry M. Hoenigswald, John Gumperz, Einar Haugen, Raven I. McDavid, Jr., Dell Hymes, John Fischer, William Samarin, Paul Friedrich, and Charles Ferguson. One bright new star on the horizon, a student of Uriel Weinreich at Columbia, named William Labov, was also invited to Lake Arrowhead to describe his dissertation research on New York City speech. This cadre of participants represented a number of quite different research traditions—linguistic geography, language contact, historical changes, ethnography, and language planning. Out of this conference-induced blending of traditions it was only natural to find terms into which each research tradition might fit. "Language and Society" and "Sociolinguistics" were the most logical choices and it was determined that two courses by these names should be offered at the 1964 LSA Institute.

John Gumperz had been carrying out earlier research in India and Norway on the differences in language used among people of various castes and social status. Those who had heard him talk about this in the past prevailed upon him to offer a summer institute course dealing with the broad issues involved in such variability. He taught the course called "Language and Society."

Charles Ferguson's research began with Bengali and Arabic studies, which led him to focus on different uses and/or varieties of those languages. By the fifties he had written about Arabic politeness and baby talk, for example. In the early sixties he, along with Gumperz, edited an issue of IJAL called "Linguistic Diversity in South Asia." He also wrote about diglossia as a language teaching problem. At the 1964 Institute he conducted a seminar in Sociolinguistics. It is often the coming together of a nucleus of scholars with the same growing concerns that frees it and lets new ideas bloom. It is not my purpose to pinpoint the creation of modern sociolinguistics at the Lake Arrowhead conference of LSA Institute alone, but rather the combination of both in a continuous period from mid-May to mid-August of 1964. Just as linguistic geographers had broken from the view of language study which treated languages as homogeneous and unified, so sociolinguists broke from structural linguistics in their treatment of languages "as completely uniform, homogeneous or monolithic in their structure" (Bright 1966:11).

In addition to Gumperz' and Ferguson's courses in sociolinguistics, the 1964 LSA summer institute provided still another impetus for the development of language variation study. Alva L. Davis, a linguistic geographer then at Illinois Institute of Technology, along with Robert F. Hogan, of the National Council of Teachers of English, secured funding for a conference on Social Dialects and Language Learning, to be held in conjunction with this same LSA Summer Institute at Bloomington. Twenty-five participants, including linguists, educators, sociologists, and psychologists, were invited. Gumperz, Labov, McDavid, and Ferguson represented continuity from the Lake Arrowhead group. All other linguists were from dialectology, language contact, or multilingualism specialties. The publications of the papers at this meeting (Shuy 1965) focused on the equality of dialects, on the need for research on urban language, on the inadequacy of past approaches to dialectology research, on the pedagogical usefulness of deeper information about language variation, and on whether non-standard varieties should be eliminated or added to by standard English.

Today, these topics seem rather common. But in the Summer of 1964 they were startlingly new issues. Several of the educators present argued, traditionally, for holding the line against substandard English. The conference came to grips with terminological issues such as "substandard" versus "nonstandard" and "culturally deprived" versus "culturally different." Haugen called into question the approach suggested by many: that we use English as a Second Language methodology to teach English as a second dialect. He pointed out that language learning and dialect learning are not the same things, despite what seemed to be similarities.

With the Lake Arrowhead meeting, with the LSA Institute, with Gumperz' and Ferguson's courses in sociolinguistics, and with the Conference on Social Dialects, the Summer of 1964 was very important for the establishment of the field of sociolinguistics. What happened afterward proves this. Many of the participants in these meetings began teaching courses called sociolinguistics at their home universities.

To most regional dialectologists, an urban study would simply use the same questionnaire and methodology in the selected city that had been used for decades in the rural Atlas research. In fact, Lee Pederson had done this in his study of Chicago speech. But Labov had brought an exciting new dimension to this work—continuous discourse, frequency of occurrence of features rather than categorical presence or absence, minority informants, and a unique guide to questioning that let the informants talk as long as they wanted on a given topic of their own choice. Some decided to use this new approach.

After Labov completed his New York dissertation, he continued his sociolinguistics studies in New York with a cadre of excellent graduate students. Meanwhile, I carried out my Detroit sociolinguistics study with the help of a few of my students at Michigan State, but perhaps more importantly, also involving Walt Wolfram and Ralph Fasold. At the same time, the Ford Foundation had funded the Center for Applied Linguistics, then under the directorship of Charles Ferguson and with the fertile ideas of William Stewart, to study urban dialects in Washington, D.C. Two years later, Wolfram, Fasold, and I moved to Washington and merged the Detroit and Washington research into a single project and formed the Sociolinguistics Program at CAL. With helpful communication with Labov and his Columbia University Associates, the three urban studies were able to make useful comparisons of urban black speech phenomena and establish the study of Vernacular Black English, and we were, justifiably, accused of a certain myopia. Our work had certainly identified some of the language diversity and change upon which the Lake Arrowhead conference had been based, but most certainly it had not dealt with all of the issues suggested, for example, by Hymes in his approach to the ethnography of communication.

Concurrent with the growth of the sort of work described above, carried out by Labov in New York and others in Detroit and Washington, D.C. in the sixties, was the development of more ethnographic research on language variation. Hymes, Gumperz, and their colleagues and students focused on language as a social fact and studied the interaction between communication and culture. Perhaps out of dissatisfaction with the generativists' limitation of "competence" to grammatical knowledge, Hymes extended the notion to "communicative competence," the most general term for the speaking and hearing capabilities of a person (Hymes 1964a). Although Newmeyer asserts that Hymes intended "communicative competence" to exclude grammatical competence (Newmeyer 1983), this was not Hymes' intention at all. Hymes did not reject grammatical competence, rather, he believed it to be a part of a larger competence that was worthy of study.

By the late 1960s, then, several strands of research approaches were fermenting and coming together. The regional dialectology strand had been around for almost a century, the language contact strand, evidenced by the work of Ferguson, Haugen, Weinreich, Fishman, and others, had strongly made its presence known, and the ethnography of communication strand had made a powerful impact in a relatively short time. All strands were concerned with language in its social context and all were composed of scholars who considered themselves to be doing linguistics. The term "sociolinguistics" began to crop up in university course catalogues, in journal articles, and in book titles. With this approaching harmony, however, were discordant tones brought about by the fact that the practitioners of this work were found in separate academic disciplines, at least as university structure defined them.

Changes from the ancestral heritage. It should be clear that modern linguistics was in severe labor pains in the mid sixties, ready and apparently eager to deliver its offspring, sociolinguistics. One might expect this child to bear certain resemblances to both its parents, linguistics and social science. One would even like to believe that the new child would bring its two parents closer together. In the period described in some detail earlier, from 1964 to 1966, the problems in doing this were well recognized. What to name this new child was discussed by the leaders in this field (Hymes 1966). How to rear this child was discussed at virtually every meeting of such scholars (training at universities). Once this child was born it would need professional conferences, journals, meetings, institutes, texts, and training centers to help it grow to maturity.

Now, one quarter of a century after those mid-sixties planning meetings, early courses, and collections of papers, it is time to take inventory of what actually happened. Did the disciplines of linguistics, sociology, and anthropology ever accomplish the rapprochement that was so eagerly wished in the sixties? Did the young child get christened with an enduring name? Did the field of linguistics come to accept sociolinguistics as one of its own offspring?

How is sociolinguistics doing in the fields of anthropology and sociology? Have specialized journals been created?

It is not accidental that many of the early sociolinguists looked to the analytical routines of sociology in addition to anthropology. Quantifiable approaches to socioeconomic status were one such routine. Census data were also found useful, along with the more sophisticated sampling procedures and data gathering procedures of sociology.

Methodology. Sociolinguists charted their own course, however, even when borrowing from sociology and, for this reason, suffered criticism from that field. It became clear early on, for example, that language data are quite different from conventional sociological data. A sociologist could interview subjects concerning voting or purchasing patterns, daily activities, attitudes, or values and still remain uncertain about the accuracy or truthfulness of their responses. It is relatively easy to stretch the truth about how many times one brushes one's teeth or exactly who one voted for, but it is much more difficult for humans to consciously change or modify the consonants or vowels they use as they produce coherent ideas in their speech.[3] This relative stability of language used in natural contexts makes a small sample of language more useful to researchers than would be an equally small sample of the type of self-report data found in other social science research.

Sociologists also argue for parting company with the methods of determining socio-economic status that are common in sociology, while acknowledging that they benefited greatly from sociological procedures, particularly in the early days of sociolinguistic research. The first large sociolinguistic research projects (Labov 1965; Shuy, Wolfram, and Riley, 1968) essentially used language data to correlate with socioeconomic status (SES) as defined by the Warner scale (1949). As knowledge and theory grew, however, sociolinguists began to ask themselves, "Why should language be selected as the variable to correlate with SES? Why not let language be the SES?" If sociolinguists were true to their belief that language is the best available window to social structure and cognition, why use it to correlate with other, less adequate windows?

With the development of sociolinguistic quantitative analysis came more sophisticated statistical analyses. It has been said that there are two types of linguistic analysts: those who search for universals (what languages have in common) and those who search for variability (how languages differ).

It became apparent that the search for language universals required less quantitative measures than the search for variability. To be sure, research

---

[3]The same essential truthfulness or validity has been noted for morphological and syntactic features as well.

in universals can use statistical analysis and it is also true that our long tradition of dialectology research had essentially avoided statistics. But as tightly focused research projects made use of multiple occurrences of language samples in different contexts, it became evident that a very important feature of language was that of frequency of occurrence, not just categorical presence or absence. For example, if a dialectologist were to interview me today and ask me the traditional Linguistic Atlas question, "What do you fry eggs in?" I could easily answer, "frying pan." Such an answer would then reside forever in the Atlas files as the lexical item used by this resident of Washington, D.C. If I were the only informant in Washington, D.C., the Atlas could claim that my utterance constitutes the norm for this item in Washington, D.C. speech.[4] Such data masks many things, the most important of which is that even in my own speech, *frying pan* is not the variant that I use predominantly. If the Atlas fieldworker were to follow me around for a day or two, hearing only every instance of my reference to this kitchen utensil, he or she would more likely hear 80% production of *skillet* and about 20% production of *frying pan.* This fictitious Atlas review, then, would have presented misleading information, having caught me in my *frying pan* mode, for whatever reason. Those of us who grew up in dialect transition areas (in my case, Akron, Ohio) may well have frequency of occurrence distinction from the onset of our language learning. Some may develop a semantic differentiation, real or imagined, when two such terms are in active production (as I discovered during my own Atlas research in Illinois in the early 1960s when I found that northern dialect informants who used *pail* also used *bucket*, but reserved the latter for the older, dented or beat-up variety of *pail.* Not surprisingly, Midland dialect informants had the same distinction, only reversed).

In the 1960s, sociolinguistic quantification resulted in rather simple statistics, usually represented in percentages. There is nothing wrong with such statistics, of course, as long as the claims are clear and accurate. In fact, such statistical representation was a tremendous improvement over previous representations of all-or-none presence or absence of a feature. As linguists became acquainted with computers, however, larger and more sophisticated routines became popular (Fasold 1984). From anthropology, some sociolinguists have borrowed the methodology of participant observation and ethnography. Although ethnographic approaches to language analysis existed for many years, it is noteworthy that the University of Pennsylvania is responsible for a burst of training and research in the sixties, one that

---

[4]To be sure, Atlas research would have more than one representative in a large urban area such as D.C. This example is, therefore, only illustrative of a point.

produced a major impact on work in this area. Dell Hymes was largely responsible for this flurry of activity.

It should be stressed that even though sociolinguists reached out for ideas and approaches from sociology and anthropology, such ideas and approaches were not borrowed in their entirety or in their purest form. They were modified to the specific purposes of the newly perceived field. Both sociologists and anthropologists might complain, with justification perhaps, that these modifications dilute or distort the purposes of their own field. However true this may be, the criticism has less force when we recognize that sociolinguistics is *not* sociology and it is *not* anthropology, per se. There are those who agree, in fact, that neither is it linguistics per se, since sociolinguists go beyond the traditional limits of linguistic analysis, but this criticism is tempered by the fact that sociolinguists recognize this fact by calling the field sociolinguistics.

From the onset of the existence of a field of study called sociolinguistics, there has been debate about whether or not there should be something called sociolinguistics at all. Labov, regarded by most as one of the major forces in this field's birth, himself objected to the term as early as 1965. For Labov, there was no need for calling this field by a separate name. He preferred that the parent field, linguistics, adjust and accept social variability within its scope. In short, Labov did not have any particular need for a concept or field like sociolinguistics. As a superb linguist himself, he would continue to do linguistics as he defined it. Not every linguist, however, was so contextually comfortable. At Georgetown University, just the opposite was the case. Partly because the National Science Foundation had made funding available for new thrusts in various academic fields, Georgetown found it politically and economically useful to use this newly emerging research area as a reference point and as a label for a newly created curriculum. Thus, the Sociolinguistics Program joined three other graduate linguistics programs at that university. Although other American universities have not, on the whole, gone so far as to label whole doctoral programs "Sociolinguistics," at many universities one can effectively accomplish much the same thing through a linguistics major.

Names. In November of 1966, when Hymes submitted his report on "Training in Sociolinguistics," no name for the field had been agreed upon. He reports that sociolinguistics subject matter was then being taught under the headings of "linguistics," "language and culture," "sociology of language," and "language behavior" as well as "sociolinguistics." Over twenty years later, the same labels appear, although among linguists at least, "sociolinguistics" has come to be the common term. Annual meetings of the

Linguistic Society of America have had sessions labeled "sociolinguistics" for over fifteen years. In fact a recent brochure describing the entire field of linguistics, distributed by the LSA, describes sociolinguistics as one of the major components of our discipline. Today sociolinguistics may be defined differently by different scholars, but there is general agreement that it includes topics such as language planning, language variability (social and regional dialects), registers, and pidgins and creoles. There is mixed agreement about whether sociolinguistics includes language change or whether the study of language change includes a subcategory of study which is sociolinguistic. Likewise, the more recent developments of discourse analysis, pragmatics, and speech acts are by some scholars considered to be a part of sociolinguistics proper and by others to be separate areas of study in themselves. David Crystal in *The Cambridge Encyclopedia of Language* defines "sociolinguistics" as, "The study of the interaction between language and the structures and functioning of society" (1987:412). Absent from the above topics are fields of study such as "the ethnography of communication" and "language and culture," which are still generally believed to be the province of anthropology, and "the sociology of language" and "ethnomethodology," which are still generally believed to be the province of sociology. Few, if any, departments of linguistics offer all of the above-mentioned topics as specializations in which students can receive training.

Outlets for publication and research. The creation of a new subdiscipline is always accompanied by the problem of where to publish theory and research. The major linguistics journals available to linguists in the midsixties were, of course, receptive to sociolinguistic work, largely because the leaders in this nascent field were well-accepted linguists. The major journal of linguistics, *Language,* was, and continues to be, open to sociolinguistics articles. *Word* was experiencing publication difficulties in the sixties but would have been receptive otherwise. *Foundations of Language* was available as long as the submissions had a bearing on linguistic theory. Among the contemporary anthropological journals, *Anthropological Linguistics, The American Anthropologist,* and the *Southwest Journal of Anthropology* were open to articles on language and culture, broadly defined.

Eventually Hymes started a new journal, *Language in Society,* which continues to be available to a broad range of topics in sociolinguistics. Fishman started *The International Journal of the Sociology of Language,* in which issues related to language planning, bilingualism, language attitudes, and other more sociological aspects of sociolinguistics find a home. *American Speech,* after a few years of dormancy, was resumed first under the leadership of John Algeo and, more recently of Ronald Butters, and continues to be a source of publication on variation in American English. *Language Planning and Language Policy* specializes in the topics of its title and serves more anthropological and sociological concerns. *Discourse Processes* was founded by Roy Freedle and is quite cross-disciplinary in its offerings, but welcomes contributions of a linguistic bent. Even more recently Labov and Anthony Kroch have started a new journal, *Language Variation and Language Change,* dedicated to more linguistic aspects of variation and change. Likewise the new interest in pragmatics has spawned the International Pragmatics Research Association, headed by Jef Verschueren, which publishes articles in that area. *Publications of the American Dialect Society* continues, as it has for a century now, to publish articles on regional and social dialectology.

In summary, a dearth of publication outlets lamented by sociolinguistics leaders in the sixties has been somewhat satisfied today and this development gives solid evidence of the emergence of sociolinguistics on the American scene.

University specializations in sociolinguistics. The definitions of any field are often slippery. The term "sociolinguistics" conjures up different things to different people. The reason for this is quite simple. It is many different things to many different people. For this reason, it will be futile to try to define it completely here. A survey of the understandings of linguists about what sociolinguistics means might yield curious results. One university administrator, a long-time friend, "assured" me recently that he would like to see sociolinguistics "remain" a vital part of Georgetown's Applied Linguistics initiative. The sociolinguistics faculty would be puzzled to hear such a statement, since they do not consider themselves applied linguists.

Through peculiar local developments, newer developments in any field seem to need to find a place on the department's shelf, for orderly housekeeping purposes. During the 1970s interest in both pragmatics and discourse analysis developed rapidly. At some universities, these fields were considered theory developments. At other universities, they were attached to language learning and teaching. Georgetown's Sociolinguistics Program saw them as extensions of the search for patterns in language variation and, therefore, embraced them as sociolinguistics. How odd it must sound, however, to a scholar who does not know the peculiar infrastructure of Georgetown, to learn that pragmatics, speech acts, inferencing, text analysis, or conversation analysis dissertations are considered well within the territory of sociolinguistics. But such are the fruits of academic departmental growth.

All academic departments are the products of the scholars who inhabit them. Sociolinguistics specialties today vary from university to university. The University of Pennsylvania excels at variation analysis, pidgins and creoles, and other areas. State University of New York at Buffalo excels at language surveys, language attitudes, and cross-cultural communication. Berkeley excels at discourse analysis, cross-cultural communication, and other areas. The University of Montreal excels at variable rule analysis and other areas. Perhaps one recurring key here is "and other areas." Many other universities have one or more sociolinguists and one or more specializations. No university offers everything that might fall under the label "sociolinguistics."

Housing. The fondly hoped-for coming together of linguistics, sociology, and anthropology, a desire which dominated much of the discussion of the leaders in the mid-sixties, can today hardly be seen to have occurred. As nearly as can be determined, linguistics currently dominates this field. Virtually every graduate department of linguistics has at least one course called "sociolinguistics." The same cannot be said for the fields of sociology or anthropology.

A more serious question is the one asked many years ago: how to get linguists adequately knowledgeable about sociological methodology. It is difficult enough for a scholar to acquire the knowledge, background, theories, and methods of one discipline, much less two. For this reason, it appears that some of the sociolinguistics research done by linguists will continue to be criticized by sociologists, and vice versa.

Where is sociolinguistics today? One definition of sociolinguistics, one which includes the language rule-governed behavior of speakers, is found almost entirely in linguistics departments. Labov foreshadowed this development some twenty-five years ago when he argued that the sheer amount of linguistic training needed to change basic linguistic research and theory was so great that linguists should probably focus on their own areas of expertise. Dialectology, both regional and social, is also found primarily in linguistics departments today, with the exception of courses in specific language dialectology located in a few foreign language departments. Historical language change continues to flourish primarily in linguistics departments. Pidginization and creolization study is also done almost entirely by linguists. The newer areas of variation study, called "pragmatics" and "discourse analysis," also flourish primarily in linguistics departments, although some versions of these topics can also be found in sociology, psychology, and communication departments.

Sociology departments continue to be the primary centers of work on social context, with language as one indicator, but the topics of language planning and language contact are shared now with many linguistics departments. Anthropology departments continue to be the major hubs of research on the ethnography of speaking and cultural aspects of language. In general, social scientists continue to be more concerned with the functions of language than with its forms.

What major changes, then, can be seen in the past quarter century? It is apparent that today the same general laments that were voiced in the sixties continue to be with us. Sociologists lament that linguists do not learn enough sociological theory and methodology. Anthropologists lament that linguists are too concerned with language forms to appreciate language functions in cultural contexts. Lingists still lament the lack of linguistic sophistication on the part of social scientists as they use language to analyze language situations. In short, the fields still operate with minimal knowledge of each other.

On the other hand, it is more common today for linguists to be concerned about ethnographic and sociological theory and methods than for social scientists to be concerned about language forms. That movement toward the rapprochement so dearly desired by those combinations of linguists, anthropologists, and sociologists who met some twenty-five years ago can be seen more clearly in linguistics departments, where the topics of social control, power, language planning, the ethnography of speaking, and functionalism are becoming more and more evident in the sociolinguistics curricula.

Then why is it that linguistics departments seem to have come to house sociolinguistics more comfortably than have departments of sociology or anthropology? Perhaps it is merely an early lead and, at some point in time, the other departments will develop their own versions of sociolinguistics as well. The lesson learned from other disciplines which create hyphenated fields may be instructive. In the forties, for example, chemistry and biology recognized the potential of cross-disciplinary overlap and created an entity called bio-chemistry. For some twenty-five years, biochemists were housed in either biology or chemistry departments and did somewhat similar and mutually comprehensible work. For the past twenty years or so, however, the chemistry department style of bio-chemistry and the biology department style of bio-chemistry have grown farther and farther apart, often leading to the renaming of departments and research disciplines.

It appears that the high hopes that academics have for cross-disciplinary intermingling is somewhat overly optimistic. All fields are too full of their own topics to admit enough topics from foreign fields to justify true duality. Hyphenation is a short-lived phenomenon which introduces pieces of new insights from other fields, but seldom complete ones. Once the field is infected with new information and insights, however, it tends to make use of only some pieces of foreign fields, especially those which further the on-going goals of the home discipline.

One might predict that sociolinguistics will develop further in sociology and anthropology, but that these developments will be quite unlike the way sociolinguistics has developed in the field of linguistics. In fact, to the extent that these three fields have developed to date, this is somewhat the case. There are few if any departments of linguistics today that would hire either a sociolinguist trained by anthropologists in the ethnography of speaking or a sociolinguist trained by sociologists in language planning or social control and power. It is equally rare that anthropology or sociology departments would hire a sociologist trained by linguists in variation analysis or language forms, in pragmatics, or in discourse variability.

Over time, academic disciplines tend to be attracted to each other, coming together briefly, grazing off each other for a few moments, then returning to their own major concerns. Under the best of circumstances, they affect each other deeply, change their approaches, and affect their knowledge. But their major concerns continue, in the long run, to dominate. We can expect sociolinguistics to be used in different ways by its forbearer disciplines: linguistics, anthropology, and sociology. And that is probably how things ought to be.

Roger Shuy
629 Beverly Avenue
Missoula, Montana 59801
U.S.A.

Pioneers

Development of Sociolinguistics in India

E. Annamalai

After training and teaching in linguistics at Annamalai University (1962–1965) and University of Chicago (1966–1971), E. Annamalai (b. 1930) has been engaged since 1971 in research and training and designing programs in CIIL (Central Institute for Indian Languages) for Indian language development, teaching, and production of learning and codifying materials. He has retired as its Director, and is at present Visiting Research Fellow at Leiden, The Netherlands.

Fishman (1992) gives the summer of 1964 as the date for the birth of American Sociolinguistics, and the place of birth was the LSA Summer Linguistics Institute. It is not that there are other national schools of sociolinguistics with different dates of birth. Modern sociolinguistics spread to other parts of the world from the U.S. after its birth on American soil. It is also not the case that there was no socially related linguistics before 1964 in the U.S. or in other countries. The LSA Summer Institute was a sociological event giving socially related linguistics academic viability and credibility as well as a name. Like other branches of modern linguistics, sociolinguistics also came to India from the U.S. From 1954 for five years Summer and Autumn Schools supported by the Rockefeller Foundation and taught largely by American linguists, trained teachers from language departments in modern linguistics. Sociolinguistics then was not a separate academic subject. The blueprint made in 1959 for the development of linguistic studies in Indian universities does not include sociolinguistics as a course of study. It states, "For a full-fledged centre of linguistics which will take care of imparting instruction in *all* aspects of linguistics at the postgraduate levelthe following subjects should be provided for: General Linguistics, Historical and Comparative Linguistics, Descriptive Linguistics, Applied Linguistics, Phonetics, Experimental Phonetics,

Indo-Aryan, Dravidian, Austro-Asiatic and Tibeto-Burman" (Linguistic Society of India 1959).

Nevertheless, the different social organization in India based on caste with a rigid hierarchy had attracted the scholarly attention of many social scientists in the U.S. and Europe for a long time. It was a natural choice to study the linguistic aspects of caste differentiation. This interest predates 1964 but follows 1954 with the publication of Ferguson and Gumperz (1960). These American linguists taught in the above-mentioned linguistics schools in India. This work was continued assiduously by Indian linguists and was for the most part a description of caste dialects, which remained descriptive in methodology and grammatical in content. There was nothing social in these studies except the name of the caste speaking the dialect given in the title. There was a proliferation of M.A. and Ph.D. dissertations on caste dialects leading toward a separate grammar for each caste. This invited a reaction to assert in a polemical and nationalist tone (Pattanayak 1976) that there are no caste dialects and they are artifacts of the sociolinguistic studies, which proliferate and perpetuate the castes contrary to the native social perception of the loss of their traditional significance. It is a different story that in this decade caste has come to be a potent and transparent political force.

By the mid sixties, Labov had entered the scene, and his worksparticularly Labov (1966)—shifted the attention to variation within the speech of a caste, with the realization that there is no invariant and discrete caste dialect and to variation and clustering of features across castes in a given geographical area taken to be coterminous with speech community. The methodology also changed to become more quantitative. This came to India later. The sociolinguistic Summer Institute organized by the Central Institute of Indian Languages in Mysore in 1972, in which Labov and Gumperz also gave courses along with others, introduced the study of Labov s linguistic variables in and Gumperz linguistic behavior of a speech community. The field studies done in the Summer Institute were published (Pattanayak 1977). The teaching of sociolinguistics as a course in the linguistic departments started in the early seventies (the University of Delhi introduced it in 1972), and research in it was strengthened by the teachers and research students trained in this Summer Institute. The seminar on "Language and Society in India," organized by the Indian Institute of Advanced Study a little earlier in 1967, also broadened the scope of sociolinguistic investigations in India (Poddar 1969).

Variation as a developmental and functional phenomenon of language also, like the caste dialect, received the attention of Indian sociolinguists before 1964 with the publication of Ferguson s *Diglossia* (1959). The Indian linguists living in a society with a long literacy tradition and large illiterate populations were greatly attracted to this linguistic phenomenon. This triggered a large number of studies on the diglossic situation in Indian languages, which extended (and diluted) the concept to include different stylistic variations like spoken versus written, literary versus colloquial, etc.

Like the descriptive concerns mentioned earlier, historical concerns were also prominent in Indian sociolinguists from the beginning of modern linguistics. Linguistic variation was studied to explain (and to predict) linguistic change. Bright and Ramanujan (1964) presented this thesis in the Ninth International Congress of Linguists. This historical interest in variation was soon extended to the study of linguistic convergence, which focussed on the lateral change in languages through contact. Emeneau s (1958) influential paper on India as a linguistic area generated many studies on areal linguistics from historical, grammatical, as well as sociolinguistic points of view. I gave a series of lectures in various universities in the early eighties on convergence, synthesizing the research done from these three points of view (Annamalai—forthcoming). The leading figure to focus on the sociolinguistic aspects of convergence and a realization of languages is Pandit of Delhi University. He also gave Indian orientation to the study of language shift by asking the question why the languages are maintained commonly in India unlike the West (1971) and sociolinguistic direction to areal linguistics (Pandit 1972).

The sociolinguistic interest in convergence gave a social dimension to the study of bilingualism and also encouraged the study of code mixing and code switching. This narrowed the distance between the study of linguistic change and language behavior. Indian linguists have done pioneering work in code mixing and switching as in convergence and areal studies.

The sociolinguistic research has a communication facet also focussing on expression of new ideas and experience and of bigroup identity through mixing and switching codes on minority-majority interactions through shifting languages and complementing domains of use, on urban and tribal material transactions through emergence of pidginized varieties, and on special settings like industrial floors, offices, and consulting rooms of professionals. It is also argued, especially by Khubchandani, that the sociolinguistic profile of India should be studied in terms of communication zones and not of language and dialect boundaries, as they are language artifacts.

It is a general perception that the multilingual India, which is multilingual not only demographically but also functionally, is an inviting and a challenging place for sociolinguistic research. The Indian sociolinguists also believe that the sociolinguistic nature of India is general. Indian multilingualism, in particular, is qualitatively different from others. The search for differentiating features—like continued language maintenance, functional complementarity between languages, fluidity of linguistic boundaries, etc.is an implicit, sometimes explicit, agenda for sociolinguistic research in India. Khubchandani (1991) is an ardent promoter of this thesis, but his research and influence are outside the institutional framework. He is joined by D. P. Pattanayak and R. N. Srivastava ideologically, though not harmoniously. This thesis claims that the western sociolinguistic theory and model do not help to characterize Indian sociolinguistic reality and an Indian theory and model should be developed. Its realization, however, remains nascent.

One of the selling points for getting modern linguistics a place in the Academia of the fifties immediately after independence has been that it is a necessary ingredient to manage problems of multilingualism and to develop Indian languages for their new roles, particularly in the domains of education and administration. Applied sociolinguistics has therefore been given attention from the beginning. The Central Institute of Indian Languages was set up in 1969 for the purpose of development of modern Indian languages by providing institutional framework, support, and opportunities for a number of young linguists, who changed their linguistic orientation towards application. Its first Director, D. P. Pattanayak, was a vocal advocate for the empowerment of mother tongues (Pattanayak 1981) followed by Dua at the same Institute (Dua 1994). The International Institute in Language Planning organized by the Central Institute of Indian Languages in 1980, which was the second one after the Institute in Honolulu in 1977, brought together linguists from developing countries in Asia and Africa and trained them in Language Planning. The Institute helped to introduce language planning as a subject in linguistic courses in India. Selected Proceedings of the Institute were published (Annamalai et al. 1986). The University of Delhi organized another Institute in Language Planning in the winter of 1987, which introduced the language management shift in this discipline. Publication of the *New Language Planning Newsletter* by the Central Institute of Indian Languages from 1985, which was published earlier from East West Center, Honolulu, serves as a channel of communication between language planners in India and elsewhere and between researchers and planners.

When I joined the Central Institute of Indian Languages in 1971 from the University of Chicago having learned contemporary linguistics from James McCawley, I had to reorient myself to the work at the Institute, as I had never studied sociolinguistics there. With this background, I saw the need for bringing the grammatical issues into sociolinguistic research to provide it with a grammatical foundation and for bringing in sociolinguistic concerns to grammatical research to provide it a social foundation. I used, for example, the mixed code to test some constraints on transformational rules and conversely used NP accessibility hierarchy to chart the course of convergence.

This approach requires the researchers to keep their interest in research on grammar and on use of language, as I have tried to keep an interest, for example, in movement rules as well as language movements.

This kind of disciplinary integration is necessary in a country like India where the number of linguists is small and the linguistic agenda is large. Moreover, the pressure on linguists in developing countries to be socially relevant is very great. They are expected not only to contribute to their discipline but also to their language and society. This integration should give better linguistics as well.

It may be true that the majority of linguists in India are sociolinguists in the sense that they write on various kinds of sociolinguistic problems. There was a big shift to sociolinguistics in the U.S. in the sixties and the training programs organized in India to catch up with it, the new positions created in the University department and the fast shifts in Chomskyan linguistics, which could not be caught up (as someone said to have the tires inflated at intervals) as funds to American universities and Summer Institutes had dried up. One more reason was the perception that sociolinguistics was a soft subject. This was based on the mistaken notion that the intuitive knowledge as a member of the linguistic community could be passed on as a research product without having to go through the rigor of theoretical and methodological application. This perception is reflected in the quality of sociolinguistic research also.

It is noteworthy that though impetus for the development of sociolinguistics in India came from the U.S. as in most other intellectual pursuits, for some of the founders of this discipline in the U.S., their Indian experience was perhaps an important motivating factor to initiate this new field of inquiry. The early works of Ferguson, Gumperz, and Bright have already been mentioned. This is the irony of sociolinguistics in India. The academic inquiry does not arise out of direct experience but comes to be accepted and pursued after it is formulated by the experience of outsiders. The basic notions of sociolinguistics, like mother tongue, language loss, language boundary, linguistic identity, bilingual competence, etc., seem to have a meaning different in the experienced reality of India from the meaning assumed in current theories, but this subjective understanding does not translate into theory. A crucial question is whether there is an Indian or a third world perspective of sociolinguistics as in sociology. If there is one, why is it not articulated assertively? Here lies the challenge for the sociolinguists in India.

What is the achievement of sociolinguistic work done in India in the past thirty years? Its contribution to innovations or refinements in theory is marginal. It is not that there are no dissenting voices. Some were mentioned earlier. But they are not in a commanding position to make an impact. There are no mechanisms or efforts to periodically review and synthesize the work done and to make a cumulative progress. There are no thematic volumes, for example, collecting cohesively Indian sociolinguistic research findings and points of view. Such volumes make international presence possible. There is no set of questions the Indian researchers share and try to find answers to collectively. The research, therefore, is diffused and repetitive.

Indian sociolinguistics has failed to excite and draw sociologists into the fold. There is no department of sociology which, for example, offers a course in sociology of language. Sociolinguistics remains an enterprise of linguists and to that extent lacks interdisciplinary depth. Indian sociology has come up with some theoretical concepts for understanding the Indian society, but they do not seem to be used by Indian sociolinguists. There is no dialogue between Indian sociologists and sociolinguists, depriving enrichment mutually.

As could be expected, the contribution of Indian sociolinguistics for the solution of language problems in social problems is minimal. But sociolinguistic research has helped us to have a better understanding of the problems at least in academia. The contribution to literacy programs, language education in schools, language use in administration and law courts, and codification efforts, such as alphabet making, script reform, technical term creation, modernization of language, etc., is of elucidating the issues, of producing materials, alphabets and terms, of giving advice to the managers of these programs, and of taking up research. Since the sociolinguists do not control many crucial variables which are of economic and political nature, the achievements in these areas are expectedly limited.

The future growth of sociolinguistics in India will depend on equipping itself with comprehensive data and theory to give answers to practical questions and on giving it a linguistic, sociological, and Indian orientation.

At the international level, sociolinguistics should absorb the general questions considered important for grammatical theory. This should include extension of theoretical underpinnings like universals and parameters to the social phenomena of language. Questions, like what the universal principles of language use are, what the universal features of multilingualism are, what the parametric variations in the rules of language use and features of multilingualism are, will call for a different research agenda. Similarly, sociolinguists should look for social determinants of linguistic structure as there are cognitive constraints. The social determinants of linguistic utterances are well recognized. Sociolinguistics in short should move into the cognitive paradigm. Another aspect of integration with grammatical theory will be interfacing the rules of language use with the different modules of grammar. The question whether there can be a separate module like the modules for co-reference, thematic rules, case relations, etc., remains open. To become a unified discipline, sociolinguistics should integrate the different theories and methodologies used to describe disparate social phenomena of language, like language variation, language use, and language behavior taking respectively speech form, speech event, and speech community as the universe of description. Finally, for sociolinguistics to be truly a universal discipline, it should take as its bedrock the ethos of multilingualism, which characterizes the majority, if not all, of the nations.

Sociolinguistics: A Personal View

Basil Bernstein

Basil Bernstein was Karl Mannheim Professor of the Sociology of Education. Senior Professor Director, Professor Director Research, University of London Institute of Education. Now Emeritus Professor of the Sociology of Education, University of London.

My contribution to the origins and development of sociolinguistics is at best tangential or perhaps even negative. My interest in language was not a primary interest. It arose out of a thoroughgoing dissatisfaction with theories of socialization which were, in the 1950s, very much influenced by functionalist role theory and, of course, by the theoretical studies of Talcott Parsons. Parsons viewed language in culture as analogous to money in the economy. The key concept in functionalist approaches to socialization was the concept of "internalization" which although it had resonances with psychoanalysis, these were rarely explored. The concept seemed to me a term pointing to the need for its own description. In the late 1950s (and still today) I was preoccupied theoretically with what was then conceptualized as the outside- inside- outside problematic, and, empirically, with problems of class specialization of the cultures of schools and families which gave rise to differential access and acquisition.

I came to the study of language by a diverse set of routes driven by the inadequacy of sociology to provide an orientation. How different today, where perhaps there is an abstracting of discourse from social structure. I drew upon work in American cultural anthropology, Russian work on speech as an orientating and regulative system (Luria and Vygotsky), within sociology on Durkheim and Mead, and especially, Casirer's Philosophy of Symbolic Forms. The discourse was somewhat distant from my work as a teacher of post office messenger boys in the East End of London, having been for three years a resident settlement worker in the area. The difference between the expected pedagogic displays and those offered became the source of a long compulsive study, the formulation of which underwent a series of transformations that took me beyond sociolinguistics. I was a passenger who both joined and departed early; consequently, it would not be appropriate for me to attempt to give an opinion on the many questions suggested by our editors. Certainly my intellectual background and orientation contributed to a sense of marginality to the developments, conceptualizations, and orientations of most of the early sociolinguists, and probably to those of today. Even when we appeared to share a common empirical problem it was clear that conceptualizations drew on different traditions and produced language descriptions separated by levels of analysis.

My introduction to linguistics consisted of a collection of samples of speech from discussion groups of lower working-class and upper middle-class male adolescents. Dissatisfied with their description, I applied to University College London to read for a higher degree in linguistics. By amazing good fortune I was sent to the Professor of Phonetics, Dennis Fry, to whom I explained my background, research problem, and occupation (school teacher). He said, "Don't bother about linguistics, go and talk to Frieda Goldman-Eisler." Perhaps these were the most crucial meetings of my career. Professor Fry encouraged me to apply for a research grant to analyze my tapes and not, as he put it, bother about linguistics. At that point he was absolutely right.

My next significant encounter with linguistics was an invitation to give a seminar in the early sixties to the Department of Linguistics at the University of Edinburgh, where I met Michael Halliday, who at that time was a lecturer in linguistics. I would say without hesitation that that meeting, and the relationship which followed when Halliday came to London as Professor at University College London, was crucial to my understanding of the workings of language in society. I was already involved in extensive research, but without any systematic theory of description that would enable me to view the data I had collected from a semantic, linguistic, and sociological perspective. I had already developed a semantic network of choices entered through a series of related subsystems forming what we called, after Halliday, the regulative context (later regulative discourse). However, what was required was a theory which could describe the specialization of *patterns of meanings* across levels of the grammar, where the unit of the analysis was above the level of the sentence; a theory where mutual translation between the languages of sociology and linguistics was possible, effective, and creative for both languages. I found this in what in those days was called "Scale-and-Category Grammar." Ruqaiya Hasan joined the Sociology Research Unit in 1964 and provided an exciting, theory-driven expansion of the research beyond cohesion analysis. We have kept up a correspondence since, and her theory of semantic variation opens up new vistas in our understanding of the role of language in the construction of consciousness and its power positionings. "My claim is that as Saussure limited the domain of linguistics, so also Labov limits the domain of sociolinguistics, which is reduced to social diagnostics, ignoring deeper issues in the role of language in the creation, maintenance, and change of social institutions" (Hasan 1992:81). Thus, the Halliday/Hasan contribution to my development is incalculable.

When I first met Halliday and Hasan, my concerns were not consciously sociolinguistic. They were driven by the theoretical and empirical necessities of the research which were then my primary concerns. I found I had little in common with the theoretical orientations of sociolinguistics in the sixties and onwards. This was entirely related to differences in the traditions we drew upon and the level of the analysis. This difference was transparently revealed at a seminar organized by John Gumperz at Berkeley in 1968. However, Dell Hymes, for me, stood apart from the micro-level preoccupations of interactive communicative/conversational analysis or correlational diagnostics. Dell Hymes' work seemed to me to be distinguished by a breadth of scholarship, vision, and generosity (rare in those days as today). Language, culture, and society were held together, and the forms of their embeddedness traced across different levels of manifestations. The direction he offered and manner of analysis was unfortunately not always followed.

To my memory, sociolinguistics in the sixties and seventies had a very selective, narrowly focussed sociological base. John Gumperz apart, sociolinguistics attracted ethnomethodologists, and as a consequence it was preoccupied with intracontextual speech displays, essentially concerned with the construction and negotiation of order as members' practical accomplishments. At that time ethnomethodology was in a rampant, radical, messianic stage, antagonistic to mainstream sociology, and sociolinguistics may well have been seen as an attractive temporary resource. Their emphasis upon members' competence—communicative competence—ensured a welcome. Competence became the focus of convergence across the social sciences embracing the study of culture (Levi-Strauss), ethnography of communication (Dell Hymes), child development (Piaget), linguistics (Chomsky), and conversational analysis (Garfinkel et al.). Thus, we have cultural competence, communicative competence, linguistic competence, cognitive competence, and finally, the competence of members' practical accomplishments. We have an extraordinary convergence across the social sciences in this period, and across disciplines with different assumptions, some structuralist, others radically opposed to structuralism.

Competence as conceptualized in the social, not the cultural sense, is not the product of any one particular culture. Cultures are always specialized, but competence is not restricted to any one culture. It is beyond the reach and restraints of power relations and their differential unequal positionings, and it is intrinsically creative and informally, tacitly acquired in nonformal interactions. They are practical accomplishments. Not necessarily intrinsic to the concept but empirically often collocating with it, is an antagonism to communication specialized by formal, explicit procedures and institutions. Thus, we have Labov's "lames" and Willis's "earholes."

The social logic of the concept competence may reveal:

1. An announcement of a universal democracy of acquisition. All are inherently competent. There is no deficit.

2. The individual as active and creative *in* the *construct*ion of a valid world of m*eaning* and practice. There can only be differences be*tween such wor*lds, meanings, and practices.

3. A celebration of everyday, oral language use and suspicion of specialized languages.

4. Official socializers are suspect, for acquisition is a tacit, invisible act, not subject to public regulation or, perhaps, not primarily acquired through such regulation.

5. A critique of hierarchical relations, where domination is replaced by facilitation and imposition by accommodation.

Perhaps we can now glimpse how the concept of competence, resonated with, was legitimated by the liberal, progressive, and radical ideologies of the heady sixties, especially those which dominated education in that period and later.

However, the idealism of competence, a celebration of what we are in contrast to how we have been positioned, is bought at a price: the abstracting of the individual from the analysis of the distribution of power and principles of control which selectively specialize modes of realization and their acquisition. Thus, the announcement of competence points away from such a specialization, away from the macro blot on the micro context, and points, instead, to "difference" as the key to understanding the selective specializings of the exploration of meanings and the forms of their realization. Some differences are legitimized as superior by dominant groups, others are judged as inferior; *but as all are competent,* inadequate communication displays on the part of those judged inferior are a function of the context, interaction, meanings, criteria, and the values in which these are embedded, created by the dominant group.

It was in this arena that the code theory was contextualized, or rather selectively recontextualized. Chomsky provided one legitimation with the judgment that the thesis "was below rationality," while Labov provided an apparent empirical dismissal. Indeed, the theory became a means of bestowing ideological purity on those who denounced it. I was, at the time essential to this intellectual field, for I had created almost single-handed a focus for the field's ritual cleansing. In this respect Labov's paper, "The Logic of Non-Standard English" achieved canonical status (see Appendix). Other views can be found elsewhere (Bernstein 1971, 1973, 1990, 1995).

There is no doubt in my mind that the difference/deficit debate which preoccupied much of the sociolinguistics in the sixties and early seventies was of little theoretical significance and, indeed, obscured more than it revealed. From another point of view, however, it was undoubtedly powerful and influential. It sucked in a steady flow of research funds and opened up new academic positions in universities. It brought together linguists, anthropologists, sociologists, psychologists, and educationalists with a common focus, and so facilitated a new interdisciplinary effervescence. It led, on the one hand, to educationalists and teachers having to reexamine their value assumptions, expectations and methods, and on the other hand, it served to legitimize what might be called pedagogic populism.

As I remarked earlier, I do not have the warrant to respond to some of the important issues raised by the editors, as I virtually ceased any relation to the field after the early seventies, although I clearly kept in contact with individuals. What I found particularly exciting about the take-off period was the opportunity to share and follow the work of Susan Ervin-Tripp, Dan Slobin, and especially Courtney Cazden. Cazden seemed to me to play a crucial dual role, informing sociolinguists through her own classroom research and exposing education (especially child development) to the new approaches and findings being developed in sociolinguistics. Alan Grimshaw played a similar analogous and crucial function for sociology. It may well be that all involved in the take-off period performed dual roles, facing towards the original discipline and outward to the new field. Perhaps with specialization of the field as an autonomous discourse, issuing its own licenses for access, study, and practice, in short with professionalization, the interdisciplinary effervescence may well have been weakened, and with that weakening there came more puzzle solving rather than new paradigms.

From another point of view I am reminded of Dell Hymes' judgment that sociolinguistics had extended the horizon of linguistics but has done little for the other social sciences. I wonder about this; certainly in my narrow experience, this seems to be the case. The *socio* of sociolinguistics seems to be very narrowly focused, selected more by the requirements of linguistics than developed by the requirements of sociology.

Very complex questions are raised by the relation of the *socio* to the *linguistic*. What linguistic theories of description are available for what socio issues? And how do the latter limit the former? What determines the dynamics of linguistic theory, and how do these dynamics relate, if at all, to the dynamics of change in those disciplines which do and could contribute to the socio? If "socio" and linguistics are to illuminate language as a truly social construct, then there must be mutually translatable principles of descriptions which enable the dynamics of the social to enter these translatable principles. These principles should facilitate descriptions of the relations between micro encounters and their macro contexts, where appropriate. Thus, the linguistic and sociological theory (for example) should be so formulated that their level of analysis in the local instance of their application, should function horizontally *and* vertically. Both theories, then, should be capable of describing ongoing, context-specific encounters, in a language that can transpose the intracontextual into the intercontextual. Central to such a linguistic theory must be the status accorded to meaning, for it is meaning which is central to a truly social theory of language. With meaning as central, we can ask: What meaning and where? Whose meaning? Why this meaning and no other? And so on. From this point of view, language becomes the interface of interrelated systems. Language as a social construct requires mutually translatable principles of description among the interface disciplines concerned with the formulations, maintenance, and change of that social construct (Hasan 1992).

Perhaps an example would be relevant here. If we take a micro context of control (parent/child, teacher/student, social worker/client, doctor/patient, prison warden/inmate), what is subject to control (i.e., selection) is the embedding of an instructional discourse in a regulative discourse. It seems to me that in order to understand the ongoing interaction and describe it, a sociological model of the *potential semantic* (even better, semiotic) is required. Such a model might take the form of a series of subsystems, each opening to a set of choices sensitive to the particularities of a context of control. Different modalities of control would act selectively on interactional realizations, and this would lead to specific emphasis on some subsystems and upon their grammar, lexicon, and paralinguistics. In this way the linguistic and paralinguistic realizations would be signifiers of modalities of control and their outcomes. Different modalities of control in turn would be signifiers of different forms of symbolic control, and these different forms of symbolic control might well be the expected relays of certain

Sociolinguistics: A Personal View   49

distributions of power, some less effective than others, some challenged more by some groups than others.

In conclusion, I am acutely conscious that most of this contribution refers to my own relation to sociolinguistics rather than to the field itself. But that may be because I am not really a field person. Perhaps, even so, such a perspective may not be entirely irrelevant to the purpose of this book.

Appendix

It might be valuable from a historical point of view to take seriously Labov's paper, "The Logic of Non-Standard English," which seems to me to have lacked such attention. It has been enthusiastically reprinted but rarely analyzed on its own terms. Perhaps this exercise might shed some light on sociolinguistics.

This opposition deficit/difference received much of its power from Labov's paper, "The Logic of Non-Standard English" (1972), in which he contrasts the arguments of two black speakers, one middle class and the other working class. He shows that the working-class youth's argument is succinct, pithy, and logical, whereas the middle-class black is verbose, redundant, and hesitant. This is an unwarranted conclusion. Both arguments are logical, as judged by rules of inference, but the modalities of the argument are different. They follow different paradigmatic forms, and in consequence they should not be judged by antitheses such as verbose-succinct, redundant-pithy, economic-uneconomic, hesitant-fluent. Larry's argument is essentially by assertion and denial: some say if you are good you go to heaven, and if you are bad you go to hell, but there is no god and so no heaven. The middle-class black is not redundant, verbose; he is producing an argument based upon a different paradigmatic form entailing rules of evidence, falsification, abstraction, generalization. The crucial difference lies not in the content but in the *form* of the argument offered by the two speakers (1972:193–94, 197).[1]

It is a matter of interest that in the endlessly recycled account of Larry's discussion of black and white gods it is rarely noted that Larry is given five probes to assist in the structuring of his argument (1972:193–94). "What?" "What happens to your spirit?" "And where does your spirit go?" "On what [does it depend]?" "Why?" Further, in another exchange (1972:217), which appears later in the paper, that may have preceded the interchange referred to above (1972:196), Larry is specifically asked what color God is, white or black, and is given three probes to focus the answer. In contrast, the question to the black middle-class speaker is, "Do you know of anything that

---

[1]The page numbers in this appendix refer to the reprint of "The Logic of Non-Standard English" published in Giglioni, P. P., ed. 1972, *Language and Social Context,* 179–215. Harmondsworth Middlesex: Penguin Books Ltd.

someone can do to have someone who has passed on visit him in a dream?" (1972:199). Not the clearest question to answer. The respondent is given no probes to assist in the structuring of his reply. The first half of the reply is concerned with the relation between dreams and reality, and the second half is concerned with whether it is possible to induce a dreamer to dream of something specific. In the light of the question, perhaps not a bad effort. However, this is not the view of Labov nor of those who recycle the quotations and interpretations unmediated by an analysis. The "liberal" ideology of white sociolinguists paradoxically here transforms difference into deficit.

Nothing is shown by this comparison because no comparison using Labov's criteria should be applied. The issue that is raised refers to the social origins of the forms of argument and the rules of their selective, contextual realization and interactional practices. It may well be the case on this analysis that the middle-class black adult has access to two argumental forms whereas the black working class may well have access to only one. This would require further investigation.

Earlier in the same paper Labov presents spoken texts of a black child who in formal experimental context was virtually silent, but when placed in a context with a friendly black adult interviewer who sat on the floor, and where the child was accompanied by his friend sharing a Coke, spoke freely and managed the interaction effectively. The example is used to illustrate the effect of context upon speech and the management of interaction, and this it undoubtedly does, but it also raises more fundamental questions. How was it necessary for the context to be changed so drastically, and what was the relation between the distinguishing features of the changed context and the management of interaction and communication? In terms of my theory an analysis of the child's speech shows that it is a restricted variant, which is precisely what it should be, given the distinguishing social features of the context. In both cases offered in the paper, the sociological level of analysis is bypassed in order to demonstrate an underlying competence, and this is not unusual where a "difference" position is to be favored, but I submit that the fundamental issue is not an illustration of a communicative competence but a question of the *controls on the distribution of sociolinguistic rules of contextualized performance.*

We shall consider in more detail Labov's second major example, taken from the speech of a black boy under different contextual constraints. It is worth spending time over these examples, as they have been received enthusiastically and repeated, usually without comment. In the first situation the boy is expected to make comments in response to the elicitation, "Tell me all you can about this." The reference is a block or fire engine. Even with six probes offered by the white interviewer the boy rarely replies in more than one nominal group (1972:185). In another context the white interviewer is replaced by a black (Clarence Robins), who interviews Leon (aged 8) (1972:186). The latter again gives minimal responses to the following question accompanied by eleven probes: "What if you saw somebody kickin' somebody else on the ground or was using a stick, what would you do if you saw that?" No other description of the contexts is given in Labov (1969). Labov's explanations are that here Leon is defending himself against possible accusations, and in the first example, it is the asymmetry of the relationship, not the ineptness of the interviewer, that is responsible for the silence.

Further, Leon is interviewed by a skilled black interviewer raised in Harlem and offered, "You watch—you like to watch television?" (Leon nods.) "What's your favourite program?" Despite eight probes Leon's replies are minimal (1972:187). Labov comments that despite the skills, sensitivities, and experience of the black interviewer, Clarence Robins, Leon is not communicative and Robins is unable to break down what Labov calls the "prevailing social constraints." For Labov, it is because the social relationship is asymmetrical, not because of the race of the interviewer. But is it? Is asymmetry a property of the form of the social relationship or is it the form of the discourse?

In all the contexts so far described, the child is positioned in an interrogative, instructional discourse, whether official within the school or informal in the case of interrogation on a moral issue or a favorite television program. This discourse is specialized, first, with respect to the child's social relation to the discourse and, second, as an interrogative of an open form. The child is positioned within a request for unique information, that is, information which only he can give. In this sense the social basis of the child's relation to the discourse is egocentric. He is differentiated from his social base and its competences, as a figure differentiated from its ground. The fact that the interrogative is of an open form intensifies the egocentric social base.

Now in the other contexts that follow, the asymmetry is no less explicit, but on the argument offered here, the child's relation to the discourse is *sociocentric* and, in consequence, he can draw upon competences which make that position possible (1972:88). Thus, when Clarence Robins sits on the floor, introduces taboo words, topics, when Leon is with his best friend, then a lively interaction takes place. Yet in this interaction the lead is taken by Leon's friend Greg. Labov argues that Greg and Leon talk as much to each other as they do to Robins, the black interviewer. In fact this is not the case. Robins makes eleven interventions, all of them *interrogative*. In other words, the asymmetry holds in the context despite its apparent informality. The interchange is lively between boys because they both draw upon common rules and shared knowledge.

In the next section, which consists of eighteen interchanges, Clarence makes six interventions, most of them explicit or implicit interrogatives, while the Greg and Leon exchanges consist almost entirely of affirmation or negations, and this pattern continues in the final sequence of exchanges. It is a little difficult to accept Labov's interpretation that "we have two boys who have so much to say that they keep interrupting each other and who seem to have no difficulty in using the English language to express themselves." These conclusions are based upon criteria that are inappropriate to the context and in an important respect are patronizing. Further, Labov's local interpretation of the exchanges seems on analysis to be unwarranted. Yet these examples of interchange (or rather the interpretations) are repeatedly quoted and virtually sacrosanct.

The view here is that we have neither expressive speech nor a rich array of grammar in one context and severely reduced speech in another. What we have are interchanges that are embedded in different social bases and thus founded upon different rules and competences. It has little to do with asymmetry. Robins maintains an interrogative mode in all contexts, and his questions press from the *outside,* whereas Greg's and Leon's affirmations, negations, and interrogations are generated from *within* the age and gender rules they both share. I agree only with Labov's conclusion: "We see no connection between verbal skill in the speech events characteristic of the street culture and success in the school." However, what is required is less ad hoc ideology and interpretation and a more systematic, general understanding of the social basis of modalities of communication and their distributive principles and differential outcomes.

The meeting of such a requirement invites an analysis of the distribution of power and principle of control that regulate and distribute, unequally, communicative performance principles which differentially position speakers with respect to interactional power and context management. This is the focus of study of the code thesis (Bernstein 1990).

Reminiscences: Beginnings of Sociolinguistics

William Bright

William Bright received his Ph.D. in linguistics at Berkeley in 1955, and taught for 30 years in linguistics and anthropology at U.C.L.A. His special interests include Native American languages, south Asian languages, anthropological linguistics, sociolinguistics, ethnopoetics, grammatology, and onomastics. He has served as editor of the journal *Language,* of the *International Encyclopedia of Linguistics* (Oxford University Press), and of the journal *Language in Society*.

As a Berkeley linguistics student in the late 1940s and early 1950s, I had the fortune to study under two distinguished disciples of Edward Sapir: M. B. Emeneau and Mary R. Haas. But paradoxically, I don't recall any reading assignments from Sapir in my classes, which were in a very Bloomfieldian tradition. There was, to be sure, a course on "language and culture" in the Anthropology Department, taught by John Rowe; but it was not in the linguistic curriculum, and I never attended it. Nevertheless, I found great stimulation in reading articles that my teachers had written in a Sapirian "ethnolinguistic" tradition, such as Emeneau's "Personal Names of the Todas" (*American Anthropologist* 1938), and Haas' "Men's and Women's Speech in Koasati" (*Language* 1944). In retrospect, my teachers seem to me to have been among the pioneers of sociolinguistics.

Another early influence on me was Einar Haugen, whom I heard lecture at the 1949 Linguistic Institute in Ann Arbor: while everyone else was debating the definitions of the phoneme and the morpheme, Haugen was offering exciting views of language contact, bilingualism, and loanwords. (My first published paper in 1952, on lexical innovations in Karuk, was inspired by Haugen's work.)

When I finished my doctoral dissertation—a descriptive grammar of Karuk, a Native American language—I found no academic jobs available in American linguistics. From Emeneau's teaching, I had a background in Sanskrit and in Dravidian linguistics; and with his support, I obtained a two-year fellowship to do teaching and research in India. This was under the auspices of the Rockefeller Foundation, which was sponsoring a program in descriptive linguistics at Deccan College, Poona. During this period I became acquainted with Charles Ferguson, who like Emeneau was a member of the advisory committee for the Rockefeller program. This program deserves special mention in a history of linguistics, since it prompted a number of Indian and American linguists to begin exploring the possibilities of sociolinguistics.

Before I left for India, it was decided that my research should be on Kannada, a Dravidian language; and I spent some time eliciting Kannada data from an Indian graduate student in Berkeley. Although I asked for data in a conversational style, my consultant gave me what I eventually discovered, once I was established in Mysore State, was pure literary Kannada. For two years I alternated teaching duties in Poona with research in Mysore; in Poona I spent more time with Ferguson, and there too first met John Gumperz. It was conversations with John that first made me aware of the possibility that a field of sociolinguistics might be developed, which would make sense of the variation that we were encountering in our fieldwork.

Several of our group, after returning from India, took part in a symposium, organized by Ferguson, on "Language and culture dynamics in South Asia," at the 1957 American Anthropological Association meeting in Chicago. (It was there that I heard Uriel Weinreich utter his often-quoted definition of a dialect as "a language with an army and a navy.")[1] The papers from that meeting were edited by Ferguson and Gumperz, and published as *Linguistic Diversity in South Asia,* 1960 supplement to *IJAL.* In the meantime, during the academic year 1958–59, Gumperz and Hymes and I were all at Berkeley; Ferguson's classic article on diglossia was published in *Word* during the same period; and the pot continued to boil.

In 1959, I accepted a position in the Anthropology Department at UCLA, as a protegé of Harry Hoijer, the dean of Sapirians; there I became involved for the first time in teaching "language and culture"—much of which was what we would later call "sociolinguistics." In 1963, at the AAA meeting at San Francisco, Hymes organized a symposium which I was unable to attend, but which was edited by Gumperz and Hymes for publication in 1964 as a supplement to AA, under the title *The Ethnography of Communication.* (This was the nucleus of the book later prepared by the same editors with the title

---

[1] See Notes, *Language in Society* 1987:26, 469.

Directions in Sociolinguistics: The Ethnography of Communication, published in 1972.) At the 1963 conference, William Labov presented one of his early papers, and promptly became a leading player on the sociolinguistic scene.

In the fall of 1963, I was also planning the UCLA Conference on Sociolinguistics that took place in May 1964, and which again involved what by now were "the usual suspects": Haugen, Ferguson, Gumperz, Hymes, Labov, and others. The resulting volume, *Sociolinguistics,* was published by Mouton in 1966. As for the term "sociolinguistics," the model was of course "psycholinguistics," which in the 1950s was becoming well established as a term and as a field. When I planned the UCLA Conference and the resulting volume, I hoped that the project could play as important a role as the Indiana University Conference on Psycholinguistics had done in 1953 (the proceedings, edited by Charles Osgood and Thomas Sebeok, were published in 1954). But the term "sociolinguistics" was used before me by Einar Haugen, and had apparently been invented in 1952 by the Texas English professor Haver Currie (who died in Austin in 1994).

The UCLA Conference in 1964 was of course followed closely by the summer seminar on sociolinguistics at Indiana University, where interested linguists and anthropologists were thrust into confrontation with sociologists; Joshua Fishman played an especially important role in building bridges between the two groups. In 1966, I helped to organize the Linguistic Institute at UCLA, where sociolinguistic offerings played an important role. However, in the same year, I became Editor of *Language,* and in the following years I spent more time on editorial work than on research. In 1972, when Dell Hymes founded the journal *Language in Society,* I was delighted to be on the editorial board; and in 1992, when I succeeded Dell as Editor of *Language in Society,* it was a special pleasure to return to a central role in the field of sociolinguistics. To the teachers and colleagues whom I have mentioned, to other colleagues too numerous to mention, and to my students from whom I have learned so much—to all these, I extend my warmest thanks!

Let me now share with you a few thoughts and recollections. For me personally, simply because it was "my baby," the most important milestone in "modern sociolinguistics" was organizing the UCLA Conference on Sociolinguistics in 1964, and editing the volume *Sociolinguistics* which appeared in 1966. I *wanted* it to be a milestone and a landmark, because I felt it was time to bring together and to label the kind of work that Gumperz, Hymes, Haugen, Ferguson, Labov, and myself had been doing; and I felt ambitious to take a role of leadership in this process. I appropriated the label "sociolinguistics"—knowing, I think, that it had been coined by Currie in 1952—hoping that it would serve to define an area of study, as the term "psycholinguistics" had done a few years earlier.

In 1966, the hot topic in linguistics was of course Chomsky's work. A possible negative aspect of this, however, was that links between anthropology and linguistics, which had been very fruitful since the time of Franz Boas, were weakened. Until July 1966, when Linguistics at UCLA changed from an interdepartmental program into a separate department, I had been a member of the Anthropology Department (which itself, when I arrived at UCLA in 1959, had been part of a Department of Anthropology and Sociology). Professor Harry Hoijer, my senior colleague and mentor in linguistic anthropology at UCLA, had been one of Edward Sapir's chief disciples, and for years a leader in "language and culture" research as well as in "pure" linguistics; but during the 1960s Hoijer felt himself increasingly alienated from the Chomskyan linguistics which abstracted language from the sociocultural matrix.

Dell Hymes' anthology, *Language in Culture and Society,* had been published in 1964; it was widely used as a text in "Language and Culture" courses, and helped to define "Ethnolinguistics" and "Sociolinguistics" as respectable interdisciplinary fields. But most people involved in these areas, like myself, found themselves relatively isolated in their academic departments: our colleagues, whether in linguistics or in anthropology, were occupied with other matters. There was even less communication with colleagues in sociology, although "Sociology of Language" seemed a potential area of fruitful collaboration. I hoped, then, that the 1966 Conference would help to put sociolinguistics "on the map."

My own interests settled around the question of variation—around the realization that uniform linguistic structure did not exist in dialects, or even in idiolects, and that linguistic description needed a way to account for variation determined by such features as social class and social situation. I was also increasingly concerned with the role that variation played in the historical change of language. From the time of the UCLA Conference onward, I became increasingly aware that such phenomena as language contact, bilingualism, and language planning could also be accommodated within sociolinguistics.

As I have suggested above, the main input to early sociolinguistics came from linguists and anthropologists; but the Indiana University Conference in the summer of 1964 enabled us to meet many sociologists and to begin interaction with them. Of the sociologists there, Joshua Fishman was the most important in terms of continuing cooperation. In subsequent years, Erving Goffman at the University of Pennsylvania and Manny Schegloff at UCLA were very important in working with linguists and anthropologists to develop sociolinguistic research.

My training had been almost entirely in linguistics; but my principal teachers at Berkeley, M. B. Emeneau and Mary Haas, had been students of Sapir's, and taught me that language was definitely a *part* of a culture. Doing field work on American Indian languages as a graduate student, I read quite a bit of anthropology and associated with anthropology students. When I was hired at UCLA in 1959, it was to teach linguistics in the Department of Anthropology (and Sociology); I continued to read in the field, and to associate with anthropology students and faculty. (I married an anthropology graduate student, Marcia Kinnamon, in 1964, and did one joint research project with her; she died in 1971.)

I would like to emphasize the importance of the Sapirian tradition in sociolinguistics. Both Emeneau and Haas were active for years in the AAA, and published many articles in what we could now call "Sociolinguistics," e.g., in the use of kinship terminology, in verbal play, and in language contact. Emeneau was a member of the committee that advised the Rockefeller Foundation in the 1950s on promoting the development of linguistics in India, and he was personally responsible for getting me to India for two years. (Ferguson was also on that advisory committee.) The fellowship holders in that Rockefeller program included Gumperz, Paul Friedrich, and others besides myself, both Americans and Indians (such as P. B. Pandit), who went on to do serious work in sociolinguistics.

I kept thinking I should learn more about sociology; but I found the discipline, and the practitioners, rather forbidding. Harold Garfinkel took part in the UCLA Conference, but I don't think anybody understood what he was saying. In later years, works of Fishman, Goffman, and Schegloff gave me more appreciation of sociological contributions.

The early work in Sociolinguistics was "problem-driven": that term has always applied to my work. I'm not much of a theoretician by nature, but I've tried to contribute to the ongoing give-and-take between problem-oriented and theory-oriented research.

My very first inspiration to do what might be called Sociolinguistics was a conversation with John Gumperz in Poona, India, in 1956. After both he and I returned to the United States, I was in frequent communication with him as well as with Charles Ferguson and Dell Hymes (both of whom I had known previously). At the 1964 conferences, I met Bill Labov and Joshua Fishman, both of whom were becoming "major players." These seem to me to have been the most influential sociolinguists in the 1960s. I think they tended to be, like me, somewhat isolated on our own campuses, but seeking opportunities to get together at annual meetings of the AAA and LSA, as well as at ad hoc conferences. I arranged for Labov to teach at the UCLA Linguistics Institute in 1966, and this turned on a lot of younger people. During that same summer, a number of us held an informal meeting at my house, to discuss the development of sociolinguistics; I remember Erving Goffman attended. There was a committee of the Social Science Research Council (SSRC) in those years which was trying to encourage sociolinguistic studies; Dell Hymes was active in it, but I don't know much about it.

My contribution to the field has probably been more in organization and in editing than in research. However, some of my early writing on the role of sociolinguistics in language change was anthologized and was moderately influential: "Social dialect and language history" (1960) and "Language, social stratification, and cognitive orientation" (1967). I think those papers raised some interesting questions that have not yet been fully answered.

Starting in 1959 at UCLA, I gave a language and culture course which included a good deal of what we eventually called sociolinguistics. In the early 1970s I started a general undergraduate course called Sociolinguistics at UCLA, but I may have only taught it once; after that it was taught by various other people. There was moderate cooperation from the Anthropology, Sociology, and English departments. In later years I gave occasional grad courses in the linguistics department on particular sociolinguistic topics, e.g., "Sociolinguistics of South Asia" and "Language Contact."

Labov used to say that the goal of sociolinguistics was to put itself out of business—that is, not to establish the interdisciplinary field as an "empire" of its own, but to help create a better and fuller linguistics, a better social anthropology, a better sociology. I think most of us agreed. But success has been only partial.

Sociolinguistics has in fact grown, and has a higher profile every year; it has attracted interdisciplinary research involving such fields as psychology, medicine, education, law, speech/communication, ethnic studies, gender studies, and literature. In some university linguistics programs, which are oriented toward "functional" approaches to language, the contribution of sociolinguistics is recognized and well integrated. In particular, in programs where discourse analysis is cultivated, there is likely to be good interaction with sociolinguistics. However, in programs which are oriented toward "formal" linguistics (generative or other), sociolinguistics continues to be seen as largely irrelevant. New papers on sociolinguistic research are much more likely to be given at the AAA meeting than at the LSA.

I have mentioned meetings, seminars, and colloquia above. The principal organizers in the early stages were certainly Gumperz, Hymes, Ferguson, and myself.

The UCLA conference volume *Sociolinguistics,* which I edited, was certainly influential in establishing the field, and has remained in print until the present. The journal *Language in Society*, which Dell Hymes founded in 1972, remains the most general and perhaps the most influential periodical in the field.

As sociolinguistics comes to include interdisciplinary work in an increasing number of fields, it perhaps necessarily becomes more diffuse. Any hope of a unified framework for sociolinguistics seems increasingly remote. But at the same time, we see an increasing number of scholars who apparently find a sociolinguistic outlook useful for work in their own fields. Of articles submitted to *Language in Society* these days, at least as many come from people with backgrounds in Education or Speech/Communication as in Sociology, Anthropology, or Linguistics. Perhaps the benefit of sociolinguistics is turning out not to be so much the improvement of linguistics, or even of sociology, as it is that of making people in these other fields more aware of sociolinguistic phenomena.

My own connections in the early days of sociolinguistics were mainly with North American scholars, to be sure, and with colleagues that we had worked with in India; P. B. Pandit, in Delhi, was a leading sociolinguist until his untimely death. Hans Kloss from Germany was an important voice at the Indiana Conference in 1964. A little later, Peter Trudgill came on the scene in England, continuing a tradition that had begun much earlier with J. R. Firth and M. A. K. Halliday, but which had previously not had much influence in the United States. Currently, there is lots of Anglo-American interaction, as reflected in the editorial board of *Language in Society:* Suzanne Romaine is an American working in England, Janet Holmes is a Britisher working in New Zealand, Lesley Milroy is a Britisher who moved to the United States in 1994.

I have mentioned that the SSRC was an important factor in sociolinguistic studies in the early days, but I had little direct contact. The Center for Applied Linguistics has, of course, always played an important role in encouraging sociolinguistics. Of the government agencies which have sometimes provided funds for linguistic research, I believe the former Health, Education, and Welfare (HEW) was important—did they not fund a lot of Labov's work in Philadelphia? But sociolinguistics doesn't seem to qualify for support from the National Science Foundation (NSF), National Endowment for the Humanities (NEH), or National Institutes of Health (NIH). In fact, I myself have been very little involved in grantspersonship, so am not well qualified to discuss this area.

I really do not know who was awarded the first doctorate in Sociolinguistics. Surely Labov's degree, under Weinreich at Columbia, was one of the earliest and most influential, especially because his dissertation was published by the Center for Applied Linguistics.

As regards a prognosis for the field of Sociolinguistics, it has certainly gotten bigger; there are now half a dozen journals that mostly publish what one could call Sociolinguistics, and the number of people who take some interest in the topic is growing steadily. But is it still "vibrant" and "vital?" I have suggested above that it has, rather, grown more diffuse. This is not necessarily a bad thing! The important issues nowadays seem to be not in elaborating sociolinguistic theory, but in finding ways to use sociolinguistics in an ever wider circle of neighboring fields. The practical applications of sociolinguistics in such areas as law, medicine, and education seem to me quite important, and they offer much room for further growth.

The Development of Sociolinguistics

Susan Ervin-Tripp

Susan M. Ervin-Tripp is Professor of Psychology at the University of California at Berkeley. She has been a Guggenheim Fellow, Fellow of the Center for Advanced Study in the Behavioral Sciences, and a member of the NAS China Delegation in Applied Linguistics.

Development of term. In a 1995 newspaper, a press dispatch about a famous Los Angeles trial identified a consultant on a Spanish speaker's testimony as a sociolinguist, without further explanation.[1] The term "sociolinguist" without hyphens was chosen by the Social Science Research Council (SSRC) in 1963 to identify its new advisory committee. The name was an analog of psycholinguistics, the interdisplinary field it had successfully brokered a decade earlier. In 1980 we find the introduction to a book by social psychologists which says "sociolinguistics has acquired such momentum over a ten-year period that it is almost unthinkable for scholars of contemporary language use to think of themselves as anything other than *socio*linguists, whatever their particular research interests" (Giles, Smith, and Robinson 1980:1).

Psycholinguistics committee. The Social Science Research Council is an organization in which directors from the constituent social sciences participate. Established in 1924 to advance research in the social sciences, it especially focuses on new fields of research, interdisciplinary proposals, area research, raising funds for workshops and conferences, and providing travel money, fellowships, and student funding.

---

[1] "Linguist's views on Rosa Lopez." *San Francisco Chronicle* March 4, 1995.

What each field brought.[2] The Committee on Linguistics and Psychology was formed after a 1951 SSRC seminar initiated by John Carroll, a psychologist with a long-standing interest in linguistics. The areas conceived for joint study at that time were mother tongue acquisition, language structure and thought, the role of dialect in social class, and the study of linguistic structure using psychological methods. A subsequent summer workshop conducted in conjunction with a Linguistic Institute laid out other areas in a monograph publishing the results (Osgood and Sebeok 1954). Participants included Thomas Sebeok, Floyd Lounsbury, and Joseph Greenfield from linguistics, Charles Osgood and James Jenkins from psychology, and six graduate students, of whom two, Sol Saporta and I, clearly remained identified later with the field of psycholinguistics.

The three central perspectives on which this summer program was based have been almost completely overthrown in current psycholinguistic research: the associative model of language learning, the Bloomfieldian model of descriptive linguistics, sequential probabilities in the information theory paradigm. Social facets of language were almost entirely absent, except as they affected conceptual categories, even though dialect was on the original agenda. What is surprising then, is why the launching of psycholinguistics was so successful. I think there are several reasons.

One reason is that the study of verbal behavior permeates much of human psychology, so many psychologists have had a need to understand language and persisted in the linkage to linguistics. This relationship was especially visible in the remarkable developments in speech perception research by the early sixties. A second reason is that the theoretical changes which next took place made the fields more compatible. The move from associative to cognitive views of learning made room for a more complex and less atomistic notion of what language was. The idea of a generative syntax suggested sweeping underlying categories, provided a framework for syntactic analysis that was congruent with cognitive psychology, and generated testable hypotheses about acquisition and second language learning. Based on these changes, there was a new wave of child language research by the late fifties and early sixties.[3]

In subsequent years, as generative grammar has become hegemonic, it has become apparent that ideologically the two fields are compatible, both moving towards less emphasis on learning, more on biological foundations, and towards an individualistic perspective on "the ideal speaker-learner," which

---

[2] A detailed review of SSRC participation in research on linguistics and the social sciences appears in Ervin-Tripp (1974).

[3] There were virtually simultaneous projects showing systematic diachronic syntactic change undertaken about 1959 in Washington by Martin Braine, in Cambridge by Roger Brown, and in Berkeley by Susan Ervin-Tripp.

permits relatively context-free experimentation on "competence." Both psychology and generative grammar seek universal generalizations about all humans. In psychology, even the study of differences presupposes that stimuli (such as tests) work the same for all. The spurt of interest in psycholinguistics owed, of course, a good deal to the leadership of Chomsky, whose view that linguistics was an aspect of the science of the mind, helped make issues central that linguists had once considered marginal.

The committee succeeded through its series of small conferences in spotlighting important issues which required cross-disciplinary work, legitimized them with funding agencies, and helped scholars to know one anothers' work. By including graduate students in small conferences, seminars, and workshops the Linguistics and Psychology Committee introduced a new generation of cross-disciplinary scholars such as Ursula Bellugi, Jean Berko, Thomas Bever, Susan Ervin-Tripp, Wallace Lambert, Eric Lenneberg, Wick Miller, and Sol Saporta. Being in this network meant getting invited to conferences, and getting on preprint paper circulation lists so that one might be abreast of new developments before the invention of the Internet.[4]

Conferences that overlapped. Issues included in the SSRC-sponsored small conferences during the life of the Committee on Linguistics and Psychology from 1952 to 1961 were content analysis, associative processes, meaning, aphasia, and linguistic universals. Several were of consequence to sociolinguists. These included a very small conference on Bilingualism in 1954 and the Style in Language conference in 1958 for which Brown and Gilman prepared their ground-breaking paper, "The Pronouns of Power and Solidarity" (1960).

The biggest enterprise sponsored by the committee was the Southwest Project in Comparative Psycholinguistics, which was John Carroll's proposal to test the Whorf hypothesis by using the comparative psychology paradigm, that is, repeating procedures in each of six language communities, Navaho, Zuni, Hopi, Hopi-Tewa, Spanish, and English. Two summers were spent doing this project, one in preparation, one in data collection, with teams of senior and junior researchers in each community, and a common field manual to guide them. Each procedure was pretested carefully. Topics included the

---

[4]The preprint circulation net worked as more than an extended library and information source. The role of these contact networks in professional placement and hence in the spread of these new disciplines is important sociologically. Until the affirmative action changes of the early seventies, however, which mandated public recruiting, the normal hiring mode in American universities was to contact friends in major universities and ask them to hand-pick candidates, a system which virtually excluded women and men in small institutions. It would take a special study to identify the additional increment of placement advantage from these conference connections. Undoubtedly, publication opportunities were enhanced for these young scholars.

effects of lexical categories on color discrimination and memory, the effects of Navaho form classification markers on color/form preferences and on memory, the commonalities and differences in synaesthesia and in semantic differential structure, the effects of language dominance on color naming, and associations in bilinguals. This study could be seen as the predecessor of the recent Max Planck studies focused on spatial categories. Joseph Casagrande, a cultural anthropologist, worked with the committee as staff member of SSRC, and joined the Navaho field team. As the only anthropologist in the planning and research group throughout, he played a major role in the Southwest Project, but had left the SSRC by the middle of the next decade.[5]

Why a sociolinguistics committee was formed.[6] While broadly cultured linguists like Sapir had written about psychological issues, linguistics and psychology had developed relatively independently of each other. But the relation of linguistics to some other social sciences was much closer. In particular, many anthropologists studied linguistics as a part of their training and as necessary to their work, and linguistic anthropologists were educated in anthropology departments. Until the fifties, it was typical for linguistics to be studied either within language/literature departments or within anthropology. As a result, linguists of the earlier generations were often multilingual, might be sensitive to aesthetic uses of language, and, if they did field work, they were aware of the role of language in the social life of communities. Only for those who studied isolated speakers, such as survival linguistics with the last speaker of a language, would that nexus become less visible. But anthropological linguists are unlikely to conceive of sociolinguistics as an interdisciplinary field since linguistics for them is in the field of anthropology.

There were other linguists who were likely to systematically consider social correlates of linguistic features, such as dialectologists and those studying dialectal change, who were concerned with geographic and social exogenous factors influencing language change.[7] The idea for the creation of a committee came from a different source. Charles Ferguson had written a classic article systematizing a type of code variation in societies, "Diglossia." In his field work and Foreign Service Institute experience he had seen the complex organization of multilingual policies, and as Director of the Center for

---

[5]Ed Dozier, a Tewa anthropologist, participated in some aspects of the project.

[6]It is clear that perspectives on the goals of the committee and its members, the theoretical issues, and so on are very different for each participant. In this review, I decided to take an institutional angle because of my committee experience and my interest in the social process of spreading new ideas, but a careful diachronic study of publications would give a deeper view of the intellectual history involved.

[7]A clear statement regarding social principles in linguistic change appears in Weinreich, Labov, and Herzog (1968).

Applied Linguistics, he was aware of the political aspects of language use and language planning. He knew that policy decisions regarding language were being made by many governments with an inadequate research basis. His goal was collaboration between linguists and sociologists on these issues when he proposed a Sociolinguistics Committee to the SSRC in 1963.[8]

By 1968 it was possible, in a memo to the committee projecting possible journals, to list these areas as comprising sociolinguistics: language and social stratification, language standardization, typology of sociolinguistic communication, acquisition of communicative competence, language problems of developing countries, pidginization and creolization. What is absent on this list is the focus on conversation structure that developed later.[9]

Members of the committee. The committee membership started out with a substantial membership of people with interests in larger societal organization, political integration, bilingualism, and ethnic relations. The senior members, who could bring prestige to the field of sociolinguistics within their professional organizations, were linguist Einar Haugen, known for his work on bilingualism, and sociologist Everett C. Hughes who had done studies of ethnic relations, including research in French Canada. Joshua Fishman was a sociologist especially interested in studies of language maintenance and language planning. Stanley Lieberson was a census sociologist interested in segregation and neighborhood patterns. Nathan Keyfitz was a mathematical demographer who studied migrations. John Useem had worked on issues of social stratification and economic development in India and the Pacific. Among the linguists were John Gumperz, who with Ferguson had edited a report on complex multilingual communities in South Asia, and Dell Hymes, whose programmatic proposal for an ethnography of speaking had just been published. The only psycholinguist, Susan Ervin-Tripp, who joined in 1966, had been studying bilinguals.

Later, the composition of the committee shifted with the replacement of Haugen, Keyfitz, and Useem, by sociologist Allen Grimshaw, who was studying race relations; linguist William Labov, working on urban dialects; Canadian sociologist Jacques Brazeau, studying relations between language communities in Quebec; and later, Charles Fillmore, relating pragmatic issues to syntax. Dell Hymes chaired the committee from 1970 to 1973, and subsequently co-chaired with Allen Grimshaw.

---

[8]I am judging from the early composition of the committee what its goals were since I did not join the committee until 1966.
[9]My memory of the activities of the committee is aided by a file of the minutes for the period of my membership.

Perspectives on the field. From the start, there were two different perspectives on the committee that later came to be called by some "macro- sociolinguistics" and "micro-sociolinguistics" or "interactional sociolinguistics."[10] On the whole, the research of the "macro" type was concerned with larger social units, and often with political categories like a named language, rather than with linguistic features as linguists identify them. Interactional sociolinguistics was concerned with processes in face-to-face interaction, analysis of transcripts, and linguistic features. This contrast was apparent, for example, in Fishman's organization of two readers in 1968 and 1971 which reflected his committee experience. He called the macro version "sociology of language." Within the readers, he used sociological subdivisions such as small group interaction, sociocultural issues, and stratification, and had sections on bilingualism, maintenance and shift of language, and language planning, which identify societal issues. Ethnography of communication, first dubbed "ethnography of speaking" by Dell Hymes (1962) appeared to be a program for the study of face-to-face interaction, but included attention to the sociocultural categorization of and attitudes toward languages and named speech varieties.

Another realignment was due to major theoretical changes within sociology. Harvey Sacks and Emmanuel Schegloff were by the late sixties beginning to develop a form of systematic analysis of conversational structure that took transcript analysis as their primary method, but treated a different level of analysis than linguists. They took as one of their goals the discovery of regularities in conversation structure, but the project eventually dovetailed with the other goals of interactional sociolinguists, such as analyzing the properties of talk in different settings and institutional frameworks, or by some, identifying indicators and markers of social identity. Gumperz used this approach in combination with fine-grained analysis of linguistic features to study cross-cultural communicative problems, for instance.

Particularly important in the early definition of an interdisciplinary field were three events. One was a symposium organized by Ferguson at the American Anthropological Association in 1957, which was edited by Ferguson and Gumperz as *Linguistic Diversity in South Asia* (1960). This publication defined issues involving superposed varieties and regional variation, aspects taken up later in Gumperz' writing on the speech community. The introduction provides definitions and identifies problems about traditional linguistic treatment of these issues, and poses strong generalizations with the hope they will be tested in a variety of speech communities, presented in a

---

[10]This split is visible in the 1990 Fasold sociolinguistics textbooks in two volumes, the macro one called *The sociolinguistics of society* and the micro one called *The sociolinguistics of language*.

mode one can recognize as typical of Ferguson's writing (e.g., in his work on diglossia and on baby talk register).[11]

In 1960–61, in a lecture to the Anthropological Society of Washington, D.C., Dell Hymes described in detail the ethnography of speaking, proposing ways in which, from the standpoint of an anthropological linguist, one sees relations of linguistic structure and social or psychological function. Here he spoke of the "speech economy of the group," and identified dimensions and strata in speaking, which he calls an "etic framework" for analysis, that is a cross-culturally possible grid for first analysis of a unit he calls a "speech event," which is the primary unit of analysis. The factors of sender, receiver, message form, channel, code, topic, and setting are not completely unfamiliar, nor are his seven functional categories that appeared later in speech act analysis. Hymes credits Jakobson, Burke, Pike, Sinclair, and Barker and Wright for his analysis. But it was Hymes' version that proved seminal for the developing field of Sociolinguistics, including his concern with socialization.

An event that was a benchmark in sociolinguistics was the symposium at the American Anthropology meetings in the fall of 1963 in San Francisco, which later appeared as a special issue of *American Anthropologist* (1964) called the "Ethnography of Communication," edited by John Gumperz and Dell Hymes. Here in a major publication, the outlines of a new field from a variety of perspectives were laid out by Gumperz and Hymes. This was the first place where Courtney Cazden identified the importance of the "situation" in research, and forecast what has continued to be an important split in educational research between transcript-centered analysis of the classroom and more traditional educational psychology.[12] My article reported experimental research on bilingualism showing substantial content variations with language. The article summarized a variety of evidence on interrelations of topic, linguistic features, setting, audience, instantiating many of the points Hymes proposed in his more theoretical presentation. Charles Frake made vivid and specific the structure of a speech event. As Bauman and Sherzer described it (1974:5), the issue contained "exemplary essays, mostly substantive treatments of phenomena relevant to the ethnography of speaking, though not undertaken under its charter, but converging and contributing toward the establishment of the field." In the same year, Hymes published his

---

[11]Behind anybody working on bilingualism at that time were two classics, the work of Haugen (1953) and of Weinreich (1953), which drew clear attention to the sociocultural context of contact.

[12]The salience of the contrast with questionnaire/testing methods has been so great in education that the term "ethnography" was adopted in educational research with the restricted meaning of "observation," overlooking all the rest of the ethnographic methods as used in anthropology.

large compendium of major works which he considered relevant to this field, *Language in Culture and Society* (1964).

Not everyone involved in these developments fully liked the idea of a hyphenated, cross-disciplinary field. Among committee members, both Labov and Hymes have occasionally made this concern explicit. Hymes has spoken of "socially constituted linguistics" and would rather see linguistics broaden in scope and presuppositions to include the issues which have appeared in these conferences. Perhaps the best evidence that radical interpenetration of disciplines has occurred is that it is often hard to tell what department a student is from. On the other hand, since the demise of the committee, some linguistics departments have hardened their boundaries to restrict their attention to formal linguistics and narrow applications thereof. For this reason, attention to the broader view of linguistics has in some cases shifted to departments of applied linguistics or anthropology.

The spread of the term "sociolinguistics." The term "sociolinguistics" appeared without a hyphen in a Chicago dissertation of Mayers (1961), but was not used in major publications until 1966 in two publications which were direct outcomes of the SSRC committee's activities: Bright's proceedings of the Lake Arrowhead conference called *Sociolinguistics*, and the special issue of *Sociological Inquiry* (also published by the *International Journal of American Linguistics*) which Stanley Lieberson assembled and called "Explorations in Sociolinguistics." Lieberson's collection of papers included major papers on societal issues of bilingualism and standardization, social change, stratification, census data on language and could thus be said to be a landmark for "macro sociolinguistics." The members of the SSRC committee continued to be major sources of lexical spread for this term.

Joshua Fishman, despite a textbook entitled *Sociolinguistics* (1970) preferred the term "sociology of language" as a title for *Readings in the Sociology of Language* (1968) and for *Advances in the Sociology of Language* (1971). And when Anwar Dil initiated his important series of scholars' collected papers, published by Stanford University Press, he called it *Language Science and National Development*, though most of the early authors he chose were sociolinguists. However, it had enormous value in making some important ideas in sociolinguistics easily available in coherent form. A University of Pennsylvania series began about the same time.

In 1967, I wrote a survey paper called "Sociolinguistics" which later was published in *Advances in Experimental Social Psychology* (1969), and in 1973 Grimshaw did a chapter called "Sociolinguistics" for *The Handbook of Communication*. By 1970 a *Sociolinguistics Newsletter* was available from the research committee on sociolinguistics of the International Sociological Association, and substantial programs on sociolinguistics began appearing at the meetings of that association. Gumperz and Hymes combined the terms by publishing in 1972 *Directions in Sociolinguistics: The Ethnography of Communication*, which in one volume included a span of work across a range of disciplines, and for the first time brought the sociologists working on conversational analysis under the tent. A 1972 Georgetown University Roundtable cosponsored with the SSRC committee was called "Sociolinguistics: Current Trends and Prospects" and summarized the state of sociolinguistics.

In 1968 the committee began discussing the great need for a journal of sociolinguistic studies, and then we see *Language in Society* and *International Journal of the Sociology of Language*, founded respectively by Hymes in 1971 and by Fishman in 1974. The titles perhaps reflected a desire by publishers to appeal to nonlinguists, but that is a guess.[13] What is most apparent in the early seventies is that just the spread of the term suggests a marked impact. The Center for Applied Linguistics was beginning to use the term in publications by 1967.[14] Publications in Quebec, Rome, Sydney, and Mexico used the term in the late sixties, some through independent invention. In 1972 Penguin published a reader, *Sociolinguistics*, edited by Pride and Holmes and *Language and Social Context*, edited by Pier Paolo Giglioli. In 1974 they added a textbook called *Sociolinguistics* by Trudgill. Dittmar's compendium called *Soziolinguistik* was published in Germany in 1973. At the 1974 World Congress of Sociologists, 140 papers were listed as sociolinguistic, including papers on speech act theory, ethnomethodology, Chicano sociolinguistics, language census, and language in terms of a variety of institutional categories like religion, government, and science education. Clearly, sociolinguistics had arrived.

Committee meetings. Membership on the committee meant not only having a chance to learn about the work and interests of other committee members; in addition, guests came to talk about their work, in order to expand the planning vision of the committee. My records show for example on various occasions visits by Dan Slobin, Aaron Cicourel, and Harold Garfinkel, and Harvey Sacks, who explained how intensive analysis of

---

[13]A revealing contrast is the history of the term "psycholinguistics" as in the journals *Applied Psycholinguitics* begun in 1970, and *Journal of Psycholinguistic Research* started in 1972.

[14]It is perhaps not a coincidence that Charles Ferguson directed the Center for Applied Linguistics in this period. For the names of some of the reports that were published, see the Reference section of this volume under the following: Pietrzyk 1967, Wolfram 1969, and Shuy 1971 (this reported a conference on social dialects from the perspective of several disciplines. Claudia Mitchell-Kernan and I represented sociolinguistics).

small group interaction permits them to avoid postulation of categories and provides a discovery method.

Conferences sponsored by committee. What was clear to anyone who was a member of the SSRC committee during this period was that all this publishing activity didn't happen by accident. It seemed to me that there were two factors involved in the success of the enterprise. One was certain individuals who took the lead, and a kind of division of labor developed. Ferguson had set up the committee, which was heterogeneous in its interests. His own experience and goals were relatively wide. He had diplomatic experience as a chair in being able to present a suggestion, let it get expanded and become a group product without his name on it. He deftly spread around commitment to the committee's activities, and reduced the territorial disputes which can occur in such groups. Later on Dell Hymes, who succeeded as chair, also promoted breadth of attention of the committee to a variety of perspectives. Another noticeable feature of certain committee members was unusual energy and public skill in creating visibility for the field through conferences, symposia at professional meetings, correspondence, and prompt publications. Others were concerned primarily with theoretical problems, and wanted small working groups to focus on intellectual issues. Gumperz was especially tuned to new developments in social theory and helped the committee see, for instance, how ethnomethodology could be relevant to the committee's goals.

The means available to the committee for building the field included conferences, workshops, and scholarships. The first major activity was a Summer Research Seminar held in Bloomington in conjunction with a Linguistic Society of America Linguistic Institute in 1964. The seminar brought together sociologists, anthropologists, and linguists to discuss languages in contact, linguistic indices of social stratification, and the relations of social and political change to the linguistic integration of societies. Papers prepared by the participants in the seminar were published in various places later, such as "Explorations in Sociolinguistics" (S. Lieberson, ed.) in *Sociological Inquiry* in 1966 and in an issue of the *Journal of Social Issues on Bilingualism* (J. Macnamara, ed.) in 1967.

During 1966–1968 alone the committee sponsored two small conferences on language as data and as obstacle in comparative sociological research (or the ethnography of asking questions), and on multilingualism and social change from the perspective of Yiddish, and planned several small working groups on formal analysis of linguistic interaction in small groups, computer analysis of texts in relation to language acquisition, language problems arising from the technological revolution in bilingual and multilingual societies, and sociolinguistic research training. A conference on censuses and language data was projected.

There were two major conferences in that period. The focus of the first was on societal issues. Developing nations are often multilingual. They must discover a lingua franca, standardize means of communication in the context of diversity, develop literacy, and find means to communicate in schools, industries, cities, and political assemblies. Political decisions about language choice affect the power of competing groups and affect unification, as the blood shed over language testifies. The papers were published as *Language Problems of Developing Nations* (1968), edited by Joshua Fishman, Charles Ferguson, and Jyotindra Das Gupta. The second conference had as its focus a linguistic phenomenon, creolization. Pidgins and creoles arise in special societal conditions, in multilingual societies where the languages are quite different and in conditions of marginality which prevent the learning of the linguistic norms of the contact group. They provide the most vivid instance of communicative need generating a code, and provide an ongoing laboratory for the study of language genesis. Both of these conferences brought together scholars who had studied similar conditions in widely varying parts of the world, and both conferences defined a range of issues for collaborative research. The second was published as *Pidginization and Creolization of Languages* (1971), edited by Dell Hymes.

Although the initial focus of the committee was on comparative issues and multilingual societies around the world, attention moved to linguistic problems of ethnic minorities and to sociolinguistic surveys. Surveys in New York, Washington, Detroit, and elsewhere were initiated independently of the committee, but many of the scholars involved were members of the committee and it played a key role in stimulating the spread of such work and of panels reporting findings.[15] For example, a symposium on sociolinguistics at the American Anthropological Association was published later in a volume edited by Smith and Shuy as *Sociolinguistics in Cross-Cultural Analysis*, and included papers on urban language issues such as Puerto Rican speech in New York. The committee has also facilitated a project on Chicano sociolinguistics.

Committee-planned conferences explored problems of classroom communication and issues on the ethnography of speaking. The latter included sessions on community ground rules, genres, scenes and roles, and the

---

[15]Recent critical analysis of the Cold War and the universities has drawn attention to the fact that much government and foundation funding of social research was motivated by political goals such as political control and domestic counterinsurgency. A detailed study of this issue in sociolinguistic work remains to be done.

definition of speech community, and was published by Richard Bauman and Joel Sherzer as *Explorations in the Ethnography of Speaking* (1974).

A 1972 Georgetown Roundtable cosponsored with the SSRC committee was called "Sociolinguistics: Current Trends and Prospects," and summarized the state of sociolinguistics. Topics included language planning, multilingualism, sociolinguistic surveys and investigations of variability in language, conversational analysis, and the ethnography of speaking. Papers were published in Shuy's Georgetown Monograph of that name, in Shuy and Fasold's *Language Attitudes: Current Trends and Prospects* (1973) and in Rubin and Shuy's *Language Planning: Current Issues and Research* (1973).

The committee's sponsorship helped in fund raising for projects which took some time, for example a project in which four scholars worked on language planning for developing nations at the East-West Center in Hawaii. An immediate product of that year was a monograph by Rubin and Jernudd called *Can Language Be Planned? Sociolinguistic Theory and Practice for Developing Nations*. Further projects on language planning followed, spearheaded by Fishman and Ferguson.

The committee's facilitative efforts also included a mailing list for the Group for the Study of Sociolinguistics, lists of graduate schools offering relevant training, and sessions on sociolinguistics at research meetings of disciplinary associations.

Conference on language socializaton. Gumperz, Ervin-Tripp, and Dan Slobin began planning a major project on language socialization in Berkeley. The goal was to pursue three research areas: cross-linguistic study of semantic, phonological, and grammatical development in children, in the tradition of earlier psycholinguistic study of child language; the development of the social functions and social rules of language in children—child sociolinguistics—and the ethnography of communication; and the study of the nexus of beliefs and practices regarding language that are the milieu of the child's language learning. The stated goal was to discover universal aspects of the process of learning to use language for communication in diverse settings.

Several Berkeley anthropology graduate students were working with three faculty members, Slobin in Psychology, Ervin-Tripp in Speech, and Gumperz in Anthropology. Research in linguistic socialization was planned by Jan Brukman, Keith Kernan, Claudia Mitchell, and Brian Stross. The project began with the development of a field manual by Slobin, Ervin-Tripp, and these students in Berkeley. The *Field Manual for Cross-Cultural Study of the Acquisition of Communicative Competence* composed by this group was edited by Slobin, who took comparative syntactic development as a career focus at that point and has subsequently been the leader in its development.[16] The manual brought together the ideas of the time about how to study phonology, lexicon, grammar in children, practicalities of using equipment and informants and interpreters, and most important for our purposes, doing a study of communicative development and linguistic belief systems. The section on communicative development was still primitive since little was known about this subject; it included study of the child's life space in terms of settings and network, peer talk, baby talk, and routines. There were sections on the social setting of linguistic behavior in terms of social categories, cultural socialization, education, usage, taboos, bilingualism, conversational structure, special styles, and speech acts. While the analysis has been superseded, it was a pioneering effort and was the first to focus on these topics. The Field Manual was widely circulated and probably had its greatest impact on the development of comparative syntax, since that was the most developed field at the time.

The second phase of the study was the preparation of dissertations based on work in Hungary, Finland, Samoa, India, Kenya, Mexico, Nigeria, and several California sites.[17] In the summer of 1968, with the aid of National Science Foundation training funds, the project brought together thirty-two students and seven field workers with faculty and visiting scholars for intensive study of the problem areas. The students had now completed their field work, along with others such as Ben Blount. Ferguson joined the three faculty to chair the phonology workshop. Ervin-Tripp and Gumperz led the two workshops on sociolinguistics, which paid particular attention to code switching, sociolinguistic rules, beliefs about language, and the social meaning of speech variation. Visiting experts came from around the world, so it was a stimulating summer.[18] Among the students were many who later became productive scholars, such as Melissa Bowerman, Carol Brooks Gardner, James Shenkein, Abigail Sher, and Merrill Swain. Student reports, such as several on baby talk register, became working papers of the Berkeley Language-Behavior Research Laboratory available through ERIC. Students reported that the most important aspect of the work-

---

[16]The project had the support of Project Literacy, the Office of Education, the National Science Foundation, and the Social Science Research Council. Also the Institute of Human Learning at UC Berkeley housed the project until it was moved to the new Language-Behavior Laboratory.

[17]Students who brought back fieldwork results based on the manual in addition to those who wrote it were Rodney Vlasek, Carolyn Wardrip, and Ben Blount.

[18]Visitors who gave public lectures included a veritable who's who: Ursula Bellugi-Klima, Basil Bernstein, Martin Braine, Courtney Cazden, Aaron Cicourel, William Geohegan, Erving Goffman, Dell Hymes, Vera John, Wick Miller, Michael Moerman, John Ross, Harvey Sacks, Emmanuel Schegloff, Roger Shuy, and Carlota Smith.

shop was cross-disciplinary training and establishing a network of acquaintance with others in the field.[19]

A subsequent related conference sponsored by the SSRC committee was organized in 1974 on Language Input and Acquisition, and published as *Talking to Children*, edited by Catherine Snow and Charles Ferguson (1977). In 1974 I organized a panel at the American Anthropological Association meetings, bringing together young scholars of language socialization who did not know each other at the time. These papers appeared as *Child Discourse* in 1977, edited by Mitchell-Kernan and Ervin-Tripp with an introduction to this book differentiating this field from psycholinguistic studies of language development. Among the participants were Ochs and Schieffelin, who subsequently have had a fruitful writing collaboration; they reinvented and extended the project conceived in the 1968 conference, refocusing both method and issues, and have been prime movers in developing cross-cultural studies of linguistic socialization. They conceive of this work as anthropological linguistics, however, not as sociolinguistics.

Local nexus. Several important developments in sociolinguistics came from the University of California, Berkeley; my personal connection with the development of the field probably would not have occurred had I not been there by chance.[20] In the early sixties, there was an interdisciplinary network, at the center of which were Hymes, Gumperz, and Lamb. Sidney Lamb was developing stratificational grammar, which included notions of neutralization and realization across language strata, allowing an easy fit for the pragmatic categories that were beginning to enter linguistic analysis. He also managed a colloquium that was hospitable to a wide range of ideas about language. There was a custom of informal cross-disciplinary language discussion, for example, a Friday lunch meeting. The notions that Gumperz and Hymes presented in the American Anthropology Association meeting in 1963 had already been discussed by them in such venues. By 1963, there were discussions of creating a center for the cross-disciplinary study of language.[21] The loss of Lamb to Yale in

---

[19] I gave a detailed description in Ervin-Tripp (1969).

[20] While the networks arising from conferences and committees are important, cross-disciplinary scholars can have problems from institutional marginalization, affecting their ability to train graduate students. John Gumperz has been in three different departments, Near East languages, Linguistics, and finally, Anthropology, and I have been in three also, Education, Speech, and Psychology. Geographic marginalization is to my mind even more of a problem, at least before the internet existed. An example of geographic marginalization was J. L. Fischer of Tulane University who was a sociolinguistic pioneer. There are many others.

[21] Ervin letter to Slobin, August 5, 1963, describing Berkeley language scene.

1964 and of Hymes to the University of Pennsylvania in 1965 severely damaged this network.

In 1967 the Institute of International Studies[22] offered to fund a language center, and asked a new anthropologist, Paul Kay, to chair it. As a result, a site was found for the Language-Behavior Research Laboratory, and Slobin, Gumperz, and I, who were all in different departments, had a place to confer, some facilities for work, and sponsorship for a working paper series.[23] Other institutions, such as Texas, developed similar series.

An important part of this mix was the informal seminar, often in homes. These seminars made students and fellow-faculty in other departments aware of what we were doing. Through them we learned of Gumperz' new work on code switching, which inverted the studies I had done by setting the language and watching how the other features of bilingual talk changed. Through them it was possible to see the careful training on close observation of the linguistic strategies used in natural groups which Gumperz provided for his students, and how he related these studies to language shift. Through such seminars, I talked about analysis of pragmatic functions in natural settings, during the ten-year period when I was studying requests. It was frequently students who visited these seminars who made a synthesis: Stephen Levinson, for instance was a participant. He and Penelope Brown took the larger step beyond faculty work to integrate with the discussions in the sociolinguistic seminars the ideas of Grice, Robin Lakoff, and Goffman, who all had been on the Berkeley faculty.

Later developments. By the seventies it had become clear that a functional analysis of language was coming from several directions, from speech act theory, from conversational analysis, and from a few psychologists who did empirical study of natural interaction, like William Soskin and Vera John (1963). Crosscutting this work was the study of how the interpretation or realization of functions linguistically was altered by considerations like power and solidarity, what came to be called "politeness," so that linguistic choices other than language, dialect, or register features could convey social meaning. This work later came to be included in pragmatics with some considerable overlap with the interests of interactional sociolinguistics. Levinson, in

---

[22]cf. note 15 for a perspective on such unexpected sponsorships.

[23]These working papers included many sociolinguistic prepublication items. Unfortunately, the LBRL faculty did not make sure the graduate students recognized working papers are not publications, so many important student studies, such as several of the dissertations in the SSRC linguistic socialization project, remain unpublished and are not available in most libraries. We lacked some strategic acumen in promoting the field and our students.

his textbook, *Pragmatics,* regards the field as "a remedial discipline born, or re-born, of the starkly limited scope of Chomskyan linguistics" (1983:xii).

In 1985 Muyskens wrote an evaluation of the field in the *Sociolinguistics Newsletter.* He pointed out that sociolinguistics was not a unified field, that it failed to have much theoretical integration. Muyskens attributed the problem to the superficiality of the levels of language related to social features. But the problems are both institutional and conceptual, as was visible in the heady early days. There is no single social science; even sociologists who work from societal statistics have little relation to those who work on face-to-face processes. There has been an astonishing inflation of knowledge, in part just from the technological changes that have made new methods available, such as video tapes and computer text searches. Scholars are becoming more, rather than less specialized. There is even more need now for the kind of intelligent integration and programmatic projections that various scholars tried to create at the beginning of the field.

History of Sociolinguistics

Interview with Charles Ferguson

Charles A. Ferguson, Emeritus Professor of Linguistics, Stanford University, founded the Center for Applied Linguistics and served as its director for eight years. His research interests range broadly and include child language, especially acquistion of phonology; sociolinguistics, particularly language planning and register variation; and linguistic studies of Arabic and Bengali.

This contribution is the edited typescript which resulted from a series of interviews conducted with Charles Ferguson (widely known as Fergie) during the summer of 1993. At the time, Fergie had been hospitalized following a series of severe strokes, and the interviews were carried out by many of his friends, colleagues, and students while they were visiting him during his recuperation.

Milestones. There were two landmark events for the beginning of modern sociolinguistics: one was in 1963, the AAA (American Association of Anthropology) meeting, which eventually resulted in *Ethnography of Communication* (Gumperz and Hymes, 1964). The meeting included a varied group of participants. It incorporated Labov's paper, where he first elaborated on his notion of phonological variables. And my article on "Baby Talk" appeared in it.

The second event took place at the 1964 LSA Summer Linguistic Institute, at Indiana University. It was a seminar on sociolinguistics, which was supported by the Social Science Research Council (SSRC) Committee on Sociolinguistics. It brought together sociologists, anthropologists, and linguists, who were doing research related to linguistics and society. The sociologists made important contributions that summer, and some of them remain committed to doing such research. But on the whole, they did not respond, so what happened was that anthropologists and linguists have carried on that kind of tradition, although you would think from the name sociolinguistics you'd be more likely to have sociologists on that list.

I think the reason for that was that anthropologists have had more of a tradition of working with language issues—having to learn the local language and maybe even writing a grammar, whereas sociologists traditionally have not.

I assumed that that seminar was going to be a landmark, the second summer especially, because that's why the SSRC committee was backing it. It did have important consequences for the field. And one thing that struck me at the time was the attitudes that different people at the seminar had toward the whole deal. It was quite clear that for some people there, any sociolinguistic study was only to improve linguistics and to make linguistics more realistic. Labov certainly had that point of view. On the other hand, there were people like Joshua Fishman who wanted something that would improve sociology; that is, put a whole new subject matter before sociologists that wasn't there before. And then you had people like Dell Hymes, who felt that what was going to evolve was some new kind of field—language in society—which would perhaps replace fields such as linguistics and anthropology and provide a new way of looking at human behavior. And then there was John Gumperz who felt that there was already a new discipline called sociolinguistics, the study of language in society. And I always thought that one characteristic of him was the way he started many sentences by "In sociolinguistics, we..." and so there was already a field there, which I could not feel myself. For me, sociolinguistics was just a loose label for phenomena relating language to society.

What has impressed me over the years is that all the people I have just mentioned have kept the same view up to the present time. I suppose I could be faulted for being too easygoing and nontheoretical. Anything that involves the study of language behavior in connection with the way society works should be done, and I didn't care whether we had some great theory for it.

Some of our colleagues considered that an ethnographic perspective, but a less respectful designation would be a nominalist point of view in medieval philosophy terms. It all depends on what you *call* things. I do not think I am a nominalist in that sense—more like an ethnographic approach, as you say. But I would not associate myself with the position that some people would attribute to me, of being interested only in correlational studies. I would resist being put in that kind of category.

Well, one other thing I wanted to say was that the summer seminar in Indiana was important because it was backed by the SSRC committee on sociolinguistics. A lot of the early American work in sociolinguistics was sponsored by the SSRC committee. It is interesting how that committee got started. I do not know all of the details,[1] but there was an SSRC committee on psycholinguistics at that time which involved Tom Sebeok and Charles Osgood, and I guess the feeling was they had had their turn, now we should move to sociolinguistics or something like that, and I think that turned out to be good, although the makeup of the committee changed a lot over time. In fact, I certainly approved of everything we sponsored.

One member of the committee that I found sensible throughout was Gillian Sankoff. She was a peacemaker, in a sense, on that committee. You knew right away when she recognized someone as behaving abominably, but she always found some way around it. She was not the only woman on the committee; Ervin-Tripp was on it for some time.

Later on Allen Grimshaw was on it also; in fact, he was co-chairman with Dell Hymes. A funny thing about that original summer of 1964, when all these sociologists, linguists, and anthropologists were to get together, Grimshaw was already at Indiana, so he said, in effect, "Can't I come?" and I said, "I don't know, who are you?" So as I remember, I excluded him and he has never stopped kidding me about that. So in a sense he was not in on the ground floor of the developments. He was, however, almost the only real sociologist who continued his interest in sociolinguistic research from day one until the present. There were others who came and went, like Stanley Lieberson. He is the author of well-known books on ethnicity and race relations, and he had some imaginative research techniques in sociolinguistics which have not been kept up by others. For example, trying to understand the movement of French versus English speech in Montreal, he examined the census returns which go by census district and you could plot the diffusion. Of course, census studies are one of his specialties. He used to know the name of every county in every state, automatically. He also did things like reading the Montreal newspapers and trying to find out which kinds of want ads required which language. Once again a wealth of information was given there for which a linguist would never think of looking; he was very ingenious. On the other hand, he got into trouble several times with that. I know one time when *I* was the troublemaker: Garfinkel and Lieberson were going to be at the same table for dinner, and Lieberson would explain how he made use of census data and of course that would be instantly denied by Garfinkel and his arguments were, I am sure, reasonable in their way. For example, he pointed out that suppose you come to the door as a census enumerator, and you ask simple questions, but suppose the

---

[1]See Ervin-Tripp, this volume.

person that responded to it is someone that has had a sex change operation. Just think what that does to your question-and-answer exchanges.

Garfinkel was not always argumentative; he would just oppose things that he thought were a matter of principle. The first time I met him was at the sociolinguistics conference that became Bill Bright's book (1966). When he stood up and asked me some question, I had no idea what he meant; it was just unintelligible as far as I was concerned, so I sort of made up an answer to a different question, which is what you can do in a situation like that. But it freaked me out that this guy asked such a far-out question. Where was he coming from? And so at the cocktail party later, I deliberately attached myself to him, to try to find out what he was like, where he was coming from, and we talked for an hour or two. At the end, I concluded, this guy is nearly insane. I ruled him out as a possible contributor to the sociolinguistics enterprise. That was my first exposure to Garfinkel. Later on I realized my mistake: Garfinkel had many important ideas and observed all kinds of interesting things, but that was not immediately apparent to me.

Sue Ervin-Tripp was at that same cocktail party, I don't know what her view of Garfinkel was at the time. I gradually developed quite an affection for him, partly because he became so predictable as the years went on, and I remember telling classes, "Garfinkel will be giving the lecture next Tuesday. Now you will notice in the first several sentences, he will use the word 'member' without explaining member of what." And I would go through a whole list of things; for example, in the first paragraph or so, he would explain that all of sociology has gotten off on the wrong track and the true kind of sociology is what he and his colleagues do. And that disciplinary identification is very important to ethnomethodologists, as they came to be called.

The early work in sociolinguistics was problem driven, although there were some who felt it was important to have a unified theory. Interestingly enough, many other social scientists (but not linguists) held the same point of view at that time. It became much more fashionable in linguistics later.

Sociolinguistics is probably still more problem driven than theory driven. None of the textbooks start off with what are the ingredients of a basic theory of sociolinguistics. Some try to do it but are not very successful.

I tend to be pessimistic about formulating a basic theory of sociolinguistics; possibly I'm unduly pessimistic. I would think that if Fishman put his mind to it, he could probably come up with a kind of theory. Of course, it would tend to focus on macrosociolinguistics [sociology of language], like the books he has written on ethnicity and nationalism and so forth, which do have theoretical positions and some theoretical propositions that are derivable from more basic ones, and so on. Even as far as Labov is concerned, he would try to embed the understanding of sociolinguistics in some kind of generative linguistic theoretical position. Whether that can be done, or whether he would be satisfied with the results, the very fact that he insists on writing variable rules, means that he accepts the notion of rules of the generative type. I think whether that is appropriate already raises a big theoretical question.

I made one, not very powerful, comment on the intellectual, social, and economic climate in that the launching of sociolinguistics occurred near the end of a lengthy period of work by an SSRC committee on psycholinguistics and people were beginning to feel that it was time to encourage a little more sociolinguistics.

Before 1964, there was no overall framework intellectually. The people with different disciplinary backgrounds were all people of good will. For example, sociologists at one 1964 session wanted to know how linguists measured linguistic distance. How do you measure how far apart languages are? They felt sure that the linguists would know that, and that sociologists could make use of such a measure. They were appalled that linguists not only had no such overall measure, but were not at all interested in developing one. As another example, I remember one day we were talking about ethnic groups and obviously we were not getting anywhere; we were talking at cross purposes and finally as chairman, I said, why don't we just abandon the notion of "ethnic group." The sociologists were appalled, but there was a peacemaker, Paul Friedrich, who patiently explained to me that the current terminology of social segmentation used "social class" for segmentation based on income, occupation, and education, and "social castes" for inherited "ascribed" status, ritual purity and endogamy, and "ethnic groups" for things like religion and food and so forth (except that the "mainstream" for some reason was not called an ethnic group). He was the only one who actually was capable of communicating across disciplinary boundaries.

Another good example of cross disciplinary misunderstanding concerned the meaning of the word "data." For the linguists, examples of actual utterances constituted data; for sociolinguists, only numerical or quasi-numerical relations counted as data.

To choose the participants for the seminar, we looked around to see who was publishing things and doing "language in society." I do not think we made any real mistakes; all those people were doing something called sociolinguistics, though if you asked which ones continued afterwards, most of the sociologists didn't continue.

For example, Everett Hughes was a sociologist pretty well known in some fields. He wrote about the societal differences between English and French speakers in Canada. And he carried out insightful analyses. He realized long before most that the issue labelled language had to do with the power being largely in the hands of the Anglos. It was the fact that some francophones were beginning to move up a little bit in big businesses and so forth, they would bring all this insistence on French, insisting on their use of the language. It was typical at that time in the 1960s that in any company like a bank or a manufacturing company, all the lower employees were French speaking, but when you got up to vice presidents and district managers, they would all be English speaking. But he pointed out the underlying economic issue that was there, which I think most people were not paying much attention to, certainly not linguists.

When urged to pick one contribution, a book or an article or something of my own to the field of sociolinguistics that stands out, I'm probably compelled to say "Diglossia" because everybody else says that. The reason is that it gives a description of a language situation that has always interested me, but also it is concerned with language change.

As I look back on that article, and ask myself whether it should be changed in any way, I have answered this question in part with the article "Diglossia Revisited" in the *Southwest Journal of Linguistics* (1991).

There are lots of examples of new areas of diglossia. I said at the time that I thought there were a couple of hundred examples of diglossia operating, and a few additional clear cases in the past. I would not disagree with that now, but if you use diglossia in the looser sense described by Fishman, there would be many more cases. But as I said in "Diglossia Revisited," there are more complications, because some of them are embedded in the larger situation and I was not very good about discussing that in the article.

There was one very important project for the development of linguistics in general, as well as for sociolinguistics, that I would like to say a few words about. I am thinking of the Deccan College project in the 1950s that brought a powerful renewal of linguistics primarily by organizing summer Linguistics Institutes. The sponsors at the Rockefeller Foundation assumed that having some Linguistics Institutes would solve India's language problems, and that did not happen. But the foundation was laid that has put India at the top of the list in Asia (except Japan) for competence in linguistics. I have often thought it would be very good to do a historical study of that whole project from beginning to end. And there are a few people around who could do it. Professor Katre, the Indian scholar who was the principal initiator of the project now lives in San José. I am sure he has very vivid memories about the whole thing. The Rockefeller Foundation funded the project, and their point man was Chadbourne Gilpatric (now deceased). Most of the faculty were Indian, with maybe two or three Americans, and most of the people are still available. That would be a fascinating story; I do not know what field of science it would be, perhaps the sociology of knowledge or something like that. How does a scientific discipline get started in a given country? That would be a fascinating study of how governments understand what it is that linguistics is and what it is that linguistics can do.

Actually a man named Pattanayak, an Indian linguist who participated in this Program started the Central Institute of Indian Languages in Mysore, which was funded by the central government and was in many ways one of the most effective research centers in the world; they had maybe seventy-five people there, all linguists working on sociopolitical questions and many of them were very language problem oriented or government policy oriented in America, which was quite a contrast with the way linguistics developed in Japan.

There were some institutes that had a significant impact on sociolinguistics. In Russia (I would have to look up the dates again, but I think it was earlier than the sixties), the Russians actually held a meeting on sociolinguistics, a conference in Moscow, and as near as I could understand it, the subject matter of the conference was, why is there so much sociolinguistics being done in America; it should be done in the USSR because it is obviously a Marxist kind of thing to do. And they were partly berating themselves for not doing more work and partly of course showing how derivative the American capitalist goals were and so forth, but it would be worthwhile to go back and look up the reports of those meetings. I have talked a little bit occasionally with Ivanov and various people that I have come into contact with over the past decade or so. I would think that someone like Konrad Koerner who cares so much about the history of linguistics, would be interested in doing something like that. There was, after all, an important beginning of sociolinguistics in France, where Meillet and others regarded language as a social institution, in particular Marcel Cohen who wrote a book called *Pour une Sociologie du Langage*, in which he talked about practically every question that sociolinguistic research has dealt with since. And he was a linguist primarily working on Hamito-Semitic languages. I think he had a social interest partly because he was an associate of Meillet's and partly because he was apparently a Communist party member, so he had some other ideological concerns.[2] I do not know how it has all happened, all I know is that for instance the term "diglossia," when it's used by a French linguist nowadays always implies the oppression of some lower classes by upper classes and I never even thought of that when I was writing about diglossia.

Apart from this diffuse interest in social science, there were particular interests that figured very importantly in some people's concerns. One is this

---

[2] See Tabouret-Keller, this volume.

business of ethnicity and nationalism of language maintenance and language shift and all the Fishman legacy. It has persisted and grown; partly it tied in with bilingualism and minority languages and so forth as a result of increased concern with these issues apart from the kind of interest which people like Labov had. Of course the question of how language changes over time is a good solid question, and Labov made an enormous contribution to that. When I went to graduate school, I was still taught that there is no way you could observe a language change in progress by its very nature. Almost single-handedly Labov changed that attitude. I think people now take it for granted you *can* study language change in progress and this is a significant part of sociolinguistic research. I was at least as much fascinated by the fact that Labov's phonological variables were very good at marking sociological variables. The social class analysis which he made use of included education, occupation, and income as main variables, and the linguistic characterization of social class membership was more sensitive to the class identity than any one of those other factors. My feeling was that that finding should have rocked the sociologists back on their heels because no sociologist thought of language as being a salient marker for class. They wanted to know whether you had a corrugated roof or indoor plumbing or what kind of car you bought, useful secondary markers, but it never occurred to them that language might be a key marker. And I think that in a way Labov did not make as much of that as he could have, if he really wanted to. From Labov's aim of wanting to understand language better, this meant that understanding language better requires using social class as a variable.

Many sociology students have never heard of Labov's work, and are prone to ask, "Where has all this stuff been?"

It just never penetrated. The same thing is even true nowadays, where there is so much talk about ethnicity and so forth. The classic textbooks on ethnicity and race relations in the United States do not have this sort of basic stuff, and I have to wonder what was driving American linguistics in the 1960s to get interested in sociological questions. I am sure that Dittmar would insist that it came from the social questions that were bothering our society at the time, and so a lot of it has to do with black versus white. Unfortunately, this got tied in with fascination with rules and so forth, whether Black English really is the same as White English or something like that.

There have been some key international players in the field of sociolinguistics. Swedes are excellent in sociolinguistic research. But I felt they are too dependent on Anglo-American research and ideas and so on. They sometimes pick up an American or British idea and run better with it than the Americans or British, but I still feel that they should pay more attention to France and to other continental research and should also go their own way sometimes. The Swedes are sufficiently competent, why should they always look at other people for a lead?

Thinking of scholars outside of Europe who were in on the early years of sociolinguistics, one of these was P. B. Pandit. He wrote a book called *India: Sociolinguistic Area*, a collection of his papers. What he did was really to introduce other variables into the scene, for example, talking about education whereas everybody before him always looked at caste.

Chaim Blanc was also somebody of international scope who always impressed me. He lived in Israel almost all his life, but he must have come from a Russian Jewish family that lived in France, something like that, and he may have been wounded in the war over Israel in 1947 or 1948, I do not know exactly the time, and he lived completely blind. He had pension money I assume from Israel, from some appropriate governmental office, to provide him with readers, and I remember he had this need for readers of French, Russian, Arabic, and Hebrew because he was at home in all those languages. He was a rare individual who crossed lots of boundaries.

Central to the launching of the field of sociolinguistics was the Ford Foundation which is still interested in language issues. It was and is very important, at various levels.

Roger Shuy, in his group at Georgetown, was set up by the National Science Foundation much to the jealousy of other departments. You can not help wondering if all the other departments asked, "Why aren't *we* getting all that help?"

People have wondered about who was awarded the first doctorate in the field of sociolinguistics. There is a good bit of talk about who gave the first course called sociolinguistics at the Summer Institute. I do not know the answer to that one. I gave a course on sociolinguistics in the summers of 1962 and 1963 in Seattle, at the LSA Summer Linguistic Institute. I was there both those years, but whether that was the first, second, or third, I have no idea. I know people have talked about that issue, but I do not know what the chronology is.

I do not think the field is as vibrant and vital today as it was a quarter of a century ago. I guess what I am thinking of is a couple of years ago when Giglioli came to me and said he was thinking of maybe editing another collection of papers like the old *Language and Social Context* (1972), and he asked where we could find a group of individuals to contribute papers worth including, and I had a very hard time coming up with a comparable set of names and topics.

The questions that initially motivated the field have not been sufficiently answered, but accounting for language change has become increasingly understood from a sociolinguistic perspective.

I found it fascinating that in the early days of sociolinguistic research in America, people for one reason or another, produced books of readings, and they had a tremendous influence. And so we not only had Fishman's *Readings in the Sociology of Language*, and Hymes' *Language in Culture and Society*, but also the Penguin book of Gigliolo, *Language and Social Context*, and they were widely read and bought. I don't know enough about the sociology of knowledge to know if that is the common way for new fields to start out, but I was surprised we didn't have more of those integrative review articles by leading scholars.

There are the two major journals, *Language in Society*, and *The International Journal of the Sociology of Language*, and I guess some people know by now that I did not approve of that when the journal IJSL was proposed, and so I locked in with the *Language in Society* journal. Anyway, it turned out that I was wrong because both have been very productive though quite different. Today, there is also the European journal, *Sociolinguistica*, which is basically an annual review.

Now there are so many new journals, among them *Language Variation and Change*, the *Journal of Linguistic Anthropology*, and *Discourse in Society*. I can not believe there is room for all of them, but then I have made that mistake before. But there is no systematic attempt at coverage, it is just an explosion. A couple of people get together and say, we really do not have any place where you can put things. I am not necessarily a great believer in central planning, although people have often accused me of that for various reasons, but I think some pondering by people active in the field of what would be a useful mix of journals might be worth while.

I think the establishment of the new journals represents some sort of fragmentation. For example, these various publications having to do with discourse analysis of one type or another. I think there is still plenty of room for more of those because you can view discourse analysis in so many different ways which serve different purposes, and most of those ways involve a social dimension of some kind, so I do not think that is an unnecessary fragmentation. There is also a kind of fragmentation which represents not different subject matter but different national groups.

Bloomington, Summer 1964: The Birth of American Sociolinguistics

Joshua A. Fishman

Joshua A. Fishman is Distinguished University Research Professor, Social Sciences, Emeritus, at Yeshiva University and Visiting Scholar, Linguistics, at Stanford University. He is General Editor of the *International Journal of The Sociology of Language* and of the book-series *Contributions to the Sociology of Language*.

Having always derived generalizations from empirical data and having a preference for initially studying even my empirical data at a lower rather than at a higher level of abstraction, I propose to reflect on the past third of a century of American sociolinguistics in that fashion as well, using the summer of 1964 as my point of departure. I was at the Center for Advanced Study in the Behavioral Sciences (Stanford, CA) during the 1963–1964 academic year, rewriting my *Language Loyalty in the United States* for publication, when I came across a notice in the *LSA Bulletin* (or was it in the *SSRC Items?*) inviting applications from those interested in participating in a Seminar on sociolinguistics that was to be part of the 1964 Summer Linguistic Institute at Bloomington, Illinois. I asked Einar Haugen, who was also at CASBS that year, and to whom I had shown several of my *Language Loyalty* chapters, whether he thought I should apply. He told me that he would be on the faculty of the Linguistic Institute that summer and would also be participating in the Seminar and he encouraged me to apply. It was already late, either very close to or even a little after the announced deadline, so he advised me to call Charles Ferguson at the Center of Applied Linguistics, rather than lose the few extra days that a letter would require. I knew Ferguson's name from his "Diglossia" article and from his paper on "Myths about Arabic," but I had no reason to believe that he would know me since my only noteworthy publication at that time was my "Systematization of the Whorfian Hypothesis" (1960). I did call him and although he seemed a little cool on the phone, he accepted my application.

Even though I applied, I really did not know whether to hope I would be selected or not. Leaving Palo Alto for Bloomington in the summer, two months before the scheduled completion of my precious year at the CASBS, could be interpreted as being doubly intrapunitive. I (and Gella and our three boys) would be exchanging one of the world's loveliest summer climates for one of the more oppressive ones, and after Bloomington we would be going back to New York, and who knew if we would ever see the Bay Area and the Peninsula again. Gella and I decided not to tell the children until we would know for sure whether my application had been accepted. It did not take long before a positive answer arrived and I spent my last month at CASBS feverishly completing a paper on "The Differences between Monolingual and Multilingual Polities" (to be published in 1966 in a collection edited by another participant in the Seminar, Stanley Lieberson). A very perceptive friend commented at the time, "Going to Bloomington must be awfully important to you if you are willing to give up two months at CASBS for it." It was important for me. I did not know what to expect intellectually (that would depend on who else had gotten selected, but with Ferguson and Haugen there, how much of a risk could *that* be?), but I did know that I did not want to continue to be without a community of like-minded scholars, as had been my lot till then.

The make-up of the seminar. When I finally met the other "seminarists" (technically we were all considered to be faculty members of the LSI and, therefore, of the University), I realized that I knew only Haugen and Leonard Savitz from before. I had met Savitz during my two years as Associate Professor of Psychology and Human Relations at the University of Pennsylvania (1958–1960). He was primarily interested in criminology and in social disorganization more generally, but he was also interested in social problems very broadly, including social problems involving language. I was always on the lookout for sociologists with language interests of any kind, so I began corresponding with Savitz, after my leaving Pennsylvania, about putting out together a set of "sociological readings" pertaining to language. Because language was my first priority and Savitz's third, I finally went ahead with this idea on my own during the year at CASBS (and, in its final and unconscionably delayed version, my *Readings in the Sociology of Language* 1968 included several papers by "seminarists" as well). I had also corresponded quite a bit with the German sociologist of language Heinz Kloss, in connection with his chapter on German in the United States for my *Language Loyalty* book (indeed, Ferguson had called me to get Kloss's address, in order to invite him to join the seminar, since, seemingly, very few other Americans were in touch with him at that time). Finally, I had at least met John Gumperz, because he used to come up from Berkeley to the weekly "linguistics seminar" at CASBS. He had let me read his manuscript on code-switching in Hemnesberget (1964) and had begun to educate me as to the manifold differences between ethnographic and survey research (even though I had already done some of the former and much of the latter). Let me add that I also knew three other seminarists at least by name: William Bright (from his spring 1964 conference on sociolinguistics, several of the preprints of which I had read), William Labov (because he had been a student of my friend Uriel Weinreich, from whom I had gotten copies of some of Labov's early papers), and William Stewart (because of his 1962 paper on typology of multilingual settings). I had neither any prior contact whatsoever with nor knowledge of Jack Berry, Paul Friedrich, Chester Hung, or Stanley Lieberson.[1]

Even if we count Ferguson as a sort of "impartial chairman," there were only five sociologists (Hunt, Kloss, Lieberson, Savitz, and myself—a refurbished social psychologist) and seven anthropologists/linguists (Berry, Bright, Friedrich, Gumperz, Haugen, Labov, and Stewart). The standing of the two groups, from the point of view of making immediate contributions to an emerging sociolinguistics, was even more unequal than their numbers alone would imply, and their interactions with one another were qualitatively quite different.[2] The sociologists, with the exception of Kloss,

---

[1] I should also mention a few of the scholars each of whom visited the seminar, separately, for a few days at a time, throughout the summer. I had met Susan Ervin (today Ervin-Tripp, ed. comment) in the same way that I met John Gumperz. She too used to come up from Berkeley, from time to time, to participate in the CASBS "linguistics seminar" and I had read (and assigned) several of her papers on bilingualism for my 1959–1960 courses on "Psychology of Language" and "Sociology of Language" at Penn. I knew Joan Rubin from her 1962 paper on "Bilingualism in Paraguay." Wallace Lambert was also a "known entity" for me because of several of his psycholinguistic studies of bilingualism. I also knew Dell Hymes from his 1962 "Ethnography of Speaking" paper (I believe that his 1964 volume of readings on *Language in Culture and Society* had either already just appeared or, at least, that its table of contents was known to most of us by then). Braj Kachru was just a young newcomer at that time. He spent some time at the LSI that summer and came to tell me about his research at that time (on Indian English), but I do not remember him coming to the seminar per se. Allen Grimshaw was in a category all by himself. He was not an official member of the seminar, but he was not exactly an outside visitor either. He was then already at Indiana University and came to some of the seminar discussions and even to some of its social gatherings. I knew him from his graduate student days at Penn.

[2] Bright left the seminar after only a week or two, due to a sudden death in his family. As a

had published little that could be immediately co-opted into sociolinguistics, although both Lieberson and I were about to publish several germane items within the next few years. Also, the sociologists did not know one another well (or even at all) prior to Bloomington, given that most of them had never interacted, directly or vicariously, before. As it turned out, they generally also had neither strong methodological nor substantive (not even language) interests in common, except for Hunt and Savitz who were both "language as a social problem" oriented. The anthropologists/linguists, on the other hand, had mostly at least rubbed shoulders before, had all read some of each other's work, and, in some cases, had a number of substantive and methodological interests in common (Ferguson and Gumperz, e.g., had worked on India- related material together and Bright too had worked in India), and their interest in language and/or society did not make them "odd balls" in their own professional circles. Accordingly, they were much more active in the seminar than were the sociologists, and the contributions that they made at that time have been more lasting vis-à-vis sociolinguistics as a field of specialization.

The anthropological/linguistic advantage. Several of the anthropologists/linguists came to the Seminar with a very tangible head start, so to speak. The Hymes/Gumperz symposium at the 1963 American Anthropological Association meeting in San Francisco (on the very day that John F. Kennedy was assassinated!)[3]—with papers by Hymes, Gumperz, Ferguson, as well as by Labov and Ervin, to mention only those who later were associated in one way or another with the Seminar—was entitled, "The Ethnography of Communication." The papers put together by Lieberson, appearing some two years later, nine of whose thirteen papers are by members of the seminar, still carried the less focused title, "Explorations in Sociolinguistics." Gumperz and Hymes started off their issue by pointing to "the good fortune of copresence in the same area over several years" of many of their contributors, something which enabled them "to have frequent discussions and to discover the common interests that link their work." Lieberson, on the other hand, started off his issue with the admission that, "there is no systematic collective effort on the part of sociologists to investigate the linguistic correlates of social behavior and, on the other hand, the influence of society on the

---

result, the bulk of the eight-week seminar consisted of eleven, rather than twelve, members (plus the chairman).
  [3]Although published in December 1964, as Part 2, vol. 66, no. 6 of the *American Anthropologist,* most of the papers were available as typescripts either by the time of the seminar or even before that.

nature of language."[4] The Gumperz and Hymes papers had a shared theme and many had a shared methodology. The Lieberson papers had neither. The Gumperz and Hymes papers were addressed to anthropologists/linguists who were already convinced of the importance of language but who may have needed to be convinced that the "ethnography of speaking" was a promising way to study and understand language in society. The Lieberman papers were addressed to sociologists who were not (and still are not) by any means convinced of the importance of language and the papers themselves provide no unifying theme or methodology by means of which they could become convinced.

The "two cultures" problem in sociolinguistics. The Seminar itself reflected and foretold many of the differences between these two publications. Some of the anthropologists/linguists at the seminar were already familiar with or sold on the ethnography of communication; indeed, to some of them "sociolinguistics" was little more than a more interdisciplinary label (or an opportunity for interdisciplinary expansion) for the ethnography of communication. The sociologists at the seminar were (with the exception of Grimshaw) quite distant from ethnography and, at best, considered it to be just another method and one with severe validational and public scrutiny problems of its own. Of course, the anthropologists/linguists were fully familiar with linguistic theory and with the collection and analysis of field data and most of them gravitated markedly toward the types of topics that could be coordinated with selected snippets of corpus. None of the sociologists at the seminar was trained in linguistics (neither then nor since) and, indeed, their work gravitated markedly toward macro-sociological concerns and methods. The result was a distinct lack of full acceptance of one another's work on the part of some of the members of each of the two subgroups of seminarists. When I presented my paper on the "Differences between Multilingual and Monolingual Polities" I was asked by one of the linguists where my "corpus" was. It was, partially, in order to avoid this kind of irrelevant question in the future (at the Seminar I asked my questioner whether he felt it was "necessary to explain the causes of World War II at the phonological level, too, merely because the subsequent combatants had initially engaged in negotiations"), that I soon returned to my earlier preference for "sociology of language" as the name of my field; no one would expect a linguistic corpus in the sociology of anything. When Gumperz presented his Hemnesberget paper, he was asked by a sociologist why his "hard data" was not presented in

---

[4]Although not published until 1966, as vol. 36, no. 2, of *Sociological Inquiry,* most of the papers by sociologists were actually presented, discussed, written and/or revised at the Seminar.

tabular form, and why he had performed no statistical tests to "substantiate his impressions."[5]

Problem-driven versus theory-driven? Or something in between?
There were many underlying reasons why sociolinguistics appeared on the scene in the early sixties. The reason that the seminar itself most fully represented was the ample availability of financial resources to support novel intellectual undertakings. The seminar was supported by the SSRC, an agency whose reason d'être is to provide research and training grants for just such purposes. Let us remember what 1964 was like, and not confuse it with subsequent years. The Vietnam war was still a relatively minor affair, entirely lacking any indication of its subsequent escalation into a full-fledged military campaign, on the one hand, or protest movement, on the other hand. Neither bilingual education nor any other minority language-related issue had yet been highlighted, either by adherents or opponents. There *was* a war on poverty and Head Start was already fully underway, but only a few advocates of Black English and William Labov's Lower East Side study realized the language potential in that connection. The Ford Foundation's International Division was not yet supporting far-flung language policy related research and its Education Division was concerned with language (under Marge Martus' aegis), but as a purely cognitive (teaching/learning) tool rather than as a societal indicator and constituent. There was still little if any outside support for a social problems-driven sociolinguistics. As for the seminar and its participants, social problems were similarly deemphasized there. Although I had definitely included the social problem and social policy components of the lamentably still ongoing attrition of U.S.A. language resources in my *Language Loyalty,* I do not remember this perspective ever coming up for discussion during the entire eight weeks in Bloomington. I had quickly learned my lesson and avoided bringing up a topic that I had tackled with so little ethnography (there *was* one ethnographic chapter however, generally overlooked, devoted to a Polish mining town in Pennsylvania) and no corpus whatsoever. If Savitz and Hunt were unhappy about this deemphasis of "language problems," they were very relaxed and nonvocal about it. All in all, I do not think that the seminar was social-problems driven or that the subsequent work of the Social Science Research Council's "Committee on Sociolinguistics" was in any way motivated along these lines. When I once quietly mentioned to Sue Ervin, who was seated next to me at a particular Committee meeting, that we were attending to language in such theoretical

---

[5]For more recent commentary concerning this paper, see Brit Maehlum. 1990. Codeswitching in Hemnesberget—myth or reality? *Tromsö Studies in Linguistics,* vol. 11, 338–55 (Tromsö Linguistics in the Eighties). Oslo: Novus Press.

terms that "the fact that people were willing to kill and be killed for their beloved language was being completely overlooked," she stopped the deliberations and quoted me. However, nothing but looks of annoyance greeted my observation. Linguicide was not on the proper level of abstraction for our Committee, just as it had not been for the Seminar.

But the Seminar was not theory driven either. Gumperz may have seen ethnography as a means of capturing basic reality and he may have looked forward to seeing it become the dominant method for the study of language behavior, but I do not think even he viewed it as anything but the best, most scientific way of arriving at a theory of such behavior. Labov was convinced that his techniques for studying linguistic variables, across formality levels and across social classes, were part and parcel of linguistics pure and simple, and that no separate field of inquiry such as sociolinguistics was either implied, necessary or desirable. His Black English work was still ahead of him, but when he finally tackled it, he did not do so in order to come up with social policy findings but in order to derive very basic language change and language variation formulations. He may have later come to think of his findings and methods as encompassing much or most of sociolinguistics, but that was not clearly the case at the Seminar and, had it been, it would hardly have carried the day in either camp. Ferguson certainly had no grand scale theory in mind and even middle range theory did not seem to preoccupy him. Ferguson was obviously disappointed with sociology by the end of the seminar. It did not seem to have anything solid to offer, and in a disciplinary way, neither by way of substance nor methodology. That may still be a valid criticism of sociology today, but Ferguson himself worked (and still works) on a very large array of fields and topics, and, in *this* sense, at least, he came (and comes) very close to sociology. Actually, Ferguson comes pretty close to epitomizing the level of abstraction that was most common at the seminar, i.e., a focus on topics (and on whatever method or methods they may have required, including the method of history), rather than on social problems, on the one hand, or on theory construction and testing on the other hand. Theoretical generalizations may be derivable from many such studies, but that is a long way off and remains "iffy" at best. I have not been too disturbed by that. Sociolinguistics, notwithstanding its constantly disorganized state, has contributed handsomely and lastingly to linguistics, and the sociology of language has done likewise vis-à-vis sociology, during the very same third of a century in which a very much "tighter" and grander linguistic theory both rose (noisily) and fell (silently).

Accomplishments of the seminar. None of the above is meant to imply that the Seminar did not accomplish much, let alone that I ever regretted giving up two months at CASBS in order to attend it. Quite the contrary. It was extremely worthwhile and shaped a good bit of the rest of my career, and continues to do so to this very day, more than thirty years later. A very considerable number of publications, courses, and conferences flowed directly from the Seminar and from the SSRC Committee on Sociolinguistcs which had sponsored the Seminar and which continued to meet for the next decade or more. The membership of the Committee was constantly drawn primarily from those who were in (or "almost in" or who visited) the Seminar during the summer of 1964. The Research Group on Sociolinguistics of the World Congress of Sociology was a direct spin-off from the Committee, since it was founded as a result of the Committee's having sent me to the WCS's Evian meeting (late August 1966) to organize a group that would help guarantee that sociolinguistics did not become a strictly American affair.

But it was not only in immediate and long-term professional recognition, organizational activity, and funding terms that the Seminar was eminently worthwhile. From the point of view of sociology, it launched or confirmed several sociologists on language-related pursuits which (have) lasted for essentially their entire academic lives. This might not otherwise have been the case had they not made the personal and intellectual connections which the Seminar facilitated. When I did a census-type study after the Seminar, I always reviewed Lieberson's recommendations in that connection. These recommendations were essentially hammered out with a group of sociologists at the Seminar.[6] I made sure to include an ethnography of speaking as well as Labovian variables in my *Bilingualism in the Barrio* (1971). This required me to work with linguists (Gumperz the chief one among them for one of the two years of that project), and after the seminar I was much readier to do so than before. I worked with linguists once more on my (our!) *Language Planning Processes* (Rubin et al. 1977). I had never been a number-cruncher pure and simple, but after the seminar it was clearer to me than ever before that the historical, cultural and micro-level aspects of any topic needed to be explored at their own levels and with their own appropriate methods and data. My *Language Loyalty* (1966) was already conceived as interdisciplinary, well before the Seminar, but after the Seminar I became incurably sensitized to the contribution that a corpus might make to an appropriate investigation. And, lo and behold, I am finally working on a corpus-related study now! I have done historical/biographical research in my *Ideology, Society and Language* (1987) and have repeatedly returned to the same field-sites for my *Reversing Language Shift* (1991). My very close friendship with Ferguson, and my continued friendship with several of the seminarists and visitors to the seminar, has continued to this very day, and they represent an important

---

[6]See his "Language Questions in Censuses," *Sociological Inquiry* 36:262–79.

segment of my social and intellectual interaction network. Several of the linguists/anthropologists formed equally important (and perhaps substantively even more interactive) linkages as a result of the Seminar. To this very day, sociolinguists usually tend to be very few in number on any one campus, and therefore they tend to rely on phone, mail, conferences, and personal visits even more than do other academicians. The Seminar provided me with a network for feedback, assistance, and even moral support that has lasted for a third of a century. These are not things to be sneezed at. From my early interactions with the Weinriechs (particularly during my graduate school years) through today I have thought of myself as a bridge between linguistics and the social sciences. The Seminar helped me immeasurably to see this as a worthy and a challenging (as well as stimulating) role.

But the above positive "bottom line" should not hide the fact that the absence of consensual theory and methodology, or even a consensual definition of whether sociolinguistics is a field and, if so, what it includes, the gulf between its "socio" and its "linguistic" subgroupings, the absence of linguistic training among the former and of sociological training among the latter, the far lesser tie of the field as a whole to sociology than to anthropology/linguistics…all of which the Seminar itself revealed, have all remained hurdles that need to be overcome by future generations of sociolinguists. The "founding fathers" did their best, but they did not, by any means, do everything that needed (let alone everything that still needs) to be done in and for sociolinguistics.

Memories

Paul Friedrich

Paul Friedrich is Professor Emeritus at the University of Chicago in the department of Anthropology, Linguistics, and Social Thought (and Associate in Slavic Languages and Literatures). He is author of *The Language Parallax* (1986) and his *Music in Russian Poetry* (1997).

I know relatively little about the institutional and academic-political origins of the American sociolinguistics which sprung up in the early 1960s. When I was invited to take part in the Los Angeles conference (1963) and then the Summer Institute at Bloomington (1964) I was focusing on rewriting my book *Agrarian Revolt in a Mexican Village* and also on far-ranging Indo-European studies. In retrospect, however, the impetus and motivation for this initial or formative stage came, if not equally, then at least strongly each from Bill Bright, "Fergie" Ferguson, "Josh" Fishman, John Gumperz, Einar Haugen, and Dell Hymes; Joe Greenberg participated as an invited speaker. Uriel Weinreich, while universally esteemed and awesomely productive, was, for whatever the reason, not central. The persons named continued to loom large during subsequent years when, for various reasons, I repeatedly declined to serve in various ways such as on the SSRC committee. With this frank acknowledgement of marginality but also, perhaps, the advantages of an almost outside angle, here are some memories of the birth of sociolinguistics.

The field or set of subfields, while keenly aware of the very audible presence of the "Chomskyan Revolution" which had begun just a few years earlier, was primarily and most radically inspired and oriented, not as a reaction to anything, but as sort of proprioceptive response to a wide gamut of what were felt to be of genuine discoveries or empirical breakthroughs that had been happening since about 1960—the sorts of things when you cry "Eureka" or the like. This could be the way one urban dialect reacted phonetically to another, or the way complex speech habits were predictably structured by specific cultural factors, or the way—crosslinguistically—national languages patterned into high and low variants along roughly the same dimensions, or even the way shifts in terms of address reflected the complex mental states of complex human beings. In each case the linguists in question had carried out intensive and extensive fieldwork or textual analysis and had come up with exciting regularities, predictions, generalizations and insights that in many cases were well beyond the conceptual resources of so-called descriptive linguistics, traditional philology and comparative work, or the burgeoning so-called theoretical linguistics. It is probably not vain to claim that the sense of excitement and shared discovery in Los Angeles and Bloomington significantly resembled the atmosphere during the early Indo-Europeanist days of Rask and Grimm, or the early Neogrammarian period of Werner's Law, or the high tide of Franz Boaz and his students immersed in Amerind, or indeed the more mathematical and formal object excitement of Chomsky and his immediate followers. The empirical discoveries and research clusterings of the nascent sociolinguistics seem to fall into three main areas.

First in my view was that language forms and patterns are always politically charged and are always ensconced in sociopolitical contexts that should not be avoided or ignored by a scientific fiction. This stance of political sensitivity in sociolinguistics took the most variegated shapes; for example, the intense work on Yiddish social lexicology and the fate of Yiddish in Europe and America was overshadowed and partly motivated by the Jewish Holocaust, then only two decades away. Political sensitivity or consciousness, intersecting with the then fashionable idea of "relevance," also motivated a great deal of the study of variability in language forms and usage which, in practice, boiled down to the differences involving immigrants, the working classes, Native Americans, and so forth in relation, explicit or implicit, to prestigious national standards; excepting Brahman India, studies of the rich and aristocratic were few and far between. Political sensitivity and the associated degrees of populism and linguistic liberalism also account for critical specific episodes, exchanges, and controversies. I particularly recall the mutually eloquent and impassioned debate at a plenary session a few years later between Einar Haugen and William Labov as to whether the LSA should take a public stand on the claim by a widely known and cited scholar that Black speech was "linguistically deprived." The political engagement and commitment, of which the above is a tiny fragment, carries with it no small irony because Noam Chomsky of "formal linguistics" is the most politically prominent and influential linguist of all time whereas his linguistics and that of his immediate followers has remained by and large deaf and mute to the political.

The second deep concern, obviously connected with the first, of this "lusty neonate" was that speech and language are only meaningfully studied in the context of situations of society, history, and ethnographic or intellectual culture: the syntax of two socially contiguous classes was exciting, not because the two classes illustrated yet another variant of recursion, but in terms of their interaction with ritual exchange and the like. The vision was, not one of pure linguistic form and social context as two necessarily interconnected phenomena, but of one overarching phenomenon that included both form and society—culture just as form interacts with meaning at all levels of the speech process of one individual. Such sociohistorical sensitivity, more typical of those sociolinguists dealing with foreign language and cultures than of those in what was sometimes a cocoon of American materials, entailed comprehensive attention to, for example, language in its organic interdigitation with the political economy and even religious history of Norway or long term polymathean and eclectic fieldwork in the adobe (and often mud) of East and West Indian villages. The sociohistorical assumptions meant that "the life of language," that is, change through time and the dynamics of use within one "synchrony" had to be argued in terms of anything from the statistics of caste to the axiomatic categories of a culture to the implications of a river boundary. Again, I felt a certain irony in all this because in their actual practice some sociolinguists were strictly synchronic (i.e., contemporary) and often neglected the historical, comparative, not to forget the prehistoric, mythological, and literary historical, aspects of sociolinguistic inquiry.

The third concern, intertangled with the first two, was also charged with ambivalence and controversy: what was the role of "linguistic form" in some conventionally linguistic sense in the rising new sociolinguistics? Barring a few individuals to whom I return below, all of the participants named above and many others had been rigorously trained in phonetics, phonology, morphology, lexicology, pre-Chomskyan syntax, and so forth. We all knew about gingival occlusives, periphrastic constructions, perhaps even ethical datives; all eight of the formative figures named in the first paragraph above, and the undersigned, had written or were to write dictionaries. The deep ambivalence about form derived from the fact that, on the one hand, we were well aware of how pure or straight linguistics, whether descriptive or TG, tended to fetishize form qua form, and yet, on the other hand, we realized the scientific value of combining latent and overt political concerns and a commitment to social context with linguistic variables that would be defined in a technically competent way: precisely defined allophones or clause types would be related (not necessarily "correlated") with precisely defined class (structure), cultural categories and attitudes, and so forth. Yet within this naturally constrained and contextualized appreciation of form, it must be emphasized that phonetic, lexical, and descriptive syntactic variables received more attention than morphological or generative syntactic ones. Moreover, we often commented on the fact that beyond most of the formative group were active and creative people, such as Allan Grimshaw, who were primarily trained in sociology and, in some cases, linguistically naive or ignorant. Thus the issue of form and its uses was attended by ironies and internal contradictions.

Fourth, and by the way of conclusion, the sociolinguistics of the sixties was marked by a humanism that, while incipient and partial, constituted one of its most essential and indeed appealing characteristics. On the one hand, practically all the participants were trying to understand language in its fullest range, depth, and association from the cultural implications of an Amerind classification to the politics of bilingual eduction at the national level. Practically all the major articles and books authored by the participants in those early years of empirical discovery and a new academic rhetoric were and remained charged with ethical, aesthetic, epistemological, political, economic, and yet other philosophically deep issues. And yet those same pages rarely go around the next corner of relating the fundamental issues of sociolinguistics to the great issues of the humanist tradition couched in terms of such fairly universal (i.e., also African and Amerind) values such as freedom, creativity, love, fate, music, irony, death, and work, as these have been elaborated on and adumbrated by thinkers from Socrates to Nietzsche and many others before and since. Another way of saying this is that a philosophy of sociolinguistics was not being written and still remains to be written—granted that in terms of the partially positivistic outlook of all the early participants it was questionable that a philosophy of sociolinguistics *should* be written. Yet another way of saying this is that the healthy empiricism and excitement about so-called "data" often left little energy for the sort of humanistic philosophizing that I am suggesting should get more time. Although it is probably asking too much of the increasingly younger sociolinguists to turn that last corner, it is part of my final point, as a relatively marginal participant, that the deepest, humanistically critical roots of the early sociolinguistics remain shrouded in a tantalizing and evocative mystery.

Origins and Milestones

Allen Day Grimshaw

Allen Grimshaw was a member and then co-chair of the SSRC Committee on Sociolinguistics (1967– 1979) and president of the Research Committee on Sociolinguistics of the International Sociological Association (1987–1994). He was a member of the Department of Sociology at Indiana University from 1959 to 1994. Currently an independent scholar/writer, he maintains his affiliation with Indiana.

Origins and milestones. When I was a graduate student at the University of Pennsylvania in the 1950s one of my fellow graduate students, Leonard D. Savitz, discovered the importance of language and language behavior for understanding sociological questions. He read widely, subscribed to *Language,* and tried unsuccessfully to educate the rest of us (including giving a paper on the topic at a professional meeting while still a graduate student). None of us paid any attention to him. Years later Savitz was one of the participants in an SSRC-sponsored seminar at the 1964 LSA Summer Institute—that seminar evolved into the SSRC Committee on Sociolinguistics (CSL)—one of the several critical events/milestones in the emergence of sociolinguistics as an intellectual enterprise in the United States. I was an informal participant in many of the activities of the seminar and gave a talk to the group about ways in which knowledge about language might illuminate sociological questions; it was not long before I became more closely involved.

Several of the participants in the seminar had participated in the UCLA Sociolinguistics Conference earlier that summer; publication of Proceedings of their conference (Bright, ed. 1966) constituted another critical event/milestone in the emergence of sociolinguistics. A special publication of the AAA edited by Gumperz and Hymes entitled *Ethnography of Communication,* published in 1965, was another important event—publication of a revised and extended version of the volume as *Directions in Sociolinguistics* marked the appearance of sociolinguistics as a multidisciplinary activity of significance (Gumperz and Hymes 1972).

During the 1964 Institute there were, if my recollection is sound, a variety of excitements. Even people who were principally interested in what came to be identified as sociolinguistics (or, as Joshua Fishman consistently said, "sociology of language") got drawn into talk about Chomsky and transformational grammar. For people with more sociolinguistic interests, the principal new foci seemed to be the work of William Labov and of Basil Bernstein. I do not recall much being said explicitly about Roger Brown and his work on address forms—everybody knew about the work and it was one of the things people told me to look at which demonstrated the value of language in use as sociological data.

The growth of interest in other cultures and languages in the post World War II period and the later concern about assimilation of immigrants and bilingual education, and so on, helped establish a base for the success and influence of the Georgetown University Round Tables, particularly in the 1960s and 1970s. I have only limited personal knowledge of the role of the Round Tables; it was considerable. I have similarly limited knowledge of the role of the Center for Applied Linguistics; some major contributors to sociolinguistics were associated with the Center.

Who was around at "the beginning?" A personal view on who "started it all" will reflect the reporter's age, disciplinary origins, substantive and/or area interests, personal networks—and happenstantial events. Linguistic anthropologists are likely to include Malinowski and Firth. Older sociologists might invoke the names of George Herbert Mead or Charles Cooley, their contemporaries are more likely to be familiar with Bernstein than with the sociologists who were involved in getting the SSRC CSL underway (i.e., Everett Hughes and John Useem; for a full listing of all members of the CSL see Grimshaw 1980). Charles Ferguson and Joseph Greenberg were founding members of the CSL; Ferguson, in particular, played a major role in the institutional development of sociolinguistics. Joshua Fishman, another early member of the CSL tried for years to establish a Section on sociolinguistics within the American Sociological Association; he was not successful. Haver Currie claimed to have invented the term "sociolinguistics"; Joyce Hertzler published an early volume on the sociology of language (1965). Carl Voegelin ran a seminar on "ethnolinguistics" for many years before interest in sociolinguistics itself became fashionable. William Bright organized the 1964 UCLA sociolinguistic conference and was responsible, in his role as editor of *Language,* for pioneer publication of sociological writing on language (by Goffmann and by Harvey Sacks and his conversation analyst associates) in that journal. Roger Brown's material on address was and continues to be widely cited. As noted above, Bernstein stirred up a considerable amount of interest early on; linguists were less than universally enthused.

I was once described as a "Hymes groupie"; Hymes' work had had a tremendous influence in my own thinking about language in use in social contexts. So also has the work of, and opportunities for personal interaction with, Bernstein, Aaron Cicourel, Ervin-Tripp, Ferguson, Gumperz, Michael Halliday, and Labov. And there are new and valued additions to my list with every passing year.

Personal interest in language in social contexts. Two events during my Indian experience contributed to my second "conversion," that to work on what I now identify as sociolinguistics; the first happened within days after my initial arrival in Bombay, the second was constituted by the research experience—and simply that of being a cultural stranger. I wanted to be a good visitor, and shortly after my arrival I asked some friends how to say "thank you" in Marathi. They said it was not possible; when I insisted they told me a highly Sanskritized phrase which became a source of great amusement for many of the bureaucrats with whom I dealt during my early months in India; I soon learned to use the English expression or none at all. Only after more extended experience did I begin to ask the question about why a behavioral item so central to our social life should be absent in another. Only after the second experience and in subsequent years of growing familiarity with sociolinguistic literatures did I begin to glimpse the outlines of an answer.

I went to India to undertake a large-scale study of the response of a major Indian urban community (Poona—now Pune, another sociolinguistic datum) to the traumatic effects of a devastating natural disaster, the Panshet-Khadakvasla floods of 1961. I, myself, interviewed a number of community leaders and individuals who had played important roles at the time of the floods and after. I then turned to construction of a questionnaire and recruitment and training of a crew of interviewers and translators. I was vaguely aware of problems of translation and attempted, through primitive methods of back-translation and triangulation, to generate a viable approximation of my English questions in the Marathi schedule. I soon discovered that some questions were deemed inappropriate or unanswerable. (I already knew that notions of appropriateness were not shared. The same friends who taught me how to say "thank you" warned me that strangers would ask me my income. Strangers did; I was stunned.) I was fortunate to have an extremely sensitive Indian associate in my work on the project, Shri R. P. Nene. His gentle corrections of my assumptions about the appropriateness of questions and how to ask them—and his further insights into the translation and interpretation of answers—heightened my feelings of uncertainty about both my methods of work and my attempts at understanding everyday interaction. I soon realized that there was more involved in resolution of these problems than a search for lexical or conceptual "equivalence," that the people with whom I was interacting had different notions about what it is polite to say, what are appropriate questions to ask, what possible answers are and what they "mean," and what are meaningful goals in life.

Language as research obstacle; language as sociological data. In terms of my subsequent intellectual life, however, my most important discovery was that of the critical importance of language as both an obstacle to understanding of the social life and a rich and neglected resource for the investigation of sociological questions. As I began to write up findings of the research and to present them at professional meetings, however, I found myself more and more intrigued by issues of language—both as it intruded in the research process and as its everyday use revealed fundamental facts about social life—and by more general dimensions of the problematic nature of comparative and cross-societal social research. These interests, and my deep conviction about the importance of comparative social research both for testing of generalizations about social patterns and processes and for learning about one's own society, led me into two new activities. First, and more transiently, I became a proselytizer for the necessity of training in and practice of comparative sociological research. With the support and encouragement of John Useem, a consortium supported by the Institute of Comparative Research (ICS) was founded to facilitate research training for graduate students and faculty in several midwestern universities; the ICS sponsored a series of summer training programs and conferences over the next decade. Shortly afterwards, again with the support and encouragement of Useem, the Social Science Research Council (SSRC) established a short-lived Committee on Comparative Research; it was soon replaced by more focused discipline, world area and conceptually-oriented Council committees. This activity engaged me deeply in worrying about matters such as conceptual contrasted to phenomenological "equivalence"; the result was that I became more and more interested in issues of language in use.

I soon realized that I could not lecture my colleagues about the importance of language unless I first learned something about language myself and then did some research to demonstrate the validity of my assertion that "we" should be paying more attention to language in use.

During the summer of 1964 the Summer Institute of the Linguistic Society of America was held in Bloomington, and I eagerly took advantage of the opportunity to meet with participants in an SSRC-sponsored seminar on sociolinguistics held in conjunction with the Institute. I was fortunate to find in Charles Ferguson, John Gumperz, Dell Hymes, William Labov, and other scholars a tutorial faculty eager to discuss and illustrate the complex relationships between language structure and social structure; these scholars and others with whom I subsequently served on the SSRC Committee on Sociolinguistics (1967–1979) continue to be valued teachers. In the decade following 1964 I became a student again, enrolling in courses in linguistics here and at the 1973 LSA Summer Institute (an extraordinarily exciting and rewarding intellectual "feast"). The courses I have taken include courses on syntax and phonology with Charles Bird, Roger Higgins, and Tim Shopen, and on linguistic field methods with William Labov and Gillian Sankoff, textual cohesion with Michael Halliday, and conversation analysis with Harvey Sacks and with Sacks and Emmanuel Schegloff. I also began to teach courses on language in use. I will turn briefly to a short account of some of the directions in which this conversion to sociolinguistics has taken me; I want first to comment on some effects of the changing world environment and a shifting disciplinary context on my sense of appropriate concerns for research and teaching.

Much of my re-education on these matters must be credited to my colleagues on the SSRC CSL—and to the controversies over the work of Basil Bernstein and that work's reinterpretation as "deficit theory" which stirred up the arena of public education in the sixties and seventies. My CSL colleagues were doing work which was impeccably rigorous and theoretically relevant; they were doing that work on issues of social "relevance," e.g., claims of varying "efficiency" of language varieties, social (economic, political) disadvantages suffered by speakers of socially-disvalued varieties, language maintenance, change and conflict, and so on. They, and other scholars were able to *demonstrate* the differences in social outcomes which followed from policy choices. The impact of the solid work they and others were doing was reduced, however, by the quantum growth in sociolinguistic publications and proposals which resulted, in these years, from a rush of (sometimes) opportunistic and (often) unqualified researchers taking advantage of funding opportunities and the faddish growth of concern with, e.g., bilingual education or gender differences in speech. After being taken for granted (and thus ignored) for many years, language was suddenly a "hot" topic. Public personages were making pronouncements about how "everybody should learn

English" and about the shortcomings of bilingual education and even about making English our country's "official language." Most people, I discovered, paradoxically continued to take language use in their own lives for granted and to simultaneously accept emergent public ideologies about language so long as those ideologies were personally unthreatening.

I went to India to study social conflict processes comparatively; I became intrigued by problems of working across languages. I began to study language as an "obstacle" and found myself discovering language as "sociological data." Studying language as an interactional resource I learned that not all language varieties are equally valued as social capital and came to recognize "language as a social problem." Through research on social accomplishment in talk I have come to comprehend some of the complexities of communicative nonsuccess and of conflict talk; this understanding has encouraged me to look for ways in which parallel processes may influence similar nonsuccess and conflict on the international as well as on the interpersonal level. Sometimes the world "outside" intrudes, of course; my interest in possibilities of research on communicative nonsuccess and conflict talk in international negotiations had an additional impetus in the realities of our troubled world, just as did the decision to teach a course on "war as a social problem."

What follows is a short version of how the research on talk developed its own intellectual momentum, driving me to deeper and deeper attempts to discover what "goes on in talk."

Intellectual climate—"Readiness" for sociolinguistic/theoretical and applied concerns. Some of the kinds of things which now constitute sociolinguistics have been going on in anthropology for a long time; the kind of focus provided by Gumperz and Hymes and the "ethnography of communication" has brought forth a specific interest in language in use in social contexts and increased interest in pragmatics. I have a sense that the kinds of interests reflected in the formation and activity of the SSRC Committee on Psycholinguistics—interests which were often rather more oriented to language in use than are some of the experimental studies which for many represent contemporary psycholinguistics—also helped create a climate for the emergence of sociolinguistics. Sue Ervin-Tripp, who served on both the SSRC committees played a significant role in bridging the emergent subfields.

While I suspect that my recollections of chronology in the early days are sometimes a tad fuzzy, I also have a strong sense that much of the interest in what emerged as sociolinguistic concerns and topics grew out of ameliorative social concerns. A number of people who became interested in the workings of language had modest, if any, linguistic training—they were initially drawn in because of concerns about success and failure of children in school, about possible discrimination in the delivery of health, legal, and other varieties of social services, about ways in which talents of speakers of socially dispreferred language varieties might be lost because of "language as a social problem." An interest in school successes and failures stimulated Basil Bernstein's early work on public and private (elaborated and restricted) "codes"; similar concerns drive his later conceptualizations of classification and framing in educational settings. An interest in communicative nonsuccess in doctor-patient interaction drew Roger Shuy's attention, differences in linguistic "self-esteem" in situations of bilingualism, Wallace Lambert's. During the 1970s professional schools, particularly of education, law, and medicine, began to develop programs which specifically attended to issues of language in use in social contexts; some participants in these programs were initially trained in linguistics and/or social sciences disciplines, substantial numbers of researchers and educators were professional in the fields who came to recognize the important sociolinguistic dimensions of practice. At least some of this recognition may have been stimulated in complex ways by other events of the times, most particularly civil rights movements.

"Problem-driven" and "theory-driven" research. The question in which various investigators were interested were by no means simply applied issues, however. If some investigators may initially have been driven by ameliorative concerns about unfairness in the delivery of health services, provision of educational opportunity, or in participation in legal institutions, from the beginning some students of these same processes were identifying and addressing theoretical dimensions of activity in these and other institutional arenas. Sometimes applied concerns seemed to lead to (or at least precede in visibility) theoretical questions; sometimes work on theoretical questions appear to have opened up possibilities for change in applied arenas. Roger Shuy descriptively identified problems in doctor-patient interaction; Aaron Cicourel has developed the theoretical apparatus of cognitive sociology in part to understand the complex cognitive and linguistic processes brought into play in negotiating diagnoses. John Gumperz developed a theoretical frame for understanding code-switching behavior, gradually moved to a refocus on the role of contextualization cues, and recently has focused on how differences in the latter in situations where speakers of different codes come into contact, generate communicative failure. Robin Lakoff described differences in men's and women's speech; William O'Barr looked at the differences described, recharacterized them as differences in "power" in speech—and then examined the role of powerful and powerless speech in influencing reactions to witness testimony in the courtroom. While I will say something somewhere about problems resulting from insularity and/or parochialism of students of language in use, I do believe that there has been two-way commerce between those who have received stimulation from theoretical questions and those whose work has been driven more by applied concerns—I think that similar commerce has occurred among anthropologists, (some) linguists, (some) sociologists, and among colleagues and co-workers located in professional schools of education, law, and medicine. Students of language use located in departments of communication and in programs in experimentally oriented social psychology have been interested in some of the same questions (both applied and theoretical); they have had very modest interaction with the first set listed.

Interdiscipline, independent subfield, or lunatic periphery? I have written elsewhere about distinctions between sociolinguistics and the sociology of language—and between micro- and macro-sociolinguistics; I have a strong suspicion that those who are responding to these sets of questions are overwhelmingly of some sort of micro orientation. There are colleagues who have thought about the micro-macro articulation (Basil Bernstein, Aaron Cicourel, and Randall Collins among them), and many of us have interests which are probably more or less affected by such issues *without explicitly* attending them. The murkiness of intra- and inter-disciplinary relations in arenas related to language in use is further exacerbated by variously foregrounded tensions over the use of so-called qualitative and quantitative methods (or, following Clifford Meehl, "clinical vs. statistical" 1954).

My own experience with sociolinguistics has been preeminently interdisciplinary. My initial interest was stimulated by a concern with working across languages and cultures; interest in some sense of language as an obstacle in research drove me to find out what sorts of solutions had been developed for the methodological *problems.* The people who were involved in the SSRC-sponsored seminar at the LSA Summer Institute in 1964 were primarily linguistic anthropologists and linguists of several orientations; there were only a few sociologists. I received extensive tutorials from Dell Hymes and William Labov and more occasional counsel from John Gumperz and Charles Ferguson, i.e., a mix of anthropology and linguistics. At my own institution I enrolled in graduate courses in syntax and phonology; primarily with Charles Bird (with whom I also co-taught courses and co-authored my favorite piece in linguistics [Ibrahim, Grimshaw, and Bird 1976]). The SSRC Committee on Sociolinguistics was always interdisciplinary in comparison and in the activities it sponsored. My major research project in recent years, the Multiple Analysis Project, has involved anthropologists, linguists, psychologists, and sociologists (with other disciplines represented in less central roles). My work on conflict talk has involved me with investigators from a number of disciplines; my projected work on the discourse of international negotiations involves Russian linguists as collaborators. Our Sociolinguistics Seminar at Indiana University has regularly drawn visitors from a range of disciplines, both as participants and as presenters. Courses on language in use at Indiana University at the upper undergraduate and graduate levels regularly draw students from around the university; sociology graduate students sometimes minor in linguistics. While there has been increasing attention to language issues within sociology, it is probably accurate to say that my personal networks (so far as research interests are concerned) over the last two decades have involved me more with anthropologists (particularly), folklorists, and linguists than with sociologists (there are obviously exceptions). I certainly do as much or more reading in other disciplines as I do in "core" sociology.

All the above said, I cannot underline too strongly my firm belief that sociolinguistics should not become an independent discipline. The strongest intradisciplinary organization interested in language in use in social contexts is surely the Society for Linguistic Anthropology. The society has about five hundred members; it has its meetings in conjunction with those of the American Anthropological Association—that embeddedness in contexts of other work on culture with a strong ethnographic orientation clearly adds to its strength. A central role of sociolinguistics in my view is not to set up as an independent fiefdom but to strengthen parent disciplines by making them increasingly aware of language in use as data (e.g., sociology) and of social contexts of use (e.g., linguistics). It might be argued that such consolidation would reduce the current diffuseness of sociolinguistic interest and literatures. I doubt that it would; in some cases (e.g., law, education, medicine) the practical and applied interests of some professionals would continue to draw them to their own fields and professions, in other cases (e.g., experimental social psychology, "communications") both substantive concerns and modes of work would keep old bonds strong and ultimately lead to further fragmentation. On simply practical grounds, moreover, this would not appear to be an optimal time in which to try to develop new university departments.

Internal to sociolinguistics. Following from what I have just said, it is not clear to me that a specifically sociolinguistic theory is either necessary or even desirable. I see the sociolinguistic enterprise (to employ a cliche) as a route to stronger and better sociologies and linguistics. I am very much in favor of what Hymes has called "a unified theory of sociolinguistic description" and I believe that it is possible to work for observationally and a descriptively adequate sociolinguistics in the sense in which Chomsky used them for linguistics. I believe it is possible to discover, define, and refine a conceptual apparatus for what goes on in talk—and that this can perhaps be done at a level at least somewhat more formal than Goffman attempted in his studies of interaction—or even in "frame analysis." I consider my own notion of *instrumentalities* employed in interactional accomplishment and the identification of constraints of *instrumentality* selection to be sociological. I consider the specification of *instrumentalities* as speech acts, or as whatever they are, to be an activity appropriately designated as some variety of pragmatics *within linguistics.* Study of specific studies of social processes of negotiation, or evaluation or conflict falls within the domain of sociology, e.g., examination of use of formulaic talk, or of humor, or of clause subordination to foreground topics, or whatever, within the domain of linguistics. There may be circumstances under which studies not clearly tied to parent disciplines can be undertaken with considerable profit. Essentially local relationships can certainly be attended in such work; if someone wants to call what it is that gets done on such occasions "sociolinguistics" I have no complaint. But I remain uncertain as to just what *sociolinguistic theory* might be. My preference for at least short-term goals is to look instead for *linguistically informed sociological theory* and, where appropriate, *sociologically informed linguistic theory.*

I guess what I have just said means that I do not know exactly what it means to talk about different roles for data in linguistics and in sociolinguistics.

Sociolinguistics has had a modest impact in making sociologists more aware of language as data (and obstacle) and in making linguists aware of the relevance of social contexts of language in use. Foregrounding of questions of pragmatics has had generally salutary effects. While there have doubtless been some improvements, my biggest personal disappointment has been that while the general public may have become somewhat more aware of the existence of *social problems associated with language* there has been little substantial success in solving those problems. I say this in awareness that programs for sensitizing school teachers, legal practitioners, and medical doctors to such problems within their own institutional sectors have become increasingly routinized in recent years. I say this also in awareness that "language planning," like bilingual education, has become a major industry. (It may well be that there are major successes of which I am simply not aware.) I suspect that my hopes/expectations have been unrealistic here; they have been elsewhere.

Yes, there are some things called sociolinguistics that I do not believe are.

Personal involvement(s). As I have several times noted, my initial activity in sociolinguistics consisted of learning about the field and in proselytizing my fellow sociologists. Some of my review essays on the field have apparently helped in that proselytical task. My major research contribution has been my long-time involvement in the Multiple Analysis Project—an activity which has resulted in two major books (1989 and 1994) and a number of other papers, chapters, and so on. As I also noted, my "favorite" research piece is on greetings in the desert—a paper co-authored with Charles Bird and Ibrahim.

I have taught courses and seminars at every level and on a variety of topics. The first such offering was at Indiana University, in the mid 1960s. I have taught courses solo and with Charles Bird, John Gumperz, and Hugh Mehan. As noted above, Indiana University has a long tradition of interest and work on sociolinguistics or sociolinguistics-related topics. Some of the initial undergraduate offerings were senior and honors seminars, and students enrolled because of that rather than because of the topics.

One of my early motivations was improvement of data collection, particularly, early on, in both domestic and comparative survey research. Struggles still go on. A second motivation was more incorporation of language materials into sociological work—and of sociological considerations into linguistics. There have been some modest successes; skeptics remain in both disciplines. A third motivation has been "consciousness raising" about language as a social problem. There has been some increased awareness; I noted above that I do not have a sense that accomplishments have been very notable. People closer to the problems may have more positive reports (i.e., Frankel or Cicourel on medical institutions, Danet or O'Barr on legal, Kjolseth on bilingualism, or Mehan on classroom interaction).

At least some of the motivating questions are the same today. Some of the theoretical underpinning remains as well, both narrower and more pretentious theories are also abroad.

From the mid 1960s onward I regularly attended meetings of the AAA; I less regularly attended the Georgetown Round Tables and meetings of the LSA. I several times attended LSA summer institutes. During my years on the SSRC CSL, I think I attended almost every conference and workshop organized by that body. As interest began to emerge in sociological circles, I was frequently asked to organize sociolinguistic sessions for ASA annual meetings. Many of the people named above came and gave papers and/or plenary sessions for sociologists. My cohort did more traveling in those days. I mentioned Voegelin's Ethnolinguistic Seminar earlier; he brought many sociolinguistic types to the Indiana University campus.

It is meaningless to assert that there could be a "single most important publication" which provided definition and visibility; that denial notwithstanding, if I have to pick a single publication it would be Gumperz and Hymes' *Directions*. Hymes' 1964 reader must also have had substantial influence; I am less familiar with what was happening then. As I think more about this question I start thinking about other early contributions—and realize that there is no possible exclusive answer.

While Austin cannot be ignored, and while any honest look at precursors would have to consider Firth and Malinowski—and perhaps Jakobson and Mukarovsky, it does appear that with the exceptions of Bernstein and Halliday the origins of contemporary sociolinguistics were primarily North American. As I have noted elsewhere (1996), much work that would now be considered sociolinguistics was being done in the USSR—even in the darkest periods.

The NSF (National Science Foundation) and NIH (National Institute of Health) have from the beginning provided some modest support. Linguistic anthropology has had support both from these agencies and from more traditionally anthropological sources (Guggenheim and American Philosophical certainly, the Smithsonian, maybe Wenner-Gren?). The Canada Council provided relatively more funding than was available in the United States. The SSRC Committee on sociolinguistics obtained support from a variety of sources—none of them terribly munificent. Substantial support for sociolinguistic work in the United States has come from private corporations with interests in communication(s); at one time Bell Labs was a major funder of research closely related to sociolinguistic concerns, in recent years Xerox has been a major funder. Support from governmental agencies has been proportionately higher in some western European countries and was considerably higher in the Soviet Union. If there is modestly more support available today than was true twenty or thirty years ago—the number of applicants has increased by several more magnitudes.

Future(s)? I used to really look forward to the intellectual excitement of SSRC CSL meetings and to activities sponsored by the Committee. The 1973 LSA summer institute was an extraordinary feast for me. The use of the terms "vibrant and vital" is absolutely appropriate for the early years. I do not have any idea of whether those now starting work in sociolinguistics are as excited as many of us were thirty years ago. I do not know whether anybody in the social sciences or the humanities is. Some of the loss of excitement may be a consequence of routinization and/or of shifts from initial exploration to the filling in of maps. Some of the shift may be some sort of cohort effect. There are many bright young scholars—and new generations are appearing (I get some truly insightful questions from students in my current graduate seminar on discourse as sociological data—and some very thoughtful ones from students in my current first year course on language as a social problem). There are still exciting things to read—and I cannot keep up. And, as I have noted, there are many sorts of problems remaining to be solved.

Some Comments on the Origin and Development of Sociolinguistics[1]

Conversation with John Gumperz

John J. Gumperz is Professor Emeritus of Anthropology, University of California, Berkeley. He has done field work in village India, urban Europe and the United States. His publications include *Language in Social Groups,* Stanford, 1971; *Directions in Sociolinguistics* (co-edited with Dell Hymes), New York, 1972; *Discourse Strategies,* Cambridge, 1981; and *Rethinking Linguistic Relativity* (co-edited with Stephen C. Levinsohn), Cambridge, 1996.

The beginning of "modern sociolinguistics." Let me start with some background. What marks the beginning of sociolinguistics for me is the break with the two dominant research traditions of the post World War II period: the descriptive linguistics of Sapir, Bloomfield, Pike, and Hockett, that focused on grammatical analysis of languages seen as unitary, internally homogeneous wholes, through direct field elicitation with native informants; and the dialectological tradition represented by Hans Kurath, Raven McDavid, and others of the Linguistic Atlas of the United States who interviewed representative native speakers in a series of communities tracing the regional and social diffusion of selected linguistic markers. The two traditions came together in my dissertation research on the Swabian dialects of Washtenaw County, Michigan and in my two years of field work on village dialects of Hindi as a member of a team of anthropologists studying rural development in a North Indian community.

---

[1]This chapter resulted from a telephone conversation between John Gumperz and Dick Tucker, which was later much edited by Gumperz.

In both studies I began by working out grammatical sketches of local talk and followed up with surveys of the use of key variants. Attempts to reconcile findings from the two types of approaches led to the realization that, to account for the role of social and regional factors in talk, linguistic field work must be grounded in the life worlds of specific localities. So that the analytical starting point should not be a specific language, dialect or style, as such terms are ordinarily understood, but the linguistic repertoire, i.e., the totality of speech variants or varieties that make up locally relevant communicative practice. It is this insight and the related realization that linguistic diversity is intrinsic to human communication everywhere that has formed the basis for much of my work since.

My perspective on sociolinguistics was initially shaped during my postdoctoral research in India with the Cornell University interdisciplinary project on rural development. I was greatly influenced by contacts made in India. S. A. Dube (then teaching at Hyderabad and later director of the Anthropological Survey of India) and his wife, Lila, spent several months in the field with our interdisciplinary research team. Other visitors to the research site included M. N. Shrinivas and Iravati Karve, the two leading figures in the discipline in South Asia, among others. Informal discussions with them and cooperation with the American anthropologist, sociologist, economist, psychologist, and political scientist team members on questions arising in the course of the fieldwork provided a unique opportunity for insights into a broad range of ethnographic research perspectives. Such intensive interdisciplinary cooperation in a research team is unfortunately rare today in social science although in science it happens all the time. I also taught in several of the Linguistic Society of India's Linguistic Institutes at Deccan College in Poona (1955 and 1956) and in Dehra Dun, Uttar Pradesh. Following the traditions established by the Linguistic Society of America, the faculty was made up of a diverse and eclectic group of linguists including Gordon Fairbanks of Cornell, Charles Ferguson, Henry Hoenigswald, and H. A. Gleason of Hartford Seminary. The South Asian faculty included world famous specialists like S. K. Chatterji, the dean of Indian linguists, as well as Prabodh Pandit and J. Burton Page, both of whom had worked with J. R. Firth of the London University School of Oriental Studies, one of the pioneers of modern sociolinguistics. We all met frequently in seminar and over the dinner table, and issues of linguistic diversity and language history loomed large in our discussions. My experience was unique. I not only spent most of two years immersed in North Indian village life, but also had opportunities to talk about my ongoing research with an unusually diverse and distinguished group of linguists and social scientists.

Origin and Development of Sociolinguistics

The events in India had a direct impact in creating interest in sociolinguistic issues in the United States. In the late nineteen fifties, the Association of Asian Studies formed a Committee on South Asian Languages, with support from the Rockefeller Foundation. Rockefeller had also supported the Deccan College institutes and had provided fellowships for South Asian graduate students and junior faculty as well as U.S. postdoctoral fellows. A main purpose of the committee was to further research on South Asian languages in the United States and to advise on the selection and training of South Asian Rockefeller fellows studying linguistics in the United States. On my return to the United States I became a member of the committee along with Ferguson, Fairbanks, Hoenigswald, and Gleason. In 1957 the committee sponsored a panel discussion "Language and Culture Dynamics in South Asia" with papers by William Bright, Uriel Weinreich, and William McCormack among others at the Annual meeting of the American Anthropological Association. The session led to a special 1960 volume of the *International Journal of American Linguistics,* "Linguistic Diversity in South Asia," edited by Ferguson and Gumperz, which has often been cited as having played a key role in the early development of sociolinguistics.

The Committee on Sociolinguistics of the Social Science Research Council, formed in the mid nineteen sixties and chaired by Charles Ferguson who had also chaired the earlier AAS committee, took part of its membership from the latter. I was active in the SSRC committee until the early nineteen seventies and I remember my informal discussions with co-members William Labov and Dell Hymes. Although our theoretical interests differed, we all shared the premise that sociolinguistic research of all kinds must build on the ethnographer's insights into the everyday life of speech communities. The difference was that Labov was interested in communities as human collectivities, while Hymes and I were concerned with language use or (to use a more current term) communicative practices as based on shared individual knowledge.

Another major influence in my own development were the associations I formed in the nineteen sixties at the University of California in Berkeley with Dell Hymes, Erving Goffman, Susan Ervin-Tripp, and with Charles Frake and others at Stanford.

Our informal discussions over the years led to the publication of the 1964 special issue of the *American Anthropologist* "The Ethnography of Communication," which formed the basis for the 1972 book, *Directions in Sociolinguistics,* both edited by Gumperz and Hymes.

Major intellectual concerns that motivated early work in sociolinguistics. My major concern all along has been with finding systematic methods of showing how linguistic analyses of everyday communicative practices can produce insights into the workings of social and cultural processes. It is for this reason that, rather than focusing on word-to-world relationships as most anthropologists had done, I began by trying to show how and by what mechanisms social boundaries come to reflect language or dialect boundaries. For example India, as a caste society, is said to be marked by clearly demarcated social divisions. It might therefore be assumed that similarly sharp boundaries exist among caste dialects. But this was not by any means always the case. The data did not show a simple one-to-one correlation between linguistic variability on the one hand and caste or other social categories on the other. Rather, it was the quality of the interaction among speakers and the prevailing norms of interpersonal relations that turned out to be the key factors in determining the relationship between linguistic and social markers. Where people were able to interact freely and able to form close ties, unhampered by hierarchical constraints, linguistic differences tended to become attenuated. On the other hand, normative social constraints on interaction of whatever kind, favored the maintenance or reinforcement of linguistic boundaries.

Over the years such findings led me to the assumption that discourse level communicative processes, such as code, dialect, or style switching, choice among lexical options or phonetic variables, and prosodic contours and shifts in rhythm or tempo, are more sensitive indicators of social process than clause or sentence level phonology or grammar as such. In my later work I argued that these selection strategies function as contextualization cues, that is as indexical, metapragmatic signs which frame the interaction in such a way as to affect the inferential processes by which speakers and listeners assess what is intended at any one point in an exchange. It is the study of such indexical signs, of the extent to which they are shared, of how and to what degree they differ in today's increasingly diverse populations, how such differences are ideologically evaluated and strategically employed either to establish ties and coopt others or to create distance and justify symbolic domination, that I believe is my most important contribution to the field. Empirical studies of contextualization processes of the kind I have proposed can deal with speaking as a reflexive process which simultaneously conveys content and information about how that content is to be assessed and ultimately enable us to analyze linguistic and social phenomena in terms of a single integrated analytical framework.

Key international scholars in the field of sociolinguistics. I do not see much explicit mention of Roman Jakobson and of the influence of his work on sociolinguistics in the current literature. The notion of speech event rests in large part on his work. Additionally, he was one of the first to call attention to the social significance and importance of indexicals. Moreover his work on poetics has influenced much current work on genre.

Another unrecognized figure is the Norwegian linguist, Alf Sommerfeld who was a pioneer in European sociolinguistics, and among the first to point out the relevance of Durkheim's social theory for sociolinguistic analysis.

I have not personally met many Russian sociolinguists, although I have read some of Desheriev's work. The major Russian figures are of course Voloshinow and Bakhtin. I am not quite sure but I seem to remember that extracts from Voloshinow's work, which has become so influential in current sociolinguistic thinking, was first translated and distributed in mimeograph form by the Center for Applied Linguistics long before the work was published in the United States. Again Roman Jakobson should be credited here with calling attention both of myself and others to this work. The influence of Russian linguistics is of course also reflected in the Prague School approach to style and language function of which Roman Jakobson was the best known representative in the United States. In the sixties, I became somewhat acquainted with the spirit of some of the Russian work through my informal contacts with him.

Neustupný is currently the major representative of the Prague School approach in the West. But there is also a growing interest in the earlier Prague School work in current sociolinguistic writing. I might have mentioned in discussing the SSRC Committee on Sociolinguistics, that the committee's perspective was also greatly influenced by the sociolinguistic working group led by Charles Ferguson at the Summer Linguistic Institute at Indiana University in 1964. Michael Halliday, whose work in sociolinguistics is strongly influenced by the Prague School, was an active participant in the discussions of this group along with others who I am sure have been referred to by contributors to the present volume. In my opinion what distinguishes the American perspective from others is the insistence that the analysis of linguistic and social processes center on real life situations in real life communities.

The first doctorate in the field called "sociolinguistics." I am not sure that there is a consensus about who received the first doctorate in sociolinguistics, nor do I know how long it is since people have been identifying themselves as having a degree in sociolinguistics: probably not much more than ten years. As far as I know Georgetown had the first formal program in sociolinguistics. Chicago, Pennsylvania, and Berkeley, where many of the most influential sociolinguists now active received their degree, have chosen not to set up organized sociolinguistics programs. The reason is that the early generation of scholars was at first reluctant to create new disciplinary boundaries and chose not to call themselves specialists in sociolinguists. Labov refers to himself as a student of language in social context, others have degrees in either anthropology, and call themselves linguistic anthropologists, or in psychology, and call themselves psycholinguists. In the present era when disciplinary boundaries are increasingly being blurred this is not necessarily a bad thing.

Early goals and achievements of sociolinguists. Even if we leave out Labovian variability studies and their universally recognized achievements in the analysis of ongoing processes of language change, there are many other areas of sociolinguistics where significant progress has been or is being made. Up to the early seventies there were relatively few scholars for whom sociolinguistics was the primary concern. That is a very accurate reflection. A major reason is that sociologists of the sixties and seventies were trained in the structural-functionalist tradition which took an instrumental view of language as a tool, something like the Morse code or a computer language, that serves as a means of conveying independently existing ideas. Basil Bernstein was among the first to question that view, by showing how family modes of communication shape an individual's social persona. Bernstein's writings had an important impact among European sociologists but in the United States his work was much criticized, and I believe misunderstood. It is only in recent years that interest in his work is reviving in the U.S., particularly among Vygotskian psychologists. Present day sociolinguistics on the other hand has many of the characteristics of a major discipline, with numerous new journals in the United States, Europe, and Asia and several new professional associations. For example, about half of the more than 3000 members of the International Pragmatics Association are working on sociolinguistic issues. The Association's journal *Pragmatics* has hosted important international debates on issues of code switching, intercultural communication, linguistic ideology, and the like. The European journals, *Multilingua, Text, The Journal of Pragmatics,* as well as the new U.S. *Journal of Linguistic Anthropology,* all regularly carry important sociolinguistic articles. And of course, *Language in Society* continues to be a predominant international sociolinguistic influence.

It would be difficult to point to any single clear breakthrough, yet there is no question that the last few decades have seen many important advances both in theory and in method. For example, until about ten to fifteen years ago, sociolinguistic research tended to be mainly concerned with explaining linguistic variability as a function of speaker attributes, relying on established methods of clause level linguistics to isolate specific linguistic markers. In recent years there has been a shift towards in-depth discourse and conversational analysis focusing on the situational and interactional accomplishment of social activities. As a result of this shift, identities and other social and contextual categories are no longer treated as givens but are shown to be in large part produced through talk. This enables us to determine how, and under what conditions, linguistic variability interacts with the sequential organization of turns at speaking, how it can affect understanding in everyday encounters, and ultimately shows how qualitative discourse analyses can shed light on basic social and communicative issues.

In another significant development, following Michael Silverstein's highly influential work on linguistic ideology, linguistic anthropologists and sociolinguists are turning to detailed studies of writings about language and political rhetoric to show how these affect the way we evaluate talk. It has long been evident that mere descriptions of linguistic features cannot account for the pervasive stigmatization that minority speakers tend to encounter in everyday life. The focus on ideology is beginning to provide empirical documentation to show that stigmatization is not just a matter of preexisting attitudes; the values in question tend to be consciously propagated by identifiable individuals and groups. Moreover, their spread and the transformations they undergo as circumstances change over time can be traced through historical analysis. Ideology also plays a significant role in the development of standard national languages as recent studies of the Basque regions of Spain and in Indonesia indicate. Looking over my own North Indian findings in the light of this work I am realizing the need to reexamine the data in the light of the political forces that I knew were at work there also but which in the early days were not directly brought into a sociolinguistic discussion.

Finally, linguistic anthropologists and sociolinguists have embarked on a series of detailed empirical studies to disprove the claims of cognitive scientists and linguists, who, basing themselves on Chomsky's claim that linguistic abilities are innate and therefore pan-human, have raised serious doubts about the Whorfian assumptions of linguistic and cultural relativity underlying much sociolinguistic research. They argue that since all human beings are genetically endowed with the capacity to learn grammar without explicit instruction, claims to the effect that linguistic variability affects the way we think and act are wrong.

The basic issue of relativity, its historical antecedents and the early attempts to test its claims are critically examined in two 1992 volumes by John Lucy. Another edited volume entitled *Rethinking Linguistic Relativity* with theoretical and empirical articles by an interdisciplinary group of linguists, anthropologists, and psychologists and edited by Stephen Levinson and myself, appeared in 1996. A main argument of this work is that Sapir and Whorf's ideas, much like other research of its time, were largely suggestive and programmatic so that the relatively uncritical attempts to test these ideas in terms of the dominant descriptivist/structuralist paradigm of the fifties, sixties, and early seventies were bound to be flawed. Yet now when Whorf's notions are reworked in the light of the last decades' theoretical developments, valid experimental tests of linguistic and cultural relativity are indeed possible. Preliminary results so far yield a number of clear cases where semantic grammatical variability relates to cognitive differences. Seen by themselves such differences may not seem too significant in view of what we now know about universals. But seeing them in terms of their effect on conversational action, these differences can cast light on major problems of intercultural communication.

I have mentioned only some of the recent developments, those which involve what I am familiar with. A critical review of the literature would reveal many more. My overall impression is that considerable progress is being made and sociolinguistics is having an increasingly important impact on related academic fields, if not sociology as such, but certainly linguistic anthropology, pragmatics, conversational analysis, Vygotskian psychology, and developmental psychology. For example, as a result of these developments, theory is being broadened in scope and methodologies are being refined. There are signs that when these methodologies are applied to the study of current social issues, many applied issues that remain from the 1970s can be resolved.

History and Development of Sociolinguistics

Dell Hymes

Dell Hymes was born in Portland, Oregon and attended local schools and Reed College there. His doctorate is in linguistics from Indiana University in 1955. He has taught at Harvard, Berkeley, and the University of Pennsylvania, where he was Dean of the School of Education 1975–1987. He is now Commonwealth Professor of Anthropology and of English at the University of Virginia. He founded the journal *Language in Society* and edited it for twenty-two years; served on the Social Science Council for several terms; and was a trustee of the Center for Applied Linguistics (1973–1978) and President of the Linguistic Society of America in 1983.

Milestone. I do not have a sense, myself, of any particular milestone in the history of sociolinguistics. My own interests were going in the direction which became absorbed by the term "sociolinguistics," and would have continued in any case.

Certainly there were high-water marks.

- The conference on sociolinguistics in 1964 at UCLA, with publication, edited by Bill Bright, in 1966.
- The formation of the Committee on Sociolinguistics of the SSRC in 1964.
- Bill Labov's 1966 monograph on New York City.
- The initiation of Language in Society *(Cambridge) in* 1972 and of the International *Journal of the Sociology of Language in 1973.*

Climate. I like to say that Chomsky is responsible for the development of sociolinguistics, because of his statement in *Aspects of the Theory of Syntax* (1965), which defined the goal of linguistic theory in such a way as to eliminate people and use.

At various times I have made a comparison to Feuerbach, as criticized by Marx. Chomsky and Feuerbach are alike in a conception of the unity of a community in terms of what A. F. C. Wallace, in *Culture and Personality,* called "replication of uniformity" as against the reality of "organization of diversity" (which carries on in a nonevolutionary way Durkheim's "mechanical solidarity" and "organic solidarity"), and in assuming a "natural" unity of the community because everyone is already the same, as against the kind of unity one observes, which integrates diverse roles, identities, interests, capacities, and the like.

If Chomsky had not wished to exclude so much and had not become so influential, the course of linguistics in the United States might have continued much as before. Analysis and models of linguistic structure had a centrality, but the field included the other interests of linguists, interests that were expanding. The narrowing of the "neo-Bloomfieldian" or "structural" movement, such that it was felt necessary to rebuild everything from a new base, was giving way to exploration. Interaction in a psychiatric interview, paralinguistics, even kinesics, literature (A. A. Hill was one such), psycholinguistics, and ethnolinguistics were adjuncts not committed to particular theories.

The reality was, and is, that many aspects of language and its use exist which attract research, yet which are outside the Chomsky goals and methodology. It is a curious irony, perhaps, that the decade of the 1960s, which saw an upsurge of political activity of a sort congruent with Chomsky's own radical perspective, also gave rise to a sense of need for knowledge about such phenomena as Black English and urban problems. Labov's discovery of attitudes or valuations, which linked behaviorally diverse speakers and styles, and his development of a replicable approach for studying such phenomena, intrinsically and effectively denied the claim that behavior ("performance") was without pattern. Linguists were still guided by the goal of finding pattern. Here was pattern in relations of behavior to social circumstances.

The proposal of ethnography of speaking addressed the same point in an anthropological or "cultural" idiom. In the 1950s many had felt that linguistics and anthropology were becoming separate. The growth of structural, or descriptive, linguistics itself, the abstractness of the phoneme and morphophoneme (it seems silly now to think that a problem, but it was for some at the time), an interest in formal models for their own sake, was one factor. I have always thought that there was a lack of interest in language on the part of many Americans. Partly it may have been that language, and sensitivity to its use, was on the "feminine" side. Partly it may have been that many Americans did not value language, knowledge of languages, and did not take differences among them seriously. (I went to a very fine small liberal arts college [Reed] where the language requirement was de-emphasized). It occurred to me that the heart of the problem was that language and culture were discussed in terms of the products of linguistic and anthropological work—grammars, etc., on the one side, ethnographies on the other. Both sought kinds of patterning, and did not see their kind of patterning in the other. Both abstracted from the sphere in which such patterning might exist, the use of language. There was patterning of language beyond the levels of grammar, patterning within the institutions and events of culture. (It is really true that one could hardly find examples of attention to that at the time.)

In both respects, then, the alternative was not the one seemingly posed by Chomsky, deep structure on the one hand, epiphenomenal mishmash on the other.

Without Chomsky, the development of an approach to urban linguistics might still have occurred. The case for a new kind of study of language in relation to culture and society would have been made, simply because someone like myself, with a degree in linguistics, employed in departments of anthropology, have an occupational requirement to worry about the connection between the two. Also the fact that studies of the use of language were being made on many different fronts in the next decade or two suggesting an emerging "climate of opinion," a "Zeitgeist," invisibly at work. It is hard to be sure, because what did occur was influenced by knowledge of what had just happened. Streams of interest affected each other through particular people and institutional connections. But speech acts were underway from Oxford to Berkeley (Austin to Searle), even if Searle did go to Massachusetts Institute of Technology for a semester as well. Garfinkel's critique of sociology was under way with its phenomenological roots. Goffman was going to continue to notice small interactional details. The growth of TESOL was bound to encourage studies of politeness and interactional repertoires.

Broadly speaking then, I would hazard a guess that "sociolinguistics" got a name because there was a slot in a paradigm to be filled. Linguistics having established itself as a new and exciting activity (newly departmentalized), it became the base of new terms. "Psycholinguistics" got off to a start early, "ethnolinguistics" gained use early on and continues (though not as a disciplinary name), "sociolinguistics" was sure to be tried. Indeed the early efforts of the SSRC committee were formulated in terms of bringing together linguists and sociologists. But "sociolinguistics" came to involve a spectrum of *social* interests in language, and some of the individuals being psychologists (Sue Ervin-Tripp), some anthropologists (myself), some linguists with anthropological connections (Gumperz).

My guess was that a range of studies of the use of language was going to develop, whatever it, or part of it, came to be called.

The sense of excitement around linguistics, and then Chomsky's linguistics, and the orientation to it in criticism of people like Labov and myself made the issue one of "what kind of linguistics," more than of "what kind of sociology," "what kind of anthropology," or even "what kind of dialect geography?"

What concerns and questions? What attracted my interest, as indicated, was concern to show that there is patterning in the use of language, and that it is culturally specific. That one has to have ethnography to understand what a language means to those who use it. This was beginning to develop. The activities beginning to be called "sociolinguistics" became a sphere in which to pursue it. Language was already seen as a central topic by many. I remember a friend on the faculty at Reed when I was there (graduated 1950), who reported that a visiting Ford Foundation representative had said that language was the "in" thing. (He would not have said "in" at the time.)

I have always considered social problems an intellectual concern. The grave defect of Chomsky's direction for those of certain political or religious backgrounds was that it turned the back of linguists on actual human conditions. A celebration of a generic ability substituted for attention to actual people.

No linguist, of course, had doubted that language was a marvelous thing. Chomsky was original in his milieu for arguing that there had to be a specific biological basis. Granting that, how much can be attributed to genetics is far from clear. The term "language" becomes deeply ambiguous. It is used for that portion that can be attributed to the biological, as if all the rest was incidental (Pinker 1989). It may be consoling to academic linguists to think of linguistic differences as superficial, but that is not much help to those who live with them, nor to those who devoted themselves to *creatively* developing the resources of a particular language. Much of what language means to people, and accomplishes for them, consists of an integration of features in ways that cut across analytical levels. What Chomsky and others can consider as condition, does not help determine what language is for those who use it. And this last is not random, but has much of pattern to be discovered and understood.

For some of us, then, there was and is a fundamental contradiction between Chomsky's political concerns and his linguistics. Not that there is anything wrong with that kind of research, but to reject other kinds is reactionary. It would leave talk about language to those who do not understand linguistics.

An important attraction in the early years of sociolinguistics was that a number of individuals, interested in its use, were marginal to their official affiliations. The idea of there being a field for studying the use—in ways relevant to social life and social problems—brought them together. Some of them sought each other out. The paths of Bernstein, Bright, Ervin-Tripp, Gumperz, Ferguson, Fishman, Goffman, Haugen, Lambert, Labov, Shuy, and others, might have crossed, but not so likely come to seem connected.

It may have been different a little later.

Interdisciplinary? As someone with a degree in linguistics, teaching in anthropology (and with affiliations with folklore), I could not be other than interdisciplinary. Concern with Native Americans leads to the same situation. Various disciplines are involved. Research itself has always been my own. There was collaboration in projects to develop the field, though, particularly, in the 1960s with John Gumperz. I did not attempt formal training in any other field; trying to keep up with fields I was already in was enough.

Problem driven or theory driven? The field of sociolinguistics was motivated by a concern with language as a problem in social life. No one problem was the concern of all (cf. Black English, bilingualism, language planning and policy, interaction in small groups). If by theory is meant a predictive theory, or something close to it, then it was not so driven. If theoretical perspective is meant, then various discipline-derived perspectives were at work. I was certain that there had to be important things to be found by studying cross-culturally how people used language. At the time almost nothing of the sort could be found in anthropological literature. (In putting together *Language in Culture and Society* [1964] I had looked hard.)

One or a few individuals? Charles Ferguson certainly was critical, through the formation of the SSRC Committee on Sociolinguistics. The field was already taking shape, but the committee was important for legitimacy and as a stimulus. It was out of discussions of the Committee that the launching of a journal emerged. One would have emerged, no doubt, but in the specific case, the first, *Language in Society*, came out of the Committee.

Joshua Fishman's devotion to a certain range of problems was also important. In any event, he left the SSRC Committee, feeling that "microsociolinguistics" was not what concerned him. Gumperz and I felt, I think, that the difference was between work at the edge of linguistics and work that did not require it.

John Gumperz was of great importance in reaching out and bringing together people at Berkeley and elsewhere. Marginality again was the probable part of the motivation. He was teaching Hindi in a South Asian program, innovatively indeed, but without much recognition for his linguistics. John organized a local production of Saturday papers with John Searle, Erving Goffman, Sue Tripp, myself, and some others, which led to a session at the AAA meetings in San Francisco in 1963, and the *Ethnography of Communication* special publication of the AAA in 1964.

California was a further factor in the presence of Harold Garfinkel at UCLA, and then of two of Erving Goffman's students, Sacks and Schegloff (dissident or maverick, to be sure). At this time there was a sense of an interest in linguistics in the social sciences for those who had been at Harvard in the Department of Social Relations. Clyde Kluckhohn had advocated it (and caused the position which led to my being hired there). At Stanford, Kim Romney, Chuck Frake, Roy Andrade had that (and in Chuck's case, Yale linguistics and anthropology) as a background. There were not that many people of any such kind. The Stanford people, I think Kim mainly, arranged a weekend conference, in which I remember twitting Harold Garfinkel that "ethnomethodology" (whose name was influenced by Goodenough, Frake, etc.) and "ethnoscience" needed a basic unit and it should be called the *Finkel*. (Embarrassing to recall.)

So at this time there were several overlapping and intersecting sources of influence conducive to thinking of linguistics as important to social science, such as aspects of the existing disciplines, particularly anthropology, linguistics, and psychology, which, together with common institutional backgrounds (Harvard, Yale, Berkeley, and no doubt others), gave a sense of affinity. The postwar thrust toward a unified social science, among the relatively much smaller number of social scientists, had not yet faded.

Later these folks would mostly go separate ways. But at the beginning of the 1960s the sense of affinity was real and important.

Although Bill Labov became identified as central, and even equivalent to "sociolinguistics," he was not happy with the term early on. He wanted what he did to be seen as linguistics, and a direct challenge to other ways of doing linguistics. His influence was soon felt, of course.

A little later in Pennsylvania (ca. 1965) a cross-department network emerged that was important. It had diverse roots—personal drives, the earlier "communication" interest of Mead, Bateson, and others, Chicago symbolic interaction, etc. For a while there were the late Sol Worth (whose work was with film, but who interacted with all the rest), Ray Birdwhistell, Erving Goffman, myself, then Bill Labov. Again, for a certain time, affinities, not a common discipline.

History and Development of Sociolinguistics

My own work. I do not really know what the contribution of my work may have been; others would have to say. I think that the anthology I published in 1964 was important to some and remained so. It showed a wide range of concerns with language in a single volume, related to more than one national tradition and geographical area. The history may be relevant. In 1957–1958 I thought of a reader in American Indian languages, to be done jointly with Harry Hoijer. That evolved into a reader in anthropological linguistics, and then into the broader title.

The notion associated with me, of course, is "the ethnography of speaking." I think it encouraged study of the use of language on the part of a number of people, in anthropology and also in language teaching. The notion expressed the twin poles of my concern: study of speaking, over and beyond language as such, and studies specific to actual ways of life. Pattern is emergent in such contexts, not the filling in of already fixed slots.

Probably quite important was the attraction of several graduate students at the University of Pennsylvania to work on a small research project, scanning anthropological literature for what could be found about the use of language. Here a quite unpredictable source has to be mentioned. The late Stanley Diamond had a grant from the National Institute of Education (as I recall), and told me he was subcontracting a bit to me. I was able to pay a few students for the work, and we met once a week at our house. One eventual result (though there was more than the published outline) was by Joel Sherzer and Regna Darnell at the end of *Directions in Sociolinguistics*. Besides Joel and Regna, other participants were Elli Ochs (Ochs Keenan), Susan Philips, and Judy Irvine. Richard Bauman was around one year. Out of all this came in part the Bauman and Sherzer book of 1974, *Explorations in the Ethnography of Speaking*, and some of Bauman's other work, much noted in folklore.

The notion of "communicative competence" was prompted as a response to Chomsky's use of "competence" from 1965 on, and I first used it publicly in a conference at Yeshiva in 1966. I believe it has been useful to people in language teaching, if only as a legitimation of what they must address, as against what Chomskyan competence would allow. I never did feel able to complete the longer English-language manuscript as a book (but it was translated into French! [Hymes 1984]).

Courses and teaching. When I arrived at Harvard in the fall of 1955, it was clear that I was to teach a course Kluckhohn had taught, and had called, "Practical Phonetics for Social Scientists," essentially the exposure of students to a variety of languages. In the spring, I think, I introduced a course, "Language in Culture," new to Harvard, but not the world, and have taught a successor to that course ever since. It remained "Language and Culture" at Berkeley, but when I left the Anthropology department at the University of Pennsylvania in 1971, I was not allowed to transfer the title and rechristened it "Ethnography of Speaking."

At Harvard the students were somewhat interdisciplinary. Jean Berko, concentrating in psychology, took it, a few linguistics students, but mostly anthropologists, as I recall.

Ferguson was at Harvard for a while at the time and we talked. Kluckhohn of course was a sponsor. Otherwise, I do not recall an active interest.

Expectations and aspirations in the sixties and seventies. I am not confident about then, or subsequently. Those of us who found each other early on have continued pretty much to pursue the concerns with which we began—Bernstein, Fishman, Gumperz, Labov, myself. Not without evolution, to be sure. Back then I had no idea what would come out of worrying about intimations of morphology in early Native American texts.

For some, the model of work developed by Labov was central, or even all-encompassing. And the N-Wave group continues to meet. Those in language teaching who saw assistance in sociolinguistics continue with their primary problems. Pidginization and creolization, which was not much more than a roomful of people twenty-five years ago, is now a specialization of its own.

I'm not sure that there is "sociolinguistics" any more. If I am right in remembering the initial impulse as a response to Chomsky, as a concern to justify study of the use of language, *as an aspect of concern with linguistics itself,* then that has been accomplished. Several terms have come to the fore as labels for study of the use of language—pragmatics, discourse, most notably, with rhetoric, communication, and others also in use, as well as the more specific "conversational analysis." There is almost no linguistics at Virginia, and my active work has been concentrated on narratives, so I do not feel sure about the present situation. When I edited *Language in Society,* through 1992, those who contributed were from a range of backgrounds.

I would be in favor of a broad term for all this inquiry, to encourage interaction and integration. "Sociolinguistics" can well be that term. Possibly the long history of "pragmatics" (going back to C. W. Morris and Pierce), a seeming neutrality as to disciplines, and the easy trinity and hierarchy of syntactics, semantics, pragmatics, gives it advantage. I have the impression that it is too easy for the truly social and cultural to be left out of account.

"Sociolinguistics" may have been affected by its identification with Labov's style of urban work. But if the term can be cultivated for its "socio-" from "social" (rather than "sociology"), it would be valuable. As I said, I would be hard put to say what "sociolinguistics" is today.

If "conversational analysis" is considered part of the field, then it is encouraging that it is becoming open to ethnographic concerns.

Careful study of *literacy* has come to the fore in many fields, including medieval studies. There is a great opportunity here, a central issue about the uses of language in relation to each other, that requires interdisciplinary effort, and for which sociolinguistics could well be the context.

Key players. I experienced the field as largely of North American impetus, but British scholars were part of it from the start. Bernstein, of course, and more generally linguists influenced by Michael Halliday, including Bernstein himself. Also that aspect of the British tradition by J. R. Firth. And Peter Trudgill's Norwich study was important, then the work of the Milroys.

At the outset I was not aware of French work, though aware of a French tradition of attention to language and society. German scholars became visible early on, including of course Norbert Dittmar. The sociologist Thomas Luckmann wrote a bit on language. Of course there is a long German tradition which does not come to the attention of Americans much.

Funding agencies. I recall the National Institute of Education as being supportive at one point. I do not remember the source of the funds for the SSRC Committee. I do not know about support today.

Degrees. I do not know of a doctorate in "sociolinguistics." At the University of Pennsylvania the degrees were in anthropology, linguistics, and later, some in education.

Prognosis. As indicated along the way, I am at a loss as to what to say. Being in an anthropology department again, I find myself with people whose horizons are pretty much limited to anthropology. (The English department is all over the map, but not with regard to linguistics.) Which may be evidence that linguistics is local. But not really. Given that my attention is focussed so much on Native Americans and narrative, I am pretty much aware of what happens with Native American poetry (which I teach), and "ethnopoetics" (a label for what I do). Both concern organized uses of language, to be sure, and accounts of the performance of narrative in cultural settings could be part of sociolinguistics. (My "ethnopoetic" work includes showing that Labov missed important patterning in his New York studies and that his framework for narrative distorts the patterning these narratives have. Maybe that makes it sociolinguistics.)

It seems clear that there will always be need for careful study of situations of the use of language, attentive to the patterns and meanings that the users themselves deploy and have. Such study may be more important, and more difficult, with increasing politicization of knowledge and identity.

There is need for articulating such knowledge as we have about such things, as against cognitive science, which lends itself to simplistic solutions (1974).

Sociolinguistics could be the framework.

The [R] Evolution of Sociolinguistics

A Personal Retrospect of the Early 1960s

Björn H. Jernudd

Björn Jernudd held appointments at Monash University in Melbourne (from 1966), the Ford Foundation in Cairo, the East-West Center in Honolulu and the National University of Singapore before joining the Hong Kong Baptist University in Hong Kong where he is Chair, Professor of Linguistics and Head of the Department of English Language and Literature.

Milestones. Disciplines and milestones construct each other. There are events that have grown in importance to become disciplinary milestones, having once been important *in a different sense*. Early events are remembered in terms of their *later* importance and, I believe, retold as chunks of a story. The story is told a little differently each time because the telling responds to the situation that prompted it, but the story firms up as time goes by. Present interests and socioacademic relations select their antecedents *ex post facto*. The disciplinary paradigm selects its canon, its classics, and textbooks—but these publications are indexical or summary statements of thought and enquiry that have multifarious social-academic histories of construction. It is difficult enough to know thyself at the moment of an event unfolding. For example, in the fall of 1962 I discussed the draft report (Jernudd and Johansson 1963) of a study of social stratification of choice of vocabulary and pronunciation in Stockholm Swedish with Claes-Christian Elert, Phonetics Lecturer at Stockholm University. He commented on a passage that probably criticized Swedish language specialists for not taking a sociolinguistic point of view. He said that I should not think that we were the first to have *thought* to do what we did, but that we should be proud of having *done* it.

Some doings, then, can be recovered out of the past, yet their record alone does not produce history. There are good reasons for others to have thought but not to have done what we think it is important to do.

Happily, the editors offer a (cop-)out: what were milestones *for you?*[1] It was an important event *for me* that I attended Charles Ferguson's course on Sociolinguistics at the LSA Linguistic Institute at the University of Washington, Seattle, in the summer of 1963. It was also an important event for me that my term paper in that course on the language situation in Tadzhikistan was eventually published by the editors Voegelin[2] in *Anthropological Linguistics* (1965). It was an even more important event *for me* that I was invited to and attended the Airlie House conference on language problems of developing nations in the fall of 1966, with a paper on "Linguistic Integration and National Development: A Case Study of the Jebel Marra Area, Sudan" (1968).

The Zeitgeist of the early sixties. While a discipline of sociolinguistics was forming, displaying unity vis-à-vis other types of linguistics, there was considerable diversity of thought, enquiry, idiom, and social structure behind work that constructed sociolinguistics (Jernudd and Neustupný 1974). Yet, I venture some guesses about a few features of the *Zeitgeist* in the 1960s that conspired to produce one particular type of sociolinguistics practiced by the "iglpers," the international group of language planners:

- There were different worlds: The East Bloc, the U.S.A., the underdeveloped and developed worlds; the cold war caused competition that benefited language study, international study and engagement with development.

- There was interest in development.

- Some of us felt excluded by entrenched interests in government and politics, yet,

- we recognized and accepted the realities of political process and central state power;

- and we believed in the good of state action, that governments could act efficiently and satisfactorily.

---

[1]Thus history is reduced to anecdote.
[2]My baby daughter [un]happily presented Carl Voegelin a bouquet of flowers on the evening of his death in Honolulu.

- There was radical change in academic paradigms, notably in the social sciences, information sciences (and technologies) and linguistics—utilitarian descriptivism and structuralism matured and were already being undermined by discourse-based critical theory, ethnomethodologies, and process-based thought and methods.
- Distances were shrinking (globalism had not yet arrived although IBM had, to Stockholm, with English as in-house language, I was told).

New nations were emerging in the cold-war decolonization period. A sociolinguistics with differential bases in the U.S.A. and the Soviet Union responded to this global restructuring (Rice 1962, Guxman 1960), the latter with an ideologically governed theory of development of national languages on the route towards an endpoint of internationalism, the former with empirical methods of fact gathering and classification of use of all languages in the new nations on the route towards modernization (with an unthought endpoint), in both cases for purposes of policy formulation and language development. Mobilization of the emerging masses and modernization of their societies were key issues and goals. There was a belief that knowledge of processes of mobilization and modernization, and description of the language situation, could be co-articulated with policy processes of decision making to inform a state (central) planning process that aimed at development; planning would implement policy and feed back information into a continuing cycle of policy and planning, of problem determination, choice of solution by decision making according to optimization theory within constraints of modelling of behavior, and implimentation. The political process itself could be so planned. There was optimism and belief in orderly, even well informed, decision making involving governments. I concluded a very brief introduction to "Språksociologi" (sociolinguistics) published in the Anthropology newsletter at Stockholm University in 1964 with (pages 3–4),

> I will mention one single practical application: a description of the language situation serves as factual input [Swedish: underlag] for decisions on language problems being taken by those governing the nation. I think first of the developing new nations where the need is immediate. But these issues are of course important also in other nations, e.g., concerning educational problems.

Intellectual concerns and contributing disciplines. My nearly accidental engagement with language (by military service placement to study Russian) revealed a wide open field of inquiry that allowed application and testing of methods and theories to language as universal communication behavior and to languages as its specimens by accident and human design. The methods were those of the social sciences—and they were available and obvious. The theories were those of sociology, chorology (the study of spatial distributions), political economy and public administration, development and social change—and they were crying out for a language dimension. Sociolinguistics as a discipline emerged later to select and order interests and activities. At the time there was no question but that whatever was thought and theorized in planning theory should apply to language. Similarly, when I planned my first field work in Sudan, I based it on chorological theory (Hägerstrand 1953): to test aspects of chorological theory on and extend them to particular-language-using populations. Conclusions and recommendations in my Sudan paper refer to social, geographical and economic determinants of the spread of Arabic; I claim that "[E]fficient language planning would take account of these terminants and might even propose, as a means of promoting language knowledge and use, the subsidizing of public transport or local products" (1968:178). During the following period of emergence of types of sociolinguistics with their respective social structures and idioms, much relevant input was lost because of neglect of thought and facts from outside it. I agree with Fishman's evaluation (1987:410) that "most sociolinguists engaged in language planning are simply too uninformed with respect to formal sociology" and that we "have benefitted far too little from the theory that has been elaborated by specialists working in other areas of social change and social planning" and feel that this evaluation can be applied also to other types of sociolinguistics.

Multidisciplinary formal training. I exchanged seminars on sociolinguistics in 1963 with Ulf Hannerz (wherefrom the brief newsletter article, 1964), he in an ethnological anthropological institution at Stockholm University and I in Phonetics.[3] At that time, Linguistics did not exist as an examinable subject much less institution anywhere in Sweden. Phonetics (at Uppsala and Stockholm, in my case, but available also at Lund) offered an umbrella for linguistic study and examination. I got my decision sciences, social and behavioral sciences training at the Stockholm School of Economics working towards my MBA. I specialized in the economics of public administration: how to improve efficiency of decision making in government. As for linguistics, in 1966 I became the first student in Sweden to be examined, by special permission, in Linguistics (allmän språkvetenskap) at Stockholm University which appointed Bertil Malmberg at Lund

---

[3]Hannerz researched *Soulside* (1969) with an affiliation at the Center for Applied Linguistics in Washington, D.C., and returned to pioneer social anthropology at Stockholm University (against fierce academic resistance).

University as examiner. The person whose leadership accomplished this was the Professor of Latin, Dean of Arts, and then Rector of Stockholm University, Dag Norberg. He had apparently decided to modernize language study at Stockholm University, and succeeded. At Uppsala, Göran Hammarström, whose seminars I followed, fought a valiant disciplinary battle on behalf of structural linguistics but decided to leave for Australia in 1965—and I followed him there in 1966.

Individuals' management of an emerging field. John Lotz, John Gumperz, and Charles Ferguson visited Stockholm in the very early 1960s, with different impact and purpose. Gumperz' lecturing must have had a considerable impact on my thought;[4] but Ferguson's interest in sitting down with the mere undergraduate me over lunch probably decided my future path in sociolinguistics. Charles Ferguson's management of the Center for Applied Linguistics, the Center's newsletter *The Linguistic Reporter,* his interest in and concern for individuals, and his lucid lectures and articles shaped sociolinguistics. Through Ferguson, I met Joshua Fishman and J. V. Neustupný who was also invited to the 1966 Airlie House conference on language problems of developing nations in the same year as both of us joined Monash University in Melbourne. Joshua Fishman took me on board a life-long journey of writing and research; Ji í Neustupný became my close friend and intellectual companion.

Later I appreciated the significance of Mel Fox' (and others', among them Elinor Barber, Frank Sutton, Champ Ward) work at the Ford Foundation (cf. Fox 1975) and through the Social Science Research Council (U.S.A.), the Center for Applied Linguistics (under Charles Ferguson's direction), and through a multitude of other institutions worldwide, to respond to and nurture individual interests and needs for contacts, conferencing, training, periods of writing and research, and books, in support of sociolinguistics in general and the international group of language planners in particular.

My one "critical" contribution to the shaping of the field—"revisited." I know I should nominate my contribution to *Can Language Be Planned?* (Rubin and Jernudd, editors, 1971) because it is a book that still sells, it reports on a cooperative, deliberate effort to develop language planning theory, and it led the way for the only major international comparative project on language planning processes (Rubin, Jernudd, Das Gupta, Fishman, Ferguson 1977). Should the book be written today, it could not carry the

---

[4]And I visited Gumperz' home in New York in 1963, and subsequently at Berkeley; but I also made a point to speak to Morris Halle at MIT!

subtitle "Sociolinguistic Theory and Practice for Developing Nations," but would have to take account of a broad range of different sociolinguistic situations at different levels of enlargement (from nation to firm), of a broad range of different interests and population groups (from women to refugees), under widely different communicative circumstances (of media, channels, information processing), and foremost, of the different ideological and real, global and local sociopolitical conditions. A dominant contemporary economic ideology favors deregulation (paradoxically enforced by controlling state institutions or supranational organizations such as the International Monetary Fund or the World Bank), the *Zeitgeist* commands attention to individual and small group rights and problems over and above positing a collective (public) interest, the struggling communities have largely been abandoned to their own fates. What has not changed, however, is my commitment in the book to resist disciplinary closure of thought and enquiry: planning theory must answer to general planning theory, problem-solving models to general problem-solving theory, economics to general economics, political theory to political science, and developmental speculation and recommendation to theory of socioeconomic change.

Sociolinguistics teaching. I taught regularly scheduled sociolinguistics courses in the undergraduate linguistics curriculum at Monash University from 1966. In 1967 an introductory course in linguistics, which included lectures on sociolinguistics, was taken by practically all students of a language in the Faculty of Arts, including Classical languages, and of Anthropology and Sociology.

At Monash University, Michael Clyne studied bilingualism among migrants. Language planning and management were virgin fields, as was sociolinguistic description (including a geographical dimension, and the study of contact) of any social group in Australia. Australian English specialists were of course aware of Cultivated, General, and Broad Australian English varieties of speaking, but their theories were utterly unsophisticated and essentially equated person with variety (as reviewed by me in 1971). Discourse was an unknown concept. It was under the circumstances easy to generate excitement among students. My unpublished files of student work and my own research held data and findings that we generated in the sixties that were not reproduced by other scholars until well into the eighties.

Maybe a close look would uncover material that could still make news. Professor Steven Muecke, Mrs. Elizabeth Thuan, Dr. Manfred Klarberg, and Dr. Helen Tebble were among those students who shared in the excitement and remained associated with the field. My immediate colleagues *in situ* with sociolinguistics interests were Michael Clyne (German), Professor

Göran Hammarström (Linguistics), and Professor Ji í Neustupný (Japanese). Elsewhere, I had acquired a mentor and colleague in Joshua Fishman. He brought me to the East-West Center (1968–69) to develop language planning theory, and then into the international project on language planning processes. He asked me to read his introduction to *Sociolinguistics* (1970) in manuscript and to comment which I did in copious detail and with unstoppable confidence *[sic!]*. And I came to share with him in the grief of Uriel Weinreich's death.

There is no question in my mind that should one single most important publication have to be identified that helped to provide definition and visibility for the sociolinguistics field of the seventies and eighties, this would be Fishman's (1970) introduction (in its several manifestations). Weinreich's *Languages in Contact* may have held all the seeds, Ferguson's diglossia article and Labov's New York study may be the most quoted by some measure (are they?), Hymes' 1956 paper the longest-lasting fruitfully repeated grid of enquiry, and so on—but Fishman's introduction to sociolinguistics/sociology of language offered a unified perspective and a program for teaching and research.[5]

Aspiration. Efficiency in government through systems analysis (McKean 1958) was an overriding aspiration which could be projected on language planning and on other problem-solving language, e.g., in language teaching (Jernudd 1968, presented at a seminar at the Stockholm School of Economics in May 1966). Further, interest in development produced interest in language planning, thus in government decision making on matters of language development and determination. Language offered an exciting area of work because it had to be regarded as an intangible good, with peculiar properties. The need for research to establish a knowledge base that allows prediction of probable language behaviors was taken for granted; on this basis, for a given problem, peoples' preferences would have to be determined along dimensions of normally conflicting goals, alternative solutions would have to be proposed as would probabilities of outcome. Our models assumed that the validity and value of decisions had to be continuously reassessed because situations change, and they change partly because of the decisions taken and implemented.

Theoretical advance in the study of differentiation of language use in society and space was another aspiration. The two aspirations were strongly

---

[5]Together with his *Readings* (1968) and *Advances* (1971, 1972) volumes, the introduction to sociology of language made up Fishman's course in the sociology of language, not sociolinguistics. The *Sociolinguistics* introduction was overtaken by the sociology of language introductions.

interrelated in that good decisions require good theory. Advance could be had by applying models from chorology (the general science of spatial distributions) and the social sciences. I simply took it for granted that theories and methods from disciplines that explain and predict social and spatial distribution of human characteristics (behaviors) would apply to language as well. I am, with Fishman (1987), disappointed but not surprised that with formation of disciplinary types of sociolinguistics this openness necessarily became constrained.[6] On what base(s) new openness could develop, I do not know but am willing to speculate: perhaps individual rights? information systems? renewed interest in public responsibility for management and restoration of habitat, not in a state (government) system but on a coalition of diverse interests?

---

[6]The problem of explaining the human language faculty was understood as a separate matter.

Sociolinguistics: Birth of a Revolution

Rolf Kjolseth

Rolf Kjolseth is Associate Professor of Sociology at the University of Colorado in Boulder. He was a founding member and elected President of the Research Committee on Sociolinguistics of the International Sociological Association during its first eight years (1966–1974) and also served on the Social Science Research Council's Committee on Sociolinguistics from 1973 to 1979.

The emergence of sociolinguistics in the U.S.A. during the 1960s was a full-blooded intellectual revolution, born on the swell of major social movements and producing a combined power which has swept across the country leaving very little untouched. Its cry has now echoed around the world and its perspective affects interest in language almost everywhere.

Perspective. How, where, when, and by whom was this triggered? Like all powerful changes in social life, this one, while not inevitable, was overdetermined, i.e., catalyzed by not one, but many events and persons. Elsewhere (Kjolseth 1971b), I offered an early analytical overview of the propitious intellectual, social, political, and economic factors in the development of sociolinguistics. My purpose here is different—to cite what I saw as some crucial events in the early phase of the field's development from my own personal vantage point as one participant.

International organization. Where I believe I made my main contribution to the development of sociolinguistics, if such there be, was as a cofounder and as the president of the Research Committee on Sociolinguistics (RCS) of the International Sociological Association (ISA) during its first eight years (1966–1974). The initiative for this development came from Joshua Fishman, representing the U.S.A. Social Science Research Council's (SSRC)

Committee on Sociolinguistics (COS) who in 1966 organized and chaired a one-day meeting on sociolinguistics immediately following the Sixth World Congress of Sociology in Evian, France. This was my first real contact with a group of sociolinguists. It turned out to be a milestone in the development of the field. Some thirty researchers and students from six countries met and agreed on the need for an organization. A board of five was elected with myself as president and including: Joshua A. Fishman, U.S.A.; Heinz Kloss, Federal Republic of Germany (FRG); Claude Metais, France; and Tom Brock, Denmark.

Our mandate was (1) to create an organization recognized by the ISA that would spread and promote the development of sociolinguistics internationally, (2) to establish a *Sociolinguistics Newsletter* that would foster contact and exchange of interests, ideas, and information, especially those which were prospective, tentative, and in progress, and (3) if successful in the first two, to organize a formal program in sociolinguistics for the next ISA World Congress in 1970.

We won recognition as a Research Committee (RC #25) of the ISA by 1968. Our *Newsletter* was launched in 1967, and by 1969 I was editing and mailing it to 502 subscriber members in forty-three countries on four continents. So much exchange was generated that I was able to organize a large and diverse program with forty-seven presenters from sixteen countries for our first RCS program at the 1970 Seventh World Congress of Sociology in Varna, Bulgaria. Fritz Sack and I edited a selection of these papers which became the first collection of its kind on the continent, and the first sociolinguistics reader in German (Kjolseth 1971a). It gave, I believe, a boost to the field in Germany where sociolinguistics soon developed very strongly for reasons similar to those in the U.S.A.—analogous movements for social justice and educational reform.

At our 1966 founding meeting in Evian, there was a strong sense that we were at the right time and place to articulate a perspective whose time had come. We felt impelled by multiple social forces and by changes occurring around the world; our scattered adherents were a potential social movement within science waiting to be organized. The subsequent explosive growth of the RCS membership and activities confirmed that initial optimism.

Within our program at the 1970 World Congress at Varna we held three open, organizational working sessions, each attended by twenty-five to thirty persons from twelve to fifteen countries. Knowing that RCs have a tendency to evolve into small fiefdoms of hierarchical, self-serving cliques, we were committed to creating organizational structures that would maximize open membership. Our by-laws were revised and expanded to rationalize our growing organizational requirements and to strengthen member participation and influence, especially that which flows from the general membership to the RCS Board. By these means we sought to democratize the day-to-day workings of the organization and ensure the direct contribution of our members to the ongoing formulation of imaginative programming and policies. A Board with clearly differentiated functions was elected: President (Rolf Kjolseth: U.S.A.), overall coordination; First Vice-President (Albert Verdoodt: Belgium), quadrennial World Congress program organizer; Second Vice-President (J. D. Desherijev: USSR), interim, regional conference organizer; Secretary/Treasurer (Evangelos Afendras: Greece and Canada), finances and membership building; and *Newsletter* Editor (Edward Rose: U.S.A.), membership communication and development.

In our second four-year period between the Seventh and Eighth World Congress, Edward Rose developed the *Newsletter* into a refined instrument of membership recruitment and involvement. As he wrote, "the full membership of the RCS is invited to join in the editorship and publication of our *Sociolinguistics Newsletter*. Let each member of the committee see himself or herself as a contributing editor." And so they did, often using the imaginatively designed tear sheets Rose provided in the *Newsletter*. Standard strong sections that he developed were: "The Teaching of Sociolinguistics" on where, how, and by whom sociolinguistics was being taught throughout the world; "Activities and Interests of Our Members" including *inter alia* research reports, agendas, works, requests for information, announcements, regional conference reports, opinion pieces, short articles, biographical sketches and addresses of members, and reports on RCS activities; "Books and Articles of Interest" with topical and annotated bibliographies, short book reviews, and announcements of new and feature issues of journals. By 1973 (Vol. 4:2) the *Newsletter* contained fifty-two pages packed with member-member communications. Over an eight-year period (1970–1978), Rose tailored the *Newsletter* in order to connect member-to-member and interest-to-interest throughout the world. By mid-1974, subscriber-membership had swelled to almost 1,000 in fifty-five countries. Managing editor Jon Driessen was elected editor in 1978. With the support of Scholar's Press and the University of Montana, he continued this membership-centered tradition and refined the *Newsletter* through 1986. In that year, the RCS Board made the, I believe, fatal decision to drop the *Newsletter* and to divert its resources to the publication of a standard journal. Three issues appeared (*Sociolinguistics*, Vols. 17–19, 1988–1990) before its demise. This sidelining of the *Newsletter* was one factor among several which account for a drastic reduction in membership. There are now (1994) fewer members (between thirty and fifty) than there once were countries represented on the RCS. Nevertheless, quadrennial and interim conferences continue to thrive. Between our first two World

Congresses in the 1970–1974 period, the RCS collaborated with regional groups in organizing five interim meetings. Two were held in Moscow, and were organized by our Second Vice-President, J. Desherijev: the first in June 1970 on "Sociolinguistic Problems of Developing Nations"; the second in June 1974 on "The Sociology of Language." Our First Vice-President, Albert Verdoodt, collaborated with the *Association Internationale de Linguistique Appliquée* (AILA) in organizing their first section on sociolinguistics at AILA's August 1972, Third International Congress in Copenhagen. Forty papers were presented and later published (Verdoodt 1974). The RCS also collaborated with the nascent Committee on the Sociology of Language of the German Sociological Association in the April 1973 "International Colloquium on The Sociology of Language and Theory of Speech Acts," held in Bielefeld, FRG. And finally, in July 1974, in conjunction with the European Institute of Applied Linguistics and AILA, we held a three-week Advanced Summer Course in Sociolinguistics, with ten teachers from six countries and sixty participants from more than twenty countries, at the new University of Linburg, Diepenbeek, Belgium. Since then, the RCS has on average organized at least two conferences between World Congresses and, without exception, the sociolinguistics programs at the World Congresses have been among the largest in the ISA.

Our second full-scale World Congress in 1974 in Toronto was an important landmark. Albert Verdoodt as First Vice-President began organizing the program four years earlier, and it grew to 160 papers from more than fifty countries. It sounds impossible, but it was not. No papers were read at the Congress. The eleven section Chairs arranged for all authors to exchange papers before the Congress, and in some sections, these exchanges went through two, or even three rounds. Thus, all the time at the Congress was devoted to discussion of the issues that had been raised in the precongress exchanges. A selection of these papers was subsequently published (Verdoodt and Kjolseth 1976). Again, as in Varna, we dedicated three full working sessions to organizational concerns, and to a revision of by-laws designed to strengthen membership recruitment, retention, and influence upon committee policy and Board elections. A very capable Board was elected: President: Albert Verdoodt (Belgium); First Vice-President: Jonathan Pool (Canada); Second Vice-President: Lluis Aracil (Spain); Secretary/Treasurer: Richard Grathoff (FRG); Membership: Fernando Peñalosa (U.S.A.); and *Newsletter* Editor: Edward Rose (U.S.A.). I became a Corresponding Board Member, and have remained so to this day.

During these first eight years (1966–1974), the correspondence needed for maintaining this degree of involvement among our internationally dispersed members and Board officers was constant and intense—and all by what we now (in the era of e-mail) call Snail Mail!

The RCS-ISA has subsequently navigated four World Congresses (1978 in Uppsala, 1982 in Mexico City, 1986 in New Delhi, and 1990 in Madrid) and is now about to present a complete program at the 1994 meetings in Bielefeld, Germany. That represents a continuous presence at eight World Congresses over a twenty-eight-year period—an impressive legacy from Joshua Fishman and the U.S. SSRC's 1966 initiative in Evian.

National organization. The most influential group in the U.S.A. for launching and promulgating sociolinguistics was the SSRC's Committee on Sociolinguistics (COS). Many of its members must be counted as the most influential persons in the field's development. They set the priorities, promulgated the paradigms, and organized the conferences that defined the shape and frontiers of the field. I learned a great deal while on the COS from 1973–1977 when Dell Hymes, another giant among the founders of the field, was its marvelously able Chair, and David Jenness its skillful SSRC staffer.

My contribution was small and mixed. One of my goals was to get a bilingual Chicano sociolinguist recruited to the Committee. This was realized when Eduardo Hernandez-Chavez, then at Stanford University, and an expert on regional and social varieties of Spanish and bilingual education (Hernandez-Chavez 1975), was invited to join in 1973.

Another goal was to organize the first National Exploratory Conference on Chicano Sociolinguistics. The central idea was to bring town and gown together by integrating academic sociolinguists with those Chicano community leaders concerned with language-related issues. Sociolinguistics owed much of its impulse to the Civil Rights movement and this conference was to embody that recognition. I formed a Steering Committee including Eduardo Hernandez-Chavez, Salvador Ramirez from my own sociology department, and Chicano activists José Angel and Luz Gutierrez from Crystal City, Texas, among others. Between 1972 and 1974, we organized the conference with the goal of fomenting collaborative research supportive of grassroots initiatives within Chicano communities. However, at the last minute, our sponsors, the Ford Foundation, challenged the appropriateness of including community leaders and activists in an "academic conference." Apparently fearing this collaboration of science and politics, they put the funds in the hands of a Chicano academic who agreed to withdraw all the names of the community participants. After this reversal, the original core organizers (including myself) made the difficult decision to encourage colleagues to join us in boycotting the conference. A small conference of academics was held, and little came of it. Ford's politics of "de-politicizing" Chicano sociolinguistics had won a round. But the campaigns for enlightened educational policies in multilingual communities continue to this day. Despite setbacks, some of their finest and most lasting accomplishments have been to increase minority community action for more active parental involvement in their childrens' schools.

Personal involvements. Much of the early work in sociolinguistics was driven by a combination of concerns about theory and about social problems. This gave it a doubled vitality in addressing concerns of both the academic and the nonacademic world. Like so many others, I resonated with this. I began graduate studies in Freiburg, Germany in 1958 where I studied phenomenological sociology, and the role of language and knowledge in the construction of social realities. These theoretical and epistemological concerns I later explored (Kjolseth 1968, 1969, 1972) in experimental studies inspired by the work of Edward Rose (1964–1965).

Practical and theoretical concerns. The civil rights, equal opportunity, and social justice movements of the 1950s and federal legislation in the 1960s focused attention and great hopes on schools, and language issues within them, as a domain in which social change was possible. Through travel, work, and study abroad, I had acquired Spanish, German, and French plus a strong interest in the social factors which inhibit or encourage language acquisition and maintenance. After marriage in Mexico, Spanish became, and has remained, the language of my home, and the first language of my three bilingual children, all of whom experienced prejudice and discrimination against their bilingualism in both school and neighborhood in the U.S.A.

As what Fishman (1966) calls a "language loyalist," I became active in a host of both practical and theoretical issues surrounding the movement for bilingual education: drafting and lobbying for bilingual Colorado state legislation, initiating, designing, and evaluating specific programs (Kjolseth 1974), acting as a consultant to existing programs, and giving expert testimony in court cases, as well as researching the forms and functions that bilingual programs across the country were taking (Kjolseth 1975, 1977, 1981, 1983, 1991). These articles, drawing attention to how and when bilingual education programs could be implemented to either foster or destroy bilingualism, were reprinted and cited with some frequency (Kjolseth 1971e), and influenced the discussion of these issues.

On the theoretical side, my 1972 article on "Making Sense: Natural Language and Everyday Knowledge in Understanding," intended in part as a constructive criticism of the undifferentiated concept of background knowledge as used in ethnomethodology, has been used by investigators in the Ethno-Inquiries.

Teaching. Both my theoretical and applied work was interdisciplinary, and radically different from my graduate program (which I finished on a three-year National Institute of Mental Health fellowship in medical sociology). When I began teaching, I declared my area as the sociology of language and not medical sociology. This first appointment was at the University of California-Davis where I went in large part because the Chair, Bennett Berger, promised to support me in introducing any new courses I wanted. He kept his word, and I added four sociolinguistic courses (two undergraduate and two graduate) during my first three years there, beginning with Sociology 174: Sociology of Language, in the Fall of 1965. The class filled easily with students from several departments. I had very little contact with colleagues in other departments, and in my own department, about half my colleagues supported me while going their own way. A quarter found my slant a bit odd, but did not bother me, and an influential quarter held me to be somehow undermining true sociology, and therefore a subversive element. This latter view influenced my resignation and move to the University of Colorado in 1971. Recently, I was somewhat surprised when I calculated that, over my past twenty-eight years of teaching, I had designed and taught ten different language-related courses, offered a total of sixty-three times, or on average 2.25 sociolinguistics courses per year.

An outstanding figure. If I had to select one outstanding figure from among the several true giants in our field, I would point to Joshua Fishman. Joshua was one of the earliest (Fishman 1965) and certainly has been one of the most original, innovative, and prolific thinkers in this field. He has done it all: micro (1967), meso (1972b), and macro (1966); synchronic (1971a) and diachronic (1985) studies; has contributed to developments in both theory (1972b) and methods (1971a); was founder (1974) and editor of the *International Journal of the Sociology of Language,* and of several publication series (1972a), as well as editing (1968a, 1968b) and authoring textbooks (1971b) and an impressively diverse library of books. I cannot begin to give a coherent typology of his prodigious and seminal works. But I repeat, he has done it all, and ask, "Who within our discipline has not learned from this scholar?" He is, I must add, one of the finest human beings I have had the pleasure of knowing in person.

Prognosis. The future of sociolinguistics, as I have pointed out elsewhere (Kjolseth 1971d), depends upon a resonating concatenation of sociopolitical, intellectual, and organizational elements. The original intellectual and organizational structures of sociolinguistics have grown and matured. The general sociopolitical climate has, however, ebbed and waned. Meanwhile, crisis has become chronic, and tremendous transformations and upheavals are becoming routine. Uncertainties abound. This "post-modern malaise," gives impulse to interdisciplinary fields. In this environment, the construction of social realities through language use has become a mainstream concern, and one of the coming challenges will be the development of a "constructivist sociology of language," exploring the spoken worlds that humans both create and experience.

Sociolinguistic Patterns[1]

William Labov

William Labov attended Harvard University (BA 1948) and Columbia University (MA 1963, PhD 1964). He was an industrial chemist 1949–1961; assistant professor of linguistics at Columbia University 1964–1970 and professor of linguistics and psychology at the University of Pennsylvania from 1971 until the present. He served as president of the Linguistic Society of America in 1979.

I have resisted the term sociolinguistics for many years, since it implies that there can be a successful linguistic theory or practice which is not social. When I first published the studies of Martha's Vineyard and New York City that form the basis of the first part of this book, it seemed necessary to make that point again and again. In spite of a considerable amount of sociolinguistic activity, a socially realistic linguistics seemed a remote prospect in the 1960s. The great majority of linguists had resolutely turned to the contemplation of their own idiolects. We have not yet emerged from the shadow of our intuitions, but it no longer seems necessary to argue about what is or is not linguistics. There is a growing realization that the basis of intersubjective knowledge in linguistics must be found in speech—language as it is used in everyday life by members of the social order, that vehicle of communication in which they argue with their wives, joke with their friends, and deceive their enemies.

When I first entered linguistics as a student, in 1961, it was my intention to gather data from the secular world. The early projects that I constructed were "essays in experimental linguistics," carried out in ordinary social settings. My aim was to avoid the inevitable obscurity of texts, the self-consciousness

---

[1]This article is the introduction to Labov's book *Patterns of Sociolinguistics* (1972) and is printed here by permission of University of Pennsylvania Press.

of formal elicitations, and the self-deception of introspection. A decade of work outside the university as an industrial chemist has convinced me that the everyday world was stubborn but consistently so, baffling at the outset but rewarding in the long run for those who held to its rational character. A simple review of the literature might have convinced me that such empirical principles had no place in linguistics: there were many ideological barriers to the study of language in everyday life. First, Saussure had enunciated the principle that structural systems of the present and historical changes of the past had to be studied in isolation (1949:124). That principle had been consistently eroded by Martinet (1955) and others who found structure in past changes, but little progress had been made in locating change in present structures. The second ideological barrier explicitly asserted that sound change could not in principle be directly observed. Bloomfield defended the regularity of sound change against the irregular evidence of the present day by declaring (1933:364) that any fluctuations we might observe would only be cases of dialect borrowing. Next Hockett observed that while sound change was too slow to be observed, structural change was too fast (1958:457). The empirical study of linguistic change was thus removed from the program of twentieth-century linguistics.

A third restriction was perhaps the most important: free variation could not in principle be constrained. The basic postulate of linguistics (Bloomfield 1933:76) declared that some utterances were the same. Conversely, these were in free variation, and whether or not one or the other occurred at a particular time was taken to be linguistically insignificant. Relations of more or less were therefore ruled out of linguistic thinking; a form or a rule could only occur always, optionally, or never. The internal structure of variation was therefore removed from linguistic studies and with it, the study of change in progress.

It was also held that feelings about language were inaccessible and outside of the linguist's scope (Bloch and Trager 1942). The social evaluation of linguistic variants was therefore excluded from consideration. This is merely one aspect of the more general claim that the linguist should not use nonlinguistic data to explain linguistic change (see the first section of Chap. 9). Throughout these discussions, we see many references to what the linguist can or cannot do as a linguist.

I might indeed have disregarded all these restrictions by the force of my own inclination and resistance to authority. But I was fortunate to encounter at Columbia University a teacher not much older than myself, whose own insight, imagination, and creative force had long since bypassed these restrictions. It is impossible for me to estimate the contribution of Uriel Weinreich to the studies reported here. I learned from him in courses on syntax, semantics, dialectology, and the history of linguistics; he supervised the work on

Martha's Vineyard (Chap. 1) which was my Master's essay, and the study of New York City (Chaps. 2–6) which was my dissertation; yet in all this he did not put forward his own view or direct suggestion about which way to turn. But with caution, restraint, and example, he helped to direct my own projects into the most profitable channels. Weinreich had an extraordinary sense of direction in linguistics; he rarely made a misstep in his own research projects, and we all profited by his insight. I have recently had the opportunity to read some of Weinreich's unpublished sketches and projects for the study of multilingualism and social variation in the speech community; I found that his thinking had anticipated my own by many years and undoubtedly played a larger part in the results given here than might appear in the overt references. More than anything else, I benefitted from Weinreich's calm conviction that we were moving in the direction that a rational and realistic linguistics must inevitably follow.

In 1966, Weinreich proposed to Marvin Herzog and myself that we write a joint paper on "Empirical Foundations for a Theory of Language Change" for a conference at the University of Texas. As we delivered it, this paper embodied the results of my own work in New York and Martha's Vineyard, Herzog's findings on the dialectology of Yiddish in Northern Poland, and Weinreich's overall insight that created the Language and Culture Atlas of Ashkenazic Jewry. This was set in a larger view of the history of linguistics that was entirely the product of Weinreich's scholarship. In the spring of 1967, when Weinreich realized that he had only a short time to live, he turned to the final revision of this paper with great energy. In the last two weeks of his life, Weinreich recast the introduction to this paper in a way that captures clearly his overall view of the nature of language and its relation to society. It states the major theme of this volume better than any passage of my own:

> The facts of heterogeneity have not so far jibed well with the structural approach to language...for the more linguists became impressed with the existence of structure of language, and the more they bolstered this observation with deductive arguments about the functional advantages of structure, the more mysterious became the transition of a language from state to state. After all, if a language has to be structured in order to function efficiently, how do people continue to talk while the language changes, that is, while it passes through periods of lessened systematicity?...The solution, we will argue, lies in the direction of breaking down the identification of structuredness with homogeneity. The key to a rational conception of language change—indeed, of language itself—is the possibility of describing orderly differentiation in a language serving a community. We will argue that

nativelike command of heterogeneous structures is not a matter of multidialectalism or "mere" performance, but is part of unilingual linguistic competence. One of the corollaries of our approach is that in a language serving a complex (i.e., real) community, it is absence of structured heterogeneity that would be dysfunctional. (Weinreich, Labov, and Herzog 1968:100–101)

Personal Views on the Beginnings of Sociolinguistics

Wallace E. Lambert

Wallace E. Lambert was educated at Brown University, Colgate, and the University of North Carolina. Since 1954 he has taught at McGill University where he is now Professor Emeritus of Psychology, with research interests in social and experimental psychology, cross-national studies and psycho- and sociolinguistics. Lambert is a Fellow of the Royal Society of Canada, a member of the (U.S.) National Academy of Education, and a former President of the Canadian Psychological Association. In 1990 he was awarded the APA Distinguished Scientific Award for the applications of Psychology.

It is not as easy as one might think to recall the very first scenarios that I was involved in where the term "sociolinguistics" was thought about or discussed. The problem is not so much with my memory system as it is with the sheer passage of time and the fading of dates and names that help fixate my first encounters with sociolinguistics. Still, I do have three scenarios that I am pretty sure of.

The first scenario from the 1960–1961 period involved a letter or two from Uriel Weinreich, a linguist, who wanted all the results and details of a study we had just completed at McGill using the "matched-guise" procedure (where bilingual speakers recited an English and a French version of a passage so that taped copies of their verbal delivery could be presented to listeners, bilinguals, and monolinguals, who were to judge the likely personality characteristics of the speakers; no mention was made to the listeners that bilinguals were being presented on the master tape). Uriel was so eager for the details that I asked him why, and he explained it was for one of his graduate students who was keenly interested in the procedure and the differences in attributions made to each of the bilingual speaker's linguistic guises.

As Uriel put it: "With this fellow we have a perfect example of the first real 'sociolinguist'." I remember arguing that from his interests he sounded more like a linguistic sociologist than the reverse, but Uriel liked the term sociolinguistics, as though linguistics needed a facelift about that time. So Uriel made me a thesis consultant for the first sociolinguist who turned out to be Bill Labov. (Incidentally, I was able to visit with Bill and family just recently to get verification of this old event.) I was satisfied with the "linguist" suffix because Bill was focusing on social class and ethnic/racial speech markers and their influence on the impressions of listeners. But the "socio" part was not nearly as impressive in Bill's work as the ingenuity around the linguistic part. In fact, had T. Parsons or R. Merton done the same studies, we would have called it "linguosociology," I figure.

The second scenario took place also in the early sixties (as best as I can recall) at one of several SSRC meetings in New York City where a mixed group of psychologists, linguists, and anthropologists were gathered to evaluate and attempt to orient a newly arrived subdiscipline referred to as "psycholinguistics." That term has always bothered me (as does sociolinguistics) because most of the psychologists in attendance were involved in studies of the "psychology of language," including the social psychology of language. The SSRC committee included Charlie Osgood, Jack Carroll, Jim Jenkins, and me as psychologists, Joe Greenberg and Charles Ferguson as linguists; and Joe Casagrande and (I'm guessing here) a man named Eugene Lounsbury and Greenberg again as anthropologists and/or sociologists. There were others there, but they have not stayed in my memory. Since most of us psychologists were the nosiest, we dominated those meetings, but in doing so, we widened the gap from the others who were more polite but not at all as excited as we were with our early studies. For example, we were focusing on such topics as verbal (or semantic) satiation, free-association norms, word frequency counts, instrumental conditioning of verbal behavior, or the measurement of stages in bilingual development. But our perspectives on language were basically foreign to the linguists, I felt, even when Chomsky visited the committee and described a new type of linguistics that in his mind made psychology "trivial." But I clearly recall Greenberg, Casagrande, and particularly Lounsbury saying that they were not interested so much in behavioral or mental studies of language as much as they were in ethnographic and more "social" aspects of language (topics such as the bilingualism of Hopi Indians, baby talk in Arabic, diglossia, or dialect variations). We needed, they argued, a more "sociolinguistic" development in our collaboration with linguists, something different from psycholinguistics. I remember clearly the arguments that psycholinguistics, fledgling as it was, was likely to be of limited interest and that there was a need for a different tack, a more "socio" one.

The third scenario was a follow-up SSRC meeting at the University of Indiana, shortly after the New York one, where a new subgroup, including new members like Einar Haugen and Josh Fishman, formalized the new field. We even opened a family-sized bottle of root beer to celebrate the launching of "sociolinguists," with a host of plans for studies to be done. Still I felt we were now talking about the sociological, social psychological, and ethnographic approach to language. Just as we had earlier anticipated that interested students might split their training between psychology and linguistics, we now had to think through a program that combined sociology and social anthropology with linguistics.

As I will explain later, I never believed in the double-major idea, but others like Sue Ervin and Roger Brown did and in their own development they demonstrated splendidly its possibilities and its value of discipline combinations. I felt that linguists like Greenberg and Ferguson politely tolerated the enthusiasm of the psychologists who played around with language, but privately I could not imagine that they would encourage their students to really go into psychology. Similarly, I for one never saw the value of my students going into linguistics, although many did, regardless of my bias. For me, each discipline had its own mess of fish to fry and each was most likely to be effective when each asked its own unique questions about language and language behavior (see Lambert 1994). The questions each group asks fit into quite different underlying hierarchies of status. Psychologists in general view sociology and ethnographic anthropology as "softer" disciplines, linked with history and culture studies, while reductionism towards the inner workings of the body and mind, as in physiology and neurology, were "harder" and more profound domains, even harder than the purely psychological. The unknown was where linguistics fit in the status hierarchies. The exactitude of linguistic descriptions was intriguing to us, and people like George Miller and Charlie Osgood demonstrated how psychologists could profit from asking psychological questions about language as a code. However, the basic fascination linguists have with the code per se worried me and made me wonder what "we" had to learn from "them" about the human interactional features of language. Regardless of this debate, psycholinguistics and sociolinguistics were both on their ways, starting in the early 1960s.

The intellectual climate of the time of sociolinguistics' appearance goes back to the post-WWII period, started in the mid forties with a wave of ex-service people returning to college subsidized with the G.I. Bill, racing to make up for time away at war. This meant no monkey business on college campuses, no seeking out easy courses, and a very serious attitude on the part of somewhat older students. Employment was high which meant that one could study and specialize on topics of personal interest. The trick was to learn something thoroughly and then shop around for the job and the setting of one's choice. The war time enemies, Germany and Japan, had taught us the dangers and horrors of rampant nationalism, racism, and tyranny. Many of us wanted to improve on society by making it more fair and tolerant (see Lambert 1992). We needed to be more informed about people and about differences in ways of life around the world, starting with ethnic, racial, and social class differences within the U.S.A. Accordingly, to focus on languages as codes or on the psychology of learning in laboratory settings seemed rather distant from the important fields of action. Topics like race relations or language usage differences due to nationality, ethnicity, or social class were fascinating because research around these issues might in time promote more open human interactions. Moreover, feelings of belonging or not belonging might be determined by such superficial characteristics as skin color, style of speech, or accent and were thus worth probing. The possibility that bilingual people might have dual membership in more than one social/cultural group was an exciting idea to many of us, as was the idea that bilingualism, developed on a broad scale, might improve inter-group and inter-nation relations. All of us in the beginning phases of psycho- and sociolinguistics shared these fundamental interests, even though we would approach them quite differently.

The possibility of joint or collaborative scholarship was in the wind in the post-war period. For instance, Harvard had formed a Department of Social Relations comprising teachers from psychology, sociology, and anthropology placing demands on students to become triple-treat specialists. Not many actually did so and eventually the attractiveness of that idea diminished. At the same time (the early fifties) the Center for Advanced Study in the Behavioral Sciences opened at Palo Alto; it defined the behavioral sciences more broadly to include political science, linguistics, history, and psychiatry as well as psychology. The "social sciences" in the mandate of the SSRC of that period comprised a somewhat different subset of disciplines, placing less emphasis on experimental psychology. The Ford and Carnegie Foundations began to encourage collaborative research and cross-cultural investigations, all at about the same time. Thus, the appearance of psycholinguistics and sociolinguistics was in tune with the times, and the times seemed to have great expectations for combinations of disciplines, as though two would be better and faster than one.

With regard to interdisciplinarianism(!), I have recently reflected on that issue (Lambert 1994) and have come to the grouchy conclusion that each discipline might be better off if it developed its own klieg light and focused it with as much precision as possible, from its own (often tiny) mountain peak of specialization, onto personal and societal events that many disciplines might find of common interest. The belief is that the combined, confluent beam emanating from various mountain peaks would really light things up if each light source were kept as sharp, separate, and unique as possible. The value of SSRCs or CASBSs, this argument goes, would be in bringing together the distinctive klieg light specialists so as to exchange interpretations of what each sees in the event of focus.

In the everyday world, however, much collaboration naturally takes place for those with a common interest in a topic like language. For instance, Weinreich and Labov asked me for details of a social psychological measurement technique. In turn I asked Uriel how we could get speakers who had flawless control over two forms of spoken English—standard and Jewish- accented speech—and he helped us find some candidates and checked out others we already had for their veridicality. (In this instance, we were conducting a matched-guise study with Gentile and Jewish listeners.) In another instance, Joe Greenberg joined us in a study of perceived closeness or distance of language sounds; Joe had a theory about that topic and we had a scaling technique that was applicable. Osgood, Casagrande, Carroll, and Sue Ervin put their heads together on a study of bilingualism among Amerindians. This type of collaboration was mutually profitable, I believe. More complex collaboration might not work as well. For instance, Dick Tucker and I had the hunch that a profitable collaboration would emerge if we could arrange a meeting of Noam Chomsky and Don Hebb at McGill. It was the era in the late sixties when Chomsky was talking about "a psychology" of language, the meeting ground of thought and language, as described in his Cartesian Linguistics. We had a wonderful day together but it quickly became clear that Chomsky was, in Hebb's analysis, too close to philosophizing, too sure of his ideas, and too far from researching anything to make any sort of collaboration possible. I am also certain that Chomsky felt he was dealing with trivialities—a trio of psychologists trying to explain the complexities of perceptual learning, Lashley's ideas about serial order, and cell assembly development and offering them as likely alternatives to some innate language acquisition device. Actually, Chomsky did not understand Lashley's thinking nor Hebb's, and they apparently foreshadowed much of his own work (see D. Bruce 1994; also D. O. Hebb, W. E. Lambert, and G. R. Tucker 1971). Nonetheless the exchange brought to light the distinctiveness of the psychology of language in contrast to the linguistics of language.

The group of individuals I see as critical to the development of both psycholinguistics and sociolinguistics have already been mentioned. (Of course other ancient mariners, from their own experiences, will see different sets of players, with different roles assigned.) Most important I think were Uriel

Weinrech, Noam Chomsky (in his later phases), and Joe Greenberg because they were able to ask linguistic questions about psychology and about social anthropology. This is more evident in Uriel's case because he enjoyed thinking about languages and ethnolinguistic groups in contact. Noam was skilled at generalizing across language groups in order to discern his type of "language universals," and this prompted him to explore the psychology of human cognition and ask profound psychological questions. Joe Greenberg was less hasty in generalizing. He was more attentive to clusters of languages that, through their similarities, formed one type of "universals" in contrast to other clusters that formed quite different universals. Joe's training made him the perfect anthropologist. Each of these people had his unique impacts on psycho- and sociolinguistics. But Uriel seemed to me to be the only one really interested in and ready to collaborate and interact cooperatively with the psychos and socios. On the psychology side, John Carroll studied and learned the linguistics needed to conduct his important work and this made his collaboration thoroughly psychological and linguistic. But Carroll kept his identity as a psychologist whereas Jim Jenkins, who had made so many valuable contributions to the free-association issue in experimental psychology, got so enraptured with Chomsky's messages that he seemed to become ashamed of his psychological past. Chomsky had that degree of charm, and we had seen effects earlier on the conversion of Sol Saporta who also negated his earlier psycho- and sociolinguistic past.

By the way of contrast, Charles Osgood was the psychologist in the early networks who animated everything he touched. Charlie was plagued in life with too many ingenious ideas, I figure. He tried his best to write them down and to research as many of them as possible. But I felt neither Charlie nor I (who also had fun trying to check out ideas through research) ever heeded or became conversant in linguistics itself. Rather, we enjoyed bouncing new schemes off linguists because they at least listened whereas our psychology colleagues wondered where we were headed. But Osgood and I were interested in the problems of meaning and meaning systems. For Charlie, the fundamental topics were (a) meaning, referred to as "mediating responses" or "little mr's," following Hull's terminology, a line of thought that brought him close to Hebb's cell assembly notions; (b) meaning systems viewed cross-culturally and cross-lingually; (c) the compound/coordinate forms of bilingualism, following from Uriel's schema; and (d) the broader notion of perceptual learning, going back to Lashley and Hebb.

In perspective, I see the beginning of psycholinguistics in particular as "theory driven," with theories drawn on from psychology, neuro-physiology, and philosophical linguistics. The beginnings of sociolinguistics, which were fused with psycholinguistics from the start, were less prompted by theories.

Rather topics or basic structures (like social class, group membership, ethnic relations) that had their moorings in ethnology, sociology, social psychology, and cross-cultural studies were examined by specialists from each discipline, not very often collaboratively, as I recall. What joined these people was a common interest in language, viewed from their own vantage points.

With regard to my own research, some of it shows the helpful influence I had from these meetings with the linguists and other behavioral scientists. The influence freed me from the restraints of experimental and social psychology by legitimizing an interest in the topic of language, while trying to remain a psychologist. At the same time, pandering to that personal interest seems to have had some influences on the shaping of the field of sociolinguistics. The research I have in mind includes the following: the development of the matched-guise technique and the studies that it generated (Lambert et al. 1960); the development of the interplay of attitudes and motives on second language learning, acquisition, or maintenance, with Robert Gardner (Gardner and Lambert 1959); the probing of bilingualism's effect on cognitive functioning, with Elizabeth Peal (Peal and Lambert 1962); the development of notion of additive versus subtractive forms of bilingualism, with Dick Tucker (Lambert and Tucker 1972) which opened us up to searching for the advantages of being bilingual and for ways to circumvent the potential disadvantages; the studies on personal address forms, studied cross-culturally, with Dick Tucker (Lambert and Tucker 1976); and the more current work with Don Taylor on the relation of individual bilingualism and biculturalism to personal maturity and a sense of worth (Lambert and Taylor 1990) which leads us to the exploration at the societal level of multilingualism and multicultural in free and open societies (Lambert 1992). As I look back, it seems that I picked up from those early social contacts a sense of the power and fascination that language generates, and with this realization I was free to return to my base as a psychologist and to ask psychological (including social psychological) questions about language (Lambert 1994). My guess is that a new wave of sociolinguists is coming on the scene now who (I am thinking here of the exciting work of Shana Poplack, Jim Cummins, Merrill Swain, Howie Giles, and Ellen Ryan) will be better combinations of socios and linguisticos! But as they work their way onto center stage, some of us will still be plodding along trying to test out or probe further the topics that we started out with way back when.

The one contribution that most excited me (and that still does) is the cross-cultural research I did with Josiane Hamers and Nancy Frasure Smith (Lambert et al. 1979). The studies involved persuaded me, at least, that ethnolinguistic groups chosen to be as "different" as can be (e.g., Japanese, Greek, Italian, American, Portuguese, British) are on analysis hardly different at all in terms of their humanity and their basic values. For instance, when we studied how various national or cultural parental groups tried to bring up their children, teach them to become independent, to live cooperatively, etc., there were few discernable cultural and national differences. In fact, the "culture" or "nation" variable was nearly completely overshadowed by apparently more fundamental variables like the parents' socio-economic standing, their maleness versus femaleness, the urbanity versus rurality, etc. In fact, the research demonstrated that samples of Japanese middle class parents are amazingly similar to middle class in France, America, Portugal, or wherever, whereas the same middle class Japanese are worlds apart from Japanese working class parents who in turn are amazingly like working class parents everywhere. Similarly, it turned out that mothers are mothers across "cultures" and different in many ways from fathers across the same cultures. And sons are sons, and daughters are daughters. The reason that groups are not reliably different one from another is that *within* group variability nearly always outweighs *between* group variability. Thus, the really different entities in the social world are individuals, not arbitrary groupings of individuals according to national or "cultural" backgrounds.

The relevance of this research to sociolinguistics, I believe, is that it demystifies "culture" and cultural "differences" and opens a way for us to develop a sense of unity among peoples around the world. If extended, it could eliminate also the fear of culture and language "differences" and substitute instead an appreciation for the variety of human expressions that the social world affords us all. There are new directions here, I feel, for sociolinguistics in the 1990s.

With regard to my teaching in the area of sociolinguistics, it usually happened in the summers or on leaves from McGill. McGill never had that much interest in any form of specialization, since we were paid to teach basic courses within our own department, but I had fun running seminars at Stanford, Michigan, Indiana, University of Massachusetts, in the Philippines, Thailand, France, and Egypt, for example, where sociolinguistic issues were of major interest. There was, and is, it seems to me, a great potential for sociolinguistics to focus on the international aspects of language because major sociolinguistic issues play themselves out on the broad international stage. For instance, language planning, language shifting and loss, the competition among languages for international interactions, the ascendance of English world wide and the concomitant fear of heritage language loss, the problems of translation, the movement of peoples, with its bilingual/bicultural demands, and hopefully, the worldwide appreciation of humanity and its fascinating diversity of expressions.

Early Developments in Sociolinguistics

Stanley Lieberson

Stanley Lieberson is the Abbott Lawrence Lowell Professor of Sociology at Harvard University. He is currently studying the social factors influencing the first names given to children, using data sets gathered from a wide variety of settings and over long spans of time. He is a past President of the American Sociological Association and a member of the National Academy of Sciences.

My own interest in sociolinguistics started without any knowledge that such a field was developing, let alone knowledge of the work that was being done. In point of fact, sociologists had been studying some linguistic dimensions of social phenomenon for many years—albeit without developing the extensive and dense work necessary for a discipline to evolve. In 1955, for example, the Random House "Studies in Sociology" series published a small book by Joseph Bram on *Language and Society*. None of the references deal with a sociological work—except for a 1953 volume by Hugh Dalziel Duncan on the sociology of literature (see Bram 1955:64–66). However, sociologists and demographers had independently shown some interest in what we would later classify as sociolinguistics. Some parts of symbolic social psychology emphasized the importance of language (I was exposed to this perspective in a social psychology course offered by the sociologist Anselm Strauss in the mid fifties at the University of Chicago). There was, for example, a remarkable paper by Schatzman and Strauss (1955) on class differences in their ways of communicating. At the other extreme, sociologists and demographers did have access to census data on language knowledge and usage from a wide variety of sources. The United States Census provided data on the ability to speak English as early as 1890; the magnificent 1920 Census monograph on immigrants by Niles Carpenter (1927) discussed the mother tongues of immigrants; mother tongue data were available for numerous censuses, albeit with the question not always consistent from year to year (Kiser 1956); and Dudley Kirk paid considerable attention to language matters in his chapter on the ethnic diversity of Europe (1946). Certainly, Hertzler was correct in his 1965 book, *A Sociology of Language,* when he described the sociology of language as "still in its rudimentary stage of development" (p. 6). Although, in different ways, sociologists encountered issues which led them to think of language matters, the emphasis was more on the *socio* than on the *linguistics* facet of the topic (a matter I will address below).

In my case, an interest (in what I would later learn is sociolinguistics) started while I was doing my Ph.D. dissertation in sociology. Briefly, I was studying ethnic residential segregation and assimilation in ten US cities during the twentieth century.[1] Being interested in the influence of segregation on assimilation, I examined the correlations between the level of each immigrant group's segregation and their proportions able to speak English. In discussing this topic with my mentor, Otis Dudley Duncan, he wondered about the linguistic situation in other countries. In particular, he mentioned the work of a demographer on the linguistic pluralism of Switzerland reprinted in a volume of demographic readings that he had co-edited several years earlier (Kurt Mayer 1956). The question stuck, even if it was not the time for pursuing it. Several years after I completed my dissertation, I submitted a proposal to the National Science Foundation to study language diversity in the entire world. It was a naive proposal, I suppose, but the Foundation saw some merit and offered to support me long enough to try a pilot study to see if I could do it.

There were four important ways in which this proposal impacted on my work in sociolinguistics. First, the grant in 1964 itself permitted me to do a substantial study of bilingualism and language diversity in Canada, with primary focus on English-French patterns.[2] (I decided against doing a pilot study to see if an extensive study were possible; instead I focused on the language situation in one particular country.) Second, one of the reviewers (surely it was a sociolinguist) mentioned publications that I was totally unaware of and that were invaluable to me. Third, because of the announcement of this grant, I was invited at the last moment to attend a summer program on sociolinguistics at Indiana University in 1964 sponsored by the Social Science Research Council (SSRC). Fourth, after that summer program, I served on the SSRC Sociolinguistics Committee between 1964 and 1970. The importance of this grant in enabling me to do research on the linguistic situation in Canada is self-evident. Below, I will discuss the influence of the three other events.

---

[1] This dissertation was completed in 1960, and later revised and published as a monograph (Lieberson 1963).
[2] Among the publications resulting were: Lieberson 1965, 1970.

As indicated, I was unaware of the rich literature that existed, even then, in the area of sociolinguistics. From both the reviewer's comments on my NSF application as well as the publications discussed in the summer program I was influenced by several of these publications. Uriel Weinreich had published a magnificent review of the literature on language contact and the unresolved issues (1953). Einar Haugen (1956) had also published a valuable bibliographical guide to bilingualism per se (during this period, my work concentrated on bilingualism and mother tongue diversity). I think it was then that I also learned about Haugen's two-volume study of bilingualism among Norwegian immigrants to the U.S. (Haugen 1953). The review of my grant application also mentioned a paper by Uriel Weinreich, dealing with bilingualism in India (1957). It was important for me on two counts: (1) it suggested some very nice demographic patterns influencing language behavior in India—patterns that I found also operating in Canada; and (2) it used a set of language diversity measures proposed by the anthropological linguist, Joseph Greenberg (1956). I used the Greenberg measures to describe mother tongue diversity and communication potential within groups in Canada and elsewhere. In addition, I expanded his measures to make them applicable for diversity and communication *between* groups (he had approached the problem only in terms of *within*-group characteristics).[3] Moreover, I developed the diversity measures for application to nonsociolinguistic topics (Lieberson 1969). There were other writings that I learned about at that period and that I recall impacting on my work. These include: the earlier book on language by Bloomfield (1933); the well-known book on nationalism and communication by Deutsch (1953), which I could never fully convert into something doable, although it was stimulating; the paper by Diebold (1961) which helped me realize how simplistic was my notion of bilingualism and the way it almost necessarily had to be used in census data; the small collection of papers in the volume edited by Frank Rice on second languages (1962), particularly the paper by Ferguson (on language and national development) and the paper by Roberts (with data on the linguistic situation in many nations, which eventually jump-started my analyses of trends and patterns in language diversity in the world); and the book on Switzerland by the political scientist, Kenneth McRae (1964).

The summer program on sociolinguistics run by SSRC at Indiana University in 1964 is a very important factor in my own development and, I believe, for sociolinguistics generally. It brought together people with strong sociolinguistic interests who were either leaders in the field or about to become leaders. Among the participants who come to mind are: Jack Berry,

---

[3] Lieberson 1964.

William Bright, Charles Ferguson, Joshua Fishman, Paul Friedrich, Allen Grimshaw, John Gumperz, Einar Haugen, Chester Hunt, Heinz Kloss, William Labov, Nathan Keyfitz, and William Stewart. There were others whom I have inadvertently left out. Further, Indiana University was also the setting that summer of the Linguistic Institute meetings. This meant that there were a large number of linguists present, some of whom where in Bloomington in order to teach a course or two on more traditional linguistic topics. Nevertheless, many had interests in sociolinguistics and would drift in and out of our discussions and workshops. In addition, there were such outside speakers brought in, as Joseph Greenberg, Dell Hymes, Wallace Lambert, and Uriel Weinreich. I have mentioned the impact of Greenberg and Weinreich on my own thinking, but have said nothing of Wallace Lambert. His innovative and imaginative social psychological work at McGill on language—particularly on bilingualism—was often discussed that summer. I got to know Wally better later on, and was always impressed (and inspired) by his intellectual verve and imagination. Moreover, there was no question that he was committed to a scientific effort to understand sociolinguistic processes.

Elsewhere, I have described other features of the summer program on sociolinguistics:

> Although much of the summer was marked by debates and disagreements, I learned a great deal from this group. There were a number of high-powered minds talking right past each other, but for someone who had never taken a course in linguistics it was absolutely enlightening. The linguists were for the most part an impressive group of people, but their way of thinking was alien to my own, which originated in what might be called the social-demography and human-ecology traditions of Chicago sociology. Many of them, but not all, were oriented toward the humanities rather than the social sciences. For some, one exception was grounds for wiping out the value of a generalization. They were largely unsympathetic to quantitative data and were certainly more interested in the linguistics part of the term "sociolinguistics." It was the elaboration of the various features of language that most excited them. The idea of using national censuses to deal with language questions was absolutely incomprehensible to some participants—and rightly so, I should think, from their perspective, which could see little value coming from a study with such crude measures of language as those used in census questions. (On many occasions I have had to argue for the proper place and application of language data from censuses; this battle

is reflected in several of my papers in this book.) But I benefitted greatly from the issues raised and was helped by valuable suggestions and references. (Lieberson 1981:380)

All of these disagreements and battles were actually productive in the sense that views were slowly modified even if we continued to follow our initial dispositions. It was impossible to be untouched by these new considerations that one had previously failed to appreciate. It may have taken one extreme statement to move someone from a position that was equally extreme in an opposite direction, but the net effect was an improvement in perspective and understanding. I was, as I say, under assault for wanting to use census data and other survey materials to deal with topics that the more linguistically minded members of the group saw as grossly inadequate and pathetically oversimplified. This made me think long and hard about how to use such data, how to test their assertions, the ways in which such data could be improved in future studies, and the problems for which such data were appropriate. My response was a paper on language questions in censuses that addressed four issues: their availability; their limitations; procedures for evaluating the data; and the kinds of problems for which their use is appropriate (Lieberson 1966a).

At the time of the summer conference, I had an invitation from *Sociological Inquiry* to edit a special issue on a topic of my choosing. Because of the stimulating events at the Indiana conference, I decided to edit an issue on sociolinguistics rather than follow my earlier disposition to deal with race and ethnic relations. The editors were very supportive of my desire to take advantage of the exciting developments that summer, even though the topic was hardly of central concern to many sociologists. The contributors to this issue, which I titled "Explorations in Sociolinguistics" (Lieberson 1966b), included (in alphabetic order): Basil Bernstein, William Bright, Harry Crockett, Jr., Joshua Fishman, Paul Friedrich, Allen Grimshaw, Einar Haugen, David Heise, Joyce Hertzler, Chester Hunt, Heinz Kloss, William Labov, and Lewis Levine (in addition, I wrote an introduction as well as contributing the aforementioned paper on language questions in the census). The volume, thanks to this fine set of papers addressing cutting-edge issues in a field moving at a rapid pace, received considerable interest: it was reprinted a year later as a special issue of the *International Journal of American Linguistics,* 33 (October 1967), and later in the year went through the first of three printings as a book published by Indiana University Press. (The support of Dell Hymes was invaluable in getting the Press to publish this volume.)

As I mentioned, there were numerous disagreements and sometimes issues that I saw as nitpicky, but I learned much. Certain underlying issues became obvious to me that summer, and they were to reappear in the years ahead—particularly during the period when I served on the Sociolinguistics Committee established by SSRC. There were some fundamental differences between most of the linguistically oriented sociologists and the handful of us with either a sociological background or a full appreciation of the complexities of social processes and how they could interact with linguistic phenomena: the former were ultimately far more intrigued with language per se and all of the nuances involved. The sociologists were, on the whole, less interested in this and more concerned with the social context of linguistic behavior. As a consequence, there were different emphases and different criteria. Data gathered in a census are indeed superficial for dealing with a variety of linguistic issues. On the other hand, some of those with purely a linguistic background seemed naive in their approach to social processes and social causes. Additionally, there was some opposition to statistical approaches—a matter where sociologists could make an important contribution if it were appreciated and desired. Related to this, there was an inability to think *probabilistically* as opposed to *deterministically*. For example, there were those who considered any general statement to be obviously false if they could cite even one case in which it did not work. For some of us, an exception hardly disproved an assertion, since we implicitly understood the propositions to be probabilistic (see the discussion of a probabilistic social epistemology in Lieberson 1992a:7–12).

During that summer, and in the succeeding years, I was particularly influenced by the linguist Charles Ferguson. "Fergie" encompasses extraordinarily broad tastes, tolerances, knowledge, and enthusiasm. He was more open than most of us to appreciating the potential utility of a wide variety of approaches proposed in the Sociolinguistics group meeting that summer, and in the years ahead when we both served on the SSRC Committee. He was helpful to me in pointing out naive omissions, confusions, or valuable references to the literature, and he could see the point of the proposed work. For Ferguson, there was a passionate commitment to the field and the desire to take the best of what could be obtained from any and all sources. Labels were irrelevant; advancement of sociolinguistics was what counted. His scholarly contribution to the development of sociolinguistics is substantial, in and of itself. But it would be inappropriate, in his case, to neglect his leadership contribution and his ability to bring a variety of people into the tent. There were some other linguists who were also impressive in the intensity of their dedication to the subject, but few could match Ferguson in the breadth of his overview.

After the summer program, I began to serve as a member of the Committee on Sociolinguistics, run by the Social Science Research Council. The Committee was both stimulating and frustrating. It was stimulating and valuable because there were (at different times) some very lively minds present. Charles Ferguson, Joshua Fishman, Allen Grimshaw, John Gumperz, Einar Haugen, Everett Hughes, Dell Hymes, and William Labov are among those who I recall overlapping with the period when I was a member. There were strains within the Committee—almost sides I would say—that revolved around issues of method, style, goals, and the like. Again, there were some with almost an antipathy towards social science: one member on more than one occasion teetered on outright opposition to social class as a useful idea for social research. For him, the ethnomethodologists were the most appealing part of sociology since their critique of mainstream sociology supported his own biases. But there were others whose views I could understand and support. Being at that time very much a demographically oriented sociologist, there was not much of a place on the Committee's main interests for me. The Committee was important to me anyway because, in effect, I was isolated and the Committee was my main interpersonal tie to sociolinguistics.

It was also a problem, of course, for the anthropologists, linguists, political scientists, and psychologists who had taken up a sociolinguistic perspective.[4] In the discussions at Bloomington and on the SSRC Committee, the successful development of psycholinguistics was a model of how sociolinguistics could progress. It became clear that was not occurring. From time to time, an invited visitor to our Committee meetings would sometimes display a remarkable lack of understanding of the simplest elements of the perspectives that were emerging. I remember one young linguist from a leading university who had not the slightest idea of seeing linguistic patterns as emerging from, and being a part of, a social order. I likewise remember, after moving to the University of Washington, offering to present a paper in the Linguistics Department colloquium. The chairman indicated that he would not allow me to present a paper since my work was not *real* linguistics.

Eventually I drifted away from sociolinguistics. I suppose if I was a program builder, or a charismatic figure, or someone with a mission in this area, I could have done more. However, it seems to me that sociolinguistics was less likely to take hold in sociology than in any of the other relevant fields. I must say that, in general, I found relatively little active interest in sociolinguistics among sociology colleagues. Colleagues did not object to my studying this topic, nor did they question the appropriateness of the subject. But they could not get particularly excited by it. At the risk of committing an injustice, it is my impression that the sociological work of Joshua Fishman—then and now, a major figure in this area—was impacting less on American sociologists than on either other sociologists overseas or scholars in other disciplines. Likewise,

---

[4]There were many in linguistics, for example, who found little use for sociolinguistics—indeed questioning whether it was an appropriate task for linguists at all.

I believe the greatest impact in the United States of the work of the British sociologist, Basil Bernstein, on class differences in speech was not in sociology. By contrast, the imaginative and provocative early work of the linguist William Labov was generating excitement and interest among many linguists and anthropologists. The closest comparable situation at that time was the work of various ethnomethodologists. But their work, original and provocative as it may have been, was more of a critique of the existing practices in the sociological discipline. For example, ethnomethodologists were challenging: they used standard data sources in sociology such as surveys or demographic forms, quantitative procedures, sociological assumptions and concepts, and were concerned with macroprocesses. My ties to the linguists, psychologists, and anthropologists at these institutions were modest at best, although I can recall a few exceptions through the years. So I was greatly dependent on the encouragement received from people whom I met in Bloomington and from my colleagues on the SSRC Committee on Sociolinguistics.

In the late sixties, I gave a graduate seminar on sociolinguistics at the University of Washington which attracted a small number of students, all in sociology. None of the students showed an interest in pursuing the topic and I never offered the course again.[5] On the other hand, I added a section on language for both my graduate and undergraduate courses on race and ethnic relations in the United States and the world. Here the topic was always of considerable interest to the students. The section dealt with language differences between groups in contact with each other, conflicts in the nation/state over language issues, assimilation, various bilingual processes, mother-tongue shift, and differences between indigenous- and migrant-subordinate groups in their likelihood of giving up their mother tongues. I believe there was not the intellectual "infrastructure" in sociology to carry forward a strong program that was "purely" sociolinguistics. Hence, it blended in very nicely as part of a race and ethnic relations course, but not as an entity in itself.

I know of several funding agencies and foundations that were playing central roles in launching sociolinguistics during the years when I initially got involved. The Ford Foundation had a lively interest in this subject and helped support a number of conferences, the extensive sociolinguistic research on language use and language teaching in East Africa, and other research efforts (thanks to Elinor Barber, at one point I benefited from a modest grant in the mid seventies); in addition, in December 1968 I attended a working conference in Dar es Salaam, Tanzania on these East African surveys. Likewise, in 1978 I attended a very stimulating conference on language spread at the

---

[5]In the early eighties, when I was at the University of Arizona, the chair of the Linguistics Department expressed interest in my offering a course on sociolinguistics, but by then my focus had drifted to other matters.

University College of Wales, Aberystwyth, that they helped fund. I have already alluded to the deep impact of the Social Science Research Council through its organization of the summer program on sociolinguistics, as well as the Committee on Sociolinguistics which met under its aegis. The Committee vigorously promoted sociolinguistics by organizing various conferences and meetings, encouraging professional associations to pay attention to sociolinguistics, supported a new journal that Dell Hymes was starting, and even made efforts to get publishers interested in starting a series in this area. A grant from the National Science Foundation in 1964, as well as a later one from them, supported my work on Canada as well as some of my other studies of multilingual situations.[6] The Center for Applied Linguistics was a very energetic and active promoter of sociolinguistics activities such as conferences and publications. There were also a variety of other sources of research support and scholarly conferences during this period. In my own case, for example, during the mid sixties I received a modest grant from the Royal Commission on Bilingualism and Biculturalism to study linguistic segregation in Canadian cities. And, since this was prior to the availability in Canada of census data on tapes, even more important was their willingness to run various segregation tabulations that I could not analyze with the published census data. There was an intense concern about linguistic issues in Canada, reflecting French Canadians' efforts at that time to alter the second-class position of French in the country. I should mention that other nations, as well as the agencies of the United Nations, supported conferences and research that addressed local concerns about language planning, bilingual education, linguistic assimilation, and other sociolinguistic issues. I think these applied issues gave a greater sense of urgency and usefulness to the work of sociolinguistics. From my vantage point, I would say that the key organizational people would include Charles Ferguson, Dell Hymes, Melvin Fox (Ford Foundation), and Elbridge Sibley (the SSRC representative in their Committee on Sociolinguistics).

There is one feature about developments in the early days that I find remarkable as I now look back. Namely, even though there were a variety of different disciplines represented, the interaction between the various participants was intense. There are twenty-two names (myself excluded) on the list of pioneers that the editors are approaching for their recollections. I met twenty of these twenty-two, even though most are not in my discipline and even though I was certainly not a central player in this development. This

---

[6]The funds of the Social Science Research Council were rather limited, at least then, so I would be reasonably confident that they received funding from other sources to support their activities in sociolinguistics. I have a vague recollection that the National Science Foundation was one of their sources of support.

reflects the intensity of interaction between people drawn into sociolinguistics from a wide variety of sources with a wide variety of interests.

I am asked to comment about my own work and how it fits in with sociolinguistics. Initially, my work stemmed from an interest in race and ethnic relations. I viewed language as an important issue to consider in understanding race and ethnic relations in almost every nation of the world. This reflected the fact that racial and ethnic groups in the same society often differ in their mother tongue (at least at the point of initial contact), and the fact that language is a central issue in societies marked by groups speaking different languages.[7] The potential contribution to sociolinguistics was only secondary to this concern. I spent considerable time studying bilingualism since that is the key mechanism if a transformation is to occur from language diversity to language homogeneity. I studied both the causes of bilingualism and also addressed the two radically different outcomes of bilingualism. First, there is the situation in which many of the offspring of bilinguals give up on their parents' mother tongue and learn the acquired tongue as their own mother tongue. This is the situation in the United States for most immigrants; somewhere along the way people with a non-English mother tongue become bilingual by learning English. In turn, they pass on English as the mother tongue to their offspring and their own ancestral language is, at best, a second language. The next generation in turn continues with English as their children's mother tongue, often passing on minimal knowledge of the grandparents' mother tongue. Thus, bilingualism is a mechanism leading towards mother tongue shift. A very different outcome occurs in many societies: people become bilingual, but they pass on their own mother tongue to their offspring—not the acquired language. Such a process continues ad nauseam, with language diversity and/or ethnic differences in mother tongue remaining stable over relatively long spans of time. On a theoretical level, I found that my societal theory of race and ethnic relations (Lieberson 1961) helped me understand which of these linguistic outcomes was most likely to occur. This theory draws a major distinction between two kinds of subordination: groups that *migrate* to subordinate positions in the receiving country; and groups that are *conquered* and thereby become subordinated. The latter, I theorize, are more likely to maintain their mother tongue; the former are more likely to shift to the dominant group's language. This works out very nicely; for example, mother-tongue shift among immigrants migrating to subordination in the United States and Canada is far more rapid than the rates among North

---

[7]See "Language and Ethnic Relations: A Neglected Problem" originally published in 1970 and reprinted in Lieberson 1981:1–18.

Early Developments in Sociolinguistics 169

American Indians and Inuits, as well as populations migrating as dominants and then conquered (as in the case of French Canadians in Quebec).[8]

This interest, in turn, generated work on related but broader questions about mother tongue diversity in nations. I became interested in national language diversity per se, and with the factors driving shifts over time, and I ended up questioning what had hitherto been thought of as the standard association between national development (industrialization, literacy, modernization, etc.) and language diversity. My initial concern also expanded into studies of the residential segregation of ethnolinguistic groups in cities, occupational demands for second language acquisition, domains of language usage (based on Fishman's use of that concept), demographic factors affecting the levels of language shift in the United States, and the linkages between national and regional language diversity.

I also moved into problems unrelated to understanding race and ethnic relations. Several papers dealt with language questions in censuses and extensions of Greenberg's measures (referred to earlier). I also addressed questions on improving sociolinguistic surveys, measuring the incidence of bilingualism, and the anatomy of language diversity. Sociolinguistics was catching; indeed, I wrote a theoretical piece dealing with how a language will spread and replace other languages. This was directed at the way English replaced French as the lingua franca of the world (Lieberson 1982).

Currently, after working for a number of years on issues quite removed from sociolinguistics, I find myself returning to a sociolinguistic problem different from any I would have visualized in the past. I am presently trying to understand the forces driving tastes in first names. I have gathered a wide variety of data on names for different nations over time. In many cases, I have information permitting me to cross-tabulate the names given to children by such parental characteristics as: socioeconomic status, race, ethnic origin, marital status of mother, and age and cohort. In addition, I can examine the influence of long-term trends in broad social, political, and economic developments. The spillover from my earlier interest in sociolinguistics is clear. I first wrote an exploratory paper on this topic for an issue of the *International Journal of the Sociology of Language* dealing with the future of sociolinguistics (Lieberson 1984).[9] Some years passed before I could fully turn to addressing naming practices as a way of studying fashion and tastes in a rigorous way (see Lieberson and Bell 1992; Lieberson 1992b). At any rate, I am moving full force into this topic at the present time, and it is fun to be doing it.

---

[8] See Lieberson, Dalto, and Marsden 1975.

[9] This paper stressed the racial and ethnic dimensions of first names, although it was by no means exclusively devoted to this matter.

Another Time

John Macnamara

John Macnamara taught high school in Dublin (Castleknock College) (1955–1958) before becoming lecturer in educational psychology in St. Patrick's College, Dublin (1960–1969). From that time he was Professor of Psychology at McGill University until his death in 1996.

John Macnamara died in Montreal on January 13, 1996 from brain cancer. John was an enthusiastic participant in this project from the earliest stages. Both of the editors remember vividly and fondly interactions with John over the past thirty years. In fact, after he relocated permanently to Canada, he lived initially with the Tucker family. During the 1960s and 1970s John made a number of important contributions to the areas of bilingualism and bilingual education and language policy and planning through his research and his scholarly writings. The editors are grateful that his manuscript was completed prior to his death.

Growing up in the new Irish Free State during the most intense efforts to revive the Irish language and coming to be a teacher of Irish with a university degree in the subject, it was inevitable that I should reflect long and hard on the relation between language and culture.[1] The reasons given for learning Irish were far-reaching and interesting, but not, I felt, convincing. The ability to read Irish, we were told, would put us in contact with all that was peculiarly Irish in the thoughts and feelings of our ancestors. Knowing Irish would enhance our distinctively Irish traits. It would, in particular, mark us as different from English people and thus justify the struggle for national independence. It would, certain authors urged, buttress our religious faith to withstand the mounting tide of materialism and heathenism.

---

[1]Preparation of this note was supported by a grant to the author from the National Science and Engineering Research Council of Canada. I am deeply grateful to my wife, Joyce Delarichelière Macnamara, for comments on an earlier version.

The reasons for my uneasiness were partly my distaste for the idea that I should try not to be like an Englishman and that I should try to be like an Irishman. It struck me as all wrong that I should try to be like, or unlike, anyone. I also doubted that a language would be an effective buttress against the ideology of our times, unless it rendered us incapable of communicating with the rest of the world. I wondered about the value of a religious faith that could survive only in such isolation.

In fairness, however, not all revivalists wanted to isolate us from the modern world. They claimed instead that the very salutations in the Irish language were Christian in form and inspiration and that in using them one became more deeply and naturally Christian. Irish literature and folklore, too, are full of legends and saints and of traditional prayers for all occasions. For example, on entering an Irish house one was expected to call God's blessing on all within. But I could imagine an atheist using the formula; just as total heathens call on the name of Jesus Christ in any alarming situation. It just seemed to me that language did not control the mind in the manner that some revivalists claimed.

My viewing of things in this way explains my interest in sociolinguistics and also the brevity of my part in it.

Later, when I studied psychology in Edinburgh, I came across a theory that looked like a generalization of the Irish revivalists' views coming out of work in comparative linguistics. This was the theory of Benjamin Lee Whorf, which I encountered in the delightful, and for me influential, book of Roger Brown (1958), *Words and Things*. There I learned that the issue could be joined at the level of psychological theory and experiment. Colorfully phrased in the language of the time the issue was whether language acted as a cloak or as a mold. If language is a cloak, it takes its form from thought, which was usually believed by the protagonists of the cloak side to be a structure that is common among people who speak even strikingly different languages; if language is a mold—the side on which Whorf threw most, but not all, his weight—then one might expect different languages to be associated with, or even cause, basically different patterns of thought. The mold theory would support the nationalist arguments with which I was familiar but uncomfortable.

The issue is deeper than at first appears, because the Whorfian view implied that the basic structure of the human mind is in some significant degree formed by the environmental input.

> Actually, thinking is most mysterious, and by far the greatest light is thrown by the study of language. This study shows that the forms of a person's thoughts are controlled by inexorable laws of pattern of which he is unconscious...And every language is a vast pattern-system, different from others, in which are culturally ordained the

forms and categories by which the personality not only communicates, but also analyses nature, notices or neglects types of relationship and phenomena, channels his reasoning, and builds the house of his consciousness. (Whorf 1956:252)

Thus, Whorfianism fitted well with the industrial-strength empiricism that prevailed in the 1950s. With behaviorism, it claimed that the structures of the mind are due, almost entirely, to environmental factors imposing themselves on the mind from the outside. In the end behaviorism as a psychological theory collapsed as quickly and completely as Russian imperialism. Whorfianism appears to have shared behaviorism's fate (see Gumperz, this volume).

My own first essay on Whorfianism arose out of my studies of bilingualism. Whorf's ideas implied that bilingualism should be a psychological tragedy. If each language begets in its speakers a distinctive understanding of the world, what is a bilingual to do with these mutually incommensurate understandings? And how is translation possible? Since I saw no reason to believe that bilinguals were in any psychological trouble, I concluded that Whorf's ideas had to be seriously misleading. I presented these views at a Georgetown Round Table in 1970 (Macnamara 1970). I still hold to those views (Macnamara 1991).

While the account given so far is accurate, it is a gross distortion of the field of sociolinguistics as a whole, because from the start the cloak/mold dispute was but a small, though important, part of the field. Sociolinguists studied language planning and political problems related to linguistic diversity. They studied the factors that influence choice of language, or dialect, or register and the effects of such choices. They studied the effect of common language on social cohesiveness and of language diversity on intergroup tensions. They studied the connection between the language of the school and the progress of children from various ethnic backgrounds in academic attainment and in social and personal adjustment. Such educational concerns occupied the first ten years of my research work as a psychologist. But this was really not me. While I was in Ireland I felt obliged to work on practical problems where my efforts were having (as I believed) a beneficial effect on schooling. When I moved to Canada, at the end of the 1960s, I gradually switched to the learning of the mother tongue where I felt the issues had to be worked out at their most basic level. The switch was not sudden or total, because from 1969 right through the 1970s, at the suggestion of Dick Tucker (then a young colleague), I taught a course on bilingualism in the Department of Psychology at McGill. In this course undergraduates were introduced to sociolinguistic issues related to bilingualism.

My research, however, was more and more in the area of child language learning. I was encouraged by the reception of my very first paper on the subject (Macnamara 1972). I stopped counting reprint requests after 1000. *Current Contents* declared it a "citation classic" in 1985. Most people did not recognize that it was really on the Whorfian problem. The paper presented evidence that the way children see and understand the world their mother is talking about is for them an important clue to the linguistic system she uses to express what she has to say. This is the antithesis of the main Whorfian claim. Susan Ervin-Tripp summed up the point more effectively: you have a fair chance of learning Russian if you watch Russian television; you have none at all if all you have is Russian radio.

One has to remember that at the time Noam Chomsky was, understandably, insisting on the assumption that syntax and semantics are autonomous in the sense that the *statement* of syntactic rules should appeal to no semantic facts. He also, incomprehensibly to me, threw the weight of his authority behind the methodological assumption that the theory of language learning could be developed without involving children's perceptual and (antecedent to language) conceptual abilities. This despite the fact that he himself freely employed evidence from semantics in arguing for purely syntactic points. The field of child language followed his methodological lead and this was the heyday of the autonomous Language Acquisition Device (LAD). By 1972 people saw that this was the wrong way to look at things. It was wrong for the same reasons as Whorf was wrong. You need a fully operational mind and a good deal of information about people and their construal of the environment to learn a language. My paper formulated this other view, which was already taking shape in people's minds. It is my impression that this view has continually gained strength in the subsequent twenty years, and that today most psychologists working on child language, implicitly or explicitly, hold something closer to this view than to the view implicit in LAD.

I am sure that the move from bilingualism to child language and subsequently to the logical foundations of cognition will seem quite radical to some. From within, the change is hardly perceptible. It looks like a continuation of interest in a single central issue, at deeper and deeper levels. I am still interested in the fundamental character of human thought and how it relates to the fundamental categories of grammar. It is this continuing interest that has led me away from what most people recognize as sociolinguistics. Whorf, in certain moods, often struck me as a gardener who delights in the variety and exuberance of nature. It is my perception that the founders of sociolinguistics, notably Charles Ferguson and Joshua Fishman, shared Whorf's delight without his (to my mind) diminution of our common humanity. In ways, I am more like a molecular biologist. I am fascinated by properties of the human mind that are common to everyone: men and women, infants and adults, professors and ploughmen, Inuits and Irish. These are properties, like the interpretation of proper names, that show up no matter what language or dialect or register a person employs. We need both types of scholar, just as biology needs the organismic approach in addition to the molecular one.

The mention of Joshua Fishman's name gives me an opportunity to set at least one record straight. During my first visit to North America, spent at Stanford in the summer of 1965 at a six-week conference on Learning and the Educational Process organized by Lee Cronbach, I saw a great deal of Joshua Fishman and Wallace Lambert, and a certain amount of Charles Ferguson. It was there that we planned the special issue of *The Journal of Social Issues* on "Problems in Bilingualism" (Volume 23, Number 2). Fishman asked me to be editor of the issue mainly to give a beginner a leg up. The idea for the issue was his, as were most of the suggestions for contributors and what they might be asked to write about. The issue was one of the journal's most successful, and I received much credit that should properly have gone to Fishman. Wallace Lambert was also exceedingly kind to me and arranged for me to spend a year at McGill as a visiting scholar in 1966–1967. It was during that year that I completed my editorial work and the issue appeared.

My way, then, has led me away from sociolinguistics to the study of universal properties of the human mind. The avenue, however, is still the same: the properties of the human mind as seen from the perspective of language. The focus, too, remains the same: cognition or the conceptual abilities of the human mind as evidenced by the semantics of natural languages. Syntax and morphology are still important, because it is the system of interpreting expressions in grammatical categories within syntactic structures that is at the focus of attention. Moreover, the whole approach has this in common with linguistics. Linguists, qua linguists, are not concerned about what people say or why they say it; rather they are concerned with explanations of why they find this arrangement of morphemes, and not that, satisfactory (or grammatical). Likewise, my work is not centrally about what people think or why they think what they do; rather it is about the general rules of interpretation that makes this, and not that, a suitable means to express whatever one thinks. My work demands some sort of naturalization papers in the philosophy of mind, linguistics, and logic as well as in psychology. More and more I work with mathematical logicians, attempting to grasp their formal systems. Most useful among these are category-theoretic approaches to model theory and I am fortunate to work in Montreal with a team of category theorists that includes Gonzalo Reyes, Marie La Palme Reyes, Houman Zolfaghari, and Michael Makkai. It is a marvel that my early concerns should have led so far. Who would have thought that the Whorfian problem had so much blood in it?

This is also the reason for my fading from the sociolinguistic scene and for my inability to reflect on what is happening there now. I was delighted, if a little surprised, to receive an invitation to describe my part in its development. I owe an explanation to dear friends for my fleeting and, perhaps, marginal role in the play.

Contribution to the History of Sociolinguistics: Origins and Development of the Rouen School

J. B. Marcellesi

Jean-Baptiste Marcellesi studied at the *École Normale Superieure de St-Cloud*. He holds a State Degree in Linguistics *(Agregation de grammaire)* and taught at the *Université de Nanterre* from 1967 to 1970, and in Rouen from 1970 to 1992. He is a professor of sociolinguistics and was head of the Linguistics Department at the *Université de Rouen* from 1970 to 1990. He also directed the Research Group 1164 (associated with the SNRS), "Sociolinguistics: The Use and Future of Language" from its creation in 1984 until 1992. Since 1992, he has been Professor Emeritus—with honor—at the *Université de Rouen*.

It was 1968, under the direction of J. Sumpf (1968), when a French publication used the title *Sociolinguistics* for the first time (issue no. 11 of the journal *Langages*). This does not mean that before this date there had not been any concerns relevant to this discipline; some of the best works of traditional French lexicology and dialectology and even comparative historical linguistics, posed the question of the relationship between language and (other) social factors, even when structuralism was dominant. In the early fifties (1952), Marcel Cohen even stated that he favored a sociology of language *(Pour une Sociologie du Langage*—the title of his book). For once, the French government seems to have anticipated scientific recognition. At the time of "the Fouché reform" in the late sixties, certificate programs in sociolinguistics (and psycholinguistics) were established at some faculties including Nanterre, under the "specialized master's degree" in linguistics. The committee had followed the suggestions of Jean DeBois, one of its members, as he mentioned at the Rouen conference on Sociolinguistics in 1978 (DuBois 1978).

Issue no. 11 of *Langages* requires some comment. Promotion of the word "sociolinguistics" was accompanied by articles typical of the French backwardness in this field. The entire edition, apart from the article by J. Sumpf himself, dealt rather with semantic analysis of P. Henry and S. Moscovici, M. Mouillaud, Launay and Goulemot, or the methodology of dialectological survey (Lerond). As for J. Sumpf's contribution on "Linguistics and Sociology," it did point out previous French work in sociolinguistics, but as far as concrete works were concerned, quoted only American references.

The structure of this field of research was the subject of a work that appeared in February 1971, conducted like the previous one by the Nanterre Faculty of Arts, which I was fortunate to coordinate. Issue no. 9 of *Langue Française* (*Linguistique et Société*, J. B. Marcellesi 1971b) clearly contained works of a more directly sociolinguistic nature, all of which helped define French sociolinguistics for the seventies. The dominant theme at that time was "the sociolinguistic analysis of political discourse," a significant change in political lexicology open to the distributional method (Provost-Chauveau, L. Courdesses, D. Maldidier) to a sociolinguistic concept of communicative competence (D. Slakta) and to Labov's method (F. Gadet 1977 and 1978), while Robert Lafont introduced the study of diglossia. The general line of thought initiated by Sumpf and the three components mentioned above constituted the first line-up of French sociolinguistic forces. But in the bibliography, as far as the French works are concerned, the term itself only appeared in two of my references, both relating to my doctoral thesis on the Congress of Tours ("Linguistic and Sociolinguistic Analysis of the Congress of Tours" 1971a). It was after this particular issue of *Langue Française* that works inspired by sociolinguistics proliferated between 1971 and 1978.

I reviewed this proliferation in no. 209 of the publication *La Pensée*, under the title "Succès d'un mot et engouement pour un champ de recherches" (Acceptance of a word and passion for a field of research, J. B. Marcellesi 1980). Since this publication is no longer available—which is to be regretted—I will quote it in detail:

> Since issue no. 11 of *Langages* (Sumpf 1968), it is evident that the word has been accepted in France, and in print, as the term itself has emerged either in the titles of works (Fishman 1971, J.B. Marcellesi 1971a, Marcellesi and Gardin 1974, Calvet 1975), journal subtitles (*Lengas*), to specify the theme of special journal issues (Quemada and Ross 1976, Encrevé 1977), or in article titles (Helgorsky 1973, Baggioni 1975, Boutet, Fiala and Simonin-Grumbach 1976, Gadet 1977). In its own way, the "Sociology of Language" is upheld elsewhere: in

the new Maspéro edition of his book in 1971, M. Cohen, who was the first in 1952 to address the panorama of issues, within the limitations inherent to the era, slightly modified the title (*Eléments pour...*), *without changing "...sociologie du langage,"* others incorporate sociolinguistics into a wider theme or dissociate themselves from it (Boutet, Fiala and Simonin-Grumbach 1976). The list of books or journals concerned with wholly or partially sociolinguistic problems which do not actually use the term is quite extensive: books dealing with the problems raised by Marcellesi and Gardin (1974), for example, Calvet (1975 and 1977) and Houdebine (1977), public opinion on linguistics (N. Gueunier 1978) or linguistic conflicts (Calvet 1974), special issues of journals on linguistics and society (J. B. Marcellesi 1971b), regional languages (J. B. Marcellesi 1975), the sociocultural aspects of language acquisition (*La Pensée*, No. 190, cm 1977), problems of Marrism (J. B. Marcellesi 1977). Likewise, journals which do not specialize in linguistics, such as *Actes de la Recherche*, attach great significance to such problems to which others devote special issues (*La Pensée*, No. 190 or *Dialectiques*, No. 20). We should note the publication of various works dedicated to the whole spectrum of problems (*Cahiers de Linguistique Sociale, Langage et Société*) or to more limited questions such as multilingual Creole communities (*Bulletin du Centre d'Études des Plurilinguismes Créoles*). Credit courses in sociolinguistics in various universities and predoctoral programs under various titles such as Linguistics, Modern Languages, are also worthy of mention.

Additional evidence is to be found in the shift towards sociolinguistics in centers initially oriented in other directions: J. L. Fossat's dialectology team in Toulouse (cf. Fossat 1978), the originally grammar-oriented group in Tours with N. Gueunier (cf. Gueunier-Khomsi-Genouvrier 1978), the Strasbourg research team with psycholinguistic origins with A. Tabouret-Keller (Hostein 1977a, 1977b, La Tour 1977), F. Francois' "Language and School" team (cf. Francois 1976, l978), and even on occasion the "Lexicology and Political Texts" group directed by M. Tournier (l975). This movement was a reinforcement for Robert Lafont's team (programmed cooperative research of C.N.R.S. 482, which edits *Lengas*), our Sociolinguistics Covariance Group (G.R.E.C.O., University of Rouen), the group of linguists around J. C. Chevalier, P. Encrevé (1977a and 1977b), and P. Bourdieu and B. Laks (1980). It is also important to mention the colloquia: the one we organized in Rouen during November/December of 1978 (Gardin and Maracellesi, eds. 1980) testifies in its way to the same movement, as witnessed by the 150 participants, the content of the Proceedings, the significance of the final round table, where all the participants had a word to say, some soliciting caution against risk of distortion, others an espousal, at least of the word, for what had earlier been called "grammatical studies" or "dialectology, in the fine tradition of Gilleiron" according to J. DuBois, or even studies devoid of any social content. One could thus detect some kind of linguistic "swing" towards sociolinguistics, suspecting at times an optical illusion caused by lack of knowledge of works which always had a sociolinguistic orientation. In any case it should be explained that as soon as this word came into use it was accepted, and also that it was a success. This must be because sociolinguistics exists and is something, whatever this may be, that is capable of arousing passion. This must not at the same time preclude criticism of an unwarranted espousal, or encouragement of what truly is an advance of knowledge in the field of research.

From then on (in relation to our early education) French sociolinguistics seemed to us to be a discipline open to philosophical study, a rigorous manner of thinking, a critical response to a political and social question.

These aspects suited the late sixties in France perfectly and, more especially, the Nanterre Faculty of Arts, the cradle of French sociolinguistics and—without there being a direct connection between the two—the birthplace of the great protest movement of the spring of 1968. During this period the University, its function of social reproduction, its established structures and the State itself were being radically questioned. While only a few large French universities had Linguistics Institutes, prestigious but separate from the usual channels of educator training, the upheaval enabled Nanterre with Jean DuBois, Rouen with Louis Guilbert, and elsewhere, to create autonomous linguistic institutes within the Modern Languages faculties, thus freeing linguists from the yoke of literary and philological tradition, opening up the recruitment of educators in advanced linguistics and facilitating a relationship with the social sciences (the primary condition for the development of sociolinguistics). One cannot say that this discipline would not have developed without this movement, but it enabled us to anticipate the discipline and to give it autonomy.

The questions which motivated us in our work revolved around the correlation between linguistic facts and nonlinguistic social facts. Did membership in a group determine the linguistic behavior of the group members? And up to what point? We already believed that interactions between the two types of phenomena were complex and multiple, that unilinearity was the exception and that multiplicity of cause and effect was the rule. That led us to define covariance in the terms of dialectics: we mainly adopted the principle of "general correspondence" advanced by Jean Dubois (1962) in his thesis on changes in the political, economical, and social lexicon at the time of the

Paris Commune in 1871. More broadly, we felt that it was necessary to reopen the debate on language, superstructure and class phenomena, and we questioned the theories of N. Marr as well as the responses given in Moscow by the traditionalists in the name of Stalin at the beginning of the fifties (J. B. Marcellesi 1977). The disciplines which can be said to have contributed to the development of French sociolinguistics at the end of the sixties were dialectology, lexicology, and social history (insofar as it generates speech)—or rather, the inability of these disciplines in providing satisfactory answers to our questions. It should be noted that the study of collective bilingualism, one of the up-and-coming areas of French sociolinguistics, barely had any roots in France to the extent that it was considered a quasi-pathological case by an entire tradition.

Most of our working relationships were with historians (such as Régine Robin). It was mostly a question of reciprocal exchange of information, though we rejected the idea of an interdisciplinary field of study. We had, rather, cross-disciplinary concepts, since we in any case dealt with the social totality, and only the perspectives, framed by disciplinary limits inherited from the nineteenth century were different. Linguists focused on the facts of language and speech because it is their task to explain these facts, but all the other phenomena were already as they always had been. As for the interdisciplinary perspectives, I more or less presented them as such in issue no. 209 of *La Pensée* (J. B. Marcellesi 1980b).

> On a more general level, the disputes revolving around sociolinguistics relied either on the principles which were supposed to define the field of study of a science, or on the examination of concrete research, or on the reputation forged by and the rights refused by linguistics proper. After assuming with Saussure that language is primarily social, we know how linguistics was developed from analyses which reduced the system to its invariable portion. This concept culminated with Chomsky's theory of transformational generative grammar. One must not think that various types of structural linguistics and/or generative grammar are unaware of or silently ignore the existence of the social differentiations of language. They simply reject from linguistics the study of cause and effect of "extralinguistics" upon language, and its symbolic value and role in society. Research in this domain is sent elsewhere, often to an indeterminate place: to anyone who wishes to become involved, sociologists, historians, politicians; but certainly not to linguists. At the same time in France, however, Meillet was concerned with sociolinguistic issues.

The primary concern in establishing sociolinguistics was theoretical, as we have already explained. What also inspired us about sociolinguistics was what we called "social linguistics," which studied the linguistic behavior of collective speakers or rather, "collective intellectual-speakers," as we said in a vision of society inspired by the Italian Marxist philosopher Gramsci. But this is also an indication that we were interested in entering into problems and debates. Gardin and I presented our positions in Marcellesi and Gardin 1974. The theory was put to the test and modified by concrete questions and field experience. Moreover, this is how the field of political discourse has been progressively displaced by the study of mass bilingualism, the problems of which were clearly exposed for us by the IDERIC colloquium and the bulletin of the Center for Studies on Multilingualism (Nice 1969) by Robert Lafont (Montpellier) and Andrée Tabouret-Keller (Strasbourg). The anthropological and sociopolitical vision of the former and the rigorous approach of the latter are very much reflected in later developments in this area (see Lafont 1978 and 1979, Tabouret-Keller 1976 and 1982 on this subject).

Our original team included J. P. Colin, D. Maldidier, and myself, at the time assistant lecturers at the University of Nanterre. We were later joined by Louis Guespin, Bernard Gardin, Mathèe Giacomo, Christiane Marcellesi, Geneviève Chauveau-Provost, Jean-Pierre Kaminker, Madeleine Briot, Françoise Madray, and Daniel Baggioni. This group sought to provide theoretical and epistemological answers on "social linguistics." It functioned like a literary circle, meeting once a month and assigning itself collective tasks. It was named GRECO ("Sociolinguistic Covariance Research Group," covariance being understood to have a dialectic definition [cf. see above]). This was how, transferring gradually from the Paris region to Rouen, it came to publish issue no. 25 of *Langue Française* ("Teaching regional languages," J. B. Marcellesi 1975) and to found the *Cahiers du Linguistique Sociale* (which are still published in Rouen). Moreover, from 1971 to 1977 (the date of his death) Louis Guilbert (1965a and b), a professor at Nanterre, gathered together the same people and a few others into a group associated with CNRS (National Center for Scientific Research) for research on "Lexical neologisms" and published several significant documents on sociolinguistics as applied to vocabulary and terminology (see also C. Marcellesi 1973). From this work the Rouen school of socioterminology, defined later by Louis Guespin during the mid eighties, was born. These two teams (the Rouen group and that founded by Louis Guilbert) converged at a critical point and were the mainstay of Rouen sociolinguistics. GRECO, strengthened after 1977 with Régine Gelber (Delamotte-Legrand) and claiming its roots in the sociolinguistic movement started in Rouen in November 1978, was able to organize the first colloquium held in France, the proceedings of which appeared in 1980

(Gardin and Marcellesi 1980. *Sociolinguistique—Approaches Théories Pratiques [Sociolinguistics—Approaches in Practice and Theory]*). From this time on the centers of interest shifted to mass bilingualism, even though interest in this subject was already patent in issue no. 25 of *Langue Française* (see above). After 1980 the group was restructured into four main areas of interest, which were promised in issue no. 209 of *La Pensée* (J. B. Marcellesi ed. 1980b). It may be helpful to review their titles and content. At first, it was a question of individual articles written by one or more authors, all contributions then went through a slow process of maturation throughout 1979. Copies of the papers were circulated which everyone read and annotated, and then the entire issue was discussed by the team. It should be noted that Françoise Madray (Madray-Lesigne), although she herself did not put her name to any article, played a significant part in the thought and editing thereof. In my article already mentioned above, "From the linguistics of crisis to crisis of linguistics: sociolinguistics" (1980b:4–21) I developed the following theme: "there have always been sociolinguistic concerns, but the success of both term and discipline is due to the latter's connection with concrete language problems. This accounts for the similarity of the blueprint of the discipline to the blueprint of the crisis." Still on a general level, Jacques Legrand spoke of "Social classes and social relations in the determination of language" (1980b:22–34). He approached "the relationship between language and social class with a vision of social relations and the internalization of language and how it is used, along with its use as a network of hierarchical mediations, historically constituted by a specific mode of production." The general concept presented in the above two articles resulted more specifically in the 1990 *Colloquium on Linguistics and Materialism* (Rouen 1990; Richard-Zappella J. 1990) and, on a documentary level, in the sociolinguistics bibliography of the year edited under the direction of Thierry Bulot initially accessed through Minitel (3161 LING) and published later (Bulot 1985, 1986, 1987, and 1988).

Three contributions provide the framework for glotto-politics, with the problems of national language, norms, and linguistic "belittling." On language, linguistic and political problems Daniel Baggioni (1980) "questioned the identification of a nation with its language," thus criticizing Austro-Marxist glotto-politics which led to the Stalinist policy of "nationalities." For him, examination of the Italian, German, and French situations profiled the diversity of ways in which a national language is formed, a product/process of a political dimension. The same author, along with J. P. Kaminker, defined two areas requiring theoretical reflection, using the concept of linguistic norms: "the theory of the state (the norm is inseparable from the nation state) and semiotics (linguistic censure is inseparable from the establishment of meaning by the listener)." Thus for them, linguistics, if suitable for refuting ordinary normative discourse, is hardly capable of dealing with matters of norms, other than in a very marginal way (Jean-Pierre Kaminker and Daniel Baggioni 1980). The third and last article in this series is the work of Lambert-Félix Prudent. Dealing with the processes of linguistic devaluation: a look at the situation in the Antilles and at Creole studies, Prudent (1980) suggests that even the "monolingual" communities sense a certain antagonism. Thus, the situation in the Antilles, where there is a conflict between French and Creole, was marked by a search for solutions of a technical nature or by colonialist or paternalistic concepts. The article concluded by defending the integration of Creole language studies with Caribbean social problems. This trio of works resulted in a glottopolitical orientation, adopted by Louis Guespin and myself, the major points of which became the 1984 symposium on glotto-politics, an issue of *Langages* devoted to glotto-politics (Marcellesi 1986), recommendations for polynomial languages, and the 1990 colloquium in Corte (Chiorboli 1991). F. Laroussi's work in 1994 also deals with this aspect.

The third theme in issue no. 209 of *La Pensée* was devoted to "Language, social relations, school." After analyzing the conditioning of language and cognitive development authors Régine Legrand-Gelber (Delamotte) and Christiane Marcellesi (1980) considered linguistic differences observed among children and demonstrated the complexity of mediations, critiqued the "notion of environment," and finally suggested "some areas for research." This was the point of departure for the group on the sociolinguistics of language acquisition, giving rise to numerous issues of *Cahiers de Linguistique Sociale* and colloquia resulting in publication (Christiane Marcellesi 1986, Régine Delamotte-Legrand 1987 and 1991).

The final group of works in 1980 concerned the pragmatic dimension of sociolinguistics. Daniel Coppalle and Bernard Gardin (1980) debated the question of "Speaking in order to dominate." After observing that there is often an "interconnection between language, speech, and power in philosophy and in linguistics" the authors linked this to "the very nature of linguistic practices which can be grasped by the study of reality and consciousness." For them, "the significance of this theme seems to indicate current data on ideological conflict." Louis Guespin (1980), in his article on "Work, language, personality, etc.," after considering Robert Lafont's book (1978), indicated (1) the need for linguistics to take into account the causal factor, which is work; (2) the dangers of a mechanistic association of work and language; and (3) the interest of a personality theory for this topic. Hence, it becomes a question of human activity, where the social aspect necessarily coexists with the individual aspect. Thus, B. Gardin began a study of the linguistic effects of social conflict in the workplace, Françoise Gardes-Madray developed a praximics analysis (see Gardes-Madray and Gardin 1989) and L. Guespin, reviving the teachings of Louis Guilbert, created his socio-terminology (see F. Gaudin 1994 on this subject).

Issue no. 209 of *La Pensée* gave an excellent account of what has been going on in Rouen sociolinguistics over the ten-plus years since 1980. Since 1984, the Rouen school of sociolinguistics has occupied a significant place in the scientific world: it has been affiliated with CNRS as well as U.R.A. C.N.R.S. 1164 SUDLA (Sociolinguistics, Usage and Evolution of Language). With this orientation for its teams it has received recognition at the highest level. I was the leader of this team until I stopped teaching in 1992. Régine Delamotte-Legrand has been in charge since January 1, 1993.

Our main publication defining the subject was the book I published with B. Gardin: *Introduction à la Sociolinguistique: La Linguistique Sociale* (1974), regularly quoted by *Les Cahiers de Linguistique Social,* University of Rouen. The first few hundred pages, mainly my responsibility, were devoted to the definition of sociolinguistics from the perspective of Marxist philosophy. The second part, written by Gardin, was an examination of possible contributions and insurmountable differences in relation to sociolinguistics by Saussure and Halliday, Volochinov, Bernstein, and Labov. Thanks to our book, the latter three authors were to attract the attention of French publishers resulting in translation and publication a few years after our book in 1974. Part three, which I worked on, described the sociolinguistic perspectives of recent work in various areas of sociolinguistics. The book is still sought after, but I suspect it suffered from the somewhat obscure and in parts too philosophical style of writing which made comprehension rather heavy going. On the other hand, many of its discussions remain of interest for researchers in sociolinguistics. I would in any case include the article from the issue of *Langages* which was devoted to Marxism (J. B. Marcellesi 1977), the relationship between Marxism and linguistics (Elimam and Marcellesi 1987), the problems of defining and delimiting sociolinguistics (Gardin and Marcellesi 1987), and, in particular, conceptual contributions to glotto-politics (J. B. Marcellesi 1979, 1981, 1986, and 1987) an area barely mentioned in the *Introduction à la Sociolinguistique.*

Our first course in sociolinguistics was offered to undergraduate and master's degree students at Rouen. It was an elective credit course for students of Modern Languages: at that time linguistics or Language Sciences did not exist at Rouen: this was only obtained at the beginning of the eighties, initially for a doctorate, then for the predoctoral thesis program, then for a master's degree and finally for undergraduates. If the discipline was established from the top down, it is because our team was first recognized on the outside at a high level, as a result of our research, and because the ministers who did not want a program in Language Sciences at Rouen gradually had to make concessions, as Rouen sociolinguistics was making a name for itself. In these conditions (no students specializing in linguistics), sociolinguistics in Rouen before the eighties either was rejected by students majoring in literature, or else, because of its propositions and its critical nature, attracted those who had experience in the area or who were seeking an answer to a social need (mainly those who already had teaching positions).

If there is a big difference between our original sociolinguistics and that of today, it is in the area of theoretic ambitions. The very success of the discipline and also the urgency of social problems today result in an attempt to assist decision-makers in solving concrete problems (scholastic backwardness, illiteracy, minority language teaching, spelling reform). But one can be in demand and sometimes even get funding, yet still not be listened to. This is the situation.

Beyond the universities already mentioned, I must mention the role played by two different undertakings in which my colleagues and I participated. After 1975 a team composed of Gobard, Ladmiral, Encrevé, Gardin, and Arnaud established a group with the aim of promoting sociolinguistics at a time when its success in France was not assured. This was the "Institute of Research into Sociolinguistics," or IRSOL. Its activity was to take the form of meetings followed by discussions, networking between researchers, and publications. If the last purpose was not fruitful, and if the attempt to establish a data file did not work out because of lack of funds, the exchanges following lectures given by very diverse sociolinguists added to the confidence in the discipline. It is noteworthy that these tasks were later assumed by the Association of Language Sciences, in particular by its newsletter BUSCIL. Once in a while, the distinguished presence of sociolinguists, Bernard Gardin in particular, provided leadership for our discipline. It would be unfair not to mention another organization, the CERM (Center for Marxist Studies and Research), later the IRM. (Institute of Marxist Research), or at least the "linguistics" section of that naturally multidisciplinary institution. For a long time led by Marcel Cohen, the CERM, then the IRM linguistics circle took an obvious interest in sociolinguistics. Then, for some years in the late seventies, the IRM circle organized debates on a whole range of issues, to one of which our team replied in *La Pensée* no. 209. Other endeavors, initiated in particular by Michel Pêcheux, also went on during these discussions.

What I feel was the most significant text in defining sociolinguistics during the seventies in France was our *Introduction à la Sociolinguistique* (Marcellesi and Gardin 1974), or at least those pages devoted to this question. We in fact considered these problems both from a theoretical and a practical point of view. Another high point was the round table discussion at the 1978 Rouen colloquium (Gardin and Marcellesi 1980a) which we summarized in our article in *La Pensée* (Marcellesi 1980). The later work which Gardin and I published in the *Handbook of Sociolinguistics* (Gardin and Marcellesi 1987) should also be mentioned. Others have defined sociolinguistics by exclusion, without mentioning any of the works that upset their theories. We believe that the tactic of "blank pages" should be condemned when it is a question of defining an area of knowledge.

With regard to any current support for sociolinguistics, it seems useful here to mention Bernard Gardin (unpublished text). Sociolinguistics seems to be here to stay and is spreading: it is now a recognized area of inquiry; one can no longer really speak of it as a discipline, but as a series of methodologies available for case studies. These days there is more interest in microsociolinguistic realities, in the details of the processes by which the social factor determines the linguistic factor and *vice versa*. One can also say that conversation analysis (North American work combined with contributions from Volochinov) has reinforced the postulate of the fundamentally social nature of language and the glottogenesis of the social phenomena. Finally, the advent of ethnomethodology has highlighted the phenomena of cooperation and "teamwork," somewhat at the expense of conflict phenomena.

There was a European, specifically French, tradition of sociolinguistics (in the domain of lexicology, dialectology...then the analysis of political discourse). The area was methodologically revived by American anthropology (Dell Hymes), by U.S. sociolinguistics, the work of Labov in particular, who extended the area of study showing it was possible to furnish empirical proof, then by the ethnography of communication.

It must be added that provocative works such as those of Dell Hymes, Gumperz (1973), and of the S.L.1 Congress at Bressanone (Brixen; see Mioni and Renzi) have enabled us to broaden the vision of Labov, to which we owe much (see bibliography under specific names).

In France, government action may take the form of grants for meetings: for example, the congress of the International Federation of French Teachers in Rio in 1981, which I carried out with very limited resources, was able to put on its program an inquiry into "the teaching of regional languages." The CNRS accepted "programmed thematic action" such as that proposed by myself and my colleagues in Corsica on "sociolinguistic individuation in Corsica." Other local activity received assistance, in particular the "Language and Work" network for which B. Gardin is responsible. It is generally these actions of "applied sociolinguistics" which are approved, particularly when it is perceived that they will solve social problems (scholastic failures, urban ghettos, etc.). But the main linguistic financing until recently was reserved for the *Atlas Linguistiques et Ethnographiques Régionaux (Regional Linguistic and Ethnographic Atlases)* and in particular the *Trésor de la Langue Française (Treasury of the French Language),* in Nancy, for many years a huge drain on funds and personnel, in incredible proportions.

I am not aware of any government or doctoral thesis before mine (defended in March 1970), which could be said to deal with "sociolinguistics." The title was *Analyse Sociolinguistique du Congrès Socialiste de Tours (Déc. 1920) (A Sociolinguistic Analysis of the Socialist Congress of Tours, December 1920).* By various essentially distributional methods I profiled (despite my initial assumptions) the non-isomorphism of vocabulary among nonlinguistic political and social groups and linguistic groups (J. B. Marcellesi 1971a). It is possible, however, that the word "sociolinguistics" has been used in the defense of a thesis, but I know nothing of this and neither does B. Gardin.

Answers to most questions yet to be asked can be found in my previous peregrinations. Explicitly or implicitly the field of sociolinguistics is doubtless less dynamic today and definitely less polemic, if at all. The main focus will no doubt be theoretical and will concern the articulation between cognitive and social issues. However, I believe more than ever that education in sociolinguistics is required. The understanding which it imparts to social relations and ethnic frontiers is an antidote to nationalism and "purification." But let me say that the truths which it contains, so contrary to the patterns of the past, are increasingly difficult to uphold against prevailing ideas, like any science; more than any science. In response to a present-day social need, (without hopes of being heard) I should like to assign it the task of destroying a pernicious ideology. This is a good indication of how sociolinguistics is and will always be, "secular linguistics," to borrow an expression from Labov.

On Safari with Sociolinguistics

Carol Myers-Scotton

> Carol Myers-Scotton is a professor in the Linguistics Program and the Department of English at the University of South Carolina. She teaches graduate and undergraduate classes in sociolinguistics as well as graduate classes in language contact phenomena and discourse analysis. Her major research interest currently deals with structural constraints on codeswitching and she is doing field work in Africa and Europe on codeswitching under an NSF grant.

My career in sociolinguistics began through an immersion in the data of multilingual African communities.[1] My major interest, however, soon became not detailing linguistic variation and its social correlates, but rather seeking out the more abstract motivations behind variation. Specifically, I have been interested in rational-action models which see societal constraints as determining an "opportunity set" of possible social behaviors (here, opportunity set = linguistic repertoire), but then which see actual linguistic choices as the product of rationally based assessments of the optimal outcomes (cf. Elster 1989). Thus, for me, sociolinguistics has always meant something quite different from what it means to variationists of the Labovian school. True, I began by emphasizing basic description of self-reported language use patterns. These studies were based on large data sets in African cities for which subjects were chosen by standard sampling procedures based on their social identities (e.g., Scotton 1972, 1976a, 1976b). Before long, however, I moved away from self-reports to naturally occurring conversations gathered from relatively few subjects, still in the African context. Yet, while data collection

---

[1] From my first publication (1965) until 1990, I published under the name 'Carol Myers Scotton' and am indexed under 'Scotton' in bibliographies. Now, I prefer 'Carol Myers-Scotton' and am therefore preferably indexed under 'Myers-Scotton'.

moved from the macro to the micro level, the goals of my analysis remained the same, as I hope will become clear.

In mid 1968 I entered the multilingual community of Kampala, Uganda, and this engulfment led to my becoming a sociolinguist. I had gone to Africa to take up a two-year appointment as the first faculty member in the newly formed department of Linguistics and African Languages at Makerere University in Kampala. The stimulus for initiating this new department was the Ford Foundation-sponsored Survey of Language Use and Language Teaching in Eastern Africa (1968–1972). The late W. H. Whiteley, who was prominent among the then handful of Africanist linguists and who would be the Survey director for Kenya, had recommended me for the Makerere position. In those days, most Africanist linguists were European, and Whiteley, who was British, was a well-known researcher on the structures of East African languages, especially Swahili. Just as it did for me, the Eastern African Language Use Survey stimulated Whiteley to turn more attention to patterns of language use than to linguistic structures. During this period, Whiteley produced a valuable sociolinguistic history of Swahili (1969). He went on to become professor of Bantu languages at the London School of Oriental and African Studies before his death in 1974. When in the early 1960s the United States discovered Africa as a research area, Whiteley was among those Africanists recruited to American universities as visitors. Whiteley spent 1963–1964 at the University of Wisconsin where he inaugurated Swahili studies.

As part of my studies for a Ph.D. in Linguistics at the University of Wisconsin, I had studied Swahili in 1963–1964 under Whiteley, and then had done field work on my dissertation in 1964–1965 in Tanzania, where Whiteley was then at the University of Dar es Salaam.

Why Swahili for me? It was a matter of chance. My getting into Linguistics in the first place was also rather accidental, but that is another story. Once committed to Linguistics, I needed financial aid. I had a friend who was studying Arabic on a fellowship and I asked him where the fellowship came from. The government had begun offering fellowships to study various "critical" languages, he told me. So, I went down the list and stopped at Swahili, reasoning that linguists were expected to know something about non-Indo-European languages, so why not Swahili? Thus, from a background including an M.A. in American and British literature, I was selected for the first batch of graduate students nation-wide who were funded under the National Defense Education Act (NDEA) to study Swahili. I received my Ph.D. in Linguistics from the University of Wisconsin in 1967, and now I may be well known as a sociolinguist among the world's Swahilists, an accomplishment which dims when one considers how few Swahilists there are in the world.

I arrived in Uganda, expecting to do research on African languages, but on the structural side of linguistics. My dissertation dealt with semantic and syntactic aspects of Swahili verb forms, and my formal training was entirely in structural areas. Since sociolinguistics was just being recognized as a subject when I was a student, I never had a course in sociolinguistics. Neither did I even take the language and culture course, offered in the Anthropology department. One of the most picturesque meanings I know in Swahili is that of the applied form of the verb -*cha* 'to dawn' as in *jua limenichea* 'sunrise overtook me'. The passive applied form is -*chewa* and means 'to be overtaken by sunrise'. What happened to me in Uganda was that I was "overtaken by multilingualism." Without knowing how it happened, straightaway I abandoned syntactic studies and became absorbed in considering how many different languages were spoken in the city, who spoke them, and what their social functions were. Of course, I was simply caught up in answering the set of questions which Joshua Fishman was making famous elsewhere at this same time and the questions which are inherent in Charles Ferguson's analysis of a diglossic society. But initially I had no inkling of their work and thus I say that my involvement in sociolinguistics was driven by the data themselves. True, in this period (1968–1970) there were few books or articles yet written which would have helped me, anyway; but even these were not available in an eastern African university library where Linguistics was just being introduced as a subject. I read what I could to fuel my new addiction: works on theory and methodology in anthropology, sociology, and social psychology. I consulted with sociologists and statisticians at Makerere on how to do large-scale surveys. Also, when I could see them, I talked to the personnel of the Ford Foundation survey mentioned above. There were conversations with the various team members, including the first three country Survey directors: Whiteley (Kenya), Ferguson (Ethiopia), and especially Ladefoged (Uganda). In this regard, I attended the December 1968 conference on language use in Dar es Salaam which the survey sponsored, with many of the leading researchers in the field as invited participants.

Thus, from the papers I heard in Dar es Salaam I now had some conception that the studies I had already begun in Kampala fit under the new rubric of sociolinguistics. Financed through one of the small grants which the Survey awarded to individual researchers, my Kampala study was my main research project during my two years in Uganda and it is the basis for the monograph published as Scotton 1972.

For this study, I opted for the methodologies of sociology and the theories of social psychology. In retrospect, I realize that my study is distinctive in aiming for this combination. Of course my methodology turned out to be similar to that of Fishman and his associates, although I had not yet read any of his works (e.g., Fishman, Cooper, and Newman 1968 on New York/New Jersey Spanish/English bilingualism). Perhaps because Fishman saw my likemindedness, he has always been supportive of my work, even though I never was his student.

Because I had few teaching duties at Makerere, because by chance my two research assistants were exceptionally reliable and very good at their work (the main one went on to work for me for twenty years), and because I had two years in which to complete the study, I was able to accomplish what in retrospect seems to be an exceptionally respectable quantitative study. For example, once subjects were selected according to predetermined sampling procedures, in only three cases out of the core sample of 223 did we make substitutions. Also, with only two research assistants involved, both of whom were local residents, we were able to maintain a high level of consistency across interviews. While I supervised data collection from afar and was involved in pretesting the interview schedule, I realized I could not interview myself because my presence would skew the responses. The interview took between 45 and 90 minutes and was conducted in the local lingua franca of the interviewee's choice. A number of structured observations in places of work and leisure confirmed our judgments that the interviewees were, in fact, reporting their patterns of language use accurately.

I learned about random samples and constructed stratified random samples in two different areas of Kampala, both of which were chosen based on my own earlier ethnographic-style observations, my preliminary systematic surveys, and the opinions of other researchers of Kampala life. The samples were stratified in proportion to the speakers of various first languages in the research sites; in order to do this, I realized that I would need a door-to-door survey of all houses to discover the first languages of heads of households (the main subjects). One site was the Naguru municipal housing estate, (N = 168); the other site was an area of private housing near Makerere University (N = 55).

Obtaining the basis for a random sample was easy enough in the Naguru housing estate, since houses were in orderly rows and each house had a number. The private housing area, however, was another matter: houses were scattered here and there, lanes had no names, and even the concept of house numbers did not exist. I hit upon the idea of having my research assistant draw a map locating all the houses in the area. Then we took on the role of "city managers," assigning numbers to each house in order to draw out a random sample.

I also supplemented these primary samples with three other smaller samples which reflected specific types of populations (e.g., a class of twenty-eight relatively high-level civil servants was interviewed; twenty subjects from the area of Kampala known to be inhabited largely by the main ethnic group in Kampala [the BaGanda] were also studied).

Thus, results were based on a core of 223 subjects who were carefully selected according to standard random sampling procedures; then this sample was augmented to 303 with three additional quota samples. Heads of households were the chosen subjects (invariably males) and in every tenth house an adult woman (generally the wife) was interviewed as well.

Given my lack of training in sociolinguistic methodology and lack of experience, I can only say that I was lucky to have made so many "right" moves regarding methodology. And more than twenty years later, the study stands up well in this respect. (Unfortunately, when it came to publishing my Kampala monograph, *Choosing a Lingua Franca in an African Capital* 1972, I did not choose well. I was inexperienced in publishing circles and I had no mentor or social network to guide me; my publisher did not publicize the book widely and let it go out of print within a few years. Many students of multilingualism, especially outside of Africa, do not even know the monograph existed.)

For other reasons, the Kampala study was to be only one of two large-scale self-report surveys which I conducted (the second was a study of a multiethnic neighborhood in Lagos, Nigeria [cf. Scotton 1976a; 1976b]; data were gathered when I lived in Lagos in 1972 because of my husband's job). Why no more surveys? As noted above, I rapidly became more interested in other aspects of the language and society interface than in detailing use patterns; I gravitated almost immediately toward the sociopsychological motivations for language choices.

This interest was already apparent in the Kampala monograph, the aspect which makes that study distinctive. The prevailing paradigm followed in other large-scale studies was what I have called the "allocation paradigm" (Myers-Scotton 1993a:48–49). I see two models under this rubric: (1) the domain model, which views linguistic choices as predictable on the basis of the domain in which they occur (e.g., Fishman 1968, 1972; Ferguson 1959 as a precursor); and (2) the binary-choice model based on situational factors and assessments of social distance between participants. This model is exemplified by tree diagrams with clear binary branching at nodes, pointing to a single language/stylistic choice as the outcome for a specific interaction (e.g., Rubin 1968; G. Sankoff 1971; Ervin-Tripp 1972; with Brown and Gilman 1960 as a precursor).

The type of data I gathered in Kampala and Lagos implied these models (i.e., my main independent variables were domains such as workplace and neighborhood and social identity features such as ethnic group, occupation, and degree of acquaintanceship). My results largely confirmed the reliability of these variables in predicting outcomes. Yet, somehow I did not see these variables as the primitive explanatory factors. The main reason for this was that these variables could not explain *all* the variation in the data; that is, either the domain model or the binary-choice model only worked so far. Thus, I looked for an explanation which could combine the role of the normative factors that were the basis for these models and "something else." My research question became slightly, but crucially, modified: it was no longer "what factors account for the data distribution?" but rather "what motivates speakers in their choices?"

My theoretical inspiration came from exchange theory in social psychology (e.g., Thibaut and Kelley 1959; Homans 1966). Pouring over the quantitative results I obtained in the Kampala survey, in an admittedly post hoc fashion, I developed an explanation for language use patterns in a model based on the assessment of costs and rewards. In this model, the individual speaker views the specific social situation through a lens shaped by his/her social profile and the general societal norms. With this as input, the speaker makes a specific language choice, looking now at the social situation through a lens consisting of his/her perception of social reality and an assessment of the relative costs and rewards of making alternative language choices. This model, and predictions specifically for the Kampala community which follow from it, appear in chapter 5 of the monograph. They include the prediction that speakers will often choose a neutral lingua franca because although the rewards may not be high, neither will the costs. (This prediction is motivated by the finding that in multiethnic contacts, Kampala speakers often used Swahili, an ethnically neutral lingua franca in Kampala. Similarly, in Lagos, speakers often used both Pidgin English and Standard English in interethnic interactions; Scotton 1976b.) In addition, a final prediction previews my future interest in codeswitching as the unmarked choice in certain types of communities (Myers-Scotton 1993a). This prediction (1972:125) is: "That for the speaker, higher rewards without high costs are possible if he *[sic!]* uses a prestige language/neutral language combination rather than either language alone among supposed peers who have some but perhaps an unequal command of the prestige language."

True, some of my publications and further research during the 1970s and into the 1980s were within at least the spirit of the "allocation paradigm"; that is, they largely detailed language use patterns, often combining such descriptions with an analysis of language policies in African nations. Scotton (1978) in Fishman's second collection of studies on language variation is such an example. It is titled *Language in East Africa: Linguistic Patterns and Political Ideologies*. And Scotton 1982b reports on research conducted in 1977 on language-use patterns of members of the Luyia ethnic group in rural and urban settings. Even very recently, some of my writings have only the express goal of describing large-scale use patterns in Africa (e.g., Scotton 1988b). Yet, in other writings, even when dealing with macro-level data, I continued to gravitate toward looking for the motivations behind language use patterns. This is clear in Scotton 1982a in the volume on language spread edited by Cooper. Here, my focus is to advance hypotheses as to why so few Africans have learned their official languages. Very recently (1990; 1993c) I have attempted to explain language policies in general, using African policies and data as primary evidence, by invoking what I have termed "elite closure" as a major motivating force.

My other major publications during the 1970s and 1980s even more clearly showed my theoretical interest in motivations behind use patterns. Scotton 1976a, titled, "Strategies of Neutrality: Language Choice in Uncertain Situations" and published in *Language,* used the quantitative data from the Kampala and Lagos studies to argue why Africans often alternate between two ethnically neutral languages in their workplace interactions (rather than relying on just one). Further, this publication goes on to propose negotiating neutrality as a universal motivation for linguistic choices in some instances. Scotton and Ury 1977, my first publication entirely on codeswitching, also makes generally applicable claims about the motivations for using two languages in the same conversation. Finally, "The Negotiation of Identities in Conversation: A Theory of Markedness and Code Choice" (Scotton 1983a) introduces the first version of my markedness model.

In formulating the markedness model, I go beyond attempting to explain codeswitching by taking on linguistic choices in general. And Scotton and Zhu 1983b shows how the markedness model can be applied to explaining the use of terms of address in the People's Republic of China. Scotton 1985 and 1988d apply the model to stylistic switches in the speech of American television talk show hosts.

By the late 1980s codeswitching had become a topic of wide interest among students of language variation of differing theoretical and methodological persuasions. I continued to develop my formulation of the markedness model to explain the social motivations for codeswitching (e.g., Scotton 1988a; Myers-Scotton 1992). This emphasis in my writing culminates in a book-length treatment (1993a).

At the same time, my interest in structural aspects of language—largely slumbering since my dissertation—was awakened by the claims of others about structural constraints on codeswitching. My African data clearly provided counterexamples to popular claims; thus, my entry to the fray on this front of codeswitching was effected. My paper at the 1987 Georgetown Round Table (Scotton 1988c) was my first major statement on structural constraints; and in the early 1990s I formulated the Matrix Language Frame model, my "full-dress" contribution to the ongoing debate (most fully explicated in Myers-Scotton 1993b).

Throughout my career, I have also done a number of studies that fall under the rubric of "language contact phenomena," beginning with Scotton and Okeju 1973, a study of lexical core borrowing into the Ateso language (spoken in Uganda and western Kenya). In many ways, I consider my work on structural constraints on codeswitching to fall under this rubric, too.

My teaching career in sociolinguistics began in 1974. I taught my first full-blown sociolinguistics courses at Yale University from 1974 to 1976. These were both graduate and undergraduate courses, listed under Anthropology where my faculty appointment was. At that time (and perhaps still), Yale was admirably free of bureaucracy when it came to offering new courses. Perhaps, too, the Anthropology Department was especially supportive of initiating new areas of study. Thus, I simply had to come up with course descriptions and I received numbers under which to offer the courses with little further ado. My courses were labeled "sociolinguistics" or variations on that name. There was a good deal of interdepartmental interest, partly because I was a member of an active, but informally organized, African Studies faculty. Open to new ideas and supportive of Africanist research, these faculty members strongly endorsed my research interests and course offerings. Undergraduate students came from many disciplines; graduate students came primarily from Anthropology, but also from Linguistics and Social Psychology. In 1976 I joined the faculty at Michigan State University and immediately instituted a joint graduate/undergraduate course titled "Introduction to Sociolinguistics" there. I do not recall that anyone ever questioned the subject matter, and the course became popular with students. I also taught a number of seminars at MSU on special topics, including "language policy" and "language contact phenomena" as well as "language and communication in Africa." Later at MSU, a sophomore-level sociolinguistics course that I initiated received the coveted designation of satisfying a humanities distribution requirement; this meant that 85 or more students were regularly enrolled. Currently at the University of South Carolina I teach both an undergraduate and a graduate introductory course in sociolinguistics. The undergraduate course is under an English department number and is titled "Language and Society" while the graduate course is under a Linguistics Program number. I also regularly teach Linguistics graduate courses in "Language Contact Phenomena" and "Discourse Analysis." The discourse offering has a socio-pragmatics component. In addition, I offer occasional seminars on such topics as "Communicating Power and Politeness through Language" and "Language and Gender."

Having reviewed the type of research and publication which has engaged me, I now raise these questions: Is this sociolinguistics? What constitutes sociolinguistics? Certainly, my work is very different from that of Labov and his followers; and I think it is fair to say that most linguists think of Labovian work as sociolinguistics. Those working within that paradigm, of course, have almost exclusively described how the incidence of variants of a socially-significant structural variable (most often a phonological variable) may be correlated with social identity factors or situational factors (e.g., socioeconomic status or careful vs. casual style). None of my work, even at its most descriptive, fits under this paradigm. The large scale descriptions of language-use patterns *do* fit under Fishman's suggested term for some of the socially based research, "the sociology of language." But, as we all know, it is sociolinguistics not the sociology of language which is a title for textbooks or conference sessions. Yet, I am referred to as a sociolinguist and my papers —whether they are on the social or structural side of codeswitching—are scheduled at conferences under sociolinguistics.

Where do I think I "belong?" I would place myself under two different rubrics. First, my work on the social motivations for linguistic choices, including my "markedness model," belongs under a recently coined term, "socio-pragmatics." As I see it, pragmatics in general deals with the *intentionality* contained in messages which is in addition to the code-based referential meanings. Some types of intentionality expand upon referential messages; I have in mind the implicatures of Grice (1975) and Sperber and Wilson (1986). Yet even though Grice and Sperber and Wilson do not seem to recognize it, other types of intentionality carry messages about the presentation of self by speakers and their negotiations in interpersonal relations. To my thinking, this is the domain of sociopragmatics. For example, Brown and Levinson 1987 on universals of politeness falls under sociopragmatics, I would argue. I am quite satisfied to include sociopragmatics under sociolinguistics as long as the term "sociolinguistics" is seen as an umbrella for various subfields, including Labovian variation studies as only one of the subfields. It is interesting that this is just what Fasold does in his recent textbook, titled *The Sociolinguistics of Language* (1992). Significantly, much of the first part of this textbook deals with what I label sociopragmatics; and variation studies take (for the first time) something of a back seat.

Why should variation studies, as they are now done, take a back seat to sociopragmatic research? I would argue that while variationists often provide very sophisticated quantitative analyses of data, the real value of variation studies largely stops at the descriptive level. That is, variationists either are not concerned with or they do not think it is possible to delve into the "black box" of cognitive motivations for choices. Conversely, sociopragmatic studies typically go on from description to propose explanations for data distribution. I would like to think that my markedness model does this for code choice in general. To this end, I argue in Myers-Scotton 1993a for an explanatory model of codeswitching, based on the possibility for speakers, as rational actors, to access costs and rewards of alternative linguistic choices. Myers-Scotton (1995) makes an even more explicit argument for rational-action models to explain linguistic choices.

While I see my sociopragmatic research under sociolinguistics, I rather wonder where studies on language contact phenomena belong; these include those on structural constraints on codeswitching, both lexical and structural borrowing, morphosyntactic convergence, and the development of pidgins/creoles. Certainly, my Matrix Language Frame model, which purports to explain the basis for structural constraints on codeswitching, is more akin to psycholinguistic concerns about the nature of language production than it is to variation studies of phonological features correlated with socioeconomic status or even social network.

One can argue that because the phenomena included under language contact come about because social groups are in contact, these phenomena have a social side. True, but I think that we sociolinguists must be careful in how grand the claims are that we make for social factors in influencing language contact phenomena. This is my subject in my recent article in *Language in Society,* titled "Common and uncommon ground: social and structural factors in codeswitching" (Myers-Scotton 1993d). Here I suggest that it is true that the social relations between groups or group-internal socially based dynamics may be important in determining which structural option is selected in a given case. But note my word option. I go on to argue that the structural set from which options are selected is cognitively-based and not open to social influences. How this is so is not yet fully understood, but I make some suggestions that some structural principles evident in codeswitching are apparently universally active (in all data sets examined to date). (Specifically, I refer to the designation of one language as dominant in setting the morphosyntactic frame of mixed constituents and the clear division in patterns of occurrence of content versus system morphemes.) Even more recently (1995) I claim that these same principles apply in the formation of pidgins and creoles and suggest they may well apply in all bilingual linguistic phenomena (including second language learning). Again, how the principles are played out (i.e., which options are taken up) does seem to depend on the social and psychological milieu present.

Thus, I close in suggesting two advances for sociolinguistics, one that enlarges the field and the other that may narrow it. First, I suggest we recognize sociopragmatics as a major category under sociolinguistics. This also means persuading pragmatists that socially relevant messages are a significant part of what is conveyed through intentionality based communication. Second, I suggest that we exercise more care and precision in the claims we make about the influence on linguistic structure of social factors.

Sociolinguistics: Some Other Traditions

Jiří V. Neustupný

Jiří Neustupný was Research Associate at the Oriental Institute in Prague (1957–1966) and Professor of Japanese Studies at Monash University, Melbourne (1966–1993) before moving to Japan where he is currently Professor of Applied Japanese Linguistics in the Faculty of Letters at Osaka University. (Address: Faculty of Letters, Osaka University, 1-5 Machikaneyama, Toyonaka, Osaka 560)

Prague School Sociolinguistics. Although the word sociolinguistics was not used, many forms of sociolinguistic studies existed before mainstream sociolinguistics came into being in the 1960s. Various comments on "language and society" figured already in nineteenth and early twentieth century introductions to linguistics; there were the theories of J. R. Firth; the Japanese doctrines of variation (isoo), spoken and written language, and linguistic life; the "study of language and society" which developed in Soviet linguistics following Stalin's intervention in 1950; the American predecessors of contemporary sociolinguistics (Boas, Sapir, Whorf, the ethnographers and others, Hymes 1964); and Prague School sociolinguistics, of which I shall say more later.

It is true that these varieties of sociolinguistics did not claim an identity separate from the rest of linguistics or (on the whole) create separate networks. Yet, the social system of science is only one of the components of a discipline: it is important and its absence weakens the case for the acceptance of the field of inquiry. However, I believe that if the word *sociolinguistics* is kept free to refer to a specific content (design) of academic pursuit as well as to its social system, many more sociolinguistic traditions will come to light and, perhaps, enrich our knowledge.

For those of us who went through the university in Prague in the 1950s the most important sociolinguistic tradition was that of the Prague School. Within the prewar and early postwar Prague School, we can identify a wealth of concepts, theories, and study areas which are undoubtedly sociolinguistic in their nature. This includes the theory of speech functions (Bühler, Muka ovský's poetic function), theories of variation (functional differentiation of the Standard Language, Vachek's theory of the written language, the Sprachbund theory, Skalička's typology), Mathesius' and Havránek's theory of language cultivation, an interest in the structure of (written) discourse, and others (Vachek 1966). Notice that most of these theories bear names other than those of Trubetzkoy and Jakobson, although Jakobson did take part in many of the projects. These theories were theoretically rigorous and connected with the overall framework of structuralism.

What most authors in this book will write about is the poststructural type of sociolinguistics (content design and social system) that developed mostly in the U.S.A. in the 1960s. It became the most vigorous poststructural variety of sociolinguistics and fully deserves the name of mainstream sociolinguistics. I believe that I am myself a peripheral member of this variety. However, I do not believe that this is sociolinguistics as such.

A portrait of the linguist as a young man. A few facts from the Prague police archives first—facts that I agree with. I was born in Prague in 1933 in a Czech family. My first degree, a sort of M.A. in Japanese Studies, was completed in 1957, after which I proceeded to postgraduate study to finalize my Ph.D. at the Oriental Institute in Prague in 1963. Two of my postgraduate years were spent in Japan. In 1966 I moved to Melbourne where I was teaching at Monash University until 1993, when I left Australia to take up my present position at the University of Osaka.

I was strongly interested in linguistics (not only in languages) since my high school years which brought me in touch with a considerable number of languages. However, it was not until just before I was to sit for the university entrance examination that my teacher of Hindi, Vincenc Po ízka, gave me a reference to the only Introduction to Linguistics produced by a member of the pre-war Prague school, Miloslav Ko ínek (Ko ínek 1948). Ko ínek, who died at the age of 46, could not finish the text and the only well-developed part of it was phonology. I thought that this was a book of great beauty which provided answers to many problems on which my secondary school teachers had nothing to say.

When I came to the Philosophical Faculty of Charles University in Prague I entered the Department of the Languages and Cultures of the Far East to study Japanese. At the same time I enrolled, outside the prescribed course, in

General Linguistics, taught at the time single-handedly by Vladimír Skalička. In his seminar the word phonology hardly ever appeared. Instead, I remember his lectures on typology, style, grammatical case, vagueness in language, the structure of lexicon, the Sprachbund, social dialects and many other topics, as they came up in the contemporary linguistic discussions. A majority of these were sociolinguistic in their nature. Although a member of the prewar Prague Linguistic Circle, he laughed at the orthodox teaching about phonological oppositions and anything that smacked of definitions and hard-and-fast-line linguistics. Skalička was to become the most important influence on my linguistic life. I also attended lectures by Josef Vachek, who commuted to Prague from Brno as a visiting lecturer to teach about the theory of the written language. Since this was in the English department, he lectured in English, an extraordinary situation for Prague in the 1950s. The English department was three floors down from Skalička's office. Another floor down within the same building, Havránek held his weekly seminars many of which were sociolinguistically oriented. I did not attend these, although I did of course read all of what he wrote. It was under the influence of Skalička and (to a lesser extent) Vachek, that I changed from an incipient structuralist to a poststructural linguist. My graduation thesis and later my Ph.D. still dealt with phonology, but at least I selected the Japanese accent, rather than segmental phonology, and analyzed vagueness in the system.

However, already as a student I commenced my own work on clearly sociolinguistic topics, such as variation. Around 1955 I was stimulated by the Russian Japanologist N. I. Konrad's article on the national language in China and Japan (Konrad 1952), and wrote a set of theses on variation in language. Since there was no other way to publish them, I nailed the text to our departmental noticeboard and received comments from other students. Later, in 1956, these ideas were presented as a paper at the Students' Academic Conference. I remember that the concept of "language block" (we would now say a "variety system") was too much even for Skalička, who questioned my inclusion of Latin in the Czech system. The theoretical framework of this paper led directly to my first sociolinguistic publication on the concept of "Oriental Languages" (Neustupný 1965). This work was theoretical in its nature and I have remained strongly committed to theory ever since.

In the 1950s, Soviet sociolinguistics of the period was readily available in Prague and everyone in the field was reading it. However, most of the material was clearly two paradigmatic stages behind and we felt its prestructural character quite strongly. American work was not totally inaccessible, but it was difficult to find except for a couple of journals. I suspected from references elsewhere that people called Ferguson and Gumperz were developing a theory of variation close to mine, but did not get access to this work until after 1965.

After graduating from Charles University, I commenced my postgraduate work at the Oriental Institute of the Czechoslovak Academy of Sciences and went to study in Japan for two years, from the Summer of 1960 to April 1962. My environment in Japan was grammatical and I was not subject to any influences from Japanese sociolinguistics, at that time already vigorous. However, the experience of a new culture resulted in my first attempts at what could be classified as an "ethnography of speaking." Some of the framework was included in an article on the theory of literary studies (Neustupný 1962) and in a draft which has never been published. This attempt grew out of Bühler's theory of functions, my university training (Skalička spoke about similar things in his seminars), and my continuing exposure to the Japanese communication system. Let me add that Shiro Hattori too had published a paper (in English!) in which he dealt with the different ways to get drunk (Hattori 1960). After I came back from Japan, probably in 1964 or 1965, Dell Hymes stopped over in Prague and later sent me much of his work on the "ethnography of speaking" published by then. This was fantastic and so much more systematic than my own fieldwork. I adopted Hymes' model and have used it ever since (e.g., Neustupný 1987). My encounter with Dell Hymes and our later contact was among the most positive influences of my sociolinguistic career.

In the 1960s the linguistic life in Prague was quite intensive and of considerable interest. Generative grammar started early and, thanks to local tradition, was not just a shadow of Chomsky. One of the most exciting developments was the theory of indeterminacy of language ("centre and periphery," Travaux 1966) in which I also actively participated. With regard to sociolinguistics, Skalička and Havránek retained their interests, and Daneš was also strongly interested. Others contributed a paper now and then, but on the whole, it would be incorrect to imagine that a specialized network of people who worked more or less in sociolinguistics alone developed. The social system of European linguistics did not encourage such specialization. It seems I was the only one for whom sociolinguistics was to become the main area of academic activity.

Becoming a sociolinguist. In the first half of the 1960s, the Oriental Institute in Prague was an extremely lively place. Ladislav Zgusta organized a group of linguists, all working together on a project describing the grammars of Asian and African languages. When I came back from Japan, I felt the need to supplement this by another project that would deal with sociolinguistic issues which were not central for Zgusta, Zvelebil, or other more senior linguists in the Institute. I think it was my stay in Japan that greatly contributed to my interest in the "socio" part of sociolinguistics. Apart from language I have always been interested in social sciences. Although my training with Skalička was linguistic, in the department where I studied Japanese we were required to study history and other aspects of Japanese society and culture. Of course, much of this was without a proper theoretical training, but we did try to compensate for this by private study. So, I was not completely naive as a social scientist when entering my linguistic career. In Japan, I became social-problems conscious—not only with regard to Japan itself but in relation to other Asian and African societies as well.

Members of the Institute who joined me were Václav Cerný (Caucasian languages), Luděk Hřebíček (Turkish), Ivo Vasiljev (Korean and Vietnamese), and Petr Zima (African languages). Quite a bit of work was published by members of this group before it was virtually abandoned when I later left for Australia. Papers published by members of the group in English or French included Vasiljev's paper on international lexicon in Far Eastern languages, Zima's paper on linguistic variation in West Africa, and my own paper, already mentioned, on the concept of "Oriental Languages" and variation in such languages (1965). The network was not particularly firm, each of its members maintaining other interests and commitments unconnected with sociolinguistics. Only Petr Zima remained faithful to sociolinguistic studies. I was young and ambitious, perhaps pushing the sociolinguistic viewpoint too strongly and putting Ladislav Zgusta, who was the Deputy Director of the Institute, in a difficult position. I still owe him my apologies. However, I have no regrets concerning the formation of the group. This, for me, was the point of no return, a point at which I was confirmed as a sociolinguist.

My papers published after 1965 still included quite a bit of phonology based on material researched at the beginning of the decade. However, gradually I turned completely to sociolinguistics both in my topics and in my participation in academic networks. I should mention that later on, in Melbourne, I added an active interest in language acquisition and teaching with a particular interest in teaching "sociolinguistic" and "sociocultural" competence (Neustupný 1987).

I moved from Prague to Melbourne in 1966. This was a legally approved move, not defection. In 1966 the process of liberalization, which later resulted in the Prague Spring, had gone so far that this was possible. After the defeat of the Prague Spring, the new Czech government proclaimed my stay in Australia illegal and I was unable to return to Prague for more than ten years; the next opportunity I had to speak to Czech linguists again was in 1990.

Within a month of arriving in Melbourne I was invited to attend the Airlie House Conference on language problems of developing nations and following that conference was given the opportunity to meet a number of American colleagues for the first time. However, it was not this event that converted me to sociolinguistics; as explained above, I was made a sociolinguist in Prague and had already selected the discipline as my principal theme of study by 1962. However, this trip gave me an associate membership in the mainstream sociolinguist network, which was particularly useful for the development of my theory of language problems. Another beneficial development, arising from the conference was my meeting Björn Jernudd who, incidentally, had joined Monash, the university at which I had just been appointed, earlier that year. He remained not only a good friend but acted as the first reader of my papers and adviser in "speaking" to the networks of mainstream sociolinguistics. As far as the development of my theory of language problems is concerned, he always provided critical and constructive comments and was not afraid to use my work; later we started jointly developing the theory of language management (Jernudd and Neustupný 1987, Neustupný 1994).

I feel that Australia provided an extremely fruitful background to my sociolinguistics. It was a society turning postmodern and as such directly *required* a variety of poststructural sociolinguist studies. With Björn Jernudd, Michael Clyne, and later John Platt at my side I did not consider myself isolated. But, of course, isolated from mainstream sociolinguistics I was—a fact I realized whenever I visited the United States.

Problems of a marginal member. I have never been a full-fledged member of mainstream sociolinguistics. Apart from geographical distance, one of the reasons was my language; but it was not only the issue of English in the narrow sense of the word. Of course, my English was bumpy at that stage but, more than that, I was writing in what Galtung (1981) would have called a Teutonic idiom. I agree that my papers must have been difficult to read, with their abstractness, excessive density, and lexicon that was marginal to English. It was not until the middle of the 1970s that Björn Jernudd could say "now you can write for American audiences." In 1973 I was invited to contribute a volume to the Stanford series on sociolinguistics, edited by Anwar Dil, but it was beyond my ability to prepare the manuscript. All my papers were in English, but they had to be strongly edited, something I did later, with limited success, when publishing my "Poststructural Approaches to Language" at the University of Tokyo Press (1978).

However, my problems went beyond those of the idiom. It was also the ideas I wrote about that did not fit. For example, one of my leading themes has always been the issue of developmental types of communication. I could see that some of my colleagues within mainstream sociolinguistics (not John Gumperz, for that matter) expected that the issue of variation would be the same in all societies. My experience, on the other hand, pointed to the need

Sociolinguistics: Some Other Traditions 207

for different models in Early Modern, Modern, or Postmodern environments. I feel that today the idea is more readily acceptable, but this was not so in the 1960s or 1970s.

Academics have often assumed that the greatest obstacle to international communication is the language in which messages are transmitted. However, to write in English is not enough. The idiom and the content which is transmitted may significantly differ not only between paradigms but between varieties of academic disciplines within the same paradigm. Linguists, too, are often (or normally?) "monolingual" and "monocultural" in the variety in which they have been trained and require adaptation to their own idiom and content selection by others. Fortunately, I had friends who were prepared to mediate and others who could accept messages even if they were formulated within a different system.

My contribution. As I mentioned above, my own work in sociolinguistics started in the theory of variation and I did continue to work in that direction in the 1970s. However, I consider myself that my main contribution has been in the theory of language problems. I intentionally say "language problems" and not "language planning" because my interest has always been wider. One of my early successful papers in this area was "Basic Types of Treatment of Language Problems." This paper was written for the 6th International Congress of Anthropological and Ethnological Sciences, held in Kyoto in 1968. After circulation for some time in its manuscript form (as was usual at that time), it was preprinted in 1970 in *Linguistic Communications*, working papers which Björn Jernudd and I launched from Monash. At the same time it was offered for publication to *Anthropological Linguistics*, but turned down. Finally, Joshua Fishman reprinted the version from *Linguistic Communications* in his *Advances in Language Planning* (1974).

If I interpret the success of the paper correctly, it was due to bringing into focus two different patterns of what was called language planning. These patterns (Japan and Czechoslovakia) were of interest because they were either unfamiliar or familiar, depending on the reader's experience. I said that the "language policy" approach to language treatment was characteristic for Early Modern societies, while the weaker "cultivation" approach characterized Modern societies. The basic fact that there were differences in approach was probably accepted by most readers. However, some were uneasy about the developmental typology (Early Modern, Modern) especially when they took "policy" or "cultivation" as the only defining features of the two approaches. Of course, there are "policies" in Modern societies and "cultivation" in Early Modern ones. For me there has never been any doubt about that, because language and reality in general were indeterminate and could not be explained by single features, each characterizing a single category.

The language treatment paper was also reprinted in my book entitled "Post-Structural Approaches to Language" (Neustupný 1978) which, apart from papers on vagueness, typology, and variation, also included another basic contribution, printed for the first time: "An Outline of a Theory of Language Problems." In this paper, written in 1973, I developed a theory of language correction and connected it with language planning. This theory has directly led to the language management framework which Björn Jernudd and I use today. Looking back at my "Post-Structural Approaches to Language," I feel that it is perhaps more timely now than it was when it was published. Unfortunately, it has been out of print for some time. However, the collection does not include any of my papers dealing with discourse; those started appearing just when the book was with the publishers.

Teaching sociolinguistics. I have not taught at all in Prague. After coming to Melbourne, I developed a course in Japanese sociolinguistics which I offered annually until the late 1980s. Apart from this I was invited by Professor Sibata to teach a general course in sociolinguistics at the University of Tokyo in 1970. This was probably the first real introduction to sociolinguistics ever taught in Japan and the course was attended, apart from a handful of undergraduates, by postgraduate students and teachers of the department.

Sociolinguistics as postmodern linguistics. Having mentioned the developmental typologies of language, I cannot but apply this theory to answer the question why mainstream sociolinguistics appeared in the 1960s and why it is still with us.

As I mentioned above, there were many sociolinguistics other than mainstream sociolinguistics, but with the possible exception of the work of some individuals, such as František Daneš, none of them was poststructural. Several reasons can be given to explain why mainstream sociolinguistics made it. Firstly, the existing tradition was by no means negligible. Just inspect again Hymes' "Language in Culture and Society" (Hymes 1964) with its detailed bibliographies. Although similar work may have existed elsewhere, the important point is that this work was available within a single national network and could be drawn on, particularly in the initial stages of the discipline. Second, the social system of American linguistics, with its financial backing, was extremely strong. There were extensive postgraduate schools, there were universities willing to employ staff, there was money to run projects and conferences. Conditions such as this did not exist anywhere else. Networks could develop and could be maintained.

Sociolinguistics: Some Other Traditions 209

Yet, the third, and perhaps most important point, was that in North America mainstream sociolinguistics grew up in a society that was changing from a Modern to a Postmodern type. The idea of accepting variation within society, social conflict, the conviction that it was necessary to look at processes rather than at fixed categories (and other features of the Postmodern) characterized not only linguistics but society as a whole. Even had there been no tradition and only a weak social system supporting the developments, a new sociolinguistics would have emerged; perhaps not as strong as it is, but still a substantial contribution to the world sociolinguistic tradition.

Out of the other three societies with which I have been connected, sociolinguistics in Czechoslovakia remained at approximately the same level during the 1970s but started rising again towards the end of the 1980s. It is fully poststructural today, but still needs time to make peace with both mainstream sociolinguistics and the tradition of the Prague School. Sociolinguistics in Japan has also entered the poststructural stage and the same question applies: how to balance the impact of mainstream sociolinguistics with the strong local tradition (Tokushuu 1988). No doubt, sociolinguistics in Australia, also a poststructural system, is vigorous, even if it lacks a unified forum for its discussions.

Mainstream sociolinguistics has developed since the 1960s by repeatedly adding new emphases, while retaining the previous ones. Discourse sociolinguistics has been the last prominent addition and the time seems to be ripe for a new sociolinguist field of study. We know that it is coming, and it may be in full swing by the time this book is published. It will be relevant not only for mainstream sociolinguistics but also for all other varieties of sociolinguistics which still may be in existence. Why not a sociolinguistics of interaction, interaction in the sense of integration of linguistic, sociolinguistic, and sociocultural competence within the same framework? Frankly speaking, I do not believe that we can create varieties of any form of linguistics at wish. History will act on our behalf.

A Note on Holism

Kenneth L. Pike

Kenneth L. Pike is professor emeritus of Linguistics at the University of Michigan; President Emeritus of the Summer Institute of Linguistics; Adjunct Professor of the University of Texas at Arlington. His scholastic efforts include research in Mixtec of Mexico 1935–1947; author of *Phonetics; Tone Languages; The Intonation of American English; Grammatical Analysis* (with Evelyn Pike); *Language in Relation to a Unified Theory of the Structure of Human Behavior; Text and Tagmeme;* and poems.

In 1948 things came together: the completion of my four books on phonology and my appointment as Associate Professor at the University of Michigan.

I was tired of phonology, and wanted to turn to grammar. But I did not want to throw away my preceding energy. When I went through my Phonemics book to summarize everything there of generalizable type, to see if it were applicable, three items seemed relevant: contrast, variation, and distribution (which in the early stages I called feature, manifestation, and distribution). Their application went smoothly in lower hierarchical levels of the grammar. Eventually, however, I struggled with the analysis of a particular language *as a whole*. English contrasted with German, all right; English had a dialect variance; but what was it distributed *into*? That gave me problems. The English language was distributed into culture and was a part of culture. It was this insight, in the spring of 1949, that then led to the writing of my book *Language in Relation to a Unified Theory of the Structure of Human Behavior*. Professor Charles Fries, through the Rockefeller Foundation, got me a grant for a year to work on the first volume of this book. The next two volumes had to wait for several more years. Then, language, cognitive structure, cultural structure, and relevant physical behavior came together.

Before this, however, another major event had occurred, without my realizing its importance. In 1935 the founder of the Summer Institute of Linguistics had me study a language in Mexico without an interpreter—lest Spanish get in my way of learning the language well. This had immense consequences theoretically, over a period of decades. Analysis combining grammar, phonology, and lexicon required a *holistic* approach. All of these had to be handled at once. And the integration of these gave me the foundation for my book *Language in Relation to a Unified Theory of the Structure of Human Behavior*. In this sense, sociolinguistics was no surprise; semiotics was no surprise; discourse analysis was no surprise. But there was a further unexpected development. In 1936, after one field term, I was asked to teach phonetics. One of the students asked, "What happens if we use no interpreter?" I said, "I will show you—I learned Mixtec (of southern Mexico) that way." That was my first "monolingual demonstration" in which—in this instance—the informant spoke Dutch (which I did not know). By gesture I elicited sounds and phrases from her, and got a starting description of some bits of her language in an hour. This monolingual approach has continued as the best example known to me of how or why a holism may be necessary.

Notes on the Development of Sociolinguistics

Edgar Polomé

Edgar C. Polomé has made many contributions to linguistics over the years including: Christee and Stanley Adams Jr. Centennial Professor of Liberal Arts University of Texas at Austin (1961–1990, on modified service since then); previously Professor of Linguistics at Elisabethville (Belgian Congo; now Lubrumbashi, Zaire, 1956–1960); Director of the Center for Asian Studies (1962–1972) and Chair of the Department of Oriental Languages (1969–1976); Fullbright Professor at the University of Kiel (1968), Team Leader of the Survey of Language in Tanzania (1969–1970).

As a student in the thirties at the University of Brussels, I had taken a course on "Sociologie du Langage" taught by the pioneer in this field, Professor Grégoire. He used his little introduction, published in Paris, as a textbook. When I started teaching in Austin in January 1960, I suggested a course in "Sociolinguistics" to my chairman, but although the term had apparently been coined by somebody in our speech department in the fifties, it seemed totally unknown to my colleagues. Anyhow, I managed to put on the program the same course as I had been teaching in French in Lubumbashi (then: Elizabethville) in Zaire (then: the Belgian Congo) from 1956 to 1960. It rested on the manual published in Paris by Marcel Cohen, but contained data (published later, see below) from my personal experience in Central Africa where I had done a lot of fieldwork, in particular in onomastics. Most of my data were however lost in the 1960 Congo Revolution.

In 1964 Bill Bright called a Conference in Lake Arrowhead, California, in which most pioneers in sociolinguistics participated. The aim was to plan the future of the discipline, and as a result many initiatives were started, Ferguson and Hymes taking the lead.

In these years, I published an article on "Cultural Languages and Contact Vernaculars in the Republic of the Congo" in *Texas Studies in Literature and Language*. In the meantime, I had been asked by E. Stevick in the FSI to come to Washington and discuss the linguistic situation in the former Belgian Congo to help them in planning the courses to develop for that area. I was mostly busy with Swahili in these days, writing a *Swahili Language Handbook* which had two editions and was used as a textbook in East African Universities. Published by the Center for Applied Linguistics, it contained diverse notes on local variation, dialects, etc. Meanwhile, I wrote papers on Swahili, on the position of Swahili among the other Bantu languages, on the earliest attestations of Swahili, and on Tanzanian linguistic policy and Swahili. I had gone back to Africa in the early sixties and visited all the areas, where Swahili was used (former Belgian Congo; Burundi, Uganda, Kenya, Tanganyika, Zanzibar, interviewing local speakers and working with local Swahili experts). Getting more involved with creolization theory, I participated in various relevant meetings and wrote two position papers on the topic: "Creolization Theory and Linguistic Prehistory" and "Creolization Processes and Diachronic Linguistics."

In the mid sixties, Charles Ferguson[1] organized a linguistic survey of Eastern Africa, with the participation of numerous scholars like Ladefoged, Whiteley, etc. I was appointed team director for Tanzania and we were in the field from the summer of 1969 to the summer of 1970. The team consisted of Peter Christopher Hill, a specialist in pedagogy from the University of London, who had been for several years headmaster of a Teacher Training College in Tanzania, and my doctoral student, David Barton. We tried to accomplish too much in the time we had in the field and as, by law, we had to leave our original notes on local inquiries and questionnaires in the country, where they happily rotted and were eaten to pulp by bugs, we were unable to process our data decently, in spite of strenuous efforts to compute what we saved, both in Texas and in London. An article, published in 1975 pointed to these "Problems and Techniques of a Sociolinguistically Oriented Language Survey." A final product however emerged from what we saved: it is the book on "Language in Tanzania" which I edited with P. C. Hill for the International African Institute in London and Oxford University Press (1980).

Meanwhile, I pursued my interest in "creolization and language change," and started applying it to other fields. A lengthy study on the linguistic

---

[1]Charles Ferguson served as Chair of the Steering Committee for the Ford Foundation-funded Survey of Language Use and Language Teaching in East Africa. Surveys were conducted in Ethiopia, Kenya, Tanzania, Uganda, and Zambia. Clifford Prator and J. Donald Bowen served successively as the Field Directors for the Survey. Among the contributors to this volume, Polomé was co-director for Tanzania while Ferguson spent a year in Ethiopia as a member of that country's team [Ed. comments].

situation in the western provinces of the Roman Empire (1983) was prepared. More studies on Swahili followed: a chapter on its standardization (1984), a study on the Creole Shaba Swahili (1985) and various other studies.

In recent years, I have devoted myself exclusively to Indo-European and Germanic linguistic, religious, mythological, and cultural studies; I have not taught sociolinguistics for years, nor done any further research in the field; being partly paralyzed by a stroke last year, I will have to stick uniquely to my present interests.

Beginnings of Sociolinguistics in the Philippines

Bonifacio P. Sibayan

Boni P. Sibayan is Professor Emeritus of Linguistics and Education at the Philippine Normal University (formerly College) where he was Dean of the Graduate School (1967–1972), President (1972–1981), and first Director of the Language Study Center which he founded in l964. He is a commissioner in the *Komisyon sa Hikang Filipino* (Commission on the Filipino Language).

Three conferences that I attended in the sixties introduced me to sociolinguistics. Two had to do with the language problems of developing nations (LPDN) and one with language planning (LP).[1]

In March 1964 upon the invitation of the late Clifford H. Prator of UCLA, I attended the conference on LPDN organized and chaired by Charles A. Ferguson, in Rome, Italy. What I remember most about the Rome conference was an audience with Pope Paul VI. The Vatican was interested in the subject of our conference, that of LPDN, because at the time, the Vatican was seriously considering the use of the native language of the people in the Roman Catholic Mass which up to that time was said in Latin. This conference impressed on me the point that the problems of language concerning the native languages of the people is an important issue.

[1] My knowledge of sociolinguistics increased with my attendance either as participant, paper reader or consultant in conferences, in the Philippines and abroad, on language surveys, language planning and sociolinguistically related topics (e.g., bilingualism, language teaching, etc.). Some of the international conferences I attended were those at Glen Cove, New York (1971), Skokloster, Sweden (1973), Toronto, Canada (August 1974), McGill University, Montreal (1975), Summer Linguistic Institute, LSA, East West Center (1977), Georgetown U. Round Table [GURT] (1978), Curacao, Netherlands Antilles (1979), East West Center (1983), the Regional Language Centre (RELC) Singapore (1971, 1973, 1987), National University of Singapore (1988), Hong Kong (1991) among others.

In April 1966 I attended the conference on LPDN hosted by William Mackey, Université Laval, in Quebec City, Canada. It was there where I met Einar Haugen for the first time. I remember his asking me what the most important problems of language in the Philippines were. I told him that our biggest problems stemmed from the use of a second language, English, for educating our people, the development of a national language and the use of the vernaculars in education.[2] I was to meet Haugen again during the 10th International Congress of Linguists in Bucharest, Romania in 1967 where I listened to him read his paper "Language Planning, Theory and Practice" in the section on sociolinguistics.

The third conference was the LP Conference at the East-West Center, Honolulu, in April 1969, which I attended upon the invitation of Joshua A. Fishman. The conference brought together scholars of various disciplines—anthropology, linguistics, sociolinguistics, political science, sociology, economics, economic planning, and social psychology—which made the point clear that sociolinguistics is or must be an interdisciplinary field of study (see Rubin and Jernudd 1971:ix). Case studies in LP in several countries including the Philippines were read. Some of the more important portions of the proceedings were devoted to discussions on the roles of nationalism, socioeconomic planning, linguistic theory, concepts which were discussed under the rubric of sociolinguistics (see Rubin and Jernudd 1971 for publication of the proceedings of that conference).[3]

For me and for us in the Philippines and for practically all those in the new independent and developing nations that were former colonies that used the colonial language, the problem of language was perhaps the most critical topic among scholars and decision makers at the time. The question on what language to use in running the business of government including education was paramount: should the colonial language or a

---

[2]In 1951 when I first read the report on language teaching in the Philippines by Prator (1950) two things struck me, namely: (1) That here was a nation, the Philippines, trying to educate its population of more than 18 million in a second (foreign) language with only one educator (Cecilio Lopez of the University of the Philippines who obtained his degree in linguistics in Germany) knowledgeable in linguistics, and (2) Prator's vivid description of the Filipino school child's practically futile efforts to learn English. While I was disturbed by the report, it was only after I had attended two conferences on language problems of developing nations (Rome 1964 and Quebec City 1966) that I realized that the problems Prator reported were *sociolinguistic problems*.

[3]It was in Honolulu where I first met Joan Rubin and Björn Jernudd. I must take this opportunity to record here one of the biggest regrets in my intellectual life, that of the lost opportunity to attain some degree of fame. During the closing session of the conference Fishman told the participants that the proceedings of the conference would be published in a volume to be edited by Rubin, Jernudd, and Sibayan. Impulsively I declined pleading having too much work in Manila. When the book *Can Language be Planned?* finally came off the press I was filled with remorse.

native language or languages be developed and used? For many ex-colonies, nationalism and language became intertwined. Many scholars from the western (developed) countries responded to the challenge posed by the problem. For many scholars the problems of developing nations and language planning became two of the central topics in launching the field of sociolinguistics.

Thus, for developing countries sociolinguistic studies were and are problem driven rather than theory driven. For many former colonies the beginnings of sociolinguistics studies and concerns had to center on the issue of language problems. What is most interesting is that the scholars who led in the attention to language problems of developing nations came from western (developed) countries, mostly North American and a number of Europeans. In the Rome conference in 1964 I was conspicuous by being the only one invited from a developing country.

Of the groups of scholars who launched modern sociolinguistics studies, I think Charles A. Ferguson, founder and first director of the Center for Applied Linguistics, and Joshua A. Fishman at Yeshiva University stand out for convening many of the early conferences. Einar Haugen should also be in the list of leaders who launched sociolinguistics studies. Most of those in the group that met at UCLA in 1964 (see Bright 1966 for the list of participants) certainly must be included among those who launched modern sociolinguistic studies.

The best candidate for the honor of defining sociolinguistics would seem to be *Sociolinguistics* (Bright 1966). See especially Bright's "Introduction: The Dimensions of Sociolinguistics" (1966:11–15).

The publication of the papers read in 1966 on language problems of developing nations (Fishman, Ferguson, and Das Gupta 1968) highlighted many of the practical and theoretical problems and subproblems that developing nations have to wrestle with and which scholars have to address.

Another important book is *Can Language be Planned?* (Rubin and Jernudd, eds. 1971) which carries the explanatory subtitle "Sociolinguistic Theory and Practice for Developing Nations."

Of the various journals devoted to sociolinguistics, the best, by far, is the *International Journal of the Sociology of Language*, edited by Joshua A. Fishman. The multilingual journal *Language Problems and Language Planning* is devoted exclusively to what the title indicates. For studies in the Pacific Rim countries, the *Journal of Asian Pacific Communication* published by Multilingual Matters Ltd. is a good outlet.

One of the most critical problems of researchers in academe is lack of finances. This is especially so in the Philippines and practically all developing countries. Most have to depend on foreign money for funding much needed research. I consider the Rockefeller and Ford Foundations particularly central to the launching of the field of sociolinguistics not only in the Philippines but in other parts of the world.

The Sibayan (1967) study was supported in part by funds from the Philippine Center for Language Study (PCLS) which was supported by a grant from the Rockefeller Foundation while the language policy survey (Otanes and Sibayan 1969) was supported mainly by funds granted to the Language Study Center of the Philippine Normal College by the Ford Foundation.

Of the individuals that worked in foundations that helped launch the field of sociolinguistics, that of Melvin J. Fox of the Ford Foundation stands out in my mind. I first met him at the Rome 1964 conference and began a long and fruitful friendship. Early in the sixties, the support for work on language internationally shifted from the Rockefeller to the Ford Foundation. I understand that the Ford Foundation's support for projects in this field is no longer as large as in the sixties.

Upon my return to Manila from the Quebec conference I went to see the late José V. Aguilar and J. Donald Bowen, co-directors of the PCLS,[4] to ask if the Center would support a study on the determination and implementation of Philippine language policy.

I was particularly concerned at the time that the people were never consulted on what they thought about the language used in the eduction of their children, a problem that was implied by Prator (1950). Teachers and other educators were simply told by policy and decision makers to use the local language (vernacular) in teaching. There was practically no preparation made for the use of the vernaculars. No training for teachers was given, no materials were prepared for their use so classroom teachers had to improvise teaching materials. Language policies were formulated in the central government without consultation with the people. I was interested in the thinking of those who carried out policy (teachers, supervisors, and administrators) and especially the people whose children were taught and affected by implementation of language policy.

I suggested that we conduct a study on what both laymen and educators thought about the determination and implementation of language policy. The late Bowen was particularly enthusiastic about the project, especially the survey on the opinions of both laymen and educators on language policy implementation.

I conducted the study on the implementation of language policy during the first semester of the school year 1966 (reported in Sibayan 1967). I did not realize the importance of this study at the time. In retrospect, it is important because it was to be considered later as the study that started the Philippine

---

[4]The PCLS was established in Manila in 1958 under the sponsorship of the Department of Education of the Philippines and the University of California, Los Angeles through the efforts of Prator with financial support from the Rockefeller Foundation.

genre of the sociolinguistically oriented survey (the term "sociolinguistics" had not yet been used in Philippine scholarly literature at the time) and its variations of (1) language use, (2) language attitudes and motivations, (3) language acquisition and proficiency, (4) bilingualism, bilingual education and multilingualism, and (5) language planning-oriented surveys (see Gonzalez and Bautista 1986 for the most comprehensive summary of seventy sociolinguistically oriented surveys made in the Philippines of which Sibayan [1967] is cited as the pioneering work). If I were to revisit that work today, I think the sampling and the methodology could be greatly improved.

In 1967 I was invited by Bowen to contribute a paper on "Language Policy, Language Engineering and Literacy in the Philippines" for publication in *Current Trends in Linguistics: Linguistics in Oceania,* edited by Thomas Sebeok of which he (Bowen) was an associate editor. The invitation gave me the opportunity to study and put down in systematic form not only the various activities and concerns in the Philippines regarding what was then referred to as language engineering later to be subsumed under language planning. More important, I wanted to give possible interpretations of the reasons and motivations for the various activities (Sibayan 1971). I am elated that this work is credited by Fishman as one of those (the others were those of Garvin, Das Gupta, and Pool) who tried to systematize and conceptualize the work in language planning (Fishman 1974:18). The revised and updated version of the article appears in *Advances in Language Planning* (Fishman 1974:221-54).

The work on sociolinguistics and psycholinguistics in the Philippines received a big boost when the group of Canadian scholars who worked with Wallace Lambert at McGill University came as consultants to the Language Study Center, Philippine Normal College in 1967–1969 under the joint auspices of UCLA and the Ford Foundation. Notable of these were G. Richard Tucker, psycholinguist, and R. C. Gardner, statistics expert who taught the use of the computer for research. Tucker spent about three semesters teaching, advising, and training faculty and students in research and writing.[5] In 1967 Wallace Lambert visited the Philippines to give a series of lectures in psycholinguistic studies.

In 1968 a massive national survey on language policy in the Philippines was conducted by the Language Study Center of the Philippine Normal College with the expert advice and assistance of G. Richard Tucker and Tommy Ray Anderson, linguist. The findings of this study (reported in Otanes and Sibayan 1969) and those of Gonzalez and Postrado (1974) were to be used later as the basis of the 1974 bilingual education policy issued by the Department of Education, Culture, and Sports on the use of English (for teaching science

---

[5]Of the long-term consultants at the Language Study Center, Tucker left the most lasting influence. He has retained a genuine and abiding interest in the work of language and sociolinguistics (and psycholinguistics, which he introduced at the Philippine Normal College).

and mathematics) and Filipino as language of instruction (for social studies and related subjects) in Philippine schools. This is significant because sociolinguistic studies were now being used as a basis for the determination and implementation of language policy in the schools. It was personally gratifying to us to have our work recognized and used.[6]

In 1975 the first institute on sociolinguistics attended by members of Philippine academe and leaders in Philippine education from the Department of Education was held at the Language Study Center of the Philippine Normal College with funds granted by the Ford Foundation. Joshua A. Fishman came as main lecturer. The other was the late Richard Noss who was on the staff of the Regional Language Centre in Singapore at the time.

Of the foreign scholars who worked in the Philippines, Prator, Bowen, Noss, Tucker, and Fishman must be credited as having had the greatest influence in Philippine sociolinguistics studies. Both Fishman and Tucker maintain their interest and influence in Philippine sociolinguistics. Fishman continues to encourage and support the publication of Philippine sociolinguistics studies (see Gonzalez and Sibayan 1988:149–51 and Sibayan and Gonzalez 1991).

Starting in 1969 two sociolinguistics courses, (1) Language problems of developing nations and (2) Sociolinguistics, were offered at the Ateneo de Manila–Philippine Normal College consortium for a Ph.D. in languages and applied linguistics. One of the members of the faculty who had returned after his studies at Berkeley shared my interest in sociolinguistics. This is Brother Andrew Gonzalez of De La Salle University (DLSU) who was responsible for making DLSU join the consortium. Brother Andrew is the most prolific researcher and writer in sociolinguistics and other linguistic areas in the Philippines today.

Brother Andrew and I mentored the first two doctoral studies in sociolinguistics in the Philippines, one on code switching in English and Tagalog under my mentorship (Bautista 1974; for the published version see Bautista 1980); the other, mentored by Bro. Andrew, is on Tagalog borrowings from Chinese [Cantonese] (Chan-Yap 1974). Earlier in 1970, a study for an M.A. degree that analyzed shifts from Tagalog to English in printed materials was awarded by the Philippine Normal College (Marfil and Pasigna 1970).[7]

Many of the questions asked in the sixties and seventies associated with language problems of developing nations are still pertinent today. However, many of the research paradigms have changed and will continue to change as sociolinguistic theory is sharpened and sociolinguistic problems are

---

[6]In 1987 the Department of Education, Culture and Sports used the findings of the evaluation of bilingual education in the Philippines (1974–1985) as bases for revising the bilingual education policy of the Philippines (see Gonzalez and Sibayan 1988:166–67).

[7]For an update on sociolinguistic studies in the Philippines, see Sibayan and Gonzalez (1991).

redefined. The sociolinguistic questions that have dominated Western (developed) countries such as "social dialect variation, immigrant languages, the relationship between formal linguistics and sociolinguistics" in contrast to the central concerns of non-Western (many former colonies and developing) countries such as "multilingualism, the development [modernization and intellectualization] of a national language, and the choice and use of language and education" and other language domains will continue to be addressed (see McElhinny 1993).

It seems to me that some of the most important issues in sociolinguistics that may have to be addressed by scholars and language users especially in developing nations are the following: (1) language, nationalism, and language rights especially with regard to minorities in both developed and developing countries; (2) language and socioeconomic development, (3) language for carrying on the affairs in what I have called the controlling domains of language, those of government (administration, legislation, judiciary), education, science and technology, national and worldwide communication (interactive), business, commerce and industry, and (4) the modernization and intellectualization of national languages in countries such as Indonesia, Malaysia, the Philippines, and many African countries will gain importance. I am told (private communication) by E. S. de Guzman, UNESCO consultant in Cambodia, that the intellectualization of Khmer in Cambodia as the chief language of work is a national problem of the highest priority.

Worldwide, the field of sociolinguistics is certainly much more vibrant and relevant today than a quarter of a century ago. More and more, both government and nongovernmental organizations will be using social research data for decision making and for programming projects; hence sociolinguistic studies will not remain mainly as data gathered in academe nor just for scholarly publications.

What are some of the practical concerns of the field? In my view, a working partnership between academic scholars and the users of language and those who make decisions on language use in government and in business and industry, science and technology may have to be forged so that sociolinguists and their work will become more useful to mankind.

From Sociolinguistics to the Anthropology of Language

Andrée Tabouret-Keller

Andrée Tabouret-Keller is professor of psychology (general psychology) at Université Louis Pasteur, Strasbourg II, France (since 1976). She was the director of Laboratoire de recherche sur la dimension sociale et les incidences psychologiques de langage (CNRS) from 1979 to 1995. Since 1988 she has been in charge of a seminar 'Anthropologie du langage' at Maison des Sciences de l'Homme (Paris).

There is a paradox inherent in the emergence of sociolinguistics in France: the main French linguists have always been sensitive to the social roots of language behavior. Among them, Ferdinand de Saussure (1857–1913) and Antoine Meillet (1866–1936) must be mentioned, but sociolinguistics as a distinct discipline was recognized only much later, around 1975, it seems to me. Still today, it remains not only relatively marginal in the way that linguistics and more generally language science and languages are taught, but above all, it shows a certain lack of coherence, split up into its various components: variously named *sociolinguistique, sociologie du language, linguistique sociale,* or *ethnolinguistique*.[1] It is symptomatic that in 1993 three books, all dealing with sociolinguistics in the broad sense, illustrating the tension between different trends, were published by the same publisher: *La Sociologie*

This paper has greatly benefited from discussion with Pierre Achard, Robert B. Le Page, René Tabouret, and Gabrielle Varro. The first translation from French into English was made by Varro, further help with the English version came from Le Page.

[1]This is also pointed out by Oswald Ducrot and Tzvetan Todorov in their *Dictionnaire Encyclopédique des Sciences du Langages*, 1972, Paris, Le Seuil, see chapter "Sociolinguistique," 84-91.

du Langage by Pierre Achard in February, *La Sociolinguistique* by Louis-Jean Calvet in July, *Le Colinguisme* by Renée Balibar in September.

And yet, *Pour une Sociologie du Langage* by Marcel Cohen, a disciple of Meillet, was already in 1956 an attempt at mapping the terrain, stating the questions, and organizing the field of desirable investigations. The publication of this book, its date, and its author plunge us immediately into the political history that has always dominated sociolinguistic history in France and still does to some extent. Many remnants and effects of World War II were still present, often painful, though we were already in a new war, the Cold War between the two great blocks. Cohen was a Marxist and a member of the French Communist Party; the notions of infrastructure and superstructure, in their economic sense, were meaningful to him. He never adopted the position of Nicholaï Marr—he was too experienced a linguist for that—but Stalin's declarations in June 1950 were food for thought for a man as constantly curious about the life of language as he was.[2] Language[3] knows no class boundaries and is not a superstructure, Stalin said. It was not an infrastructure either. What was it then? We discussed this endlessly. Cohen's answer was: it is a social fact—from that point of view, he had remained Meillet's student—a *particular* social fact, said I. He did not disagree, but asked, "In what way?" Cohen was nearly seventy when I knew him and he remained faithful to Marxism, for him dialectical materialism, and to the class war.

I saw Cohen because I was myself at the time a member of the French Communist Party and it seemed to me that "socialism" was a better warrant of social justice than "capitalism"; we still thought then that fairer laws would produce more civilized men. However, I also met him because a totally different question intrigued me already. In my native province, Alsace, in the northeast of France, the everyday language was the Alsatian dialect, the Germanic dialect of Alsace. The language of the school was French, in which I learned to read and write just before the Second World War; then during the Nazi occupation I studied in German, and after that in French once again. The *Yiddish* spoken in my street was already disappearing though a few survivors still spoke it. How could everyone live his life, his own life, in such circumstances in which what is so readily called

---

[2]From the end of the fifties on, I was often invited by Marguerite and Marcel Cohen to their house in Viroflay. Marcel Cohen was extremely lively, his curiosity always aroused by everything that concerned the real ways people talk. We read with pleasure his column "Regards sur la Langue" in *L'Humanité*, published in book form by the Editions Sédès in Paris. He was obstinately opposed to the idea of studying language in itself and for itself and never wanted to know about structural phonetics which, for him, were an idealistic construct.

[3]The Russian word *yasic* is translated "language." See the French translation of Stalin's declarations published in the *Pravda* from May to June 1950, in *A Propos du Marxisme en Linguistique* by J. Staline, Ed. de la Nouvelle Critique, 1951.

History swept you along before you even noticed its movement? Where was the choice, the freedom to speak this or that language? In those years (the beginning of the fifties) I did a Diplôme d'Etudes Appliquées in psychology, in which I compared the school achievements and the intelligence of Alsatian-speaking children in Alsace and of French-speaking children in Burgundy, a region I chose because it was also wine growing. Paul Imbs[4] was one of my examiners, a member of my jury, and had lent me Uriel Weinreich's *Languages in Contact,* where I discovered a real project with all the questions that research in this field had to answer. André Martinet's preface was a revelation:

> "We shall now have to stress the fact that a linguistic community is never homogeneous and hardly ever self contained...But it remains to be emphasized that linguistic diversity begins next door, nay, at home and within one and the same man. It is not enough to point out that each individual is a battle-field for conflicting linguistic types and habits, and, at the same time, a permanent source of linguistic interference. What we heedlessly and somewhat rashly call "a language" is the aggregate of millions of such microcosms many of which evince such aberrant linguistic comportment that the question arises whether they should not be grouped into other "languages." What further complicates the picture, and may, at the same time, contribute to clarify it, is the feeling of linguistic allegiance which will largely determine the responses of every individual. This, even more than sheer intercourse, is the cement that holds each one of our "languages" together: It is different allegiance which makes two separate languages of Czech and Slovak more than the actual material differences between the two literary languages." (Weinreich 1951:vii)

With the encouragement of Martinet, who had helped me obtain a scholarship, I went to work with Weinreich during the summer of 1962 for a few weeks, after having attended the 9th International Congress of Linguists in Cambridge (Mass.). It is there that I heard the expression *sociolinguistics* for the first time, used by S. K. Chatterji speaking about the linguistic situation in India. He spoke in the session presided over by A. M. Badia-Margarit, who many years later invited me to the sociolinguistic circle of Barcelona, then completely illegal. These were the last years of the Franco régime, and it was under Franco's portrait that I gave a lecture on the necessity and inevitability of bilingualism. The two other people presenting papers

---
[4]Before becoming director of the *Trésor de la Langue Française* he was at the time a professor at the University of Strasbourg.

during the same session as Chatterji were V. Pauli (Sweden) who already then proposed to theorize language policy, and myself, on the sociological study of bilingualism in the Toulouse area;[5] the study of the shrinking use of the *Langue doc patois* was based on demographic and sociological data such as age, profession, proximity to urban centers, and presence of immigrants. We had all learned the elements of general linguistics in the little textbook published under that very title by André Martinet in 1960, in which chapter 5 presents language as a human institution which reflects life in society. It was clear that though one might separate out the structures of a language, one could not separate living language from its social context.

My second serious encounter with the expression *sociolinguistics* was once again in the United States, during the 1966 seminar at Airlie House (Virginia). J. A. Fishman, C. A. Ferguson, and J. Das Gupta, with the help of the *Committee on Sociolinguistics* of the Social Science Research Council, had brought together thirty or so colleagues to think over the linguistic problems of developing countries. In their presentation, signed by the three organizers, it is stressed that "most American linguists continue to be only marginally interested in language development" and that "sociolinguistics itself is still a very fragile flower, cultivated only at a handful of universities, and focused primarily on microphenomena at the level of the speech act in face to face interaction" (1968:x). In this volume, published in 1968, many titles already use the term sociolinguistics.

In 1969, I defended my thesis in psychology called *The Bilingualism of a Child before Age Six. An Alsatian Case Study (Le Bilinguisme Chez l'enfant avant Six Ans. Étude d'un Cas Alsacien)*. In its way, the choice of subject typifies the emergence of sociolinguistics in France as a politically marked field. It was impossible to imagine any kind of "neutral" sociolinguistics in the way one spoke (too readily in my opinion) of the "disciplines" in the natural sciences. If sociolinguistics were a discipline, then it must belong to the cultural sciences, which are necessarily interdisciplinary (man is a social human being blessed with speech); it cannot be neutral. No doubt that that also spurred us: the idea that we were contributing to set the foundations of an authentic anthropology, both enlightened and committed. More than a scientific movement or a theoretical need to develop knowledge, the question was what form a certain number of political realities could take in the academic universe. And first and foremost were the wars themselves

---

[5]*Proceedings of the Ninth International Congress of Linguists,* ed. by H. Lunt, The Hague, Mouton, 612–21. In 1972 this text appeared in an expanded version in English, in J. A. Fishman, *Advances in the Sociology of Language,* The Hague, Mouton, 365–86 and the same year, in Russian in V. I. Rosenweig (dir.), *Iazikovie Kontakti,* Moscow, 170–82.

and their sociopolitical and linguistic secondary effects. Many parts of Europe were swallowed up, annexed, or occupied, tossed about from one State to another. Alsace, my province, changed hands six times between 1871 and 1945, being shuttled back and forth between Germany and France. The Nazi claim that the Reich must extend as far and wide as to include wherever the German language was spoken (as far as oak-trees grew, it was also said!) made a profound impression on us, at least on me. But we were also marked—I am speaking of those of my generation, born sometime between the two world wars—by the policy of linguistic assimilation applied in the French State. It was more blatant in 1945 in Alsace than elsewhere: apart from the fact that there French had since the nineteenth century represented social mobility and urbanization, the language in 1945 came to represent a highly centralized, Republican type of power. The walls said: "It's chic to speak French." For a long time our languages, French and German, not to mention the Alsatian dialect, as a Germanic dialect, were to remain prisoners of political implications.

In other French provinces, the use of regional languages, the various dialects of Occitan, Breton, Picard, and many more had given way to French, the legal language (since François I in the sixteenth century!), the language of the public school ("obligatory, free and nondenominational," 1882), of the administration, centralized and therefore French speaking. The anti-Nazi war, the geographic proximity of Spain still controlled by Franco, the social changes consequent in the already noticeable dwindling of the farming population and thus of the local languages accompanied by unprecedented urbanization, and a consequent enlargement of the purely French-speaking middle classes: all these factors helped to form a resistance to the modern exercise of power by the State, taking the form (among many other symptoms) of the defense of local languages. In Francoist Spain, the defense of regional languages, mainly Catalan and Basque, actually represented the front of the anti-Franco struggle, a very broad front including farmers, workers, and intellectuals. Thus, it was that the fledgling sociolinguistics in France was nourished by two academic schools of thought deeply involved in the defense of minority languages and the awakening of regional identities. Jean-Baptiste Marcellesi [see Marcellesi, this volume], of Corsican origin and a Communist too, co-authored with Bernard Gardin the first French sociolinguistic reader, *Introduction à la Sociolinguistique, la Linguistique Sociale* (1974). Robert Lafont applied the concept of "diglossia" with his own definition in the Occitan regions and evolved a materialist theory of language (Praxematics 1973, 1983). Like Marcellesi, Lafont remained a linguist above all: the reality of language as a social praxis must be studied through actual language facts. Some years later, in 1977, Pierre Achard founded *Langage et Société*, a journal of working papers whose authors were called upon to abide by the principle that they must defend their publications before the audience of those they had studied and those they wished to address.

One of the underlying preoccupations of my thesis was to address the idea, widely popularized by the local Alsatian press of the time, that bilingualism was bad for the child, not only from a linguistic but also from a moral point of view. I had wanted to describe a case of bilingual acquisition in a family, of whom there were many such in Alsace, in which the parents were neither linguists nor worried that their children might be linguistically retarded due to their bilingualism; the thought never crossed their minds. According to my thesis, bilingualism was not bad for the child; what could be bad were the social, political, historical, institutional, economic, and psychological conditions which surrounded his socialization. Two observations may interest the reader today. (1) At first, no publisher in France was eager to publish the thesis, because, so they thought, there was no public for it;[6] and (2) this work was in fact multidisciplinary, borrowing methods and theories from psychology, sociology, and linguistics, and thus did not fit into the disciplinary distinctions of the time. To this day, I have held on to the principle of multidiciplinarity for the vast field of study now known as *sociolinguistics*. My teaching in this field at the University of Strasbourg began in 1960 with psychology students to whom I lectured about the *Social Psychology of Language* which was new and, it seems to me, unique in France at that time; it is certainly that which has been the most consistent topic in the research training I have given over the years to a number of French and foreign doctoral students; in many cases the background concern of the latter was a claim for freedom of thought and speech in their country of origin; although this had to be recognized, it had to be disentangled from research practice proper. Since 1980, the program has become both more precise and more subtle, as it has centered on the *social dimensions and the subjective effects of language*. The main funding agency in France is the *Centre National de la Recherche Scientifique*, which endows research units, mostly located in universities, with permanent funds over periods of four years: it is not sociolinguistics as such that is funded but research projects on specific topics in *sociolinguistique*, the decision depending on a national elected board, called *Sciences du Langage*, from 1981 until 1990, and now *Langage, Communication et Représentation*. It is increasingly difficult to get endowed, particularly in sociolinguistics, because of the impact of computer sciences on linguistics and the general shrinking of public

---

[6]I handed out about one hundred mimeographed copies, fewer in France than abroad, in fact.

money to support research independently from industry. Additional funds may be provided on a contractual basis; in my case they came mainly by the way of consulting missions about language policies or language education policies in European countries like Catalonia, the Basque Country, Alto Adigo, the Valle d'Aosta, etc.

Two major events intervened in my disciplinary positions, first during the 1960s and then in the 1970s. First there was the experience of psychoanalysis in the early 1960s; it makes the question of the relationship between man and History and between man and his own history even more complex. How can one link the uniqueness of one's own subjective experience to one's experience as an institutionally supported person? to one's experience as one individual among others in a necessarily social series? Secondly, there was fieldwork done in Central America, in Cayo District of what was in 1970 British Honduras, taken up again in 1978 and pursued in the same District, of what had now become independent Belize. It was an international undertaking led by Robert B. Le Page, and it taught me yet another sort of complexity.

Compared with the European situations I was used to, where the more or less political centralization within each nation-state has imposed the focused use of a dominant standard (Le Page 1978) and dialects of a fairly predictable though somewhat diffuse relationship to that standard, the situation in Belize was far more complex, minimally focused, due in part to the official role of a standard English known in various degrees to most of the inhabitants—native speakers of some variety of Creole or Spanish or Maya or Garifuna—primarily as a written language but the vehicle of their education (Le Page and Tabouret-Keller 1985). There the dynamics of language contact, of constant interactive pidginization and subsequent more general spread of varieties of Creole as *lingua franca,* make the discovery of statistical regularities uncertain. As everywhere else one set of parameters defining the individual was easy to set out: the names by which people identify their language and the groups they feel they belong to—ethnic, socioeconomic, religious, political, etc. Our basic data were first of all the names they themselves used, other terms to describe their language and their social structure being excluded from our method of interview. It was possible also to name a person's institutional and legal relationships and kinship even if the kinds of relationship which would in Europe bond a person to ordered aspects of his or her social and cultural environment and circumstances were in Belize—at least at that time and to our understanding—less set and less steady. As everywhere else the dimension of man as subject of words, those out of which his history, his culture, his identity, and his subjective conduct are built, calling in permanence for renewed sense, were neither given nor transparent. An existence precarious, ephemeral, calling to mind the analogy made by the Venerable Bede of the sparrow flying from the winterstorm into a quiet room and then again into the storm.

Sociolinguistics did not spring fully armed from Minerva's head; there is no "first" thesis, no "first" author, because from the start, the name *sociolinguistics* referred to interdisciplinary problems, and methods taken over from other disciplines. University requirements have made it necessary to turn it into a discipline and it is of course possible, within its broad spread with fuzzy edges, to define unified areas of inquiry. But it seems to me that they are unified due to a methodological artifact: one limits oneself to social networks, or to linguistic markers, or again to an empirical reality such as code switching, or to the bilingual acquisition of language. I doubt that the accumulation of research and results is productive as such of a discipline; sociolinguistics has developed at varying rhythms and with varying means, even in those countries that could pay for this luxury. In the many more numerous countries which have no such means, there are new sociolinguistic realities to discover. It is regrettable, besides, that the predominance of literature in English constitutes an obstacle for English-language authors who do not read what is written in other languages.

The field of sociolinguistics seems as vibrant and vital as it ever was: sociolinguists as such, but not unlike other human scientists, are concerned by the new nationalisms and ethnicisms, in Europe and elsewhere, in which sociolinguistic ingredients play a more or less important part, but generally they are not among those to which politicians and economists would pay attention. From a fundamental point of view, *sociolinguistics* research goes on bringing to light many complex phenomena which call for more integrated and new theoretical models that should be put to the test, providing stimulus for new representations. Practical concerns imply a huge realm of applications: the use of language and its regulation. From a theoretical point of view, the most urgent questions today do not seem to me to be exactly sociolinguistic; rather they concern the definition of the object of the human and social sciences. That question raises another one about the definition of the specific objective of sociolinguistics. To say that each language act is a sociolinguistic fact solves nothing because the same fact can be approached from many angles, marked by different disciplines. I was struck when I discovered in the program of the 4th International Congress of Applied Psycholinguistics (Bologna, June 1994), under the heading *Psycholinguistics as a Multidisciplinary Connected Science,* many communications which needed to change nothing at all to be included in the program of a Congress which could be called *Sociolinguistics as a Multidisciplinary Connected Science.* My own evolution is towards an integrative discipline, an Anthropology of Language with new dimensions trying to integrate sociolinguistics and the psychology of language in its broadest sense that is inclusive at least of the social psychology of language and of psychoanalysis.[7]

We would have to be enlightened and able to say how man is not only simply alive, in the biological sense of the term, but also human due to the manifold effects of culture, both imbedded in and refracted by language, how he can manage the constraints of becoming an individual, be at one and the same time a "person" (a specific construction in each society in his own times) and a subject of words. How, too, this undertaking is thwarted, in indefinitely repeated ways, how transgressing the laws of humanity becomes possible, leading to murder or to madness. Such considerations are the line of horizon which organize the painting. Why draw such a line if not because it is from there that the questions keep coming, giving new impetus and meaning to research in sociolinguistics as in the human sciences generally, questions which concern man who, as a speaking human being, is never free from words for his pleasures and pains.

---

[7]The monthly seminar *Anthropologie du Langage* which I hold at *La Maison des Sciences de l'Homme* (Paris) since 1988 follows this purpose.

Journal Editors

Reflections about (or Prompted by) *International Journal of the Sociology of Language (IJSL)*

Joshua A. Fishman

Joshua A. Fishman is Distinguished University Research Professor, Social Sciences, Emeritus, at Yeshiva University and Visiting Scholar, Linguistics, at Stanford University. He is General Editor of the *International Journal of the Sociology of Language* and of the book-series *Contributions to the Sociology of Language.*

In the beginning. It was 1970 when Peter Coutinho of Mouton (The Hague; now Mouton de Gruyter [Berlin]) invited me to become the General Editor of a journal that would pertain to the same field as the one I had defined or implied in my then highly successful *Readings in the Sociology of Language* (1968). It took me well over a year to make up my mind, because I had previously been the editor of *The Journal of Social Issues* and I knew that editorship entailed a lot of work, particularly so since neither secretary nor assistant was to be made available to me either by the publisher or my home University. I finally agreed, however, and since I was given carte blanche to do so, I opted for a journal that would be (a) interdisciplinary, reaching far beyond the field of linguistics (particularly, beyond narrowly linguistics-focused sociolinguistics), (b) truly international in content, and (c) macro-level oriented with a special concern for the status of indigenous and immigrant minority language communities. The resulting journal *(International Journal of the Sociology of Language)* celebrated its twentieth year and its 100th issue in 1993 and a complete index available by the end of 1994. The index can be used to check out many of the hunches and comments that constitute the present reflections.

Initially (and for the first few years), three issues a year appeared and, for a while, these were also simultaneously published as issues of the journal *Linguistics*. In this fashion, *IJSL* began with an appreciable subscription base. Nevertheless, for several years I found it was difficult to fill out three issues a year with qualitatively acceptable material. Little by little, however, the amount of such material increased and then four and, soon thereafter six issues were published per year. At present (January 1994), all issues through the very end of 1995 have already been commissioned, further indicative of the amount of qualitatively superior material now being received and approved by the editors, Editorial Board members, and invited reviewers. In order to cut the current publication backlog from two years to one, it would be necessary to publish issues at the rate of one per month. This is an indication not only of the acceptance of the *Journal* but of the increased size of the corpus of researchers whose work is perceived as being broadly sociolinguistic in nature.

International emphases. The same growth that has been experienced in connection with the thematic issues (the latter constituting at least five out of every six *IJSL* issues) has also occurred in connection with the material received for the once-a-year "singles" issues (initially edited by Robert L. Cooper, Hebrew University [Israel], and, since 1988, by Florian Coulmas, Chuo University [Japan]) and the thrice yearly reports on "small languages and small language communities" (edited since 1989 by Nancy Dorian, Bryn Mawr College [USA]). Indeed, during both 1992 and 1993 no "singles" issue was published in order to ease somewhat the publication backlog in conjunction with thematic issues. However, the thematic issue is more than merely the characteristic format of *IJSL*; it is a format that has permitted the *Journal* to aggressively seek out work in various parts of Europe, Africa, Asia, Latin America, and Oceania that would not ordinarily come to international attention in any organized and integrated fashion. By means of this format, *IJSL* has provided the worldwide sociolinguistic endeavor with difficult-to-achieve entrée into China, Korea, the Magreb, and Poland in the recent past, just as the Czech Republic, Hungary, South Africa, Sub-Saharan Africa, Morocco, Aboriginal Australia, and Latin America are on the publication agenda for the immediate following years. The international nature of *IJSL*'s editors and Editorial Board members is counted upon to foster ongoing and ever greater internationalization of its substantive coverage during the years ahead. The goal in this connection is not merely to provide North American and EC (the European Community) readers with a window to the realities of the "exotic" world, but, even more importantly, to enable more sociolinguists from outside North America and the EC to bring their theories and findings to more general attention and recognition.

Innovative formats and services. Another unique contribution of *IJSL* has been the "focus issue" which brings monograph-length publications to the reader, each immediately accompanied by ten or more expert critiques/commentaries and a rebuttal by the monograph author. The greater length available to authors via the focus approach and the built-in criticism and feedback provided by the critics/commentators have both enabled *IJSL* to break out of the usual unidirectional mold of most other academic journals. Additional innovative formats are urgently needed, particularly in conjunction with the communication revolution that has been spawned by the personal computer, electronic mail, and microfiche publication. Sociolinguistic thought has been particularly and surprisingly slow to recognize the sociolinguistic implications of the communication revolution that surrounds us all. The inability of sociolinguistic journals to save the *Sociolinguistic Newsletter* from virtual (and the *Sociolinguistics* journal from actual) oblivion, via cooperative ventures of the types that brought *IJSL* into the world, is an indication of the vulnerability which results from rigid adherence to the time-honored tradition of impervious walls between journals in the same field. *IJSL* is currently exploring (and is interested in exploring even more actively) innovative cooperative and electronic means of serving the sociolinguistically oriented researcher, instructor, and student.

Such newer approaches also provide some hope of breaking out of the virtual dependence of all our current journals on high-cost institutional subscriptions, at the expense of low-cost, individually tailored and interactive access. The only journal in our field to have encouraged specialized less expensive spinoffs and electronic access and retrieval (at least to some extent) is *LLBA* (Linguistic and Language Behavior Abstracts). Its efforts along these lines should be carefully watched for our more general edification. Greater use of *IJSL* in the instructional and student research processes would be particularly desirable and, thus far, very little attention has been paid to how this can be accomplished via the newer electronic means now being perfected or becoming more widely available.

Problems of sponsorship. The absence of a strong organizational voice for sociolinguists as a whole during the entire period of the past two and a half to three decades (and the absence of any such voice at all at this time, insofar as journals focusing entirely on the sociolinguistic endeavor are concerned), is definitely a sign of the professional marginality and tentativeness of this field. The nearest approach to such a status is that followed by *LPLP* (*Language Problems and Language Planning*), but that journal is sponsored by an Esperanto oriented organization, on the one hand, and by a private publisher, on the other. At any rate, although it is an exceedingly fine journal, it focuses only on an important corner of the field, rather than on the total field by any stretch of the imagination. All of the other core journals are publisher owned and (as in the case of *IJSL* itself) even publisher oriented. They are "for profit" ventures and would not long survive the prolonged economic downturn that required university libraries to seriously decrease the number of journals to which they subscribe. Although we may be slowly coming out of such a downturn at the present time, even that is not yet entirely clear, and there may still be serious attrition in the number of journals, particularly among the ones with smaller circulations, during the coming few years. This makes it even more urgent—above and beyond the intellectual and training reasons advanced above—for interjournal cooperation and for low-cost/high-circulation alternatives or add-ons to be implemented between one journal and another instead of the splendid and costly isolation which is currently the status quo.

"Then" and "now." It is worth thinking back to the differences between "then" and "now" (i.e., the period when the current sociolinguistic journals were founded and the present period), to gain perspective on *IJSL* and the other major journals in this field. The momentum and enthusiasm of a new field which was obtained has now largely been spent and, along with it, there has vanished that "the sky's the limit" sense of the mid sixties to mid seventies (insofar as the availability of funding in support of promising new undertakings is concerned). The coming into being of the core sociolinguistics journals in the industrial and commercial heart of the Western world, precisely when that world was in a period of marked ascendancy, should alert us to the distinct probability of the future coming into being of South and East Asian journals, on the one hand, and of Germany-based journals, on the other hand, in the relatively near future (if current economic trends continue unabated). Although such future journals will probably continue to be primarily in English (with some more or less ceremonial recognition of local languages as well) just as are all of the current core journals, their emphases will probably be more practical and applied than are those of today. This would not be undesirable, in and of itself, but if carried to an extreme, would also not be an unmixed blessing. Sociolinguistic theory can also prosper on applied problems, of course, but these problems do exact their toll and influence the direction of attention as well.

The importance of journals. In our field, journals are of even greater importance than they are in better established fields. There are a few universities that offer advanced training (or even more than two or three courses) in the entire sociolinguistic area and, accordingly, few sociolinguists have colleagues and a critical mass of advanced students with whom they can discuss their work on their own campus. Because of the virtual absence of professional organizations specifically for this field, there are no regular conferences devoted to it. There is, of course, The International Working Committee on Sociolinguistics of the International Sociological Association (which I helped establish, with the blessings of the American SSRC Committee on Sociolinguistics, at the Evian ISA Conference in September 1965), but it meets only once in three years and has a policy of encouraging attendance by accepting for presentation any and all papers that are submitted to it. The number of sessions on sociolinguistics at any of the annual meetings of the American Sociological Association or of the Linguistic Society of America is small indeed. As a result, our journals carry more responsibility for advancing the frontiers of the field than would be the case for more commonly and intensely developed fields. The journals virtually constitute the "leading edge" of the discipline and, therefore, it behooves us all to give our sociolinguistic journals, more (and more sympathetic) attention. They are the stimuli that not only keep us all informed and that stretch us intellectually, but they are the connective tissues which keep us together as a community of interest on an ongoing basis.

Unmet challenges. There are still many new worlds to conquer for sociolinguistic journals, *IJSL* included. I will mention only one here and now, one which I have continued addressing (but have never quite been able to clinch) for the past decade or more. The active participation of sociologists and political scientists (and, if possible, also economists and historians) seems to me to be indispensable for a fully mature sociolinguistic enterprise. There have recently been some signs of movement, finally, on this front, but far too little given that so much time and hope has been put into this matter. But without professional social science input, both our field and our journals are not only misnamed but, what is worse, are conceptually amateurish. Our journals can render yeoman's service in finally consummating the long heralded marriage between our field and the social sciences, even more so than can the universities with their traditional departmental barriers. If I were to nominate one index by which to measure the conceptual and methodological progress of the sociolinguistic enterprise during the next decade, it would be the extent to which social scientists from traditional social science departments have begun to publish in our core journals, with 1993 taken as the baseline.

Language in Society

Dell Hymes, founding editor

Dell Hymes was born in Portland, Oregon and attended local schools and Reed College there. His doctorate is in linguistics from Indiana University in 1955. He has taught at Harvard, Berkeley, and the University of Pennsylvania, where he was Dean of the School of Education 1975–1987. He is now Commonwealth Professor of Anthropology and of English at the University of Virginia. He founded the journal *Language in Society* and edited it for twenty-two years; served on the Social Science Council for several terms; and was a trustee of the Center for Applied Linguistics (1973–1978) and President of the Linguistic Society of America in 1983.

Language in Society was conceived as concerned with sociolinguistics, in an inclusive sense of the term. The first issue (1972) had an introduction which discussed the concerns of the journal. The inside cover had a short statement.

> *Language in Society* is concerned with all branches of the study of speech and languages as aspects of social life. Preference is given to contributions of general theoretical or methodological interest. Contributions may vary from predominantly linguistic to predominantly social in content, but are expected to involve both poles of the journal's field of concern in some explicit way. The journal seeks to aid in strengthening international scholarship and cooperation in this field and from time to time will carry a set of articles reflecting the state and interest of sociolinguistic research in a specific country or region. In addition to original articles, the journal publishes reviews of current books, brief accounts of work in progress, and notes and comments on points arising out of recent publications. (Editorial Policy, *Language in Society*)

Given my background, I was responsive to work in anthropology and linguistics, and to some extent education and literature.

I did not know the distribution of readers among fields.

There was no formal relationship of cooperation, but from time to time I would suggest some other journal as more appropriate for a submission. Exchanges with other journals were helpful in keeping informed as to their foci, and other work of contributors.

The demise of journals has been predicted for some time now. I cannot speak for a younger generation, but I find them still of value. For one thing, I am less likely to lose a copy of a journal. I do not know if it is because of age or the times that I read journals less and less. I think it has much to do with the increase in correspondence, and the time taken simply to deal with that.

I would guess that *Language in Society* and *International Journal of the Sociology of Language* have been the most important. For those who work in conversational analysis, the picture would probably be different.

Language in Society has an editorial board. I used it regularly for evaluation of manuscripts. That indeed was the main consideration in changes of membership. Not an evaluation of the people, but of needs of the journal in terms of what was coming to hand.

It certainly is important to have a range of viewpoints and knowledge. I have found women members among the most reliable and helpful to authors. I have tried to have an international representation on the board. In one or two cases it was so that issues could reach a certain country. I have taken ethnicity and nationality into account in seeking readers of manuscripts.

There have been occasional embarrassments in delay in publication, or in finding oneself obliged to publish something one was not enthusiastic about (after a long process). The other characteristics or articles and authors have not been a factor, so far as I know.

One development has been an increase in the regular attention to language in the *Annual Review of Anthropology* and a journal such as *American Ethnologist* as well as an increase in the number and variety of journals.

I was pretty much open to whatever arrived, and seldom sought particular pieces. But journals can have an important role in encouraging positive directions in sociolinguistics.

If there is a sense that sociolinguistics needs to be given direction, and revitalized, then active editorial planning could be immensely valuable at this time.

There are so many alternative outlets and networks associated with each, that good work of whatever kind seems publishable. (Perhaps continued hidden rotting of the social economy, inability of libraries and scholars to subscribe and support, may make that statement false). But indications that certain kinds of work are welcome would probably be noticed. And networks could be tapped through the editorial board.

Perhaps it would be worthwhile, or at least interesting, to discover what associations people have with the term "sociolinguistics," in relation to the other broad terms current in regard to the study of language.

My own answer would be that the term has been most associated with urban studies, but that its potential as a broad, general term for the social study of language could be activated.

Language as a Social Phenomenon: A Perspective on the Emergence of Sociolinguistics

Humphrey Tonkin

Humphrey Tonkin was professor of English at the University of Pennsylvania from 1966 to 1983, when he became President of Potsdam College of the State University of New York. In 1989 he joined the University of Hartford as President. He has chaired the board of the Center for Research and Documentation on World Language Problems since 1974 and is an editor of *Language Problems and Language Planning.*

The Center for Research and Documentation of World Language Problems[1] was set up in the 1950s by Ivo Lapenna, of the London School of Economics, to coordinate and promote the study of communication problems caused by language differences, particularly in international settings such as diplomatic conferences and intergovernmental organizations. Lapenna, a Yugoslavian émigré and a specialist in international public law, was also a lifetime supporter of Esperanto as a solution to the international language problems, and his Center came into being as an offshoot of the Rotterdam-based Universal Esperanto Association. His firm belief that "language is a social phenomenon" (Lapenna 1958:60–71) animated Lapenna's tenure as a leader of the Esperanto movement; he was firmly of the opinion that the acceptability of Esperanto depended not so much on its linguistic features as on political and economic factors—a sentiment widely shared by thoughtful linguists, regardless of their disposition towards Esperanto, but not always acknowledged

---

[1]Center for Research and Documentation on World Language Problems, c/o The University of Hartford, West Hartford, CT 06117–1599.

by some of the more enthusiastic supporters or energetic detractors of the language.

As a speaker and user of Esperanto, Lapenna was a linguistic maverick. Outside observers tend to see the Esperanto-speaking community as a collection of *advocates,* devoted to the cause of promoting their language as a means of international communication and, given that the jury may still be out, possibly right or possibly wrong. But in reality they are primarily a community of *users,* who communicate through a language that some say is impossible and others say lacks expressive powers. As practitioners of an alleged impossibility, they are apt to challenge received opinion, and hence the Esperanto movement and the phenomenon of Esperanto itself have implications for the linguistics community that go beyond the question of whether or not Lazar Ludwik Zamenhof's language is destined to sweep the world.

Lapenna believed that objective study of the political and economic context of language was a necessary accompaniment to the advancement of Esperanto. He thereby set in motion the development of a program of investigation that, rooted in partisanship though it was, moved beyond its initial motivation to take in a part of what is today known as sociolinguistics. Some have called this area of investigation, the study of the interaction of languages in a macrosocial context, *interlinguistics,* though others limit this term to the comparative study of constructed language intended for international use (Tonkin, in Janton 1993; Schubert and Maxwell 1988).

But many of the papers that Lapenna's Center produced were little more than data collection, and others were partisan, if well-argued, defenses of Esperanto. Serious scholars who happened also to speak Esperanto were eager for a more objective forum and wished at the same time to persuade their colleagues to enter the field, believing that this would increase the visibility of Esperanto in scholarly circles and enhance its academic respectability. A series of conversations involving Lapenna, Victor Sadler, and me, along with various others, resulted in the founding of the multilingual journal *La Monda Lingvo-Problemo,* The World Language Problem, whose first issue appeared in January 1969. The original intention was to have the Center publish it, but, at my urging, conversations were opened with the publisher Mouton, which agreed to serve as a publisher with the Center's support. Sadler, a psycholinguist trained at University College London, became the first editor, gathering around him a distinguished editorial board, including, in addition to Lapenna, the Austrian Eugen Wüster, the Australian Arthur Capell, the Russian E. A. Bokarev, and the Italian Bruno Migliorini.

Early articles in *LMLP* included historical surveys, by Lapenna himself, of the role of official and working languages in the League of Nations and the United Nations family, and studies of the language problem in diplomacy

(Ralph Harry), official suppression of language use (J. B. Rudnyckyj), Puerto Ricans in New York (Joshua Fishman), national development and language diversity (Jonathan Pool), language problems in the International Court of Justice (Julien-Maurice Lambert), and language and education in India (Lachman Khubchandani). The journal also published numbers of articles having a more direct bearing on the interests of Esperanto speakers, including articles on the nature of interlinguistics (Reinhard Haupenthal) and on planned languages (Manfred Mayrhofer) and their literature (Willem Verloren van Themaat). Articles appeared in a range of languages, but primarily English, French, and German, each with an extensive summary in Esperanto.

A total of thirteen issues appeared under Sadler's editorship. He was succeeded in 1973 by Richard E. Wood, a Germanist and linguistic polymath educated at Hamburg, Cambridge, and Indiana, who was at that time chairing the Department of Languages and International Studies at Adelphi University. After a rather erratic period in which the journal was published only with considerable delays, it ceased publication with its eighteenth issue and was transformed in 1977 into *Language Problems and Language Planning*, still under Wood's editorship and still published by Mouton, but now with a multilingual title that proved confusing in the extreme to librarians and bibliographers (the language of the title changed with each issue, in a misguided effort to establish language parity). Volume 1 of *LPLP* (the title was largely the brainchild of Jonathan Pool) was launched in 1977, and the journal appeared three times a year, more or less regularly. In 1980 it migrated to the University of Texas Press. Richard Wood, by now teaching at King Saud University in Saudi Arabia, produced his last issue in 1984, and I took over as managing editor that fall. Ultimately, beginning with Volume 14 (1990), when the journal migrated again, to John Benjamins Publishing Company in Amsterdam, I succeeded in putting together a three-person editorial team, consisting of Klaus Schubert, then with the commercial firm of BSO in the Netherlands and now at Fachhochschule Flensburg, Germany, Probal Das Gupta, then at Deccan College and now at the University of Hyderabad, India, and myself.

I have always felt a little sheepish about my own role with *LPLP*. Trained primarily as a literary scholar, I entered sociolinguistics largely as a facilitator. My entry into the field, if so grand a title is warranted, was an article that reviewed some of the absurd assumptions made about language in attacks on Esperanto by assorted scholars and nonscholars who should have known better (Tonkin 1968). During my years as director of the Center founded by Lapenna (I assumed this role in 1974), I sought to broaden the range of scholarly work in and around Esperanto by creating a climate conducive to serious scholarly work within the Esperanto movement and by encouraging other scholars to examine some of the issues raised by the notion that a created language could establish itself as a functioning speech community (Wood 1979). Such a notion, based on a set of observable facts in the Esperanto movement, flew in the face of certain perceived ideas about the origins of languages, the nature of language change, and the development of communities of meaning. The biological fallacy—that languages are "natural," that they "grow"—was belied by the phenomenon of Esperanto, which seemed to establish, incontrovertibly, that languages are products of society, not of botany. They change and they are not used in accordance with biological principles, but as a result of social pressures and demands.

Esperanto was also unique in that it derived largely from written texts, that its structure was the work of a single individual, and that its speech community grew up as the vehicle for the language rather than the other way about. In short, it raised questions of great importance about the social role of languages.

Our Center began to organize activities intended to examine such questions. We sought out collaborators around the world, connected with serious scholarly endeavors such as the Department of Esperanto Studies at the University of Budapest or the Centre de documentation et étude sur la langue internationale in Switzerland. We made common cause with the United Nations, whose Office of Conference Services now organizes an annual conference jointly with the Center, at which problems of translation and interpretation, international language policy, and the politics and economics of language are examined. The first of these conferences took place in 1983 (United Nations sponsorship began in 1984) and dealt with language in the context of World Communications Year (Tonkin 1983a). The conference was intended primarily to demonstrate to the United Nations and UNESCO that language had a crucially important role to play in the development of communications policy. It should perhaps be added that the gap remains: specialists in communications pay very little attention to language, and it is not at all unusual for entire volumes on international communications policies to appear with no mention of language differences at all; this is one area in which the influence of sociolinguistics has been minimal.

Meanwhile, our efforts to interest the scholarly community in the phenomenon of Esperanto, through *LPLP* and through our sponsorship of events and publications, continued to gain ground. The objective study of Esperanto led Toon Witkam and others to consider its use as a black-box language for machine translation systems, leading to the Distributed Language Translation project, and its by-products in syntax and semantics, many of them the work of Victor Sadler and Klaus Schubert (Maas 1991, Sadler 1991, Neijt 1986). The historical Ulrich Lins moved in a different direction, writing a history of

Esperanto under totalitarian regimes, picking up on a preliminary article on this subject jointly authored with Sadler (Sadler and Lins 1972, Lins 1988). The linguist Detlev Blanke completed a comprehensive survey of planned languages in their political and social context (1981), leading in due course to a number of other surveys of related ground (Large 1985, Blanke 1985, Eco 1993), and the sociologist Peter Forster explored the sociology of the Esperanto movement (1982). As the *MLA International Bibliography* shows, with its annual crop of two or three hundred entries on Esperanto, this effort to give Esperanto studies a place in the scholarly sun has been at least partially successful (see also Symoens' bibliography of dissertations 1989).

LPLP, whose editorial board includes such familiar figures as Joshua Fishman and Dell Hymes, has now become a respected sociolinguistics journal. While we favor articles that are broad in their reach and break new theoretical ground, we also publish case studies and related materials, as well as reviews. But we continue to feel that what might be called the international relations of languages remains an underrepresented field in linguistics generally and sociolinguistics specifically. Little work has been done on the interaction of languages in conferences or other international deliberations, our linguistic knowledge of international negotiations remains primitive, and the role of language in peacekeeping operations or international military operations has been little studied (Müller 1986). Nor do we have any clear idea about the informal accommodations made to language difference in international organizations, international corporations, or any of the other formal structures that cross national boundaries. Indeed, the Center's work in some of these areas can be regarded as pioneering (see, for example, Edwards and Tonkin 1984, Jastrab 1984, Michel and Sonntag 1984, Müller 1984, Pearl 1996). For the most part, sociolinguists remain biased towards grassroots language use, and their studies of language policy and language use tend not to extend to international settings.

One important concept that entered the range of interest of our Center at a fairly early stage was the concept of discrimination on grounds of language. The concept, little recognized at the time, is still inadequately distinguished from race and ethnicity as a social problem of great complexity. It intersects with the study of language and power and its subset, the study of language and colonialism. Through its contacts with UNESCO, the Esperanto movement entered the field early, organizing a seminar on international aspects of language discrimination with such participants as Claude Hagège and Louis-Jean Calvet (Lo Jacomo 1986), and arguing for the inclusion of the language dimension in UNESCO's controversial debate over the New World Information and Communication Order. When the right to communicate arose as a concept, my colleagues and I were quick to argue that language choice and language policy are fundamental elements in its application (Tonkin 1983b, Tonkin 1984). Furthermore, if technology is the hardware of communication, language is the software, and software incompatibility is as much an affliction to social communication as it is to the operation of computers.

In short, the role of the Center for Research and Documentation on World Language Problems has been, ever since its founding in the 1950s, to push at the limits of orthodoxy in linguistics, and to raise questions that do not fit easily within the pigeonholes of the discipline. To the extent that thinking of this kind has had an effect on the field of sociolinguistics, this has come about because of the relative openness of sociolinguistic thought and the willingness of its practitioners to reexamine received assumptions about language. It is my own strong hope that this process will continue, and also that the intersection of sociolinguistics with such fields as politics, economics, and communication studies will expand.

Early Institutional Supporters for the New Field

Center for Applied Linguistics: Interview with Rudolph C. Troike

Interviewer: Christina Bratt Paulston
October 18, 1994

Rudolph C. Troike is Professor of English and former department head (1990–1995) at the University of Arizona, Tucson. He was previously on the faculty at the University of Illinois (1980–1989) and the University of Texas at Austin (1962–1972). He served as Director/President of the Center for Applied Linguistics in Washington, D.C. from 1972 to 1977.

Do you see a critical milestone...a conference, publication, that marked the beginning of sociolinguistics as a field? I think from where I was in Texas [the University of Texas at Austin] at that point what really sparked an awareness was the publication of Labov's dissertation in 1966. There had been some local interest on the part of Haver Currie[1] in the speech department. When the term sociolinguistics began to surface in the literature, I remember he wrote a note in which he pointed out that he was the first person to have used the term in a publication, but he never really did very much with it beyond that point. He was not really active.

What do you see then, as the "climate of the times" that Labov's dissertation landed in? There were several things at Texas, mainly because we had Edgar Polomé on our faculty at the time. He brought a European-oriented perspective on sociolinguistics and looked at it in terms of Indo-European history and things of that sort, mythological texts and Indo-European religion, that kind of direction. He actually taught a seminar in it.

---

[1] Haver Currie, then Assistant Professor of English, University of Houston, in an article published in 1952. Died in 1994.

Do you see sociolinguistics having an all North American impetus or do you see it coming from what is a European link with this?
I don't really know because at the time I didn't have much interaction with Polomé. He is the person to comment on that. But it did seem to stir some latent philological sense because he was delving more deeply into culture, language, and society than most linguists had been dealing with, up to that point, at least American linguists. (The exceptions would be people like Charles Ferguson and John Gumperz.)

To go back to your original question, two other aspects of the climate of the times were of a purely linguistic nature. I think there was a growing dissatisfaction with the limitations and sort of narrowness of purely structural linguistics. So there was more and more dissatisfaction out there, but nobody really had a clear handle on it because linguistics at the time was structuralist and transformationalist. It left all these other things outside the pale. I think that there was such a sense of excitement about sociolinguistics because it suddenly provided a way to start legitimately treating some of these other issues.

Then there was the external socio/political situation that so much influenced Roger Shuy's work and a lot of Labov's work and others, of course, and my own as well. That was the emerging school desegregation/civil rights settings that were so active at that point.

Who would you say were some of the other players, individuals who were part of this launching of a new field?
At Texas we also had David DeCamp, but nationally there were William Stewart and Roger Shuy (especially with Ralph Fasold and Walt Wolfram) working out of the Center for Applied Linguistics, who had an enormous impact; Shuy really demonstrated on a much larger scale the use of the techniques that Labov had developed.

How else would you say it had an impact on the Center?
Well, the very lively awareness or belief that this kind of research could really have a significant effect on social/educational policy. Through the work of Shuy and others, the Center for Applied Linguistics came to be a major national player in sociolinguistic research and application.

Who were some of the major funding agencies during your years as president of CAL, that you sought at that point, who were behind this early development? The Ford Foundation was a major source, also the National Science Foundation got on board.

Was there any one person in the NSF who was pushing for this? I'm not sure who at NSF was responsible for language then. Paul Chapin has been very supportive since he came to direct the Linguistics program.

I think NSF has always had a sense of the importance of the social sciences area and especially so with linguistics, and social responsibility for the work that they support.

There was also at that time, in the Office of Education a research office (back in those days where the people were organized along content lines), so there were some people in the Office of Education, such as Doris Gunderson, who had some understanding and awareness of the relation of social science to education, for supporting initiatives there.

The whole Bilingual Education Act and all of that work must have had some impact on Washington. Again, on the research side, that was coming out of the Office of Education; they were supporting some research activity.

Which do you see as having more of an impact on the Center and on research—the civil rights movement or the bilingual education area? I think it's hard to separate them. Overall, I would probably say the civil rights movement. Language rights were part of civil rights.

The unfortunate thing in that regard and peripheral to this point is that the foreign language profession, as you well know, having helped in sponsoring the initiation of bilingual education, divorced itself from it to some extent, so the Center was one of the few places to maintain linkage.

Why did the foreign language people do that? I think that ultimately their interests are directed to the countries outside where the languages are spoken. They shy away from the domestic situation.

And they don't want to muck it up with nonstandard Spanish? Right, exactly. In fact I remember some people at the University of Texas counseling Mexican-Americans not to go into bilingual education because they didn't think their Spanish was good enough.

These attitudes were pervasive...there seems to be considerable insularity in the foreign language teaching profession which focuses on the training of people on the secondary level and these completely disconnect with all these children coming to school on the elementary level who already have language competency.

How about telling us about some of your own work. Is there any one contribution, of any kind, conference, book which stands out as an important contribution for shaping the field? Before I jump into that, let me go back to an earlier question, and mention Al Hayes. Al contributed to sociolinguistics at CAL by bringing people together in conferences and things like that. He deserves to be remembered for that.

I could suggest one eminent contribution of yours if you are lacking words. How do you see the conference that you put on in Mexico with Modiano.[2] How do you see that as fitting in with what we've been talking about? This was the First Inter-American Conference on Bilingual Education in Mexico City in November 1974. Actually, I don't see it fitting too directly; except as an aspect of concern for minority education. Of course I have always had a strong interest in Latin America and indigenous languages throughout the Americas. I was trying to bring about an awareness and connection between people working in the field throughout the hemisphere. And it did perhaps produce some temporary connections and it did show quite remarkably the insularity of the United States and of people working in bilingual education in the United States vis-à-vis Latin America.

And vice versa. So I don't know; the publication itself may have had an impact on people reading it as part of their training program and things like that.

And that conference on bilingualism helped in bringing Latin and North Americans together. So don't dismiss your first conference as having little importance. It was an exciting event, but there hasn't been very much continuation of contact between North Americans and Latin Americans, regrettably. However, the conference did help to stimulate contacts within Latin America. (Inter)connectedness seems to stop at the border here.

What would you think are your own most important contributions? I would say in the area of scholarly publication, the paper that I did on receptive and productive competence in the Georgetown Round Table.[3] Because to me it continues to be a live topic in terms of looking at bilingualism or

---

[2] Nancy Modiano. Last working in Chiapas, Mexico. Died in 1993. The conference papers were published as Proceedings of the First Inter-American Conference on Bilingual Education, Arlington, VA: Center for Applied Linguistics, 1975.

[3] Receptive Competence, Productive Competence, and Performance. *Papers of the 20th Annual Georgetown University Round Table Meeting*, 63–69. Washington, D.C.: Georgetown University Press, 1969.

multi- dialectalism or whatever level you want to look at—and still a very neglected area, namely, productive output. I guess on the applied side, the *Handbook of Bilingual Education*[4] Muriel[5] and I did together has been the most widely used publication, in fact, in that field. It's hard to go anywhere without running into somebody who has not cut their teeth on it.

When did you first give a course in what you might call sociolinguistics or anything associated with it? I don't have the dates at hand, but it was probably around 1968, at the University of Texas. I had a very successful seminar on sociolinguistics. There was a good group of graduate students, and we did some interesting things. The connection there, incidentally, is not a publication as such, but through the NDEA (National Defense Education Act) Summer Institute in English we had in Texas, I got acquainted with the people at the Texas Education Agency. That's where I met Mary Galvan,[6] for example.

Is she still working? Yes, although she's more and more retired these days especially since her husband died.
That opened the door for me to work with the Texas Education Agency in the field of school desegregation in the state. They became convinced that linguistics was the cutting edge in trying to break down attitudinal barriers, so working with Mary we organized a combined research-teacher training activity in East Texas and we had a number of cooperating schools there. Mary and one of my doctoral students, Riley Smith, went out and did tape-recorded interviews of children in the schools. Another doctoral student, Bill Garland[7] did some of the analysis of the data. We put that data into a training package that we sent back into the schools and used that to try to educate the teachers about language differences.

That must have been one of the earliest attempts in the country. I believe it was. It is interesting that we were disinvited back into one district because the superintendent or somebody got the notion that the word "dialect" was a code word for civil rights, so we were told we were *personae non gratae* and not to come back and give any workshops there. But the principle of that whole project was the idea that knowledge-driven, data-based training is the

---

[4] A *Handbook of Bilingual Education,* Washington, D.C.: ERIC Clearinghouse for Linguistics, 1970; Revised edition, Teachers of English to Speakers of Other Languages, 1971.
[5] Muriel Saville, then Assistant Professor of English, Texas A&M University, now Professor of English, University of Arizona, Tucson.
[6] Mary McKinney Galvan, then English consultant in the Texas Education Agency, Austin; subsequently President, TESOL.
[7] Now Professor, Department of Linguistics, University of New Mexico.

best way to change social attitudes, and we were enormously proud of the results. In one of the small districts that we worked in, the year following our work there, for the first time in the history of the school, a black girl was elected homecoming queen. This was quite remarkable, especially considering that this was a small town in East Texas that had always had segregation. Also, I should extend this discussion in a different direction: a critical element in our success was the hookup with Roger Abrahams, who at that time was working in black folklore from a performance-oriented point of view. He and I realized that there was a good way to connect what we were doing coming out of sociolinguistics to what he was doing, coming out of the folklore side.

His real background is in English. He was in the English Department there with me doing folklore. He was aware of what I was doing with the schools and he had the feeling he wished he could apply his field of knowledge so we got together and it just worked out to be a very exciting combination.[8]

An important one. So, what you are saying then, is that this early work that you saw in Texas was problem driven rather than theory driven. I think that it is probably true; I wouldn't say that of Labov, but of a lot of the people I would say it was true. **And from CAL's viewpoint? Did you ever see it shift over to theory-driven or did it stay problem-driven?** I've always believed in seeing problems as an opportunity to do basic research that could be used to test theory, and in applying theory-generated findings to the solution of practical problems. That's the ideal and that's what we did in Texas. There shouldn't be an opposition between theory and application. I think that at CAL Walt Wolfram developed a nice kind of symbiosis in the work he and Donna Christian did in West Virginia. They were looking at trying to test theory as well as looking at social-educational issues and trying to relate the one to the other.

What is your forecast for the world of sociolinguistics? Where do you see it going and what do you see as its more pressing issues? I'm distressed to see a considerable decline of interest in it as such over the years, but I guess this has happened because of the loss of what are seen as pressing social problems and lack of a funding agent to push things. There's a kind of mellowing out in a way that has moved it especially into the arena of discourse analysis and I think in some ways that is where some form of active or interesting research is emerging at this point. So I don't foresee for some

---

[8]The project is described in "The East Texas Dialect Project," in A. C. Aarons et al., eds. *Linguistic-Cultural Differences and American Education* (Special anthology issue of the *Florida FL Reporter*), 1969, pp. 152–53. A further result of this collaboration was the co-edited collection, *Language and Cultural Diversity in American Education,* Prentice Hall, 1972, which includes the preceding report.

time that sociolinguistics per se is going to be a particular arena for new development. Some of the more important work is going on in the area of restructuring language change.

You used the word "exciting" several times in describing the earlier works. Did I hear you right in saying that excitement has abated somewhat? Very much so.

That can't just be due to the disappearance of funding. No, I think it has to do with the emergence of a new paradigm and the realization of possibilities that people haven't been aware of or conscious of before. There were parallel excitements in the early work of Chomsky, but now it's hard to find anything equally exciting going on.

Center for International Education U.S. Department of Education: The Evolution of Sociolinguistics

Dick Thompson

Dick Thompson's career has bridged the academy, where he has held professorial appointments in Chinese linguistics as well as senior management positions, and the federal international education community, where he served in senior policy management positions directing the activities of the U.S. Department of Education's Center for International Education. Now retired, he served as Director of International Centers, Research, and Fellowships and Professional Lecturer in Chinese at Georgetown University's School of Languages and Linguistics.

Milestones. Headlines in newspapers all across the country and around the world on October 4, 1957 told of the Russian satellite at that moment streaking around our "shrunken nuclear-nervous globe" at 18,000 miles an hour.

This was the critical milestone that marked for me the beginning of "modern sociolinguistics." Of course, I did not realize this at the time. In fact, unlike with the death of President Kennedy, I do not even know what I was doing at the time. The strategic impact, however, was being assessed before the ink was dry. In plain language, the Russian scientists had beaten the American scientists—American education had failed.

The remedy, the National Defense Education Act (NDEA), was on the books within the year. The general provisions of the Act established that the security of the nation required the fullest development of the mental resources of the country and set forth to correct as rapidly as possible the existing imbalances in education programs that had let an insufficient proportion of the nation's population into the study of science, mathematics, and modern foreign languages. What the general provisions, however, failed to do was to state in operational terms what these imbalances were and what would constitute a sufficient proportion. This would set the stage for the most significant strategic national foreign language policy planning effort in American history, and its major focus and impact was on what we refer to today as the LCTLs (less commonly taught languages).

What was so important about this milestone was the enormously vast and unprecedented impact that this had on the nation as a whole and education in particular at all levels; and that the event was externally motivated. Robert Ward, in commenting on this century, noted that

> ...we are in the process of outgrowing yet one more boundary—the national frontier—long accepted as the natural limit of most, though not all, of our more absorbing and normal concerns and activities... both Government and peoples are in the process of learning, and accommodating to, the extent to which conditions and decisions "abroad" are capable of continuously and vitally affecting their lives, fortunes, and well-being at home. (1977:1)

Sputnik provides us with a truly global reminder of our dependence on external events to serve as catalysts for needed education planning and policy development. Consider also the negative impact of World Wars I and II on the study of German, and the role of World War II as a positive impact on foreign language education, especially the less commonly taught languages and the development of incipient area studies programs, and the training of Chinese, Korean, and Vietnamese specialists in the military language schools in response to the Korean and Vietnam conflicts. Chinese enrollments surged in response to the detonation of the first Chinese atomic bomb, while the oil crisis had similar effects on the study of Arabic.

The social climate of the times. In a retrospective look at the Sputnik event, Former Commissioner of Education Ernest Boyer stated: "I don't recall a period when we focused so single-mindedly on education, and when the schools were so linked to a national purpose. There was an almost electrifying awareness of the importance of education nationally" (*The Washington Star* 1977:1).

The fabric out of which NDEA was woven came primarily from the separate threads of the several concerned programs and interests that had represented both the commonly and less commonly taught languages in the World War II and post-World War II era. NDEA was the largest and most critically massed attack on modern foreign language research and training in history. It was more important than any of the earlier programs that preceded it, yet owed its very existence to the efforts of all of the linguists, foreign language teachers, and education specialists who contributed to the major foreign language programs that preceded it, as well as to the thousands of teachers and faculty in the colleges and universities throughout the country who supported and participated in the various programs under NDEA VI.

The earlier efforts included the Intensive Language Program of the American Council of Learned Societies (1941), the Army Specialized Training Program (1943), the Program in Oriental Languages of the American Council of Learned Societies (1952), the Foreign Language Program of the Modern Language Association (1952), the Nine-Point Statement of Foreign Language Program Policy of the Modern Language Association (1956), and the Foreign Language Program Five-Year Plan (1957). The leadership of the field was poised to not only participate in the formulation of the Act itself, but once enacted to be available for public service in its administration.

The intellectual climate of the times was primed for the programs and projects that followed. Although the immediate catalyst (or was it provocation) was sputnik, the MLA five-year plan laid the groundwork for an important part of what was to become the National Defense Act, and called for the following five steps: (1) encourage more Americans to study foreign languages, (2) improve and modernize foreign language institutions at all levels of instruction, (3) encourage the study of uncommonly taught languages by the creation of new programs and scholarships, (4) foster more research and experimentation in language learning and the development of new tests and teaching materials, and (5) establish pilot programs in selected states to serve as delivery systems for the new methodology.

What was formerly merely possible, was made desirable through the five-year plan and necessary by sputnik. Had there not been a sputnik, we surely would have had to invent one. This fortuitous convergence of events set into motion educational improvements, projects and activities on a national scale, and required not only a federal bureaucracy to manage them, but the application of national language planning concepts in a nontraditional manner.

Motivating questions. Unanticipated and significant financial resources had become available to address the issues outlined in the general provisions, to correct the imbalances that had led an insufficient proportion of the nation's population into the study of modern foreign languages. The obvious, unanswered question was "what is a sufficient proportion?" This and many other questions were left to the Office of Education to manage.

We lacked a relevant national strategic foreign language planning policy. Language planning as traditionally discussed in the literature had focussed on the kinds of problems facing the developing countries, such as the identification or modification of a national language, the development or revisions of writing systems, or planned language change. We needed to develop a language planning approach which could enable us to deliver the right language in the right amount at the right time to the right people for the right reason, and to define all of this within the context of a language and area studies mandate.

And we needed an interdisciplinary approach. A major difference in the teaching of the commonly and uncommonly taught languages derives from the widely differing organizational patterns of the two fields. In teaching such languages as French, German, and Italian, much of the focus had been on a more narrowly interpreted introduction to the culture through literature. With the less commonly taught languages this focus was not possible since, unlike the case of Western European culture, little or no instruction had traditionally been available in the history, economics, politics, and culture of the countries and areas under study. Thus, the field of "language and area studies" was both interdisciplinary, by necessity as well as by statutory mandate, and interregional. Area studies specialists in the traditional disciplines organized broadly based, integrated language and area studies programs at the institutional level, and organized themselves as a field through a network of area studies associations.

Extensive cooperative arrangements were developed in support of intensive summer and academic year study abroad. An organization of directors of National (language and area studies) Resource Centers has also been formed to further national coordination. But what is important to understand is that the "field" is a derivative of the institutionalization of foreign language and area studies programs in American higher education. External organizations or activities that function on a national level, such as the joint ACLS/SSRC regional committees, and the federal review panels, rely on the contributed expertise of the foreign language and area studies specialists that maintain the national programs at institutions of higher education.

My work. At the time, and having been trained as a theoretical linguist, I never really thought of my work as contributing to the development of the field of sociolinguistics. My formal involvement with the field began when I joined the U.S. Office of Education in the sixties. Our work was "problem driven" as we had responsibility for administering Title VI of the National Defense Education Act (now HEA). The congressional mandate talked about the fullest development of mental resources, correcting imbalances in educational programs, and insufficient proportion of our population with knowledge of foreign languages. It was left to the Office of Education to make these determinations. This was classic supply-side theory.

The early years were characterized by gathering data and setting priorities. The first major Conference on the Neglected Languages (Fife and Nielsen) charted the neglected languages and established priorities for these languages. In all, the U.S. Department of Education has funded 149 surveys, studies, and conferences designed to provide the Department with the information it needed to effectively manage the business of Title VI. Other landmark studies included: periodic surveys of foreign language course registrations in IHEs by the MLA; The Foreign Language Attainments of Language Majors in the Senior Year, by John B. Carroll; Present and Future Needs for Specialists in Linguistics and the Uncommonly Taught Languages; A Survey of Materials for the Study of Neglected Languages; *Language and Area Studies Review,* Survey of Materials Development Needs in the Less Commonly Taught Languages in the United States; and two RAND surveys of Federal Support for International Studies: The Role of NDEA Title VI and The Education and Careers of FLAS Fellowship Recipients by the Rand Corporation.

From the extensive surveys, studies and conferences we developed exhaustive matrices. For example, the matrix for materials development needs in the less commonly taught languages listed the tools of access for the study of a foreign language across the top and the major languages identified for development down the left side. Whenever a dictionary, reference grammar, or textbook was developed an X was placed in the box for that item. The list was predominantly empty of Xs and the job was gap filling. It almost did not matter what project was funded, the task was so great.

The periodic surveys and the matrices developed in-house enabled the Department of Education (ED) to base decision making in its annual research competitions upon a thorough knowledge of what materials had been developed for what languages and what were the remaining high priority materials development needs. Since the Department of Education shared this information with the public when the competition was announced, this also served as a guidepost for the field to direct subsequent research in areas of comparative need.

In addressing the question of an imbalance in educational programs that had led an insufficient proportion of our population into the study of foreign languages and related area studies, similar matrices were also developed. The base-line study *Language and Area Studies Review* (1973) provided hard data on the number of current specialists and the production rate of new specialists at the various programs throughout the country. This data was organized in a variety of ways but permitted the development of records which displayed the information by language and by discipline and world area. This gave the Department of Education supply but not demand data and led ED to develop a "comparatively underrepresented" approach to funding for its Foreign Language and Area Studies (FLAS) fellowships program.

Using this information the Department initially established disciplinary priorities by world area in awarding FLAS fellowships, and encouraged institutions to make some awards in the comparatively underrepresented disciplines such as economics or sociology (for most world areas) and away from history or political science. Although voluntary, the Department achieved some modicum of success in this approach as additional monies were sometimes made available to institutions that reassigned their fellowships. ED maintained detailed records on the production of specialists based on information supplied by the institutions receiving FLAS awards to keep current the supply information from the *Language and Area Studies Review*. The subsequent RAND surveys again provided additional supply and utilization-of-skill data.

In addition to utilizing comparative underrepresentation of certain disciplines in the current specialist pool as a factor in the awarding of quotas of fellowships to institutions, ED used other information in matching disciplines to languages and in allocating funding for fellowships to the various world areas. Information on the comparative difficulty of learning other languages by Americans developed by the Foreign Service Institute of the Department of State as well as the Defense Language Institute was one factor; the more difficult the language, the more time-on-task required and the longer a fellow in Category IV languages such as Arabic, Chinese, Japanese, or Korean would need to hold a fellowship in order to reach a level of language proficiency equivalent to a student in a Category I language such as Spanish.

Another factor considered was the period surveys of registrations in foreign language courses conducted by the Modern Language Association (MLA). Although applicant institutions to the FLAS program included enrollment data from their institutions, the national picture was provided by the MLA. An increase in undergraduate enrollments nationwide meant that more students would be entering their graduate studies with prior study, and for certain languages a FLAS award could only be made at the advanced levels. The Foreign Language and Area Studies Centers, now called National Resource Centers (NRCs), formed the nucleus of the institutionalization process. The overall goal was to produce the specialists and informed citizenry required to advance the national goals articulated by the authorizing legislation. The strategy to achieve the goal was the long-term funding of Centers. Through the Centers, both graduate and undergraduate, interdisciplinary programs for the study of foreign languages and areas were developed. These Centers attracted the top scholars and became repositories for much of the nation's research and training and through them the institutionalization of "the field." It was only natural that these Centers would train the needed manpower.

I am not sure anyone knows how the initial decisions on the number of Centers for each world area were decided, but in retrospect, it seems that these decisions were reasonable. Institutions of higher education willing to make strong commitments to the development and long-term maintenance of Centers were rewarded with funding. There seemed to be an awareness on the part of these institutions of the national need and the role their institutions could play. A natural symbiosis developed between these Centers and the Department of Education. It was largely through this strategy that the Department was able successfully to begin addressing the questions posed by the legislation.

Summary and prognosis. Looking back on the early national language planning efforts, what stands out is the early recognition of the need to develop a language planning approach different from the current models used at the time relevant for societies with quite dissimilar language problems such as the selection or modification of a national language, the development or revision of writing systems, or problems of widespread literacy. Björn Jernudd suggested that language planning efforts should not continue to be limited to the developing nations, but that language planning should recognize language as a societal resource.

In the late 1960s and early 1970s, there were discussions at the Georgetown University Round Table (GURT) on language resources and the national interest. Monthly meetings of the Interagency Language Roundtable discussed language planning problems faced by the participating agencies and constituted an ad hoc, pan-governmental policy circle.

People like Joshua Fishman, Einar Haugen, Ji í Neustupny, Chaim Rabin, Joan Rubin, Das Gupta, and Björn Jernudd wrote extensively on the subject. Convinced that the national language planning efforts of the United States, as then practiced by the Department of Education, would benefit from a theoretical base, and following the earlier suggestion of Jernudd and embracing Fishman's criticism that practitioners of language planning have not yet turned to language planning research as a guide to their own procedures, I presented a paper at the Conference on Language in American Life entitled "Long-Range Planning and the Future of Language Study in the United States." In this paper I proposed what I called a "human resources-oriented typology." As I look back on this work, I believe the approach was sound. What has, however, proved elusive for the strategy has been the inability to get anyone to provide data on demand or need.

Problems with the Bowen and Sosa *Prospects for Faculty in the Arts and Sciences* (1989) have recently been pointed out in the Chronicle of Higher Education. Subsequent area studies faculty prospects data partly based on the Bowen and Sosa report have related problems. This is only one of the problems disrupting the planning process. Predictions of academic demand rely upon accurate replacement data, which are hard to come by, and upon reliable information about new faculty positions.

The RAND *Foreign Language and International Studies Specialists: The Marketplace and National Policy* study investigated both supply and demand questions. They reached the same conclusion as the earlier GAO *Report*:

> Deciding whether specialist supply and demand is a problem that impinges on national objectives to the point of warranting political intervention is a value question, properly resolved by political processes. It is very difficult to demonstrate that any specific, observed national need for specialists does or does not exist; so many factors go into the attainment or failure of a national objective that it is virtually impossible to point a finger at either the importance or the inconsequentiality of specialists to the outcome. (Berryman et al. 1979:xvii)

The above notwithstanding, prudent allocation of federal monies for programs deemed by the Congress to be important to our national well-being will continue to require thoughtful data collection and planning. The language planning branch of sociolinguistics will continue to play an important, though largely behind-the-scenes role. There have been recent calls for national strategic planning in the less commonly taught languages by organizations external to the field. Congress appropriates monies to the federal agencies and holds them directly accountable for proper administration of the programs. The executive branch must retain *direct* national strategic planning as a tool to achieve their goals. The "field" as represented by the national resource centers and their specialist faculties will continue to perform a critical advisory function in the planning.

Ford Foundation: Personal Reflection

Mel Fox

Melvin J. Fox was a Program Officer with the Ford Foundation from 1951 to 1987. For many of those years he specialized in Language in Development serving in both the New York office as well as in Lagos, Nigeria as the Foundation's Representative for West Africa. As a Foundation staff member concerned with Language education issues, he participated in the conference at the University of Michigan in 1958 which led directly to the founding of the Center for Applied Linguistics on whose Board of Trustees he later served.

I appreciate being invited to participate in this project on the history and development of sociolinguistics. Although I was never a properly initiated, and therefore a legitimate, member of the "Club of academics, government officials, and educational entrepreneurs" (e.g., Trux Russell and Ken Mildenberger) that nurtured the growing academically centered sociolinguistics stream, I considered myself to be a friend of the field. My participation after the Ann Arbor Conference,[1] and more continually (for about fifteen years) after the establishment of the Center for Applied Linguistics (CAL), was entirely reactive and marginal, due to an accident of my location at the Ford Foundation. Though the record may disclose that I played a role in the establishment of both the first stage of CAL (1959–1965) as a part of

---

[1]The Ann Arbor conference was convened at the University of Michigan in 1958. Discussion focused on a range of topics related to the current state of applied linguistics, the potential contributions of (applied) linguistics to education and national development, and the need for a central clearinghouse or organization to coordinate work in this area. The participants recommended the establishment of such a center, and the Center for Applied Linguistics was begun in 1959 with an initial grant from the Ford Foundation. The proceedings of the conference comprise a special issue of *Language Learning*, published in June 1958.

the Modern Language Association, and the second stage as an independent organization, that too was the aftermath of the Ann Arbor Conference engineered by others.

I have always looked upon Charles Ferguson as the godfather of sociolinguistics; he certainly facilitated and encouraged (maybe at times guided) my participation after the founding of CAL in February 1959. Also the Rockefeller Foundation did much more than the Ford Foundation, or any other foundation, to nurture the *early* roots of sociolinguistics.

Subsequently, the Ford Foundation provided substantial support to this developing field by means of grants to support domestic activities such as those of CAL, international activities such as the Survey of Language Use and Language Teaching in East Africa, and support for individual scholars.[2]

Over time, the Ford Foundation's work contributed to a recognition and understanding of the prevalence of language problems in many countries in all parts of the world and at every stage of development. The Foundation came to realize the potentially productive link between its international and its domestic language activities. The role of language came to assume decisive importance in relation to the Foundation's core concerns for improving the human condition, for extending the benefits of modern science and technology, and for responding to the contributions and needs of the excluded and the disadvantaged. I was pleased to have been able to participate—at least vicariously—over the years in this contribution.

---

[2]The Foundation's activities in those early years are described in three reports by Fox: *Language in Education,* a Ford Foundation report, 1975; *Language and Development: A Retrospective Survey of Ford Foundation Language Projects, 1952–1974.* 2 Vols. 1975; and M. J. Fox and M. Abdulaziz, *Evaluation Report on Languages Used and Language Teaching of Eastern Africa.* New York: The Ford Foundation, 1978.

International Centre for Research on Bilingualism: The Sociolinguistics of Language Contact

William Francis Mackey

William Francis Mackey is a Fellow of the Royal Society of Canada and the Royal Academy of Belgium and sometime member of government language commissions in Canada and Europe. He is the founding Director (1967) of the International Centre for Research on Bilingualism, expanded in 1990 as the CIRAL (Centre for Language Management Research) at Laval University where he is currently research professor. He has authored over two hundred articles and two dozen books on language contact, language policy, sociolinguistics, and language education.

It would be difficult for me to pinpoint any one event that marks "the beginning of modern sociolinguistics." Since the day I began studying linguistics at Columbia University in 1943, my interest inevitably drifted to those "peripheral" considerations that pointed to the relations between language and life, like the external history of the language I happened to be analyzing. I admittedly found very little support for my curiosity.

So in 1946, I went on to Harvard where I came in contact with four original thinkers about language. In 1946, I attended a fascinating course by George Kingsley Zipf (of Zipf's Law) on "Language and the Dynamics of Society" in which he launched some of his new ideas, like the speaker-hearer economy later published in his introduction to human ecology (Zipf 1949). Coincidentally, I was studying the anthropological dimensions of language under Clyde Kluckhohn, a disciple of Edward Sapir. I was registered in the department of Comparative Philology under Joshua Whatmough and was exposed to his quasi-Darwinian theory of selective variation in language drift (Whatmough 1956). I maintained contact with him briefly after I left Harvard, but the mentor with whom I maintained the most lasting relationship was the great semanticist, I. A. Richards, whose contextual theory of meaning long remained basic to my thinking (Ogden and Richards 1923).

Not one of these scholars had accepted the restrictive linguistic agenda of the Establishment of the time whereby linguistics was to be confined to what could be rigorously proven—the study of language forms within a structuralist paradigm associated with the names of Bloomfield and Bloch. Although this paradigm was what one was supposed to follow in order to become a trained linguist, the restricted view did not appeal to me, and following the direction of my favorite New England poet, Robert Frost, "I chose the path less trodden by." And I paid the price, as I learned years later while reading a review of one of my books on bilingualism in 1976. The reviewer concluded that my book was not "in the main stream." Although I considered this as a compliment, it was not meant as such.

In the intervening time, I had accepted a post as senior lecturer at the University of London (1948–1951), where I came in contact with people whose view of linguistics was less restrictive. One of these was J. R. Firth (1957) with whom I had the pleasure of sharing a table in the staff dining room. As I got to know him, I also found that I shared with him the Saussurian notion that linguistics was a branch of the yet unfounded science of the study of language in society, and not the other way round.

As I thought about this over the years, it seemed to me that society had to be central to language, since there could be no society without it—and no language without society. And as society changed so did language, even though the rate and direction of changes were seldom taken into account (Mackey 1983b). What had interested me was the social phenomena associated with language contact, language change, with the life and death of languages. It seemed evident to me that one could not explain such phenomena simply by looking at linguistic structure. Even linguists working within the structuralist paradigm had to go beyond it to describe situations of language contact. It was with such linguists that I associated when I returned home.

A unique opportunity was provided in 1965 when UNESCO commissioned me to organize an international symposium on bilingualism to be held on the occasion of the Canadian Centennial (1967). Given a free hand and a generous budget, I was able to convene an international organizing committee composed of Einar Haugen, Werner Leopold, Wallace Lambert, Joshua Fishman, and Uriel Weinreich whom I had met a year earlier at UCLA where I was LSA visiting professor. (Sadly he could not attend our symposium because of an illness which was soon to claim his life.) On the suggestion of this committee the symposium was to be a small, closed, week-long affair devoted exclusively to the problems of the description and measurement of bilingualism. Ten papers were to be commissioned on the state-of-research on the linguistic, social, psychological, demographic, political, and educational aspects of bilingualism, its description and measurement. These papers, along with ten commissioned comments were preprinted and distributed six months before the meeting. This carefully prepared and well-focused symposium treated questions which seem as valid today as they were at the time. It was the joint work of leading people from different disciplines, different countries, and different perspectives. The proceedings, edited by my then student, Louis Kelly, appeared two years later from the University of Toronto Press (Kelly 1969). They were to become a blueprint for what was to follow.

The context within which such academic meetings had been commissioned included a popular interest in bilingualism, minority language rights and the spectre of separatism. In Quebec, activities of the National Liberation Front were causing concern nation wide. The reaction of the federal government was to create a Royal Commission of enquiry into the language question, particularly as it affected French-English relations. The commission launched a multimillion dollar research program into every aspect of the problem—social, economic, educational, political, cultural, and linguistic. One of the first surprises was the discovery that although these language problems had long been of paramount national importance, there was not a single department in any university where such questions were a subject of study, since departments being discipline oriented did not consider such questions to be central to any field of knowledge. They were of interest only insofar as they helped explain certain phenomena like language change, political conflict, educational backwardness, and the like.

When this was pointed out to the academic community, the Canadian Association of Universities, through its executive, decided that there should be some place in the country where one could document and study the phenomenon of collective and individual bilingualism. The obvious place it seemed would be in French Canada where language questions were felt as being most important. One of the four universities in Montreal would be appropriate. But which one? In the context of intense interethnic conflict prevailing at the time, this was no easy decision. Perhaps partly for political reasons, the more peaceful atmosphere of Quebec City was preferred (Mackey 1978). Accordingly, the authorities of Laval University were approached. Their acceptance was, of course, contingent on the possibility of obtaining adequate funding. This funding would have to come from private sources, since it would have been politically unfeasible for any government to favor one university over another. Because at the time I was the only one at Laval University engaged in research on bilingualism, I was recruited to prepare a series of proposals for the creation of a center for the academic study of bilingualism and its occurrence under various conditions in different regions of the world, particularly in Canada. It was to be an interdisciplinary center with an international outlook. After several proposals, budgets, and site visits, the university received word a few days before the end of the year that the Ford Foundation had set aside a fund of half a million dollars to provide seed money for the founding of a center. Accordingly, at its first meeting of the year (January 1968), the University Senate created the International Center for Research on Bilingualism; the CIRB (Centre International de Recherche sur le Bilinguisme) appointed me as its first director.

My first action was to create an international advisory board composed of the very people who were so successful in organizing the international symposium the year before. Stressing the primacy of documentation in this as yet unstructured field, the policies they recommended enabled us to gather the largest multilingual collection on bilingualism and related questions (Mackey 1982). Because of this, I was able to attract to our center scholars like Heinz Kloss from Germany and his research associate Albert Verdoodt from Belgium, and for shorter periods specialists from Finland, Switzerland, Czechoslovakia, England, France, the Soviet Union, Spain, Greece, China, and a number of other countries in Africa and Latin America (e.g., Savard and Vigneault 1975). After my term of office expired in 1971, I stayed on as research professor.

My immediate successor, the eminent geographer Henri Dorion, gave a new impetus to the center by launching an ambitious publications program. Likewise, each succeeding director, Jean-Guy Savard, Lorne Laforge, and Jean-Denis Gendron (of the Gendron Language Commission) left his individual imprint. After a generation of research, documentation, and publication (some 250 titles), we noticed that the sociolinguistic climate which had made possible the creation of our center was rapidly changing, along with the corresponding programs of research support. If the center were to survive, it could no longer do so as a freestanding (nonfaculty) institution. It was therefore reorganized within the faculty of letters which brought in a number of its successful research groups in language planning, language, didactics, and terminology. It was renamed in 1990 as an international center for language management research, the CIRAL (Centre International de Recherche en Aménagement Linguistique) under the directorship of the current professor of sociolinguistics, Denise Deshaies. The ongoing ICRB research programs were maintained, particularly those launched by Heinz Kloss (The Written Languages of the World and the Linguistic Composition of the Nations of the World) and continued by his long-time co-editor (and former student of mine), Grant McConnell. I have remained an associate and supporter of this important research program since it is supplying indispensable data for large-scale sociolinguistic research like the measurement of such dimensions as language vitality (Laforge and Mc Connell 1990; McConnell 1991). These macro- sociolinguistic studies have been complemented by the micro-sociolinguistic studies of the new team (McConnell and Gendron 1993).

As for myself, I became involved in such studies only indirectly since my main focus had been on problems related to language contact. Yet as I look back on my list of publications dating from 1943 to 1993 (some two hundred articles and two dozen books) I estimate that half of them contain a social, if not sociolinguistic component (e.g., Mackey and Ornstein 1979). Yet it was only after I was assigned the task of preparing the state-of-the-art report for the plenary session on sociolinguistics of the XIII International Congress of Linguists that I was obliged to take a wide look at the entire field. The experience was enlightening for I found that within the short period of a decade what was called sociolinguistics had evolved from a collection of loosely connected language studies with social components into an expanding theory-directed discipline (Mackey 1983a). I also found that in some parts of the world the field had been co-opted by movements of political activism rampant in the sixties. One could practice, for example, a neo-Marxist sociolinguistics.[1]

What was confusing about this development—and at times disconcerting—was the political appropriation of sociolinguistic terminology. Political activists were putting their own spin on terms like *diglossia* (a type of social repression through language dominance) and *polynomic* language in the context of sociolinguistic irredentism. This to me was unfortunate since I had long insisted on the creation of a standard terminology.

The need became evident early on, when I was faced with the task of tagging a half dozen descriptors to each of our 20,000 titles so that these could form part of a usable data bank. Since terms evolve over time, it was also important to index and date some of the most frequently used ones. A good example is the term *diglossia* for which I attempted by way of example a chronological typology (Mackey 1989a). So that, when I was asked to do a piece on terminology for a review on sociolinguistics, I welcomed the opportunity to dig deeper into the jungle. On preparing the article, I found that each school of thought seemed to have its own "theoretical metalect" composed not so much of new or special terms but mostly of the meanings it gave to usual ones (Mackey 1990). Or there would be a refusal to adopt a term on ideological grounds and a new one would be invented. For example, one

---

[1] For another interpretation, see Andrée Tabouret-Keller, this volume.

author writing within the framework of Hegelian ideology would formally reject the term *diglossia* and invent a new term like colingualism (Mackey 1989b). The new term was seen as a more fitting label for situations where two or more standardized written languages divide up the functions of literary language. In other contexts, this situation had been called (since 1970) *literary diglossia* (Mackey 1993).

In summary, I still believe that to understand the varied and increasingly multilingual literature on sociolinguistics today, one would need an international thesaurus of ideas and corresponding terms. Hopefully, the coming generation of sociolinguists will find the means and motivation to tackle this important task.

Summer Institute of Linguistics: What Does SIL Have to do with Sociolinguistics?

Gloria E. Kindell

Gloria Kindell has been a member of the Summer Institute of Linguistics since 1956. She worked in Brazil in the areas of linguistics, literacy, bilingual education, and curriculum development, and is currently an international sociolinguistics consultant.

The purpose of the Summer Institute of Linguistics (SIL) is to serve the ethnic communities of the world in meeting their deepest needs through seeking to assist them in all areas of language development.

In 1935 SIL began working with a few minority languages of Mexico. Since that time the work has expanded to over 1,400 languages in more than fifty countries. Historically, our field work has focused on language and culture learning, linguistic analysis, and language development in the areas of orthography design, literacy and bilingual education programs, as well as the production of pedagogical materials and literature, including portions of the Bible. SIL members serve in partnership with ethnolinguistic groups to assist them in developing physical resources and personnel in order to achieve community goals relating to areas of expertise of the organization. Our primary, but not exclusive, interests in the field of sociolinguistics are language survey and language development.

Historical perspective. In the early years SIL field linguists worked primarily with fairly isolated, rural, monolingual speech communities. Most of them concentrated on addressing practical sociolinguistic matters. A few also contributed several academic publications in the field. For example, Kenneth Pike described topics in the ethnography of communication such as tone puns in Mixteco (Pike 1945b, 1946) and the mock Spanish of a Mixteco Indian, demonstrating "(1) the prestige of bilingualism in a monolingual community, (2) cultural pressure toward the assimilation of loan words, (3) phonetic, tonal, dialectal, and grammatical interference with a person attempting to speak a foreign language, (4) humor based upon linguistic phases of cultural pressures, (5) deliberate linguistic modification as the mechanical device to express this humor" (Pike 1945a:224). His *Language in Relation to a Unified Theory of the Structure of Human Behavior* (Pike 1954) clearly describes language as a societal phenomenon. Later he dealt with topics such as language and dialect spread and change (Pike 1960) and conditions and steps for successfully stimulating change (Pike 1961).

Richard Pittman first published the *Ethnologue* in 1951, providing linguistic, sociolinguistic, and demographic information on the languages of the world (see Grimes, this volume). It seems that Marvin Mayers' study of the Pocomchí of Central America (1960) was the earliest Ph.D. dissertation in the field of sociolinguistics to be produced by an SIL member.

Beginning in the early 1960s SIL began to recognize the need for more sophisticated language survey techniques. Gene Casad's book (1974) on recorded text tests for measuring inherent intelligibility among related dialects is based on that research (see Grimes, this volume). In the 1970s SIL began to examine reasons for uneven results in its language programs: ongoing use of literature in the indigenous language is not always achieved. Wayne Dye's research (1979) and encouragement to identify the factors making for or hindering successful programs, together with the increasing number of complex multilingual societies in the world, significantly changed the techniques used in our language surveys to determine needs for language development and the shape our language programs would take. As a result of this new focus, sociolinguistic courses were introduced in the SIL pre-field training package, SIL members went into advanced study programs in sociolinguistics, and SIL both participated in and acted as sponsors of sociolinguistic conferences.

Training in sociolinguistics. Recognizing the need for expertise in sociolinguistics, SIL has encouraged graduate study programs in the field. To date fourteen of its members have earned advanced degrees in sociolinguistics per se, most of us from Georgetown University, others from the École des Hautes Études en Sciences Sociales, Paris, University of Pennsylvania, University of Reading, England, University of Texas at Austin, University of Western Australia, and University of Yaoundé, Cameroon. Many others have

Summer Institute of Linguistics 281

earned degrees in related fields such as applied linguistics, with an emphasis on sociolinguistics. We deeply appreciate the help and encouragement of our professors, advisors, and mentors. They respected our field experience and encouraged us to specialize in areas that would contribute to the work of SIL.

Since 1977 SIL has included sociolinguistics in its pre-field training package. A variety of different courses are offered in Australia, Canada, Great Britain, Germany, Singapore, and the USA. Currently the foci of these include: an introduction to language in social context, with special focus on language use and how different sociolinguistic contexts affect it; sociolinguistic research in language use in multilingual societies; and the practical application of sociolinguistic principles to language development programs.

Conferences. SIL has organized, participated in, and acted as sponsors of several conferences and workshops emphasizing sociolinguistic topics, including:

1967 Conference on Language Survey. Cuernavaca, Mexico (Casad 1974).

1976 Workshop on Language Variation and Survey Techniques. Ukarumpa, Papua New Guinea (Loving and Simons 1977).

1977 Language Survey Issues. Mexico City.

1981 Sociolinguistics Survey Conference, hosted by Charles Ferguson, Shirley Brice Heath, and John Rickford. Stanford University (Huttar 1982).

1983 Assessment meeting.

1984 Sociolinguistic Survey Meetings, Asia Area SIL. Manila, Philippines.

1987 Asia Area Conference of SIL on Survey Data Collecting and Interpreting. Baguio City, Philippines (Casad 1992).

1987 Stanford Conference on Vernacular Literacy, hosted by Shirley Brice Heath and Charles Ferguson (Shell 1988).

1987 Workshop to adapt the FSI oral interview test for preliterate language situations, with Thea Bruhn of the FSI as consultant. Dakar, Senegal (SIL 1987).

1988 Round Table on Assuring the Feasibility of Standardization within Dialect Chains. Nairobi, Kenya (Bergman 1989).

1989 International Language Assessment Conference, with the participation of John W. Oller, Jr. Horsleys Green, England (Kindell 1991).

1990 Strategic Planning and Review (SPAR) Conference. Horsleys Green, England.

1993 International Language Assessment Conference 93. Horsleys Green, England.

1997 International Language Assessment Conference 97. Horsleys Green, England.

We are indebted to several scholars outside of SIL who have made substantial contributions to our conferences and to the J. Howard Pew Freedom Trust for funding conferences and publications.

Publications. Currently the *Bibliography of the Summer Institute of Linguistics* (1992) lists some 800 academic works in the general field of sociolinguistics. Broken down into more specific areas these are, approximately: Creole studies, 40; dialect studies, 40; ethnolinguistics, 95; language surveys, 80; languages in contact, 40; language policy, 55; literacy and bilingual education, 150; orthography, 150; and sociolinguistics in general, 150. The *Bibliography* also lists 12,200 minority language titles and 250 dictionaries and vocabularies, each representing some degree of SIL members' involvement in language development.

Language survey. SIL's language survey activities currently include establishing lexical similarity between languages and dialects, conducting comprehension testing, assessing second language proficiency, describing contact situations, describing patterns of language use and attitudes, assessing ethnolinguistic vitality, and assessing the potential for standardization and/or computer assisted related language adaptation (Buseman 1991; Weber et al. 1988, 1990). Currently we have survey teams in ten countries in Africa, Eurasia, South Asia, Thailand, and Papua New Guinea.

Several SIL members have recently applied sociolinguistic concepts to the development or extension of language survey tools and techniques. General works include Ted Bergman's compilation of selected survey articles to form a survey handbook (1989, 1990), Frank Blair's introductory manual for small-scale language surveys (1990), and Catherine Showalter's annotated sociolinguistic questionnaire (1991). John Wimbish (1989) has developed a computer program, WORDSURV, for systematic lexical comparison of dialects.

In the area of assessing second language proficiency, SIL personnel have developed the Second Language Oral Proficiency Evaluation (SIL 1987; see Grimes, this volume), and the Sentence Repetition Test and Reported Proficiency Evaluation (Radloff 1991). Others have modified and used Casad's Recorded Text Test (1974) and a variety of self-report questionnaires.

Of SIL's many contributions to the field of language use and attitudes research, three have generated considerable interest. First, Steve Quakenbush (1986), during his twelve-month Agutaynen sociolinguistic survey in the Philippines, observed language proficiency and use, then interviewed over 200 people, using an integrated questionnaire on attitudes, use, and proficiency which he had developed. The proficiency section of the interview consisted of yes-no "Can you...?" questions involving specific language skills associated with FSI levels of proficiency. Second, as part of a survey of four related dialects of southwest Burkina Faso, Stuart Showalter (1991) devised a language attitudes questionnaire modeled on a matched-guise approach, including questions about shared ethnic identity, interethnic contact, awareness of neighboring language and dialects, and judgments of the personal character of speakers of those varieties. Third, Stephen Schooling (1990) applied social network theory to the problems of language maintenance and shift in Melanesia. He used the network concept to construct a typology of bilingualism, and suggests the theory as a potential universal tool for predicting language maintenance.

Of SIL survey reports there is no end, but one of the more recent is a five-volume report of a sociolinguistic survey of northern Pakistan, edited by Clare O'Leary: Volume 1, *Languages of Kohistan* (Rensch, Decker, and Hallberg 1992); Volume 2, *Languages of Northern Areas* (Backstrom and Radloff 1992); Volume 3, *Hindko and Gujari* (Rensch, Hallberg, and O'Leary 1992); Volume 4, *Pashto, Waneci, Ormuri* (Hallberg 1992); and Volume 5, *Languages of Chitral* (Decker 1992).

Language development. In cooperation with host country entities and local communities, SIL engages in language development efforts suited to specific situations. To facilitate the practical application of theory to language development programs, SIL has developed *A Manual for Strategic Planning and Review for Language Programs* (Bendor-Samuel and Bendor-Samuel 1996). This SPAR manual is used by field administrators, consultants, and language program teams to continually assess the sociolinguistic environment in which each program develops, and determine suitable approaches to development tasks. An in-house manual for strategic planning on the entity level is used for an overall language program strategy for field entities. Landweer (1991) describes a prioritizing device for initiating language programs in Papua New

Guinea. Prettol (1992) has developed an expert system for language planning decisions.

Several SIL members have investigated sociolinguistic factors influencing language development programs. These five are representative: Clinton Robinson (1992) presents three case studies (from India, Tanzania, and Cameroon), in his discussion of language choice in rural development. Roland Walker (1987) has developed a model for explaining and predicting the acceptance of vernacular literacy, based on quantitative data from a language use and attitudes questionnaire he developed. Marilyn Henne's research among the Quiché (1985) identified such factors as a negative cultural-linguistic self-image, lack of a historical domain for written Quiché, and loyalty to the local dialect rather than to the language as a whole. Henne (1991) lists twenty-four diagnostic categories in her comparative analysis of language development programs in three of Guatemala's language groups. On the basis of eight sociolinguistic factors, Doris Porter (1991) identified five types of language-culture groups in the Philippines, with implications for language survey and language development program planning. From his experience in Cameroon, John Watters (1991) identified three socioeconomic factors which deserve special attention: the homogeneity of the linguistic community, the openness of the community to change and to better living conditions, and the presence at the local level of a middle-aged leadership.

Recently SIL has begun to see the potential of nonprint media for effective communication in language development programs (Malmstrom 1991) and currently offers training in audio and audiovisual techniques.

Future directions. The sociolinguistics staff in Dallas is currently working on an electronic field manual for language survey and development which consists of information and tutorial modules, a decision-making expert system, annotated bibliography, and a glossary of terms. This is part of a larger project, including linguistics, anthropology, language learning, and translation, which SIL expects to distribute on CD ROM in 1995.

The Ethnologue, Language Surveys, and Sociolinguistics

Barbara F. Grimes

Barbara Fornasero Grimes has been a member of the Summer Institute of Linguistics since 1951. She has worked on *Ethnologue: Languages of the World* since 1953, and has been Editor since 1971. She was involved in applied linguistic field work in the Huichol (Uto-Aztecan) language of Mexico from 1952–1967 and 1979–1980, and in the Hawaii Creole English language from 1986 to the present.

Introduction

Investigations by members of the Summer Institute of Linguistics (SIL) in sociolinguistics have usually been project driven. That means we have sometimes struggled with issues in the field before others, and at other times we have profited from the work of others.

Our work has been synthesized in successive editions of the Ethnologue, which is perhaps the broadest contribution by SIL to the field of sociolinguistics. Some linguists, who would like the Ethnologue to list only what they consider "languages" from a structural viewpoint, have been unhappy with our including languages which they consider to be only dialects, nonstandard languages, creole languages, deaf sign languages, and language varieties which need to be considered separate because of the language attitudes of their speakers. Dialogue on these issues, as well as problems arising from language surveys, have led to many of our insights in the field of sociolinguistics. The same dialogue in turn has stimulated some investigators to apply similar criteria to their data in these areas.

Richard S. Pittman started the Ethnologue in 1951 as a focal point within SIL for tracking certain kinds of linguistic, demographic, and sociolinguistic information about the languages of the world (Pittman 1951–1969). Before that, Meillet (1924, 1952) had described a few hundred languages, and *The Book Of a Thousand Tongues* (North 1945, Nida 1972) listed languages which had printed Bibles or Bible portions. Later language lists were given by Voegelin and Voegelin (1964–1966, 1977), Katzner (1975), and Ruhlen (1975, 1987). Since the seventies the Ethnologue has provided information for a growing audience. The editors have had interaction with specialists in many geographic areas and language families, and with the editors of the *Oxford International Encyclopedia of Linguistics* (Bright 1992) and the *Comparative Austronesian Dictionary* (Tryon and Ross 1995).

A National Science Foundation grant to Joseph Grimes in 1963 for producing concordances of natural language text by computer made it possible to put the Ethnologue data into data base format in 1971. *Word Lists and Languages* (J. Grimes 1974) included a subset of the information from the 1974 Ethnologue. The data structure was expanded to include language header records, using the GIPSY information system at Oklahoma University, and assisted by people at the Oil Information Center at Oklahoma University. This computerization expanded the Ethnologue coverage during the 1970s. Joseph Greenberg's group investigating language universals at Stanford University also looked at this GIPSY implementation as a way of organizing their data.

The data base was moved to Cornell University in 1976, in cooperation with people in the Chemistry Department and at the New York State College of Veterinary Medicine. The data base was transferred to a personal computer beginning in 1979. In 1988 Shoebox, developed by John Wimbish of the Summer Institute of Linguistics, was adopted as an editorial tool for the data base, with limited distribution in machine readable form. The Ethnologue data have been available through Internet since about 1991 through David Stampe of the University of Hawaii. An electronic Ethnologue for PCs is currently being prepared by the Summer Institute of Linguistics and Global Mapping International.

Language versus dialect

Because Pittman and others in SIL were engaged in research on minority languages, and producing literature for their speakers, they were interested in the ability of people to communicate. They considered a language to be a cluster of one or more dialects, whose speakers can understand each other without necessarily having had previous contact, because of the linguistic similarity of the dialects. The idea of inherent intelligibility as a useful criterion identifying dialects of a single language, and separating one language from another, grew up within the framework of American descriptive linguistics (Voegelin and Voegelin 1977:4, 357).

When Kenneth L. Pike and others began studying minority languages of Mexico in 1935, they were told there were fifty-two "languages" in that country. Pike began with Mixteco, and others studied other languages. They became aware that many of the so-called "languages" had regional varieties whose speakers could not understand each other. Linguists and others had been influenced by traditional names, in many cases imposed administratively by the Aztec Empire, in labeling what they considered to be a "language."

Dialect intelligibility

Testing methods. Turner of the Summer Institute of Linguistics participated in the first filed work that tested related language intelligibility directly (Hickerson, Turner, and Hickerson 1952), based on the suggestions of Voegelin and Harris (1951). By the early 1960s, John Crawford of SIL began working with other SIL field linguists to make language surveys include systematic testing for inherent intelligibility. He built on the earlier work mentioned above, as well as that of Biggs (1957), Pierce (1952, 1954), and discussions by Wolff (1964, 1967). This empirical work resulted in refinements to the Voegelin-Harris paradigm, concurrent with Sankoff's field experience with Buang (1969). The resulting procedures involve playing a recorded personal narrative text sample from one language variety for a sample of speakers of a related variety, and testing their understanding with content probes about the text. The methods have been field tested in most of the large dialect groupings in Mexico, as well as in other countries, and further refined over a period of many years. Some of the results were described by Bradley (1968), Kirk (1966, 1970), Stolzfus (1974), and Egland (1978). The method was described in detail by Casad (1974) and J. Grimes (1988b).

Centers of communication. The data from the intelligibility testing produced evidence of dialect continua. The investigators then struggled with the same question other linguists have also faced: Can we talk about separate languages in a direct continuum or dialect chain situation? In response, J. Grimes (1974) applied operations research logic to find optimum centers of communication, showing that all dialects in a continuum can be adequately covered up to a threshold level from an optimal subset of those dialects in producing literature or planning education programs.

Lexical similarity and intelligibility. Simons (1979) compared the results of ten major surveys in which linguists had investigated both dialect intelligibility and lexical similarity, in an attempt to find a predictable relationship. The results, however, showed that lexical similarity can be used with confidence only for determining lack of intelligibility, not for predicting intelligibility (B. Grimes 1988a, J. Grimes 1988a). The lexicon is only one of the linguistic factors that affect understanding. Grammatical and discourse differences do not show up in vocabulary lists, but can have major influences on intelligibility. This coincided with a general disillusionment on the part of linguists with the accuracy and utility of groupings based on lexicostatistics.

Structure and intelligibility. F. B. Agard preferred a structural way to distinguish languages over a sociolinguistic criterion. He investigated the kinds of phonological change that took place in Romance during dialect divergence, and found that certain kinds of changes point to distinct languages (1975, 1984). M. Milliken (1988) compared the results of intelligibility testing with the kinds of phonological change distinguished by Agard, for certain Scots and American English varieties, and later for Zhuang varieties (Milliken and Milliken Mainstream Sociolinguistics), and found significant agreement.

Intelligibility threshold between language and dialect. In the earlier intelligibility surveys, the investigators in Mexico had begun with the supposition that a mean intelligibility test result of 70% or higher between language varieties indicated that the two are dialects of the same language. Kirk (1970), however, was told by Mazatec speakers that certain Mazatec varieties were easy to understand, and others were difficult. He compared their perceptions with the results of intelligibility testing, and found the marginal area to be between 75% and 90% intelligibility (Casad 1974:83–85).

Now, with over thirty years of comparing the results of testing with field experience, the consensus of investigators is that Kirk's findings among the Mazatec may be on the low side: 85% to 90% intelligibility or below between language varieties indicates they function as separate languages. Speakers of varieties with 85% to 90% intelligibility or higher tend to have functional access to the other variety, including access to complex and abstract discourse (Eugene Casad, personal communication, J. Grimes 1988b).

Voegelin and Voegelin (1977:357), in discussing Zapotec of Mexico say, "Longacre...lists seven different languages, among some of which (according to de Angulo and Freeland 1933) there exists mutual intelligibility, and hence different dialects rather than different languages." In the dialogue on approaches to dialect continua, this represents a quite different starting point: any degree of intelligibility is assumed to indicate dialect of a single "language." But in preparing literature and educational materials, it has proved more important to consider the levels of intelligibility that enable speakers to have functional access to another variety, or hinder them from doing so.

"Mutual" intelligibility. Because of morphophonemics and other factors, inherent intelligibility between two varieties is rarely equal in the two directions. Voegelin and Harris (1951) hoped that intelligibility testing would approximate a measure of linguistic similarity and distance, so they averaged the scores, and called it "mutual intelligibility."

The term "mutual intelligibility," however, has led to misunderstandings in at least two ways: (1) Averaging test result differences hides important information from the investigator who wants to know about actual understanding, giving the impression that the intelligibility in one direction is higher and in the other lower than it really is. (2) Simons (1979:34–35) points out that if "mutual" understanding were required in both directions, speakers on Santa Isabel in the Solomon Islands would need literature in seven language varieties, whereas if functional understanding is required in only one direction, literature in three varieties is adequate. For these reasons, many of us prefer the term inherent intelligibility.

Bilingual overlay. It was assumed in Mexico that few American Indian language speakers were bilingual in other minority languages, but that bilingualism was almost entirely in Spanish. Where this was true, samples as small as ten speakers were adequate to test the inherent intelligibility of other indigenous varieties for an entire group.

When investigators in the Philippines, Africa, and elsewhere used the same sampling procedures, however, it turned out that the mean scores were often inflated, because there was so much bilingual learning of related varieties. This kind of bilingual overlay (B. Grimes 1986a, 1987) on top of inherent intelligibility can take place among speakers in a region close to the other dialect area, or among persons with more outside contact than other speakers. It proved necessary to screen out individuals who have had such contact from the population sample being tested, because they are incapable of representing true inherent intelligibility. Now we realize that some of this kind of mixed intelligibility and bilingualism is present in Mexico, too.

G. Sankoff (1969:839–40) used the term incipient bilingualism for bilingualism in a related variety that does not include a great deal of learning, but does require some. However, bilingual overlays occur in related varieties which have any degree of inherent intelligibility, and where the speakers may differ widely in the amount of learning they have done.

Language bending. Jim Ellis of SIL describes how people in Micronesia modify their speech in the direction of a related language in order to communicate with speakers of that language (ms.). They call it language bending. William Moulton described the same kind of phenomenon for Swiss German varieties (ms.); and Leonard Newell has mentioned it taking place among Ifugao speakers in the Philippines (personal communication). Although these situations could impress the casual observer as cases of dialect intelligibility, they are actually a form of behavior based on some learning of the other variety through contact, which is rarely equally accessible to all members of a speech community.

Bilingualism

In 1977 a conference was organized in Mexico City by Karl Franklin of SIL to discuss language survey issues. It was recognized that we knew how to compare the phonological systems of languages and to test dialect intelligibility, but did not know very much about evaluating the bilingual proficiency of entire populations or relating these phenomena to language attitudes.

Levels of bilingual proficiency. From the time I began working on the *Ethnologue* in 1954 (B. Grimes 1974–1992), I received occasional reports that speakers of certain languages were "50% bilingual" or "100% bilingual," without saying how good they actually were at performing. It occurred to me in 1981 that the proficiency levels used by the United States Department of State Foreign Service Institute (FSI) offered a possible model for describing speakers of a language in terms of their distributions at different bilingual proficiency levels, to give a more accurate global picture of a bilingual situation. I presented this idea at a survey conference in 1981, organized by George Huttar of SIL, at Stanford University, with Charles Ferguson, Shirley Brice Heath, and John Rickford as consultants (B. Grimes 1985a). At first I encouraged field linguists to make such estimates for the languages with which they were familiar, based on their field experience (B. Grimes 1984).

Oral interview testing. In a course on language surveys (taught at SIL at the University of Oklahoma from 1984 to 1987, and at SIL at the University of Texas at Arlington from 1988 to 1992 by Joseph Grimes and myself), I attempted to adapt the earlier FSI oral interview techniques (Adams and Frith 1979) to minority language situations, so that with representative sampling, distributions of bilingual speakers' proficiency levels could be given for languages where no linguist yet had extensive experience (B. Grimes 1986a).

In 1987 the Pew Foundation sponsored a workshop in Dakar, Senegal, organized by Ted Bergman of SIL. Thea Bruhn, Head of Testing for FSI, guided us in adapting the current FSI oral interview test for preliterate minority language situations, where the investigator may not be fluent in the languages involved in the test. The procedure is called the Second Language Oral Proficiency Evaluation, or SLOPE (SIL 1987; B. Grimes 1987, 1992; Bruhn 1989; Blair 1990:67–70).

The main modification of the FSI test for SLOPE involves adding a bilingual First Language Assistant to the testing team who has the same mother tongue as the person being tested. The Assistant explains the procedures to the Subject in their mother tongue, thus avoiding the use of written materials. He also conveys to the testing team what the Subject has understood during the portion of the test that focuses on comprehension.

Sentence repetition test. About 1986 an SIL survey team in South Asia began developing a sentence repetition test (SRT) for testing bilingual proficiency under Carla Radloff (1991). It is based on the observation that although people can mimic short utterances they may not understand, they are unable to mimic longer, more complex utterances unless they understand them.

Testing methods compared. The SLOPE and SRT methods were compared in 1991 in Cameroon by SIL investigators, with assistance from Thea Bruhn of FSI, Carla Radloff, and Barrie Wetherill, a statistician from the University of Newcastle upon Tyne. They found that SRT can be useful to distinguish FSI levels 1 to 2+, but is unable to distinguish levels 3 and higher reliably (Hatfield et al. ms., Wetherill and South ms., J. Grimes in press).

Language attitudes

SIL investigators in Colombia found inherent intelligibility among dialects, or lack of it, to be as important there as it is in Mexico and elsewhere.

However, in the Vaupés River area of Colombia and Brazil, cultural values and attitudes of speakers of Eastern Tucanoan languages had to be taken into account, in addition to information about inherent intelligibility, in making decisions about where separate literature and educational materials were needed (B. Grimes 1985b). In order to preserve lineage through their system of exogamy, people cannot marry within their own language group (Jackson ms., Sorenson 1987). However, one spouse must not speak the other's language, although she or he understands it. Each speaks his or her own language to the other. Children learn the language of both parents, but identify with the father's language.

In a few cases, two language varieties which are inherently intelligible to each other's speakers are treated socially as separate languages, so that people from the two groups can intermarry. In other cases, speakers of distinct languages still cannot marry due to other cultural factors. It is important that these cultural distinctions be reflected in decisions regarding which languages literature and educational programs should use.

Soon after SIL began to work in Africa around 1962 it became evident that language attitudes needed to be investigated before making decisions about where separate literature was needed. In some situations ethnic attitudes are so strong that although speakers of one language variety may understand another, either through inherent intelligibility or bilingualism, they will not accept literature or educational materials in the other language. In cases like those in the Vaupés and Africa, the Ethnologue treats the language varieties as separate languages because that is the way they function in society.

Nonstandard language varieties

In Sabah, Malaysia, many minority language speakers are said to be becoming bilingual in something called "Malay," and it is sometimes assumed that they do not need written materials in their vernaculars because children are learning Standard Malay in School. However, the variety of Malay used in everyday life is Sabah Malay, not Standard Malay, the national language. The use of the term "Malay" obscures the difference between the two varieties. Field linguists report that Sabah Malay is closer to Indonesian than to Standard Malay. J. Echols of Cornell University estimated (personal communication) that Indonesian and Bahasa Malaysia have about 81% lexical similarity.

Similarly, C. Grimes (ms.) and B. D. Grimes (ms.) describe significant differences between Ambonese Malay and Indonesian, which have about 81% lexical similarity; yet many people consider Ambonese Malay to be a dialect of Indonesian.

In my work on the *Ethnologue*, I became aware of this and similar situations with Irianese Malay and Indonesian, and within Javanese, Ilocano, Nepali, Portuguese, Spanish, German, Italian, Rumanian, Arabic, and Chinese, among others (B. F. Grimes 1986b), where language varieties without any official status are considered to be "dialects" of a major language, even though they are different enough that their speakers have to learn the standard variety as a second language.

It is difficult for mother tongue speakers of a nonstandard variety to learn the standard variety if the two are very different. But it is even more difficult for second language speakers of a nonstandard variety to speak or use written materials in the standard variety if they are significantly different, and still more difficult for speakers of minority languages whose second language proficiency in the nonstandard variety is limited. These four different groups, with respect to mother tongue versus second language speakers of both standard and nonstandard varieties, are often not distinguished from each other when outsiders are making decisions about literature and education.

The nonstandard varieties are often treated as though they were the "low" variety in a diglossic kind of situation, even though their speakers may have varying degrees of proficiency in the standard or "high" variety, including no proficiency. The nonstandard varieties are often stigmatized by users of the standard variety, and it is assumed that they are not real languages.

Nonstandard languages also include many Jewish and Gypsy languages, which have been listed in the *Ethnologue* since 1974 (B. F. Grimes 1992:927).

Creoles

Creole languages are usually treated by the dominant language users in much the same way as nonstandard varieties, and tend to be even more stigmatized (B. F. Grimes 1989, ms.). For comparing creoles based on the same acrolect, or for testing intelligibility among creoles with a postcreole continuum, it became evident to me that the language samples need to be from the basilect, for two reasons: (1) It is likely that speakers of the basilect have less access to the standard language than speakers who can use the mesolect, so any written materials should probably be in the basilect. (2) Mesolectal speech is closer to the acrolect than basilectal speech is. Therefore, the mesolects of related creoles are closer to each other than the corresponding basilects of those creoles, and a more easily understandable to the speakers. Investigators can get a distorted idea of the closeness of creoles if they compare or test the mesolects.

Because creoles ordinarily have significant grammar differences from their acrolect and from other creoles with the same acrolect, it is even less useful to compare lexical similarity among creoles and their acrolect and try to find out about inherent intelligibility than it is with natural languages.

Since SIL began work in Papua New Guinea in 1958 and Suriname in 1968 we have been interacting with scholars in creole linguistics. George Huttar coordinated an SIL survey of Caribbean creoles in 1981, after I submitted a report on creole languages of the area in 1977. John Sandefur (1984) and others have been active in promoting the Kriol language of Australia, Pijin of the Solomon Islands, and Sea Islands Creole of the United States.

Creole languages have been listed in the *Ethnologue* since 1969 (B. F. Grimes, 1992:927–28).

Deaf sign languages

James Kakumasu of SIL was one of the earliest linguists to describe a deaf sign language in linguistic terms (1968). SIL investigators have completed a survey of sign language varieties in Mexico. They confirm what had been previously reported, that, with a couple of exceptions, there do not appear to be significant differences throughout the country (Faurot et al. ms.). Similar surveys are contemplated for other countries.

Since 1988 deaf sign languages have been listed in the *Ethnologue* (B. F. Grimes, 1992:928–29). It may provide a more complete listing than is available elsewhere.

Language endangerment

SIL investigators have been investigating and describing minority languages for sixty years. Many of these have fewer speakers than the median size for languages in the world (5,200), and many are considered to be endangered. The *Ethnologue* has always given special attention to documenting those languages, as well as the others. J. Grimes and I have been in contact with Michael Krauss and other linguists concerned about the possible demise of such languages. J. Grimes (1986 ms.) has been studying the relationship of language size to language endangerment, based on the population estimates that are available for 85% of the languages in the *Ethnologue*. We attempt in the *Ethnologue* to document other kinds of information that are relevant to language demise or survival, in addition to language size.

Remembrances

In Memoriam: Einar Haugen

Christina Bratt Paulston

Christina Bratt Paulston is professor of linguistics, director of the English Language Institute, and former chair (1974–1989) of the Department of Linguistics, University of Pittsburgh. She has lectured and done fieldwork around the world in such places as Azerbaijan, India, Peru, Tanzania, and Spain, among others. She has published in the fields of language teaching, teacher training, language planning, bilingual education, and sociolinguistics. She was President of International TESOL in 1976 and trustee of the Center for Applied Linguistics from 1976 to 1981.

Einar Haugen's "Dialect, Language, Nation" is standard reading for my Sociolinguistics course. Sometimes I tell the students as a Burkean "representative anecdote" about the first time I ever saw Haugen. They sit spellbound in dumb disbelief at Academia's ways, no doubt vowing they would never get into such a bind.

The scene was the general business meeting in St. Louis at the 1971 Linguistic Society of America Meeting. (I remind those of the readers not yet born at this time that this was the very end of the turbulent sixties, Civil Rights Act and action, and, I am afraid, a lot of pious posturing.) A man asked for attention, was recognized, and, in short, he asked the meeting to vote to officially censure Arthur Jensen and his 1969 "How much can we boost IQ and scholastic achievement?" I remember a very sympathetic murmuring and buzzing in approval from the audience. At this point a dignified man stood up, looking like a professor out of a European movie. It was Professor Haugen. He said with decorum that while he had not read Jensen's article and while he was not in agreement with its content (the first speaker had summarized it briefly), he was willing to defend any man's right to his ideas and something to the effect that Academia was the marketplace of ideas.

He asked as an afterthought how many of us had read the actual article. I remember very well trying not to feel smug (I was only a lowly assistant professor after all) as I raised my arm together with five others. Six people out of some two to three hundred people had actually read the article, but that did not stop that august meeting from going ahead to vote to censure Jensen. It was not one of LSA's proudest moments. My students simply cannot believe it. But it was another time and another climate and it took a great deal of courage for Professor Haugen to object at that time. Many years later, I asked him. Courage, he said, not really. We should not have done that, you know, it was not right. Einar Haugen was a gentleman in his scholarship, as well as in his life, not a claim that fits all sociolinguists engaged in jihad. I have never forgotten that occasion although it is a remarkably hard lesson, not just to acknowledge, but to follow. And no, I do not remember how I voted myself; I can only hope I at least abstained. Those were turbulent days which took gravitas to oppose.

Let Haugen reminisce himself:

> The second period runs from 1961 to the present, and represented a return to problems raised in my dissertation of thirty years before. The stimulus came from an invitation to participate in a symposium on Urbanization and Standard Language organized by Paul Garvin at the 1958 meetings of the American Anthropological Association in Washington, D.C. This was the first time I used the word "language planning" in public, a topic which continued to occupy me for a number of years. As suggested above, the immediate data on which I could work were Norwegian, where controversy over the national language was more than a century old. While the language planners in that country saw their task as one of healing a national wound and bringing the written and spoken languages of the people together, the effect proved to be more divisive than unifying. Again I found, on looking into the parallels in other countries, that there were many striking similarities, not only with situations of conflict, but also with the development of the great standard languages, such as French and English. I found that one could see the users of the standard or national language as a speech community on a higher level, but in principle similar to any face-to-face speech community with a unified dialect.
>
> While one result of my researches was a book on the Norwegian language controversy under the title of *Language Conflict and Language Planning* (1966), the other result was that I found myself in the midst of an awakening interest in problems of language development. The inbreeding of American linguistics as a purely structural and grammatical discipline was being attenuated by the creation of the Center for Applied Linguistics under the leadership of Charles A. Ferguson (1959). By the time of the UCLA Conference on Sociolinguistics in the spring of 1964

a whole new atmosphere had been created, one in which anthropologists, sociologists, and dissident linguists like myself could feel entirely at home. The name of the discipline, if such it is, might be new, but the idea was old, and like M. Jourdain who discovered he had been speaking prose all his life, I discovered that I had been a sociolinguist all my life. But even so, the emphasis is on the root of the word, the linguist. Without a solid background in linguistic analysis and observation there can be no good sociolinguistics. (1972:342–43)

Addendum to **The Early Days of Sociolinguistics**

Since the publication of *The Early Days of Sociolinguistics*, it has come to our attention that Heinz Kloss was a member of the National Socialist Party from the mid 1930's—see Christopher M. Hutton, *Linguistics and the Third Reich: Mother-Tongue Fascism, race and the science of language*. London: Routledge, 1999. As Kloss consistently denied any association with the Nazis, we thought we should call this new information to the attention of our readers.

(Christina Bratt Paulston and G. Richard Tucker)

Heinz Kloss went to considerable pains, several times, to convince Uriel Weinreich and me that he had never been a member of the Nazi party and that he had even been a most unwilling member of the German forces toward the very end of World War II. Hutton's revelations pertaining to Kloss, among others, confirm those of other postwar scholars who have investigated the "racial" views and activities widely shared among German intellectuals during the years of Nazi rule. Kloss was, in many ways, a very fine scholar and his case is highly instructive for sociolinguistics today because, even more than most other language scholars, we run the risk of being co-opted by revisionist ideologies and pervasive societal assumptions when doing so can facilitate our professional mobility. I am not at all sure how many of us (myself included) could resist such temptation. It is now obvious that Heinz Kloss could not.

(Joshua Fishman)

Heinz Kloss and the Study of Language in Society

William F. Mackey and Grant D. McConnell

William Francis Mackey is a Fellow of the Royal Society of Canada and the Royal Academy of Belgium and sometime member of government language commissions in Canada and Europe. He is the founding Director (1967) of the International Centre for Research on Bilingualism, expanded in 1990 as the CIRAL (Center for Language Management Research) at Laval University where he is currently research professor. He has authored over two hundred articles and two dozen books on language contact, language policy, sociolinguistics, and language education.

Grant McConnell began his career in 1968 as research assistant to Dr. Heinz Kloss at the International Center on Bilingualism (ICRB) at Laval University. He later became co-director of the International Languages' project, and finally, Director of the International Research Program at the newly named center—International Center for Research on Language Planning.

Comments by William F. Mackey. Not being discipline oriented, Kloss harbored neither the conception nor the pretension of contributing to the foundation of a new field of knowledge. His conception of the sort of work he was doing can be inferred through the name he gave to the small research center he founded in Marburg in the early sixties: the *Forschungstelle für Nationalitäten und Sprachenfragen.* In the twenty years during which I was associated with Kloss, I do not remember ever having heard him using the term "sociolinguistics." In my introduction to his authoritative *American Bilingual Tradition* in 1972, I identified him as "a leading authority on ethnic law," a characterization which pleased him. Yet he contributed a number of basic sociolinguist concepts.

Between the Great Wars—after the fall and rise of modern Germany—there developed a political and cultural interest in German minorities abroad including those in the United States. Heinz Kloss had studied these minorities and became the leading authority in this area. His much quoted work on German in America later attracted Joshua Fishman who had been working on the survival of language minorities in the U.S.—a survey which he later edited and published under the title *Language Loyalty in the U.S.A.* This academic contact between Kloss and Fishman developed into an enduring friendship maintained through contacts at numerous small meetings and symposia.

Since most language and nationality questions seem to have arisen within contexts of ethnic and language contact, we (the CIRB board of directors including Einar Haugen, W.E. Lambert, Werner Leopold, and Joshua Fishman, who made the suggestions) thought that Kloss' wide experience in this area could be of help to us in designing the research program of this new center (the International Center for Research on Bilingualism) which had started operations in 1968.

What was needed, in addition to our considerable investment in international and interdisciplinary documentation on bilingualism, was a number of basic research programs dealing with the social, political, psychological, and linguistic aspects of language contact. One of the first contracts I submitted as director of the Center included an invitation to Kloss to come and work with us; the first document I commissioned from him was a research program on *"Research Possibilities on Group Bilingualism."* Kloss had come to our Center with his new research assistant, Albert Verdoodt, who had just published a book on bilingualism in German-speaking Belgium. Both Kloss and Verdoodt worked on this commissioned document which was later published in our new series of in-house reports (Series B-18).

It was while preparing this document on group bilingualism that Kloss conceived his distinction between what he called "status planning" as opposed to "corpus planning"—a distinction which was simply a logical corollary of his *Ausbau* concept, part of his famous distinction between varieties which became "languages" by *Ausbau* (development) as opposed to languages by *Adstand* (interlingual distance). This important distinction grew out of his need to classify and weight characteristics of the languages of the world on which his center in Marburg had already gathered statistical data. Kloss was unaware that similar data had been compiled by our eminent geographer Henri Dorion. When Dorion succeeded me as the director of the Center, he handed over all the language data to Kloss and the two data banks were merged to create the nucleus of two large-scale and long-range research programs, one on the linguistic composition of the nations of the world and the other measuring the modes of use of these languages, mostly written languages. These projects were launched with the help of two of Kloss' research assistants, Dr. Irmgard Vogel of Heidelberg and Grant D. McConnell of Laval. What Kloss had in mind was a permanent language observatory recording the facts and the fates of the languages of the world.

Kloss had elaborated some of the basic concepts of sociolinguistics well before the beginning of the Second World War—concepts such as "language maintenance" in 1927. Although Kloss did not use the term "sociolinguistics," he was writing, as early as 1929, about what he called "the sociology of linguistic groups."

Kloss devoted much of his research to the establishment of these foundations. He insisted on obtaining all the facts, factors and variables, of language in society before venturing into any type of generalization. He saw that much depended on degree and relative differences, which explains his concern for accurate quantification. This led to his two main projects devoted to the linguistic composition of the nations of the world and to the degree and modes of use of the world's languages.

Kloss also contributed to what became one of the most seminal seminars in contact linguistics (The International Seminar on Bilingualism, at the University of Moncton in 1967). In his much-quoted comments on the question "How can we describe and measure the incidence and distribution of bilingualism?" Kloss introduced concepts such as "residual bilingualism," "replacive bilingualism," "implicit passive bilingualism," and "diglossic bilingualism" (Kelly 1969:296–316).

Additional comments by Grant McConnell. Sociolinguistics came to the fore during a revolutionary type period, that is, societies, and in particular western societies, were no longer content with their legacy of post-Victorian standards, but were groping for something more international and more universal in scope. This in turn led to a search for new frontiers both internal and external. Institutions from government to education to family began a long, sometime painful transformation that is still continuing today, and language too came to be seen differently as were the communities that spoke these languages. Both came to be viewed not only by linguists, but by society at large, as worthy of respect and study in themselves, for even they were perhaps not so backward and deficient as had been imagined, and might even have something to teach us in our restructuring of the new social framework and ontological order.

All of the above was fertile ground for a meteoric growth of the new discipline of sociolinguistics and this advance was compounded by a relatively prosperous period, which opened up research not just on particular languages but of aggregate groups of languages and communities both within and beyond conventional political contexts. This eventually evolved into full-blown sociolinguistic surveys that were carried out in numerous countries and in most continents of the world. Kloss was a pioneer in this regard insofar as he was interested in the survival and spread first of the German language and communities, then later of most languages and communities throughout the world. Some of his early articles date from the 1920s, but this long term interest culminated in the 1970s when he initiated two worldwide statistical surveys at the ICRB namely: *The Linguistic Composition of the Nations of the World* and the *Written Languages of the World: A Survey of the Degree and Modes of Use* (Laval University Press). Both surveys represented the macrosocietal line of research in its broadest expression.

The discipline of sociolinguistics was of course from its early days quite broad in its coverage, and early on a number of "lines" of research were discernible. Therefore seminal questions varied for each line of research. For example, the theme of "bilingualism" really covered a number of such lines, ranging from individual language learning or unlearning, involving physiological, psychological, and sociological change, to "language planning" which could cover both corpus and status issues. Undoubtedly, it would be a useful exercise to try to delineate all major questions, but suffice it to note that *Language in Society* took on a life of its own. It seems to me that the grand investigation was to delineate on one level language corpus variation with reference to the social structure (class, caste, ethnic group, etc.), and on another level to determine language use in terms of the impelling social, ecological factors influencing this patterned use.

It is obvious that the interdisciplinary mixture involved: psychologists, political scientists, social anthropologists, and to a lesser extent sociologists, economists and geographers, who together with some of the linguists, formed a new collegiality within the new discipline of sociolinguistics. Those with a psychology formation had a tendency to favor issues of individual bilingualism and language learning, but as an extrapolation of these, community survival as well. Political scientists were rather macro oriented and tended to concentrate on language policy, laws and planning within specific policies. Social anthropologists were language and community oriented. Linguists were either corpus oriented (and in that case were largely concentrated on the delineation of language varieties or registers in terms of local social variation), or were status oriented (and in that case much broader language and social categories were established). This also led to the tendency of Kloss and others to elaborate broad typologies of both language and social characteristics. Through the influence of Kloss, I was attracted to the macro and status-oriented line of investigation, perhaps because it had a global, internationalist vision that reflected an international order in the making.

Due to its relatively short history and its content, sociolinguistics seemed interdisciplinary by its very nature. But even early on, it was acting as a discipline in its own right. Surprisingly, in my experience activities in formal joint research were the exception rather than the rule. People came into sociolinguistics with their own background formation and more or less continued a line of work in the new paradigm that was closely associated with their earlier formal training. Methodological approaches and concepts were probably more often expanded than they were discarded and new ones adopted. Joint integrative research experiments, in which concepts had to be formally reworked and methodologies radically modified to satisfy all points of view, proved difficult if not impossible in practice. This may have been because the new discipline of sociolinguistics represented more of an extension and an amalgam rather than a radical break independent of earlier formations.

Kloss himself was neither worried nor concerned about discipline boundaries as his work area was largely interdisciplinary. At times his focus was on language laws (or lack thereof) or community rights affected by them, at other times he was concerned with the statistics of language demography including language distribution on an international scale. Yet again he might turn his attention on the mechanics of language use and their positive effects on language change in the language planning process which he named *Ausbau* (building on/up) in German, and at another time on the definition of "language" itself and his concept of interlanguage distance or Abstand, which for him also required a sociological input in order to make any sense.

I would characterize the early work as largely "problem driven," as it was largely due to a conceptual expansion in the world view. This in turn had a dramatic effect on the orientation of traditional disciplines, which partly imploded and thereafter expanded with the new label *sociolinguistics*. With this broadened horizon or framework of reference the new amalgamation of sociolinguistics was formed. This expanded world view posed new problems and new questions that did not fit into the old framework and the old disciplines.

Kloss' work was largely problem oriented. He relied heavily on fact finding and the inductive process to build up a case, whether it be largely description, descriptive-comparative as in his numerous typologies, or hypothetical in nature. Theory for him in this new discipline seemed not unimportant, but a long way off, when so much basic work needed doing.

What Kloss hoped to accomplish was a sociolinguistic and demolinguistic description of the world's languages. This involved a systematic gathering of statistics on languages, language communities and their distribution, but also included detailed data on social usage patterns and on language products of all kinds (books, newspapers, etc.). The basic idea was a unique, uniform, well structured data bank of the above, that would allow for comparisons and typological constructs, and that would perhaps in turn allow for the generation of hypotheses regarding external social factors instrumental in language pattern formations. This goal has only partly been realized, but progress has indeed been made, and indeed continues on today, but it is largely concrete, practical and applied, whereas on the theoretical side progress has been slow. This lack of theoretical ambition seems at the same time to have diminished expectations for the field and perhaps too, diluted the mix of scholars and shortened the list of outstanding questions. Even on the descriptive front where progress has been substantial, the coverage on the macro level is still spotty and incomplete, whereas on the micro level, although many hundreds if not thousands of studies have been done, not having any common data base, hypotheses, or methodological framework, they are largely incomparable.

Uriel Weinreich (1926–1967): A Sociolinguistic Appreciation[1]

Joshua A. Fishman

Joshua A. Fishman is Distinguished University Research Professor, Social Sciences, Emeritus at Yeshiva University and Visiting Scholar, Linguistics, at Stanford University. He is General Editor of the *International Journal of the Sociology of Language* and of the book-series *Contributions to the Sociology of Language*.

As one gets older, one inevitably begins to write obituaries for one's teachers who were, quite naturally, of an even older age. However, in, the present case, I am writing about a contemporary and a childhood friend, who, had he not been cruelly struck down by illness in the very midst of an exceedingly fruitful career, might have lived to reap even richer rewards of recognition and gratitude than those which he attained in the roughly two and a half decades of his professional endeavors. Thus, this is a doubly or triply painful obituary to write, but one that is long overdue, both personally and in terms of the recognition that is due to Uriel Weinreich from all those engaged in the greater sociolinguistic enterprise. We often do not know, or pause to reflect, on how Uriel contributed, directly and particularly indirectly, to that enterprise.

Since others have already prepared appreciations and bibliographies pertaining to Weinreich's life and work as a whole viz. Z[anvl] D[iyamant] 1960,

---

[1]Based, in large part, on recollections reinforced by letters to or from Uriel Weinreich and on deposit at the Joshua A. Fishman and Gella Schweid Fishman Family Archive, Special Collections, Stanford University, Stanford CA 94305. Comments (on an earlier draft) received from Charles Ferguson, Joseph Greenberg, and Bina Weinreich are gratefully acknowledged.

307

Herzog 1967, Kahn 1969, Malkiel 1967, 1968, Schaechter 1982, there is considerable justification to limiting these comments to the sociolinguistic area, particularly since his name and work have sometimes been overlooked in conjunction with this field of specialization. Of course, his seminal *Languages in Contact* (1953c; 8th printing 1974) cannot be overlooked, even more than 40 years after its initial publication, by all those who work on language switching in the speech of bilinguals, for, if it *is* overlooked, that is done at one's own considerable peril. It has stood the test of time very admirably and continues to be much read and cited to this very day. It brought to the American scene not only a superb (and European research-and-theory informed) conceptual and empirical analysis of the manifold linguistic, psychological, and societal factors that influence the interaction between languages, but it also provided an entrée to a wealth of generally unknown references (572 of them!) and examples in several very diverse languages (besides English, also Danish, French, German, Hebrew, Polish, Romansh, Russian, and Yiddish) that most Americans were ill equipped to peruse and had, therefore, never examined comparatively. In short, it was a tour de force, for it made what had hitherto often been considered, on these shores, to be a somewhat disreputable phenomenon (one usually lumped together under the pejorative rubric of "interference," rather than under the more neutral designation "transfer" that some utilize today), indeed, a phenomenon presumably engaged in primarily by uneducated and otherwise nonstatusful speakers, into a rich field of very fashionable empirical, theoretically, and richly sociolinguistic exploration (see Haugen's review 1954). Unfortunately, Weinreich was not granted the time he so desperately needed in order for him to be able to revise it, as he soon continually had in mind to do.

His pathbreaking "Explorations in Semantic Theory" (1966; first published as a book in German 1970; subsequently published as a book in English 1972; and subsequently also translated in Portuguese) deserves to be equally (if not even better) known in sociolinguistics, and for two good reasons. First of all, it propounded a theory of meaning that was profoundly cultural and sociosituational. Secondly, it appeared on the scene when "Uriel Weinreich" was already a name to conjure with and when the basically antisociolinguistic thrust of the Chomskyan revolution was still at full throttle. Uriel's semantics constituted one of the first major antidotes to Chomskyanism (more specifically, to the then reigning Fodor-Katz model thereof) and a very crucial indication that there were, after all, other fruitful approaches that could and should be explored in linguistics, a stance which is more fully developed in his posthumous *On Semantics* (1980). Those of us who were dedicated to sociolinguistic work, at whatever level of abstraction, were and should always be grateful that "Explorations in Semantic Theory" was completed and published before Uriel succumbed. In some sociolinguistic circles, his two above-mentioned works were viewed as legitimating documents. Even those who required no such legitimization or laying on of hands were pleased that the linguistic end of the sociolinguistic enterprise had achieved sufficient status to engender, or at least to invite, more respect for the sociology of language as a whole.

Less well known are several of Uriel's works that are closer to the macro end of the sociolinguistic enterprise. In this category, I find most memorable major segments of his dissertation focusing on Swiss-German and Romansh bilingualism and bi-dialectalism (1951), utilizing pre-Fergusonian diglossic notions of "upper" and "lower" varieties and providing a very highly and sociofunctionally differentiated definition of language "prestige." This is a work which really deserves to have been published, because from it was derived his justly famous and much more theoretically and linguistically focused *Languages in Contact* (1953c, later also published in German, Spanish, Russian, Italian, Japanese, and Parsi). His papers on bilingualism in India (1957), on the Welsh struggle for their language (1944, published in Yiddish when he was still an undergraduate student!), and on the Swiss-Romansh efforts to save their language (also in Yiddish, 1953a) all deserve to be reread. Certainly also in this same category is his documentation and condemnation of the Russification of minority languages (1953b) under the Soviet regime. Finally, the *Language and Culture Atlas of Ashkenazic Jewry* (vol. 1, 1992, vol. 2, 1995; additional volumes in press), regardless of what names were finally affixed to it by others when it belatedly began to be published roughly a quarter century after his death, is a brilliant foundation stone for a dialectalogically sophisticated sociolinguistics, something still in the offing, as well as for a truly refined and quite revolutionary "dialectology at a distance" along more general lines.

Having mentioned very briefly some of Uriel's best known and less well known contributions to sociolinguists at large, I would like to devote some of my remaining remarks to certain generally unknown contacts that he had with our field. In 1954 I asked Uriel (whom I had gotten to know well through working together with him, his brother Gabriel, and several others, starting in 1943, on various Yiddish-related youth activities) whether he would be interested in jointly formulating a societal view of language. We both agreed to try to sketch out in writing what we were interested in. My draft turned out to be so sociological in nature, and his so linguistic, that we let the matter drop, since it was far from clear at that time who would or could build a bridge between them (a goal which I did not consciously set for myself until a full decade later, but which my contact with both

Weinreichs had strongly imbedded in my mind). However, Uriel continued to observe and comment on my work from time to time. (I particularly remember his favorable remarks concerning my 1955 review of John Carroll's account of American linguistics at mid-century; for Uriel's own review of this same book see his 1953d and for his much more exhaustive critique of the work of Hockett, see his 1960 "Mid-Century Linguistics: Attainments and Frustrations.") He subsequently offered to be among those who recommended me for a year of research and writing at the Center for Advanced Study in the Behavioral Sciences (CASBS, Stanford, CA) in 1963.

As fate would have it, Uriel intersected with the 1964 "birth" or coalescence of American sociolinguistics, which, as readers of this volume well know, occurred (under Charles Ferguson's gentle direction) at the Summer Linguistic Institute held at Indiana University in Bloomington, Indiana. Both Chomsky and Uriel were invited to give back-to-back Forum Lectures that summer, and both spoke to standing-room-only audiences. Uriel and his wife Bina (also a childhood friend to both Gella and me) stayed with us during their visit to Bloomington and we hosted a reception "for sociolinguists only" in their honor. Uriel greatly enjoyed chatting with the members of the "Sociolinguistics tribe" that evening, one of whom, Bill Labov, had just recently been his own doctoral student, thereby constituting yet another Weinreichian link to American sociolinguistics. Uriel commented to me after the reception that the interests of the Institute participants were very varied and that this implied that the newly forming field would have to contend with at least as great a diversity of topics as he and I had unsuccessfully tried to contend with a decade earlier. Uriel spent the following year at CASBS himself and that was the year that Joe Greenberg and Jack Berry invited a small group of Africanists and sociolinguists to come together at the Center to discuss needed urban language research in Africa. I, being among those invited, was able to pay a return visit to Uriel (and his family) in Palo Alto. He then remarked to me that there appeared to be more folks with my "type of sociolinguistic interests" than he had supposed. Soon thereafter, I completed my *Readings in the Sociology of Language* (1968; a major paper by Uriel ["Is a structural dialectology possible?"] and another by Max Weinreich were published in this collection), but by the time this volume was ready to go to press (after years of procrastination by the publisher), it was already necessary to dedicate it to Uriel's memory.

Finally, I come to the topic of Uriel and Yiddish, something that brought us together even more than did sociolinguistic matters, but which has very definite sociolinguistic associations as well. Uriel was the elder son of an intellectual and activist Yiddishist family. His father, Max Weinreich, was the doyen of Yiddish studies, first in Europe and then, after 1940 in the U.S.A.

(That was the year in which the elder Weinreich and Uriel arrived in this country by crossing the Atlantic, escaping the Nazi onslaught on the abrogation of the Stalin-Hitler pact; Uriel's mother, Regina, and his younger brother, Gabriel, arrived subsequently, crossing the length of the Soviet Union and the Pacific.) Yiddish was not only always spoken at home, but it was the object of constant attention, concern, and conscious effort, not only throughout the entire day, but even in one's dreams at night as well. Both Uriel and I (with our respective spouses, Bina and Gella) had been raised with this view and value uppermost in our minds. Our original arena of contact was the work of our respective pro-Yiddish youth clubs (his—and theirs—in New York, and mine in Philadelphia), the Yiddish youth journal that we (and others) coedited, the federation of Yiddish youth clubs that we (and others) organized, the youth-centered Yiddish events that the federation and its member clubs sponsored, the courses that the YIVO Institute for Jewish Research (then: Yiddish Scientific Institute-YIVO), of which Max Weinreich was the Scientific Director, organized on our behalf, etc. Later, when Uriel was writing his text *College Yiddish* (1949; the 5th rev. ed. appeared in its 5th printing in 1990), I offered suggestions based on my experience with successful and unsuccessful Spanish texts and courses. It was a foregone conclusion that we both spoke only Yiddish to each other, to our spouses, our children, and our closest friends.

Many of Uriel's writings in Yiddish and on Yiddish (several of them jointly authored with Bina, a well-known Yiddish folklorist in her own right) unfortunately tend to be somewhat overlooked today, in view of his prominence far above and beyond the bounds of that language alone. I say "unfortunately," because all of his Yiddish-focused writings followed the adage of his father: "Work on Yiddish can avoid provincialism by aiming to make a theoretical contribution to general knowledge; if that can be done via studies of esoteric African languages, it can also be done via studies of Yiddish!" Rakhmiel Peltz, who now heads the Yiddish studies program at Columbia, is, therefore, rendering a most commendable service to one and all of us by preparing a volume devoted to those very works. Their intellectual importance was fully recognized by Yakov Malkiel's comment that "the twenty minutes that it took him [Uriel] to read, before a well-attended meeting of the Linguistic Society of America, his [1952] paper on '*Sa'besdiker losn* in Yiddish: A problem of linguistic affinity'...transformed a practically unknown young man into an enthusiastically applauded natural leader of the new generation" (Malkiel 1968:132).

When I decided to undertake doctoral work in social psychology (1948), doing so in New York and at the express suggestion of Max Weinreich, Uriel congratulated me on the grounds that such specialization could be easily related to the Yiddish concerns that we both had. It was not at all clear at that time that I would focus on language from that point of departure. Soon thereafter, however, I won a prize at the YIVO for student-conducted research (1949; published in Yiddish in 1951 and [partially] in English in 1952), and Uriel wrote to me from Switzerland, where he was engaged in his doctoral dissertation fieldwork, congratulating me on the fact that all of my subjects knew English natively, so that English could be treated as a constant and the subjects could be justifiably compared solely on the basis of how well they knew Yiddish. When I published my *Yiddish in America* (1965), Uriel thanked me for making it possible for him to more easily explain the Yiddish secular cultural milieu to his students at Columbia University (where he had begun to teach Yiddish in 1952, and became the first incumbent of the Atran Chair in Yiddish Language, Literature and Culture, in the Linguistics Department in 1957). Thus, although we had both intellectualized and, therefore, generalized our initial interest in Yiddish in order to encompass and define an entire area of scholarly endeavor, our involvement with Yiddish never ceased. Uriel taught courses with a heavy dosage of Yiddish data and wrote papers based on Yiddish linguistics even when he became chairman of the Department at Columbia and was ostensibly teaching courses in dialectology, lexicography, semantics, language planning, etc. During his year at CASBS, when he was already fully alerted to possibly serious health problems, he, nevertheless, spent the lion's share of his precious remaining time on completing the *Modern English-Yiddish, Yiddish-English Dictionary* (1968, reprinted 1977). During his final pre-hospitalization week, he disregarded his own state of health in order to preside at the orals of a student (Don Miron, subsequently an internationally famous researcher in the field of Yiddish literature).

So much for Uriel the scholar, teacher, and Yiddishist. However, Uriel the person should by no means be left out of the equation. Uriel had the capacity to be a warm and loyal friend and at the same time to respect the other's need for privacy. Although trained from childhood on to become a professor (Joseph Greenberg tells of Uriel's class presentation, for a course that Greenberg was teaching at Columbia in the late forties, "...which already showed all of the markings of superior scholarship and of a professorial career in linguistics, when he was scarcely more than 20 years old!"), Uriel, nevertheless, joked easily and frequently and was relaxed and informal around family and friends. His good judgment made him an ideal friend to call upon when one had a problem to discuss. He never forgot his friends when he and his family were abroad, dropping them little notes to say he was thinking of them. Uriel also read widely outside of his areas of professional specialization and had a particularly keen interest and appreciation for poetry. He was a natural leader of any group or undertaking in which he participated, but he was also somewhat reluctant for his leadership to be pointed out or stressed. He was often a quiet presence, rather than an overt spokesperson, but it was often his ideas and suggestions that prevailed. He was the kind of friend one misses more, rather than less, with the passing of time.

All in all, Uriel cannot be fully understood without attending to the constant interweaving of his Yiddish and his general linguistic interests, or to his involvement in Yiddish-speaking society in addition to his involvement in academia. But his interest in the Yiddish societal reality that he knew so well and prized so highly was also related to a general interest in small and threatened languages, and to the bilingual world that the speakers of such languages inevitably inhabited. His *Languages in Contact* contains an appendix on the issue of bilingualism and intelligence, an issue which was even more confused and maligned then than it is today. The clarification of that psycholinguistic issue and the fostering of sociolinguistic endeavors plus societal appreciation pertaining to bilingualism and the threatened languages round about us all, are significantly indebted (more so than is generally appreciated) to Uriel Weinreich. He was not only an outstanding Yiddishist, linguist, mentor, friend, and teacher, but a genuine and very natural stimulator and appreciator of much sociolinguistic research, theory, and social action the world over. Like Edward Sapir, with whom he had much in common, Uriel Weinreich always saw language as imbedded in social and cultural reality and viewed any effort to separate this trio as artificial but as impoverishing as well.

Epilogue

The Development of Sociolinguistics as a Field of Study: Concluding Observations

G. Richard Tucker

Dick Tucker was Professor of Psychology at McGill University (1969–1978) and Director of the Center for Applied Linguistics (1978–1991) before assuming his present position as Professor of Applied Linguistics and Head of the Department of Modern Languages at Carnegie Mellon University.

The recollections of the development and evolution of the field of Sociolinguistics provided by the contributors to this volume seem remarkably "coherent." In reviewing their cumulative story, I was struck by the salience of five cross-cutting themes. First, these recollections describe an interdisciplinary field whose approximate beginning can be pinpointed with reasonable accuracy. Second, the field appears to have emerged in response to a number of well-articulated and compelling social issues. Perhaps, as a partial consequence, the early activities were problem, rather than theory, driven. Third, the available evidence points to the importance of a small number of key individuals whose vision and leadership by virtue of their role(s) in convening national and international conferences, the publication of their own research, and their compilation of others' work was absolutely essential to the nurturing of the young field.

Fourth, although there seems to be a shared belief that the early work was, for the most part, problem driven, it appears nonetheless that a number of important differences characterized the underlying premises, beliefs, or motivations of the North American researchers in contrast to those from other countries. Finally, although the contributors do not, for the most part, comment on the availability of support for their work, I propose to say a few words about the financial climate in which activities in the field emerged. The early initiatives prospered at least in part because of continuing "patronage" from a small number of organizations and associations, and because of the availability of ample funding from private as well as public sources for initiatives such as conferences, surveys, the establishment of graduate programs, and publications. Let me turn now to a brief consideration of each of these five themes.

A landmark event? As contributors to this volume indicate, the formal "emergence" of sociolinguistics as a separate discipline[1] can be attributed to a series of complementary activities which occurred during 1963 and 1964. Charles Ferguson taught a course on Sociolinguistics at the University of Washington in 1963 which profoundly affected Björn Jernudd and presumably countless other students. A symposium was also convened that fall at the American Anthropological Association meetings in San Francisco (in fact several individuals remembered vividly that the session was in progress when they learned of the assassination of President John F. Kennedy) which resulted in the publication of *The Ethnography of Communication* (Gumperz and Hymes 1964). The formation of the Committee on Sociolinguistics in 1963 by the Social Science Research Council, modeled on their earlier support for the area of Psycholinguistics, clearly was instrumental in helping to sustain the momentum for this area (Ervin-Tripp 1974; Grimshaw 1980). The Committee continued to hold regular meetings and to sponsor activities until 1979.

Four additional events during 1964 were critical. These included: (1) the convening of a conference at Lake Arrowhead by Bill Bright, and the subsequent publication of the resulting volume *Sociolingistics* (1966); (2) the Summer Research Seminar on Sociolinguistics that was held in Bloomington at Indiana University in collaboration with the Summer Institute of the Linguistic Society of America (this eventually resulted in the publication of special issues of *Sociological Inquiry* [Lieberson 1966] and the *Journal of Social Issues* [Macnamara 1967]); (3) a conference on Social Dialects and Language Learning held in conjunction with the same LSA institute which included an overlap of participants from the sociolinguistics research seminar (resulting in the publication of a collection of papers with the same title [Shuy 1965]); and (4) the publication of the

---

[1] According to Kjolseth (1978), the salient defining characteristics by which a discipline distinguishes itself are: (1) a distinct manner of defining its subject matter, (2) a specialized language by which it defines its subject matter, (3) distinctive hypotheses and questions, and (4) a distinctive set of methods which are used. I believe that the field of sociolinguistics fulfills these criteria; Christina does not think it completely meets criteria (2) and (4).

The Development of Sociolinguistics as a Field of Study 319

comprehensive and influential anthology, *Language in Culture and Society* by Dell Hymes (1964).

Most of our contributors identified the seminar that summer, in particular, as a crucial turning point for themselves personally and for the emerging discipline. We are particularly fortunate that five of the eleven surviving key members of the core group of participants that summer (Bright, Ferguson, Fishman, Friedrich, and Lieberson) have contributed to the present volume, as well as four of the seven members who "visited" the seminar regularly[2] (Ervin, Hymes, Grimshaw, and Lambert), and two of the surviving four members who served on the original Research Committee on Sociolinguistics of the International Sociological Association (Fishman and Kjolseth).

The perspective provided by some of our overseas contributors was slightly different. For Sibayan and for Tabouret-Keller, the opportunity to participate in a series of conferences on language problems in developing countries (at Airlie House, VA in 1966; Fishman, Ferguson and Das Gupta, 1968; at Laval University in Canada in 1967; and in Honolulu in 1969 [Rubin and Jernudd 1971]) proved to be the important demarcation point. In contrast, for Annamalai the support provided by the Rockefeller Foundation for a series of South Asian initiatives in the late 1950s was critical to nurturing an interest in linguistics in South Asia. This work was followed a number of years later by summer seminars in India involving individuals such as Ferguson, Gumperz, and Labov.

Thompson, on the other hand, provided a very different and quite intriguing view concerning the defining moment for the field. He argues that the advent of sociolinguistics as an organized discipline can really be traced to October 1957 with the launching of Sputnik which led (perhaps directly) to the drafting and passage of the National Defense Education Act in 1958 which in turn led the Modern Language Association to implement a coherent five-year plan designed to: (1) encourage more Americans to study foreign languages, (2) modernize foreign language instruction, (3) encourage the study of the so-called less commonly taught languages by providing fellowship support, (4) encourage research on language learning and teaching, and (5) experiment with the development and implementation of pilot foreign language teaching programs. He recalls this chain of events as setting the stage for "the most significant national foreign language policy planning effort in American history," and observed that for him at least this marked *de facto* the beginning of the field of sociolinguistics.

---

[2]See Fishman, this volume.

The term sociolinguistics. Almost parenthetically it might be noted that there were several interesting observations about the introduction and use of the term *sociolinguistics*. A number of contributors noted that the term was first used by Haver C. Currie in 1952 in an article in the *Southern Speech Journal* while Marcellesi notes a French preoccupation with the relationship between language and social factors as evidenced by the title of a book by Cohen which appeared in 1952 *(Pour une Sociologie du Langage)*. In fact Polomé reports that he attended a course, "Sociologie du Langage," taught by a Professor Gregoire at the University of Brussels during the 1930s, and that he himself taught such a course on several occasions in Lubumbashi (then Elizabethville), Zaire between 1956 and 1960.

In summary, although contributors ascribe slightly different emphases to events of the late 1950s and 1960s, it does seem clear that the origin of Sociolinguistics can be traced to a small number of events which occurred within a relatively short period of time. What can be said about the social, the economic, and the intellectual climate of those times? What was it about the period that led to the launching of the field?

The prevailing zeitgeist. Contributors provided two quite different, albeit complementary, characterizations of the social, economic or intellectual climate of the 1960s that seemed to underpin the launching of the field. A number of individuals from North America and Europe (typified by the comments of Grimshaw, Kjolseth, Shuy, Tabouret-Keller, and Troike) noted that the coalition among linguists, sociologists, and anthropologists was a natural outcome of the movement for social justice and for educational reform; an interest in confronting racial segregation, poverty, and the intractability of social structures. For his part, Lambert, a social psychologist, describes the heightened interest following the conclusion of the Second World War in making (American) society a fairer and more tolerant one. This theme was later to be explored more fully in work by individuals such as Shuy (1965) and Labov (1970; but see the appendix to Bernstein's contribution for an alternative perspective on Labov's important paper).

Among a number of others, the catalytic force was the growing awareness by individuals such as Ferguson and Mackey that policy decisions involving language were being taken by numerous governments, often without an adequate research or knowledge base. Ferguson, in particular, saw an understanding of problems involving ethnicity and language, and of language maintenance and shift as critical ones to explore. Myers-Scotton recalls being literally "overtaken" (in the sense of the passive applied form of a Swahili verb) by multilingualism in Africa while Sibayan notes so eloquently that "for those in developing nations, problems related to language were the most

The Development of Sociolinguistics as a Field of Study   321

critical topic [emphasis ours] for scholars and decision makers"—a theme echoed by Neustupný and by Grimes and Kindell describing the work of those affiliated with the Summer Institute of Linguistics (SIL). As Hymes observes, studies of the use of language emerged on so many varied fronts that one had to conclude that a zeitgeist was inevitably at work.

Within this prevailing social and intellectual climate, it was inevitable that a few individuals should be recognized by their peers for the roles that they played in the development of the field.

Who provided the early leadership for the field? Available evidence—anecdotal as well as substantive—points to the importance of a small number of key individuals whose vision and leadership were absolutely essential to the nurturing of the new field. Although it may be somewhat rash to single out any one individual, from my own perspective, it seemed to me that the name of Charles Ferguson, or "Fergie" as he is widely known,[3,4] identified by a majority of the contributors as the principal architect for the field by virtue of his central role in convening national seminars (such as the Bloomington meeting in 1964) or international conferences (e.g., the Rome conference in 1964), the publication of his own research (Ferguson 1959; or Ferguson 1964), and for his role in the compilation and distribution of his and others' work (e.g. Ferguson and Gumperz 1960; or Ferguson, Fishman, and Das Gupta 1968). This should perhaps not be surprising since Ferguson was also the founding head of the Center for Applied Linguistics (CAL), and a number of meetings were called under CAL's aegis, and a great deal of information was disseminated through CAL's newsletter, *The Linguistic Reporter*, which began publication in 1959 when CAL was founded.

The identification of "Fergie" as the instigator of much of what was to follow was supported by the contributions of others such as Fishman, Gumperz, Hymes, and Labov in the development of the field. They, too, through their participation in conferences, their teaching, their writing, and their editing helped to define the parameters of the field. Indeed each of the participants in the original Bloomington seminar became pioneers for their work in the area (see Fishman's description of the backgrounds and the contributions of himself and of Berry, Bright, Ferguson, Friedrich, Gumperz, Haugen, Hunt, Kloss, Labov, Lieberson, Savitz, and Stewart, each of whom participated in the 1964 Bloomington seminar).

---

[3]Lieberson, this volume.
[4]It should be added that the name of Marcel Cohen also was mentioned frequently as providing early impetus and leadership to the development of the field. Since he wrote only in French, his work may have unfortunately been largely inaccessible to many monolingual English speakers.

The nature of the work. What about the agenda for the field? Could it accurately be described as having been theory driven or was it more likely problem driven. A substantial number of our contributors (including Ferguson, Grimes, Grimshaw, Kindell, Kjolseth, Lambert, Macnamara, Sibayan, Shuy, Tabouret-Keller, and Troike) remember that their work was, for the most part, problem driven, although for Friedrich, Marcellesi, Myers-Scotton, Neustupný, and Pike, the impetus was more theoretical in nature.

I was intrigued, however, by the vivid recollections of several individuals such as Annamalai and Sibayan of important differences which they believe characterize the underlying premises, beliefs, or motivations of the North American researchers in contrast to those from developing countries. Annamalai, for example, notes that a "Western sociolinguistic model" does not adequately depict Indian reality, and that Indian multilingualism is qualitatively different from that found in other places (although I do not read such an inference into the recollections of Myers-Scotton based upon her East African experiences). In a somewhat similar vein, Sibayan observes important paradigmatic differences between the factors which motivate the work of those in Western countries, which he depicts as driven by an interest in social dialect variation and immigrant languages with a focus on *formal* linguistics and sociolinguistics versus the conditions or factors motivating those who work in developing nations which he identifies as multilingualism, the development of national language(s), and the choice and use of language(s) in education. Let me turn now to the last of the cross-cutting themes which relates to the sources of support for the early work.

Support for sociolinguistic work. There was substantial public and private support for this type of work during the 1960s and the 1970s. I base this observation upon the recollections of contributors (for example Annamalai, Fox, and Shuy), and on my own personal involvement (which was both direct since I worked as a project specialist in language education with the Ford Foundation in Southeast Asia from 1967 to 1969, and in the Middle East and North Africa during 1972–1973 and again in 1976–1977, as well as somewhat more indirectly since I served as head of the Center for Applied Linguistics from 1978 through 1991).

Annamalai describes the nature of the support and interest in language activities shown by the Rockefeller Foundation in India. It had also provided the early support for the Philippine Center for Language Study in Manila, as well as for comparable activities in Africa. Likewise, there was massive assistance, both direct and indirect, from the Ford Foundation during that time. According to Fox (this volume and 1975a, 1975b), the Ford Foundation provided direct support amounting to more than $40 million for language

The Development of Sociolinguistics as a Field of Study   323

activities in more than thirty-five countries during the 1960s and the 1970s. This support made possible the convening of conferences, the carrying out of language surveys, the development of national resource centers, and the advanced training of future generations of scholars. The retrospective survey compiled by Fox (1975a) details the contributions of the Ford Foundation during this period. As Fox noted in the concluding section of his report:

> Ford Foundation experience over the last two decades has shown that...to be effective, work on language must take account of how the use of language relates to the linguistic and cultural setting, as well as the different social, economic and political realities in which development takes place....certain basic facts emerge from the diverse experience of the Ford Foundation.
>
> It is desirable to obtain a picture of the total setting in which language problems emerge, and the sociopolitical factors either in the society as a whole or in a particular institution, or in the particular sector or community, that must be taken into account in charting solutions. (Fox 1975a:146)

Certainly, the Ford Foundation was a major benefactor for this emerging discipline of sociolinguistics. Foundation officials were guided by Fox's observation:

> Beyond the object lessons and suggestions made for external aid efforts to work on problems of language in relation to educational change, the absolute, unchanging centrality of language to social, economic, and political development remains. (Fox 1975a:148–49)

Indirect assistance from the Ford Foundation was also critical in that it helped to support the work of organizations such as the Social Science Research Council and the Center for Applied Linguistics which directly helped to nurture the development of this new field. Additionally, as both Ferguson and Shuy noted, support from public agencies such as the National Science Foundation was essential to the development of graduate training programs in sociolinguistics at American institutions of higher education (e.g., the program at Georgetown University). As well, the individual and collective contributions by members of organizations such as the Summer Institute of Linguistics throughout this formative period (see Grimes, Kindell, and Pike) should not be underestimated.

Thus, in summary, a set of factors seemed to converge in the 1960s and 1970s which included a cohesive group of individuals intrigued by the notion of substantive dialogue and collaboration across disciplinary, institutional, and national boundaries; the increasing prominence of a number of social or educational problems in which language could be viewed as a critical ingredient; and a readiness of public and private sources to underwrite the costs of embarking upon a venture of substantial proportion to explore more fully various aspects of the multiple roles of language in educational, occupational, and social issues. As Dell Hymes so aptly noted, the "*zeitgeist* was inevitably at work" and it was to continue to gather momentum over the decades that followed.

References

Achard, Pierre. 1993. La sociologie de langage: Que sais-je? Paris: Publication of the University of France.
Adams, Marianne Lehr and James R. Frith, eds. 1979. Testing kit: French and Spanish. Washington, D.C.: Foreign Service Institute, Department of State.
Afendras, Evangelos. 1969. Sociolinguistic history. Sociolinguistic geography and bilingualism. Quebec: Centre International de Recherche sur le Bilinguisme.
Agard, Frederick B. 1975. Toward a taxonomy of language split (Part one: Phonology). Leuvense: Bijdragen 64(3-4):293-312.
———. 1984. A course in Romance linguistics 2: A diachronic view. Washington, D.C.: Georgetown University Press.
Ammon, Ulrich, Norman Dittmar, and Klaus J. Mattheier, eds. 1987. History of sociolinguistics as a discipline. In Sociolinguistics: An International Handbook of the Science of Language and Society 4:379-469. Berlin: de Gruyter.
Annamalai, E. 1986. The sociolinguistic scene in India. Sociolinguistics 16(1):2-8.
———, Björn H. Jernudd, and Joan Rubin, eds. 1986. Language planning: Proceedings of an Institute. Mysore: Central Institute of Indian Languages.
———. (forthcoming). Convergence: A study in Indian languages. Pune: Linguistic Survey of India.
Backstrom, Peter C. and Carla F. Radloff. 1992. Languages of northern areas. Sociolinguistic survey of Northern Pakistan 2. Islamabad: National Institutes of Pakistan Studies and Summer Institute of Linguistics.

Baggioni, Daniel. 1975. Orientations actuelles en sociolinguistique. La Pensée 182.

———. 1977. Contribution à l'histoire de l'influence de la "Nouvelle théorie du Langage" en France. Langage 46:90–116.

———. 1980. La langue nationale, problèmes linguistiques et politiques. In J. B. Marcellesi (ed.), Langages et sociétés. La Pensée 209:36–49.

——— et Jean-Pierre Kaminker. 1980. La norme, gendarme et bouc émissaire. In J. B. Marcellesi (ed.), Langages et Sociétes. La Pensée 209:50–63.

Bakhtine, Mikhail. 1977. Le marxisme et la philosophie du langage: Essai d'application de la méthode sociologique en linguistique. (Tr. from Russian by Marina Yaguello.) Paris: Minuit. (First ed. in Russian published under the name of V. N. Vološinov.)

Balibar, Renée. 1993. Le colinguisme: Que sais-je? Paris: Publication of the University of France.

Bauman, R. and J. Sherzer, eds. 1974. Explorations in the ethnography of speaking [2nd ed. 1989]. New York: Cambridge University Press.

Bautista, Ma. Lourdes S. 1974. The Philipino bilingual's competence: A model based on an analysis of Tagalog-English code switching. Ph.D. dissertation. Ateneo de Manila University, Philippine Normal College Consortium in Linguistics.

———. 1980. The Philipino bilingual's competence: A model based on an analysis of Tagalog-English code switching. Pacific Linguistics, Series C, No. 59. Canberra: Australian National University.

———. 1991. Code switching studies in the Philippines. International Journal of the Sociology of Language 88:19–32.

Bean, S. 1974. Linguistic variation and the caste system in South Asia. Indian Linguistics 35(4):277–93.

Bendor-Samuel, Margaret and David Bendor-Samuel. 1996. A manual for strategic planning and review for language programs. Dallas: Summer Institute of Linguistics.

Bergman, Ted G., ed. 1989a. Proceedings of the round table on assuring the feasibility of standardization within dialect chains. Noordwijkerhout, The Netherlands, September 1988. Nairobi: Summer Institute of Linguistics.

———, ed. 1989b. Survey reference manual: A collection of papers on the assessment of Bible translation need. Dallas: Summer Institute of Linguistics.

Bernstein, Basil B. 1966. Culture and linguistics. Memorandum.

———. 1971. Class, codes and control 1: Theoretical studies towards a sociology of language. London: Routledge and Kegan Paul.

——. 1974. Class, codes and control 2: Applied studies towards a sociology of language. London: Routledge and Kegan Paul.
——. 1975. Language et classes sociales: Codes sociolinguistiques et contrôle social. Paris: Minuit.
——. 1975. Class, codes and control 3 (revised): Towards a theory of educational transmissions. London: Routledge and Kegan Paul.
——. 1990. Class, codes and control 4: The structuring of pedagogic discourse. London: Routledge and Kegan Paul. (Also New York: Routledge, Chapman and Hall.)
——. 1995. Pedagogy, symbolic control and identity: Theory, research, and critique. London: Taylor and Francis.
Berryman, Sue E. et al. 1979. Foreign language and international studies specialists: The marketplace and national policy. Santa Monica: The Rand Corporation.
Biggs, Bruce. 1957. Testing intelligibility among Yuman languages. International Journal of American Linguistics 23:57–62.
Blair, Frank. 1990. Survey on a shoestring: A manual for small-scale language surveys. Summer Institute of Linguistics and the University of Texas at Arlington Publications in Linguistics 96. Dallas.
Blanke, Detlev. 1981. Plansprache und Nationalsprache: einige Probleme der Wortbildung des Esperanto und das Deutschen in konfrontativer Darstellung. Linguistische Studien, Reihe A. Arbeitsberichte 85. Berlin: Akademie der Wissenschaften der DDR.
——. 1985. Internationale Plansprachen: Eine Einführung. Berlin: Akademie-Verlag.
Blom, Jan-Petter and John J. Gumperz. 1972. Social meaning in linguistic structures: Code-switching in Norway. In John J. Gumperz and Dell Hymes (eds.), Directions in sociolinguistics, 407–34. New York: Holt.
Bloomfield, Leonard. 1933. Language. New York: Holt.
Bourdieu, Pierre. 1979. Attention régulière au problème sociolinguistique en général, noter le nº 25, janvier 1979, le pouvoir des mots.
Boutet, Josiane, Pierre Fiala, and Jenny Simonin-Grumbach. 1976. Sociolinguistique ou sociologie du langage. Critique 344.
Bowen, William G. and Julie Ann Sosa. 1989. Prospects for faculty in the arts and sciences. Princeton University Press.
Bradley, C. Henry. 1968. A method for determining dialectal boundaries and relationships. América Indígena 28:751–60.
Bram, Joseph. 1955. Language and society. New York: Random.
Bright, William. 1952. Linguistic innovations in Karok. International Journal of American Linguistics 18:53–62.

———. 1955. A grammar of the Karok language. (Published along with texts and dictionary as The Karok language. University of California Publications in Linguistics 17, 1957.)

———. 1960. Social dialect and language history. Current Anthropology 1:424-25.

——— and A. K. Ramanujan. 1964. Sociolinguistic variation and language change. In Horace Lunt (ed.), Proceedings of the 9th International Congress of Linguists, 1107-14. Cambridge: MIT Press.

———, ed. 1966. Sociolinguistics: Proceedings of the UCLA Sociolinguistics Conference, 1964. Janua linguarum, Series maior 20. The Hague: Mouton.

———. 1967. Language, social stratification and cognitive orientation. In Stanley Lieberson (ed.), Explorations in sociolinguistics. Sociological Inquiry 36(2):313-18.

———, ed. 1992. International encyclopedia of linguistics, 4 vols. New York: Oxford University Press.

Brown, Penelope and Stephen C. Levinsohn. 1967. Politeness: Some universals in language usage. Studies in International Sociolinguistics 4. Cambridge: Cambridge University Press.

Brown, Roger. 1958. Words and things. Glencoe, Ill.: Free Press.

——— and Albert Gilman. 1960. The pronouns of power and solidarity. In Thomas Sebeok (ed.), Style in language, 253-76. Cambridge: MIT Press.

Bruce, D. 1994. Lashley and the problem of serial order. American Psychologist 49:93-103.

Bruhn, Thea C. 1989. "Passages": Life, the universe, and language proficiency assessment. In Georgetown Round Table on Languages and Linguistics, 1989, 245-54. Washington, D.C.: Georgetown University Press.

Bulot, Thierry. 1985. Bibliographie sociolinguistique française, fasc. 1; 1986 fasc. 2; 1987 fasc 3; 1988 fasc. 4. Cahiers de Linguistique Sociale, University of Rouen.

Buseman, Alan. 1991. Tutorial for dialect adaptation with Ample and Stamp: Computer assisted dialect adaptation, using the AMPLE and STAMP programs. Waxhaw, N.C.: JAARS.

Calvet, Louis-Jean. 1974. Linguistique et colonialisme: Petit traité de glottophagie. Paris: Payot.

———. 1975. Pour et contre Saussure: Vers une linguistique sociale. Paris: Payot.

———. 1977. Marxisme et linguistique. Paris: Payot.

———. 1993. La sociolinguistique: Que sais-je? Paris: Publication of the University of France.

Capell, Arthur. 1966. Studies in socio-linguistics. Janua linguarum, Series minor 46. The Hague: Mouton.
Carpenter, Niles. 1927. Immigrants and their children. Washington, D.C.: Government Printing Office.
Casad, Eugene H. 1974. Dialect intelligibility testing. Summer Institute of Linguistics Publications in Linguistics and Related Fields 38. Norman: Summer Institute of Linguistics of the University of Oklahoma.
———. 1992. Windows on bilingualism. Summer Institute of Linguistics and the University of Texas at Arlington Publications in Linguistics 110. Dallas.
Chan-Yap, Gloria. 1974. Hokien Chinese borrowings in Tagalog. Ph.D. dissertation. Ateneo de Manila, Philippine Normal College, De la Salle University Linguistics Consortium.
Chiorboli, Jean. 1991. Les langues polynomiques, Pula 3–4. Université de Corte.
Chomsky, Noam. 1965. Aspects of the theory of syntax. Cambridge: MIT Press.
Cohen, Marcel. 1952. Pour une sociologie du langage. Paris: Michel Albin.
Coppalle, Daniel and Bernard Gardin. 1980. Discours du pouvoir et pouvoir(s) du discours. In Jean Baptiste Marcellesi (ed.), Langages et sociétés. La Pensée 209:99–113.
Crystal, David, ed. 1987. The Cambridge encyclopedia of language. Cambridge: Cambridge University Press.
Currie, Haver C. 1952. A projection of sociolinguistics: The relationship of speech to social status. Southern Speech Journal 18:28–37.
de Latour, Charles-Henri. 1977. Le système de parenté dans les grandes ensembles de Montbéliard. Bulletin de Psychologie 35:510–20.
Decker, Kendall D. 1992. Languages of Chitral. Sociolinguistic survey of Northern Pakistan 5. Islamabad: National Institutes of Pakistan Studies and Summer Institute of Linguistics.
Delamotte-Legrand, Régine. 1987. Education linguistique. Cahiers de Linguistique Sociale 11.
———, ed. 1991. Sociolinguistique et didactique.
Deutsch, Karl W. 1953. Nationalism and social communication: An inquiry into the foundations of nationality. Cambridge: MIT Press.
Dialectique. 1977. La politique des langages...
Diamant, Zanvl. 1960. Uriel Vaynraykh. Leksikon fun der nayer yidisher literatur 3:366–67. New York: Kultur Kongres.
Diebold, A. Richard. 1961. Incipient bilingualism. Language 37:97–112.
Dittmar, Norbert. 1973. Soziolinguistik: Exemplarische und kritische Darstellung ihrer Theorie, Empirie und Anwendung. Frankfurt: Athenäum Fischer Taschenbuch Verlag.

Dua, Hans R. 1994. Hegemony of English: Future of developing languages in the Third World. Mysore: Yashoda Publications.
Dubois, Jean. 1962. Le vocabulaire politique et social en France de 1869 à 1872. Paris: Larousse.
———. 1980. Interventions à la table ronde finale. In Bernard Gardin and Jean-Baptiste Marcellesi (eds.), Sociolinguistiques: Approches, théories, practiques. Paris: Publication of the University of France and Publications of the University of Rouen.
Dye, T. Wayne. 1979. The Bible translation strategy: An analysis of its spiritual impact. Ph.D. dissertation. Pasadena: Fuller Theological Seminary. (Pub. 1980. Dallas: Wycliffe Bible Translators.)
Eco, Umberto. 1993. La ricerca della lingua perfetta nella cultura europea. Rome: Laterza.
Edwards, Jane and Humphrey Tonkin, eds. 1984. Language behavior in international organizations. Report of the Second Annual Conference on Language and Communication, Center for Research and Documentation on World Language Problems, New York, December 15, 1983. New York: Center for Research and Documentation on World Language Problems.
Elimam, Abdou and Jean-Baptiste Marcellesi. 1987. Language and society from a Marxist point of view. In Ulrich Ammon, Norman Dittmar, and Klaus J. Mattheier (eds.), Sociolinguistics: An International Handbook of the Science of Language and Society 4:443–52. Berlin, New York: de Gruyter.
Ellis, Jim. 1991. Language intelligibility testing across Micronesia. Sixth International Conference of Austronesian Linguistics, May 20–24, 1991.
Elster, Jan. 1989. Nuts and bolts for the social sciences. New York: Cambridge University Press.
Emeneau, Murray B. 1958. India as a linguistic area. Language 32:8–16.
———. 1938. Personal names of the Todas. AA 40:205–23.
Encrevé, Pierre. 1976. Labov: Linguistique et sociolinguistique. (Introduction to Sociolinguistique, trans. of Sociolinguistic patterns, by William Labov [1972] ; tr. by Alain Kihm), 3–16. Paris: Minuit.
England, Steven Thomas. 1978. La inteligibilidad interdialectal en México: Resultados de algunos sondeos. Mexico: Instituto Lingüístico de Verano.
Ervin-Tripp, Susan. 1969a. Summer workshops in sociolinguistics: Research on children's acquisition of communicative competence. Social Science Research Council Items 23:22–26.

———. 1969b. Sociolinguistics. In L. Berkowitz (ed.), Advances in experimental social psychology 4:51–165. New York: Academic. (Republished in Joshua A. Fishman [ed.], 1971, Advances in the sociology of language 1: Basic concepts, theories and problems, 15–151. The Hague: Mouton.)

———. 1972. On sociolinguistic rules: Alternation and co-occurrence. In John Gumpers and Dell Hymes (eds.), Directions in sociolinguistics, 213–50. New York: Holt.

———. 1974. Two decades of council activity in the rapprochement of linguistics and social science. Social Science Research Council, Items 28(1):1–4.

——— and Claudia Mitchell-Kernan. 1977. Child discourse. New York: Academic.

Fasold, Ralph W. 1984. The sociolinguistics of society 1. Language in Society 5. Oxford: Blackwell.

———. 1990. The sociolinguistics of language: Introduction to Sociolinguistics 2. Language in Society 6. Oxford: Blackwell.

Faurot, Karla, Dianne Dillinger, Andy Eatough, Steve Parkhurst, and Albert Bickford. 1993. The Mexican sign language survey. ms.

Ferguson, Charles A. 1959. Diglossia. Word 15:325–40.

———. 1962. The language factor in national development. Anthropological Linguistics 4(1):23–27. (Also in Frank A. Rice [ed.], 1962. Study of the role of second languages in Asia, Africa, and Latin America, 8–14. Washington, D.C.: Center for Applied Linguistics.)

———. 1964. Baby talk in six languages. American Anthropologist. 66(6):103–14.

———. 1991. Diglossia revisited. Southwest Journal of Linguistics 10(1):214–34.

——— and John J. Gumperz. 1960. Introduction. In Charles A. Ferguson and John J. Gumperz (eds.), Linguistic diversity in South Asia: Studies in regional, social, and functional variation, 13:1–12. Bloomington: Indiana University Research Center in Anthropology, Folklore, and Linguistics.

——— and John J. Gumperz, eds. 1960. Linguistic diversity in South Asia: Studies in regional, social, and functional variation. Indiana University Research Center in Anthropology, Folklore, and Linguistics 13 (International Journal of American Linguistics 26:3, part 3) Bloomington.

Firth, John R. 1957. Papers in linguistics (1934–1951). London: Oxford University Press.

Fishman, Joshua A. 1951. Tsveyshpakhikeyt in a yidisher shul. Bleter far yidisher derstiung 4:22–44. (1952, partially published in English as: Degree of bilingualism in a Yiddish school, and leisure time activities. Journal of Social Psychology 36:155–65.)

———. 1955. The study of language: A critical review. Journal of Social Psychology 41:169–79.

———. 1960. Systematization of the Whorfian hypothesis. Behavioral Science 5:323–39.

———. 1965. Yiddish in America: Socio-linguistic description and analysis, Publication 36. (International Journal of American Linguistics 31:2, part 2). Bloomington: Indiana University Research Center in Anthropology, Folklore, and Linguistics.

———. 1965. Who speaks what language to whom and when? Linguistique 2:67–88.

———, ed. 1966. Language loyalty in the United States: The maintenance and perpetuation of non-English mother tongues by American ethnic and religious groups. Janua linguarum, Series maior. The Hague: Mouton.

———. 1967. Bilingualism with or without diglossia: Diglossia with and without bilingualism. Journal of Social Issues 23(2):29–38.

———, ed. 1968. Readings in the sociology of language. The Hague: Mouton.

———. 1970. Sociolinguistics: A brief introduction. Rowley, Mass.: Newbury.

———. 1971. Sociolinguistique. Brussels and Paris: Labor et Nathan.

———, ed. 1971. Advances in the sociology of language 1. Basic concepts, theories, and problems: Alternative approaches. The Hague: Mouton.

———, ed. 1972. Advances in the sociology of language 2. Selected studies and applications. The Hague: Mouton.

———. 1972. Domains and the relationship between micro- and macro-sociolinguistics. In John J. Gumperz and Dell Hymes (eds.), Directions in sociolinguistics, 435–53. New York: Holt.

———, ed. 1974. Editor's introduction, Language planning and language planning research: The state of the art. In Advances in language planning. Sociology of Language 5:15–33. The Hague: Mouton. (Also 1974, Linguistics 119:15–34.)

———. 1985. The rise and fall of the ethnic revival: Perspectives on language and ethnicity. Berlin: Mouton.

———. 1987. Conference comments: Reflections on the current state of language planning. In Lorne Laforge (ed.), Proceedings of the International Colloquium on Language Planning May 25–29, 1986, Ottawa. Québec: Laval University Press.

———. 1987. Ideology, society and language: The odyssey of Nathan Birnbaum. Ann Arbor: Karoma.
———, ed. 1987. Advances in the study of societal multilingualism. The Hague: Mouton.
———. 1991. Reversing language shift: Theoretical and empirical foundations of assistance to threatened languages. Avon: Multilingual Matters.
———. 1992. Foreword: What can sociology contribute to the sociolinguistic enterprise? In Glenn William, Sociolinguistics: A sociological critique. London: Routledge.
———, Robert L. Cooper, and Roxana Ma Newman, eds. 1971. Bilingualism in the barrio. Bloomington: Indiana University Press.
———, Charles A. Ferguson, and Jyotirindra Das Gupta, eds. 1968. Language problems of developing nations. New York: Wiley.
Forster, Peter G. 1982. The Esperanto movement. Contributions to Sociology of Language 32. The Hague: Mouton.
Fossat, Jean-Louis. 1980. Pour une autre sociolinguistique: La dialectologie sociale: Actes du colloque organisé du 27 novembre au 2 décembre 1978 par le GRECO, Université de Rouen, Faculté des Lettres de Mont-Saint-Aignan, 605–26. In Bernard Gardin and Jean Baptiste Marcellesi (eds.), Sociolinguistique: Approches, théories, pratiques, II, 343–693. Paris: Publication of the University of France.
Fox, Melvin J. 1975. Language and development: A retrospective survey of Ford Foundation language projects 1952–1974, 2 vols. New York: The Ford Foundation.
——— and Betty P. Skolnick. 1975. Language in education: Problems and prospects in research and training. New York: The Ford Foundation.
——— and M. Abdulaziz. 1978. Evaluation report on languages used and language teaching in Eastern Africa. New York: The Ford Foundation.
———. n.d. Language education in developing countries: The changing role of the Ford Foundation. New York: The Ford Foundation.
François, Frédéric. 1976. Classes sociales et langue de l'enfant. La Pensée 190:74–92.
———. 1978. La différenciation socioculturelle des enfants: Quelques réflexions linguistiques. In Langue de l'enfant, classes sociales, école.
Friedrich, Paul. 1970. Agrarian revolt in a Mexican village. Englewood Cliffs: Prentice-Hall.
Gadet, Françoise. 1978. La sociolinguistique n'existe pas, je l'ai rencontrée. Dialectiques 20:99–118.
———. 1978. Labov et la sociolinguistique. Nouvelle Critique 110:72–3.
Galtung, J. 1981. Structure, culture, and intellectual style. Social Science Information 20(5):817–56.

Gardès-Madray, Françoise and Bernard Gardin. 1989. Parole(s) ouvrière(s). Langages 93:1-125.
Gardin, Bernard. 1976. L'apprentissage du français par les travailleurs immigrés. Langue Française 29.
—— and Jean Baptiste Marcellesi, eds. 1980. Sociolinguistique. Approches, théories, pratiques. vols. 1, 2. Paris: Publication of the University of France and University of Rouen Publications.
—— and Jean Baptiste Marcellesi. 1987. The subject matter of sociolinguistics. In Ulrich Ammon (ed.), Sociolinguistics, 16-25. Berlin; New York: de Gruyter.
Gardner, R. C. and Wallace E. Lambert. 1959. Motivational variables in second-language acquisition. Canadian Journal of Psychology 13:266-72.
Garfinkel, H. and H. Sacks. 1970. On formal structure of practical actions. In J. McKiney and E. Tiryakian (eds.), Theoretical sociology, 337-66. New York: Appleton.
Gaudin, François. 1994. Pour une socioterminologie. Publications of the University of Rouen.
Giglioli, Pier Paolo, ed. 1972. Language and social context: Selected readings. Harmondsworth: Penguin.
——, ed. 1973. Linguaggio e società. Il Mulino. (Revision of Language and social context, Penguin Books).
——. 1973. Introduzzione. In Linguaggio e società, 5-44. Il Mulino.
Giles, H., Philip M. Smith, and W. Peter Robinson. 1980. Social psychological perspectives in language: Prologue. In H. Giles, P. M. Smith, and W. P. Robinson (eds.), Language: Social psychological perspectives. Oxford: Pergamon.
Gonzales, Andrew and Leticia T. Postrado. 1974. Assessing manpower and teaching materials for bilingual education. Manila: United Publishing.
—— and Ma. Lourdes S. Bautista. 1986. Language surveys in the Philippines. Manila: De La Salle University Press.
—— and Bonifacio O. Sibayan. 1988. Evaluating bilingual education in the Philippines: 1974-1985. Manila: Linguistic Society of the Philippines.
Grice, H. Paul. 1975. Logic and conversation. In Peter Cole and Jerry Morgan (eds.), Syntax and semantics 3, 41-55. New York: Academic.
Grimes, Barbara D. 1988. Exploring the sociolinguistics of Ambonese Malay. Fifth International Conference on Austronesian Languages, Auckland, January 1988.
Grimes, Barbara F., ed. 1974, 1980, 1984, 1988, 1992. Ethnologue: Languages of the world. Dallas: Summer Institute of Linguistics.

———, ed. 1984, 1988, 1992. Ethnologue Index. Dallas: Summer Institute of Linguistics.

———. 1984. Second language proficiency report. Notes on Linguistics 31:26–30.

———. 1985a. Comprehension and language attitudes in relation to language choice for literature and education in pre-literate societies. Journal of Multilingual and Multicultural Development 6(2):164–81.

———. 1985b. Language attitudes: Identity, distinctiveness, survival in the Vaupés. Journal of Multilingual and Multicultural Development 6(5):389–401.

———. 1986a. Evaluating bilingual proficiency in language groups for cross-cultural communication. Notes on Linguistics 33:5–27.

———. 1986b. Regional and other nonstandard dialects of major languages. Notes on Linguistics 35:19–39.

———. 1987. How bilingual is bilingual? Notes on Linguistics 40a:3–23.

———. 1988a. Why test intelligibility? Notes on Linguistics 42:39–64.

———. 1988b. On bilingual proficiency thresholds. Notes on Scripture in Use 16:1–10.

———. 1989. Special considerations for creole surveys. Notes on Linguistics 41:47–63.

———. 1992. Notes on oral proficiency testing. In Eugene Casad (ed.), Windows on bilingualism, 53–60. Summer Institute of Linguistics and the University of Texas at Arlington Publications in Linguistis 110. Dallas.

———. 1993. Evaluating the Hawaii Creole English situation. Second International Language Assessment Conference, Horsleys Green, England, June 2–9, 1993.

Grimes, Charles E. Ambonese Malay: A brief orientation. ms.

Grimes, Joseph E. 1974. Dialects as optimal communication networks. Language 50:260–69.

———. 1974. Word lists and languages (Technical Report No. 2). Report to the National Science Foundation on Grant GS-312995 and Grant GS-1605. Ithaca: Department of Modern Languages and Linguistics, Cornell University.

———. 1986. Area norms of language size. In Benjamin F. Elson (ed.), Language in global perspective: Papers in honor of the 50th anniversary of the Summer Institute of Linguistics, 5–19. Dallas: Summer Institute of Linguistics.

———. 1988a. Correlations between vocabulary similarity and intelligibility. Notes on Linguistics 41:19–33.

———. 1988b. Interpreting sample variation in intelligibility tests. Georgetown University Round Table in Language and Linguistics 1988, 138–46. Washington, D.C.: Georgetown University Press.
———. 1993. Population sizes of endangered languages. Linguistic Society of America, Los Angeles, January 1993.
———. 1995. Language survey reference guide. Dallas: Summer Institute of Linguistics.
Grimshaw, Allen D. 1973. Sociolinguistics. In Ithiel de Sola Pool and others (eds.), Handbook of communication. Chicago: Rand McNally.
———. 1980. Sociolinguistics at the council, 1963–1979: Past and prologue. Items 34(1):12–18.
———. 1987. Sociolinguistics vs. sociology of language: Tempest in a teapot or Profound academic conundrum? In Urlich Ammon (ed.), Sociolinguistics: An International Handbook of the Science of Language and Society 1:9–15. Berlin: de Gruyter.
———. 1989. Collegial discourse: Professional conversation among peers. Norwood: Ablex.
———. 1996. Sociolinguistics in post-union Moscow: A non-systematic personal view. In Jeff Harlid (ed.), East European sociolinguistics after the fall. The Hague: Mouton.
——— and Peter J. Burke. 1994. What's going on here? Complementary studies of professional talk. Norwood: Ablex.
Groupe de recherche sur la covarience sociolinguistique puis de l'U.R.A. n.d. Cahiers de linguistique sociale. University of Rouen, Centre National de la Recherche Scientifique. 1164.
Guespin, Louis. 1971. Le discours politique. Langages 23.
———. 1976. Types de discours, ou foncionnements discursifs? Introduction to Typologie du discours politique. Langages 41:3–12.
———. 1980. Langage et travail, de l'anthropologie à la théorie de la personnalité. In Jean Baptiste Marcellesi (ed.), Langages et sociétés. La Pensée 209:114–29.
——— and Jean Baptiste Marcellesi. 1980. Pour la glottopolitique. Langages 83:5–34.
Gueunier, Nicole, Emile Genouvrier, and Abdelhamid Khomsi. 1978. Les français devant la norme. Paris: Champion.
Guilbert, Louis. 1965a. La formation du vocabulaire de l'aviation, vols. 1 and 2. Paris: Larousse.
———. 1965b. Le vocabulaire de l'astronautique. Publications of the University of Rouen.
——— and J. Peytard. 1973. Les vocabulaires techniques et scientifiques. Langue Française 17:128.

Guilléron, Jules and Edmond Edmont. 1902–1910. Atlas linguistique de la France. Paris: Champion.
Gumperz, John J. 1954. The Swabian dialect of Washtenaw County, Michigan. Ph.D dissertation. University of Michigan.
———. 1969. Sociolinguistics in South Asia. In Thomas A. Sebeok (ed.), Current trends in Linguistics 5, 597–606. The Hague: Mouton.
———. 1973. La communità linguistica. In P. P. Giglioli (ed.), Linguaggio e società, 269–80. Il Mulino.
——— and Dell Hymes, eds. 1964. The ethnography of communication. American Anthropologist 66:6, part 2 (Special publication). (Rev. ed. 1972, published as Directions in sociolinguistics: The ethnography of communication.) New York: Holt.
Guxman, M. M., ed. 1960. Voprosy formirovanija i razvitija natsional'nyx jazykov. Moskva: Izdatel'stvo Akademii Nauk USSR.
Haas, Mary R. 1944. Men's and women's speech in Koasati. Language 20:142–49.
Hägerstrand, Torsten. 1953. Innovationsförloppet ur korologisk synpunkt (The innovation process from a chorological point of view.) Lund: Gleerupska university bokhandeln.
Hallberg, Daniel G. 1992. Pashto, Waneci, Ormuri. Sociolinguistic survey of Northern Pakistan 4. Islamabad: National Institutes of Pakistan Studies and Summer Institute of Linguistics.
Halliday, M. A. K. 1978. Language as social semiotic: The social interpretation of language and meaning. Baltimore: University Park.
Hannerz, U. 1969. Soulside: Inquiries into ghetto culture and community. New York: Columbia University Press.
Hasan, R. 1992. Meaning in sociolinguistic theory. In Kingsley Bolton and Helen Kwok (eds.), Sociolinguistics today: International perspectives, 80–119. London: Routledge.
Hatfield, Deborah, Carla Radloff, Ted Bergman, Marie South, Barrie Wetherill. 1993. The Cameroon study: A comparison of second language proficiency testing methods. Second International Language Assessment Conference, Horsleys Green, England, June 2–9, 1993.
Hattori, S. 1960. Gengogaku no hoohoo (Methods in linguistics). Tokyo: Iwanami shoten.
Haugen, Einar. 1953. The Norwegian language in America: A study in bilingual behavior, 2 vols. (vol. 1. The bilingual community, vol. 2, The American dialects of Norwegian, (iii), 319–695). Philadelphia: University Press of Pennsylania.
———. 1954. Review of Uriel Weinreich, Languages in contact. Language 30:380–88.

———. 1956. Bilingualism in the Americas: A bibliography and research guide. Alabama: University Press.
———. 1966a. Linguistics and language planning. In William Bright (ed.), Sociolinguistics: Proceedings of the UCLA Sociolinguistics Conference, 1964, 50–66. The Hague: Mouton.
———. 1966b. Language conflict and language planning: The case of Modern Norwegian. Cambridge: Harvard University Press.
———. 1972. Author's postscript. The ecology of language. Stanford: University Press.
Hebb, D. O., Wallace E. Lambert, and G. R. Tucker. 1971. Language, thought, and experience. Modern Language Journal 55:212–22.
Helgorski, Françoise. 1973. La sociolinguistique aux Etats-Unis et en France. Le Français Moderne, 387–409. (Bibliography pp. 409–15.)
Henne, Marilyn G. 1985. Why mother tongue literacy has failed to take root among the Maya Quiché: A study in the sociology of language in a field program of the Summer Institute of Linguistics, 1955–1982, Guatemala, Central America. M.A. thesis, University of Texas at Arlington.
———. 1991. Program planning for larger language groups: Same or different? In Gloria E. Kindell (ed.), Proceedings of the Summer Institute of Linguistics International Language Assessment Conference, Horsleys Green, 23–31 May 1989, 121–30. Dallas: Summer Institute of Linguistics.
Hernandez-Chavez, Eduardo, Andrew D. Cohen, and Anthony F. Beltramo, eds. 1975. El lenguaje de los Chicanos: Regional and social characteristics used by Mexican Americans. Arlington, Va.: Center for Applied Linguistics.
Hertzler, Joyce O. 1965. A sociology of language. New York: Random.
Herzog, Marvin I. 1967. Uriel Weinreich bibliography. Language 43:606–10.
Hickerson, Harold, Glen D. Turner, and Nancy P. Hickerson. 1952. Testing procedures for estimating transfer of information among Iroquois dialects and languages. International Journal of American Linguistics 18:1–8.
Homans, George. 1966. Social behavior and exchange. In Edwin P. Hollander and Raymond G. Hunt (eds.), Current perspectives in social psychology, 447–57. New York: Oxford University Press.
Hostein, Bernard. 1977. Le système scolaire français: Place de travailleurs migrants. IRFED.
———. 1977. Langues, langage(s) et parole dans la vie d'adolescents des milieux migrants. Bulletin de Psychologie 335:483–501.
Houbedine, Jean-Louis. 1977. Langage et marxisme. Paris: Klincksieck.

Huttar, George L., ed. 1982. Sociolinguistic survey conference. Notes on Linguistics, special issue 2. Dallas: Summer Institute of Linguistics.
Hymes, Dell. 1962. The ethnography of speaking. In T. Gladwin and W. C. Sturtevant (eds.), Anthropology and human behavior, 13–53. Washington, D.C.: Anthropological Society of Washington. (Repub. 1968. In Fishman (ed.), Readings in the sociology of language, 99–138.)
———. 1964. A perspective for linguistic anthropology. In Sol Tax (ed.), Horizons of anthropology, 92–107. Chicago: Aldine.
———. 1964. Introduction: Toward ethnographies of communication. In John J. Gumperz and Dell H. Hymes (eds.), The ethnography of communication. American Anthropologist 66(6), part 2:1–34.
———, ed. 1964. Language in culture and society: A reader in linguistics and anthropology. New York: Harper.
———. 1966. Teaching and training in sociolinguistics. Report to Social Science Research Council, 1 November 1966.
———, ed. 1971. Pidginization and creolization of languages: Proceedings of a conference held at the University of the West Indies, Mona, Jamaica, April 1968. New York: Cambridge University Press.
———. 1974. Foundations in sociolinguistics: An ethnographic approach. Philadelphia: University Press of Pennsylvania.
———. 1984. Vers la competance de communication. Translated by France Mugler. Paris: Hatien Credif.
——— and J. J. Gumperz, eds. 1964. The ethnography of communication. American Anthropologist Special Publication, 66(6), part 2.
Ibrahim ag Youssouf, Allen D. Grimshaw, and Charles S. Bird. 1976. Greetings in the desert. American Ethnologist 3, 4:797–824.
International Days of Sociolinguistics, Rome, 1969. 1970. Giornate internazionale de sociolinguistica. Rome: Tip. V. Ferri.
Jackson, Jean. ms. Language, marriage, and the tribe: The Bara Indians of the Vaupés, Colombia.
James, Heidi, Elizabeth Masland, and Sharon Rand. 1989. An investigation into bilingualism measurement methods. First International Language Assessment Conference, Horsleys Green, England, 1989.
Janton, Pierre. 1993. Esperanto: Language, literature and community. Edited by Humphrey Tonkin. Albany: State University of New York Press.

Jastrab, Marie-Josée. 1984. Organizational vs. individual bilingualism: The case of the United Nations Secretariat. In Jane Edwards and Humphrey Tonkin (eds.), Language behavior in international organizations, 6–58. New York: Center for Research and Documentation on World Language Problems.
Jensen, Arthur. 1969. How much can we boost IQ and scholastic achievement? Harvard Educational Review 31:1.
Jernudd Björn H. 1964. Språksociologi (Sociolinguistics). Anthropolognytt 3(2):1–4.
———. 1965. The language situation in Tadzhikistan SSR. Anthropological Linguistics 7(3), part 2:76–83.
———. 1968. Linguistic integration and national development: A case study of the Jebel Marra area, Sudan. In Joshua A. Fishman, Charles A. Ferguson, and Jyotirindra Das Gupta (eds.), Language problems of developing nations, 167–81. New York: Wiley.
———. 1968. Is self-instructional language teaching profitable? International Review of Applied Linguistics in Language Teaching 6(4):349–60.
———. 1971. English in Australia. Review of W. S. Ramson, ed. English transported: Essays on Australian English (1970). Kivung 4(1):50–63 (Also in Linguistic Communications 3:95–112).
——— and Tommy Johannson. 1963. Preliminär rapport över språkligt social undersölning (Preliminary reports in applied linguistics) 2, IATS, Stockholm University. Results published as: A sociological study of the Stockholm region. Svenska Landsmål, arsh, 1968. 140–47.
——— and J. V. Neustupný. 1974. On the development of modern sociolinguistics: Some data on the sociological idiom. Paper prepared for the section: The sociology of language as a discipline. Eighth World Congress of Sociology. Toronto, August 16–23, 1974.
——— and J. V. Neustupný. 1987. Language planning: For whom? In L. Laforge (ed.), Proceedings of the International Colloquium on Language Planning, 69–84. Ottawa: Laval University Press.
Kahn, Leybl. 1969. Uriel Vaynraykh in ershtn yugntruf. Yugntruf 17/18:8 and 16.
Kakumasu, James. 1968. Urubu sign language. International Journal of American Linguistics 34:275–81.
Katzner, Kenneth. 1975. The languages of the world. New York: Funk and Wagnalls.
Kelly, Louis G., ed. 1969. Description and measurement of bilingualism. Toronto: University Press.

Khubchandani, L. M. 1984. Sociolinguistics in India: The decade past and the decade to come. International Journal of the Sociology of Language 45:47–64.

———. 1991. India as a sociolinguistic area. Language Sciences 13:265–88 (Pune: University of Poona).

Kindell, Gloria E., ed. 1991. Proceedings of the Summer Institute of Linguistics International Language Assessment Conference, Horsleys Green, 23–31 May 1989. Dallas: Summer Institute of Linguistics.

Kiparsky, Paul. 1979. Panini as variationist. Current studies in linguistics 7. Cambridge: MIT Press. (Repub. 1984 in Word: Journal of the International Linguistics Association 35:194–97.)

Kirk, Dudley. 1946. Europe's population in the interwar years. Princeton: University Press.

Kirk, Paul L. 1966. Proto-Mazatec phonology. Ph.D. dissertation. University of Washington.

———. 1970. Dialect intelligibility testing: The Mazatec study. International Journal of American Linguistics 36:205–11.

Kiser, Clyde V. 1956. Cultural pluralism. In Joseph J. Spengler and Otis Dudley Duncan (eds.), Demographic analysis: Selected writings, 307–20. Glencoe, Ill.: Free Press.

Kjolseth, R. 1968. Structure and process in creative conversation: An exploratory study of gesture dialogue. Ph.D. dissertation. Department of Sociology, University of Colorado, Boulder.

———. 1969. We the gods: The member's natural constitutive account of creation, evolution, and revolution in their small language community. Offset research monograph. Department of Sociology, University of California at Davis.

———. 1971a. The research committee on sociolinguistics: Report, January 1971. Sociolinguistics Newsletter 2(1):3–5.

———. 1971b. The research committee on sociolinguistics: Guidelines. Sociolinguistics Newsletter 2(1):6–8.

———. 1971c. Die Entwicklung der Sprachsoziologie und Ihre sozialen Implikationen. Introduction to Rolf Kjolseth and Fritz Sack, Sociolinguistics Newsletter 2(1):9–32. Reprinted in translation as The development of the sociology of language and its social implications. In Sociolinguistics Newsletter 3(1):7–10, 24–29 (July 1972), and in expanded form in Joshua A. Fishman (ed.), Advances in the study of societal multilingualism, 799–825. The Hague: Mouton.

———. 1971d. Zweisprachige Erziehungsprogramme in den Vereinigten Staaten: Assimilation oder Pluralismus? In Rolf Kjolseth and Fritz Sack, Sociolinguistics newsletter 251–75. Reprinted in translation as Bilingual education programs in the United States: For assimilation or pluralism? in Bernard Spolsky (ed.), The language education of minority children: Selected readings, 94–121. Rowley, Mass.: Newbury House; and in Paul Turner (ed.), 1973, Bilingualism in the Southwest, 3–27. Tucson: Arizona University Press; and in Francesco Cordasco (ed.), 1976, Bilingual schooling in the United States: A sourcebook for educational personnel, 122–40; and (revised version with addendum) in Paul R. Turner (ed.), 1982, Bilingualism in the Southwest (2nd revised edition), 3–23. Tucson: Arizona University Press.

———. 1972. Making sense: Natural language and everyday knowledge in understanding. In Joshua A. Fishman (ed.), Advances in the sociology of language 2, 50–76. The Hague: Mouton.

———. 1975. Educación bilingüe en balance: una inversión en el éxito (Bilingual education on balance: an investment in success). Un Nuevo Día (July 1975), 15–16.

———. 1977. Bilingual education: For what and for whom? Review article of W. E. Lambert and G. R. Tucker, Bilingual education of children: A study of equal language maintenance through free alternation. Rowley, Mass.: Newbury, 1972. Language in Society 6(2):247–63.

———. 1978. The development of the sociology of language and its social implications. In Joshua A. Fishman (ed.), Advances in the study of societal multilingualism, 799–825. The Hague: Mouton.

———. 1981. A critical analysis of the state of bilingual postsecondary education. In Narcissa Jones (ed.), Bilingual higher education: Foundations, policy, and practice. (Report of proceedings of a bilingual education summer institute, Seton Hall University, Aug. 24–29, 1979), 142–51. State of New Jersey: Department of Higher Education.

———. 1983. Cultural politics of bilingualism. In Allen D. Grimshaw (ed.), Sociolinguistics today: Language as a social problem. Society 20(4):40–48.

———. 1991. W(h)ither ethnic languages and bilingualism in the United States? Crisis and the struggle between hegemony and humanism. In James R. Dow (ed.), Language and ethnicity: Focusschrift in honor of Joshua A. Fishman, 207–23. Amsterdam: Benjamins.

―― and Fritz Sack. 1971. Zur Soziologie der Sprache: ausgewählte Beiträge vom 7 Weltkongress der Soziologie (Toward a sociology of language: Selected contributions from the Seventh World Congress of Sociology). Sonderheft Nr. 15 der Kölner Zeitschrift für Soziologie und Sozialpsychologie. Köln: Westdeutscher Verlag.

―― and Victoria Patella. 1974. Evaluation of the 1974 Title I summer bilingual-bicultural program in Lincoln and Lafayette elementary schools. Research monograph. Boulder, Colo.

Kloss, Heinz. 1927. Berufserfassung und Spracherhaltung. Der Auslandsdeutsche 10(22):754–56.

――. 1929a. Nebensprachen. Vienna: Braumüller.

――. 1929b. Sprachtabellen als Grundlage für Sprachstabellen als Grundlage für eine allgemeine Soziologie der Sprachgemeinschaften. Vierteljahresschrift für Politik und Geschichte 2:103–17.

――. 1977. The American bilingual tradition. Rowley, Mass.: Newbury House.

――. 1974. Linguistic composition of the nations of the world. Quebec: Laval University.

――, Grant D. McConnell, and Albert Verdoodt, eds. 1989. The written languages of the world: A survey of the degree and modes of use, 3: Western Europe/Les langues écrites du monde: Relève du degré et des modes d'utilisation, 3: Europe Occidentale. Laval University Press.

Koerner, Konrad. 1991. Towards a history of modern sociolinguistics. American Speech 66(1): 57–70.

Konrad, N. I. 1952. O natsional'nom yazyke v Kitae i Yaponii [On the national language in China and Japan]. Uchenye zapiski Instituta vostokovedeniya 4:5–29.

Korínek, J. M. 1948. Uvod do jazykospytu [Introduction to Linguistics]. Bratislava: Slovenská akadémia vied a umeni.

La Pensée: Classes sociales, langage, éducation... 1976. Paris: ENSCP.

Labov, William. 1965. Stages in the acquisition of standard English. In Roger Shuy (ed.), Social dialects and language learning, 77–104. Champaign, Ill.: National Council of Teachers of English.

――. 1967. The social stratification of English in New York City. Washington, D.C.: Center for Applied Linguistics. (Also 1966, Dissertation Abstracts, Ann Arbor.)

――. 1970. The logic of non-standard English. Proceedings of the Georgetown University Round Table on Language and Linguistics 1969. Washington, D.C.: Georgetown University Press.

――. 1976. Sociolinguistique. Paris: Minuit.

――, ed. 1977. Lengas: Revue de sociolinguistique. Centre d'Études Occitanes, Université de Montpellier.

———. 1978. Le parler ordinaire: La langue dans les ghettos noirs des États-Unis, 2 vols. Paris: Minuit.
Lafont, Robert. 1978. Le travail et la langue. Flammarion.
———. 1979. Recherches sociolinguistiques dans le cadre des situations de diglossie. Rapport scientifique, R. C. P. 482. Centre National de la Recherche Scientifique.
———, Françoise Madray, and Paul Siblot. 1983. Pratiques praxématiques: Introduction à une analyse matérialiste du sens. Rouen: Cahiers de Linguistique.
Laforge, L. and G. D. McConnell, eds. 1990. Language spread and social change (International Center for Research on Bilingualism Publication A-22). Quebec: Laval Univesity Press.
Laks, Bernard. 1977. Contribution empirique à l'analyse socio-différentielle de la chute des /r/ dans les groupes consonantiques finals. Langue Française 34:109–25.
———. 1980. L'unité linguistique dans le parler d'une famille. In Bernard Gardin and Jean Baptiste Marcellesi (eds.), Langages et sociétés. Paris: Presses universitares de France.
Lambert, Richard D. 1973. Language and area studies review. Monograph 17 of the American Academy of Political and Social Science. Philadelphia. (See especially chapter 8, Conclusions and recommendations.)
Lambert, Wallace E. 1992. Challenging established views on social issues: The power and the limitations of research. American Psychologist 4:533–42.
———. 1994. The importance of being psychologists. Paper presented at a symposium held at York University, May 6–8.
———, J. Hamers, and N. Frasure-Smith. 1979. Child rearing values: A cross-national study. New York: Praeger.
———, R. C. Hodgson, R. C. Gardner, and S. Fillenbaum. 1960. Evaluational reactions to spoken languages. Journal of Abnormal and Social Psychology 60:44–51.
——— and D. M. Taylor. 1990. Coping with cultural and racial diversity in urban America. New York: Praeger.
——— and G. Richard Tucker. 1972. Bilingual education of children: The St. Lambert experiment. Rowley, Mass.: Newbury.
——— and G. Richard Tucker. 1976. Tu, vous, usted: A social-psychological study of address patterns. Rowley, Mass.: Newbury.

Landweer, Lynn M. 1991. Schlie-Landweer priority allocation assessment device: Rationale paper. In Gloria E. Kindell (ed.), 1991, Proceedings of the Summer Institute of Linguisics International Language Assessment Conference, Horsleys Green, 23–31 May 1989, 49–67. Dallas: Summer Institute of Linguistics.
Langue de l'enfant, classes sociales, école. n.d. Université René Descartes.
Lapenna, Ivo. 1958. Retoriko. 2nd ed. Rotterdam: The Author. (1st ed. Paris, 1950.)
Large, Andrew. 1985. The artificial language movement. Oxford: Blackwell.
Laroussi, Foued. 1994. Minoration sociolinguistique au Maghreb. Cahiers de Linguistique Sociale 22.
de Latour, Charles-Henri. 1977. Le système de parenté dans les grandes ensembles de Montbéliard. Bulletin de Psychologie 35:510–20.
Legrand, Jacques. 1980. Classes sociales et rapports sociaux dans la détermination du langage. In Bernard Gardin and Jean Baptiste Marcellesi (eds.), Sociolinguistique: Approches, théories, pratiques, 22–35. Paris: Publication of the University of France and Publications de l'Université de Rouen.
Legrand-Gelber, Régine. 1980. Nécessité d'une démarche sociolinguistique en pédagogie de la langue maternelle: Les évidences et leur dépassement. Actes du Colloque organisé du 27 novembre au 2 décembre par le GRECO, Université de Rouen, Faculté des Lettres de Mont-Saint-Aignan. 583–94. In Bernard Gardin and Jean Baptiste Marcellesi (eds.), Sociolinguistique: Approches, théories, pratiques, 343–693. Paris: Publication of the University of France.
———, Régine and Christiane Marcellesi. 1980. Langage, rapports sociaux et école. In Jean Baptiste Marcellesi, Langages et sociétés. La Pensée 209:85–88. IRM.
LePage, Robert. 1978. Projection, diffusion, or steps towards a sociolinguistic theory of language. St. Augustine, Trinidad: Occasional Papers of the Society for Caribbean Linguistics 9.
——— and Andrée Tabouret-Keller. 1985. Acts of identity: Creole based approaches to language and ethnicity. Cambridge: University Press.
Lepschy, Giulio, ed. 1994. History of Linguistics 1. London: Longman.
Levinson, S. 1983. Pragmatics. New York: Cambridge University Press.
Lieberson, Stanley. 1961. A societal theory of race and ethnic relations. American Sociological Review 26:902–10.
———. 1963. Ethnic patterns in American cities. New York: The Free Press of Glencoe.

———. 1965. Bilingualism in Montreal: A demographic analysis. American Journal of Sociology 71:10–25. (Repub. in Joshua A. Fishman. 1972. Advances in the sociology of language 2: Selected studies and applications, 231–54. The Hague: Mouton.)

———. 1966. Language questions in censuses. Sociological Inquiry 36(2):262–79. [Also published in 1967 as Indiana University Research Center in Anthropology, Folklore, and Linguistics Publication 44; supplement to International Journal of American Linguistics 33(4), part 2.]

———. 1970. Language and ethnic relations in Canada. New York: Wiley.

———. 1981. Language diversity and language contact: Essays by Stanley Lieberson. Selected and introduced by Anwar S. Dil. Stanford: University Press.

———. 1982. Forces affecting language spread: Some basic propositions. In Robert L. Cooper (ed.), Language spread: Studies in diffusion and social change, 37–62. Bloomington, Ind.: University Press.

———. 1984. What's in a name? Some sociolinguistic possibilities. International Journal of the Sociology of Language 45:77–87.

———. 1992a. A brief introduction to the demographic analysis of culture. Sociology of Culture Section Newsletter 6:21–23.

———. 1992b. Einstein, Renoir, and Greeley: Some thoughts about evidence in sociology. American Sociological Review 57:1–15.

——— and Eleanor Bell. 1992. Children's first names: An empirical study of social taste. American Journal of Sociology 98:511–54.

———, Guy Dalto, and Mary Ellen Johnston (Marsden). 1975. The course of mother tongue diversity in nations. American Journal of Sociology 81:34–61.

———, ed. 1966. Explorations in sociolinguistics. Special issue of Sociological Inquiry 36 (Spring). Reprinted (1967) Indiana University Research Center in Anthropology, Folklore, and Linguistics Publication 44 (International Journal of American Linguistics 33(4), part 2).

Linguistic Society of India. 1959. Report of the blueprint committee on the development of linguistic studies in Indian universities. Pune: Deccan College.

Lins, Ulrich. 1988. Die gefährliche Sprache: die Verfolgung der Esperantisten unter Hitler und Stalin. Gerlingen, Germany: Bleicher.

Lo Jacomo, François, ed. 1986. Plurilinguisme et communication. Paris: Société d'Études Linguistiques et Anthropologiques de France.

Loving, Richard and Gary F. Simons. 1977. Language variation and survey techniques. Workpapers in Papua New Guinea Languages 21. Ukarumpa: Summer Institute of Linguistics.

Lucy, John A., ed. 1992. Language diversity and thought: A reformulation of the linguistic relativity hypothesis. Cambridge: University Press.
Maas, Heinz Dieter. 1991. Studien zur machinellen Übersetzung: die Reihe Distributed Language Translation. Language Problems and Language Planning 15:66–77.
Mackey, William F. 1978. Organizing research on bilingualism: The ICB story. McGill Journal of Education 13(2):116–27.
———. 1982. International bibliography on bilingualism/Bibliographie internationale sur le bilinguisme. (Centre International de Recherche sur le Bilinguisme Publication F, 2nd ed.) Quebec: Laval University Press. (1st ed. 1972.)
———. 1983. Sociolinguistics: The past decade. In Shirô Hattori and Kazuko Inoue (eds.), Proceedings of the Thirteenth International Congress of Linguists, 39–51. Tokyo: Proceedings Publishing Committee.
———. 1983. Sociolinguistics and synchronic fallacy (Inaugural lecture to the Royal Academy of Belgium). Academiae Analecta 45(4):79–90.
———. 1989. La genèse d'une typologie de la diglossie. Revue québécoise de linguistique théorique et appliquée 8(2):11–28.
———. 1989. Review of "L'institution de français: Essai sur le colinguisme des Carolingiens à la République" by Renée Balibar. Journal of the History of European Ideas 11. Paris: Publication of the University of France.
———. 1990. A terminology for sociolinguistics. Sociolinguistics 19:99–125.
———. 1993. Literary diglossia, biculturalism and cosmopolitanism in literature. Visible Language 27:40–67.
——— and Jacob Ornstein, eds. 1979. Sociolinguistic studies in language contact: Methods and cases. (Trends in Linguistics 6.) The Hague: Mouton.
Macnamara, J. 1970. Bilingualism and thought. In James E. Alatis (ed.), 21st Annual Round Table, 25–45. Washington, D.C.: Georgetown University Press.
———. 1972. The cognitive basis of language learning in children. Psychological Review 79:1–13.
———. 1991. Linguistic relativity revisited. In R. L. Cooper and B. Spolsky (eds.), The influence of language on culture and thought, 45–60. Berlin: Mouton de Gruyter.
———, ed. 1967. Problems in bilingualism. Special issue of Journal of Social Issues 23(2). Ann Arbor.
Malkiel, Yakov. 1967. Uriel Weinreich, 1926–1967. Language 43:606–10.

———. 1968. Necrology: Uriel Weinreich, Jakob Jud's last student. Romance Philology 22:128–32.
Malmstrom, Marilyn. 1991. My tongue is the pen: How audiocassettes can serve the nonreading world. Dallas: Summer Institute of Linguistics.
Marcellesi, Christiane. 1973a. Approche synchronique du vocabulaire de l'informatique. Thèse de troisième cycle, 2 vols. Paris: Nanterre.
———. 1973b. Le langage de techniciens de l'informatique: Quelques aspects de leur vocabulaire écrit et oral. In L. Guilbert and J. Petard (eds.), Les vocabulaires techniques et scientifiques. Langue Française 17:59–71.
———. 1977. Aspects socio-culturels de l'enseignement du français. Langue Française 32.
———. 1978. Les problèmes de l'analyse sociolinguistique en milieu scolaire. In Langue de l'enfant, classes sociales, école, 40–51. Université René Descartes.
———, ed. 1986. École ici...là-bas. Cahiers de Linguistique Sociale No. 8.
Marcellesi, Jean Baptiste. 1971a. Le congrès de Tours (déc. 1920): Études sociolinguistiques. In Maria Roger (ed.), Le Pavillon. Diff. Publications, University of Rouen.
———. 1971b. Linguistique et société. Langue Française 9.
———. 1975. L'enseignement des langues 'regionales'. Langue Française 25.
———. 1977. Langage et classes sociales: le marrisme. Langages. 46. Paris: Larousse.
———. 1979. Quelques problèmes de l'hégémonie culturelle en France: Langue nationale et langues régionales. International Journal of the Sociology of Language 21:63–80.
———. 1980. Crise de la linguistique et linguistique de la crise: La sociolinguistique. In Jean Baptiste Marcellesi (ed.), Langages et sociétés. La Pensée 209:4–21.
———, ed. 1980. Langages et sociétés. La Pensée 209.
———. 1981. Bilinguisme, diglossie, hégémonie: Problème et tâches. In Jean Baptiste Marcellesi (ed.), Bilinguisme et diglossie. Langages 61:5–12.
———, ed. 1981. Bilinguisme et diglossie. Langages 61.
———, ed. 1986. Glottopolitique. Langages 83.
———. 1987. Corse et théorie sociolinguistique: reflets croisés. In l'Ile Miroir: Actes du Colloque Aix-en-Provence, 165–79. La Marge Ajaccio.
———. 1991. Polinomie, variation et norme. In Jean Chiorboli (ed.), Les langues polynomiques, 331–36. Université de Corte.
———. n.d. L'individuation sociolinguistique corse. Études corses 27. Archives Départementales.

―― and Bernard Gardin. 1974. Introduction à la sociolinguistique, la linguistique sociale. Paris: Larousse.

―― and Abdou Elimam. 1987. Language and society from a Marxist point of view. In Sociolinguistics: An International Handbook of the Science of Language and Society, 1:443–52. Berlin: de Gruyter.

Marfil, Alice and Aida Pasigna. 1970. An analysis of shifts from Tagalog to English imprinted material. M.A. thesis. Manila: Philippine Normal College.

Martinet, André. 1960. Eléments de linguistique générale. Paris: Colin.

Mayer, Kurt B. 1956. Cultural pluralism and linguistic equilibrium in Switzerland. In Joseph J. Spengler and Otis Dudley Duncan (eds.), Demographic analysis: Selected readings, 478–83. Glencoe, Ill.: The Free Press.

Mayers, Marvin K. 1960. The Pocomchí: A sociolinguistic study. Ph.D. dissertation. University of Chicago.

McCaulay, Ronald K. S. 1988. What happened to sociolinguistics? English World Wide 9(2):153–56.

McConnell, G. D. 1991. A macro sociolinguistic analysis of language vitality (International Center for Research on Bilingualism Publication A-23). Québec: Laval University Press.

―― and J. D. Gendron. 1993. International atlas of language vitality (Centre International de Recherche sur le Bilinguisme Publication G-13, G-14 et seq.) vol. 1 (India): vol. 2 (Western Europe). Québec: Centre International de Recherche en Aménagement Linquistique.

McDavid, Raven I. 1948. Postvocalic /-r/ in South Carolina: A social analysis. American Speech 23:129–203.

McElhinny, Bonnie. 1993. Review of sociolinguistics today: International perspectives. Ed. by Kingsley Bolton and Helen Kwok. Language 3:614–16. London: Routledge.

McKean, Roland L. 1958. Efficiency in government through systems analysis. (The Rand Corporation.) New York: Wiley and Sons.

McRae, Kenneth D. 1964. Switzerland: Example of cultural coexistence. Toronto: The Canadian Institute of International Affairs.

Meehl, Clifford. 1954. Clinical vs. statistical prediction: A theoretical analysis and review of the evidence. Minneapolis: Minnesota University Press.

Meillet, Antoine. 1921. Linguistique historique et linguistique générale. Paris: Société de Linguistique de Paris.

――. 1924. Les langues du monde. Paris: E. Champion. (1952. Les langues du monde, nouvelle édition. Paris: Centre national de la recherche scientifique. H. Champion.)

Michell, Tony and Selma Sonntag. 1984. Multinationals: Linguistic interfaces as a retarding factor in the growth of firms. In Jane Edwards and Humphrey Tonkin (ed.), Language behavior in international organizations, 59–80. New York: Center for Research and Documentation on World Language Problems.

Milliken, Margaret E. 1988. Phonological divergence and intelligibility: A case study of English and Scots. Ph.D. dissertation. Ithaca: Cornell University.

——— and Stuart Milliken. 1993. System relationships in dialect intelligibility. Second International Language Assessment Conference, Horsleys Green, England, June 2–9, 1993.

Mioni, Alberto and Renzi. 1977. Introduction à Aspetti sociolinguistici dell' Italia contemporanea. (Actes du Congrès de la S.L.I. de Bressanonc: 2 vols.) Rome: Bulzoni.

Moulton, William G. 1985. Mutual intelligibility among speakers of early German dialects. Germanica Conference, Georgetown University, Washington, D.C., July 1985.

Müller, Kurt E. 1984. Language problems during multinational military operations in Korea. In Jane Edwards and Humphrey Tonkin (ed.), Language behavior in international organizations, 81–99. New York: Center for Research and Documentation on World Language Problems.

———. 1986. Language competence: Implications for national security. New York: Praeger.

Murray, Stephen O. 1983. Group formation in social science. Edmonton, Alberta: Linguistic Research.

———. 1994. Theory groups and the study of language in North America: A social history. Amsterdam: Benjamins.

Muysken, P. 1985. 20 years of sociolinguistics? Sociolinguistics 15(2):12–19. [Newsletter of the research committee on sociolinguistics, International Sociological Association]

Myers-Scotton, Carol. 1990. Elite closure as boundary maintenance: The evidence from Africa. In Brian Weinstein (ed.), Language policy and political development, 25–41. Norwood, N.J.: Ablex.

———. 1991. Making ethnicity salient in codeswitching. In James R. Dow (ed.), Focus on language and ethnicity: Essays in honor of Joshua A. Fishman, 95–110. Amsterdam: Benjamins.

———. 1992. Codeswitching in Africa: A model of the social functions of code selection. In Robert K. Herbert (ed.), Sociolinguistics in Africa, 165–180. Johannesburg: University of the Witwaterstrand Press. (Keynote address, International Symposium on Sociolinguistics in Africa, University of the Witwaterstrand, South Africa, 2/90.)

———. 1993a. Common and uncommon ground: Social and structural factors in codeswitching. Language in Society 22:475–503.
———. 1993b. Duelling languages: Grammatical structure in codeswitching. Oxford: University Press (Clarendon).
———. 1993c. Elite closure as a powerful language strategy: The African case. International Journal of the Sociology of Language 103:149–63.
———. 1993d. Social motivations for codeswitching: Evidence from Africa. Oxford studies in language contact. Oxford: University Press (Clarendon).
———. 1995. A lexically-based production model of codeswitching. In Lesley Milroy and Pieter Muysken (eds.), One speaker, two languages: Cross-disciplinary perspectives on code-switching, 233–56. Cambridge: University Press.
———. 1995. What do speakers want? Codeswitching as evidence of intentionality in linguistic choices. In Pamela Silberman and Jonathan Loftin (eds.), SALSA 2 (Papers from the Symposium about Language and Society at Austin). Austin: University of Texas, Department of Linguistics.
———. 1997. 'Matrix language' and 'morpheme sorting' as possible structural strategies in pidgin/creole formation. In Arthur Spears and Donald Winford (eds.), Pidgins and creoles: Structure and status. Amsterdam: Benjamins.
Neijt, A. 1986. Esperanto as the focal point of machine translation. Multilingua 5:9–13.
Neustupný, J. V. 1962. Gengogaku to bungeigaku [Linguistics and the science of literature]. Eigo seinen [The Rising Generation] 108(3):1–3.
———. 1965. First steps towards the conception of 'Oriental languages'. Archiv orientální 33:63–92. [Reprinted as chapter 8 of Neustupný 1978.]
———. 1978. Post-structural approaches to language. Tokyo: University Press.
———. 1987. Communicating with the Japanese. Tokyo: Japan Times.
———. 1994. Problems of English contact discourse and language planning. In Thiru Kandiah and J. Kwan Terry (eds.), English and language planning: A Southeast Asian contribution, 50–69. Singapore: Times Academic Press.
Nida, Eugene A., ed. 1972. The book of a thousand tongues, second edition. New York: United Bible Societies.
North, Eric, ed. 1945. The book of a thousand tongues, first edition. New York: United Bible Societies.

Ogden, Charles K. and I. A. Richards. 1923. The meaning of meaning. London: Routledge. (Reprint. 1957.)
O'Leary, Clare F., ed. 1992. Sociolinguistic survey of Northern Pakistan, vols. 1–5. Islamabad: National Institutes of Pakistan Studies and Summer Institute of Linguistics.
Orton, Harold et al. 1962. Survey of English dialects. Introduction and 4 vols. in 12 parts. Leeds: Arnold.
Osgood, C. E. and Thomas A. Sebeok, eds. 1954. Psycholinguistics: A survey of theory and research problems. (Report of the 1953 summer seminar sponsored by the Committee on Linguistics and Psychology of the Social Science Research Council). Indiana University Research Center in Anthropology, Folklore, and Linguistics and Memoir 10 of International Journal of American Linguistics, supplement to International Journal of American Linguistics 20(4). (Also in the Journal of Abnormal and Social Psychology, supplement to 49(4).) Baltimore: Waverly. (Repub. 1965, Bloomington: Indiana University Press.)
Otanes, Fe T. and Bonifacio P. Sibayan. 1969. Language policy survey of the Philippines. Manila: Language Study Center, Philippine Normal College.
Pandit, P. B. 1972. India as a sociolinguistic area. Pune: University of Poona.
———. 1977. Language in a plural society: The case of India. Delhi: Dev Raj Channa Memorial Committee.
———. 1979. Perspectives on sociolinguistics in India. In William C. McCormack and Stephen A. Wurm (eds.), Language and Society: Anthropological Issues. The Hague: Mouton.
Pattanayak, D. P. 1975. Caste and language. International Journal of Dravidian Linguistics 4:97–104.
———. 1981. Multilingualism and mother tongue education. Delhi: Oxford University Press.
———, ed. 1978. Papers in Indian sociolinguistics. Mysore: Central Institute of Indian Languages.
Paulin, G. 1971. Monolingües y bilingües en la población de México en 1960: Estadísticas del proyecto sociolingüístico. Mexico City: Universidad Nacional Autónoma de México, Instituto de Investigaciones Sociales.
Peal, E. and Wallace E. Lambert. 1962. The relation of bilingualism to intelligence. Psychological Monographs No. 646.

Pearl, Stephen B. 1996. Changes in the pattern of language use in the United Nations. In Curt E. Müller (ed.), Language status in the post-cold-war era. Papers of the Center for Research and Documentation on World Language Problems, 29–42. West Hartford, Conn.: University Press of America.

Pierce, Joe E. 1952. Dialect distance testing in Algonquian. Internationl Journal of American Linguistics 18:203–10.

———. 1954. Crow versus Hidatsa in dialect distance and in glottochronology. International Journal of American Linguistics 20:134–36.

Pietrzyk, Alfred. 1967. Selected titles in sociolinguistics: An interim bibliography of works on multilingualism, language standardization, and languages of wider communication. Washington, D.C.: Center for Applied Linguistics.

Pike, Kenneth L. 1945a. Mock Spanish of a Mixteco Indian. International Journal of American Linguistics 11:219–24.

———. 1945b. Tone puns in Mixteco. International Journal of American Linguistics 11:129–39.

———. 1946. Another Mixteco tone pun. International Journal of American Linguistics 12:22–24.

———. 1954. Language in relation to a unified theory of the structure of human behavior. Glendale, Calif.: Summer Institute of Linguistics.

———. 1960. Toward a theory of change and bilingualism. Studies in Linguistics 15:1–7.

———. 1961. Stimulating and resisting change. Practical Anthropology 8:267–74.

———. 1967. Language in relation to a unified theory of the structure of human behavior. (2nd ed.) Janua linguarum, Series maior. The Hague: Mouton.

Pinker, Steven. 1989. Learnability and cognition: The acquisition of argument structure. Cambridge: MIT Press.

Pittman, Richard S., ed. 1951. Ethnologue. Glendale, Calif.: Wycliffe Bible Translators. (Rev. eds. 1952, 1954, 1958, 1965, 1969.)

Podder, A. 1969. Language and society in India: Proceedings of a seminar. Shimla: Indian Institute of Advanced Study.

Polomé, Edgar. 1963. Cultural languages and contact vernaculars in the Republic of Congo. Texas Studies in Literature and Languages 4:499–511.

———. 1975. Problems and techniques of a sociolinguistically oriented language survey: The case of the Tanzania survey. In S. Ohanessian, C. Ferguson, and E. Polomé (eds.), Language surveys in developing nations: Papers and reports on sociolinguistic surveys, 31–50. Arlington, Va.: Center for Applied Linguistics.

———. 1979. Studies in diachronic, synchronic, and typological linguistics. In Bela Brogyanyi (ed.), Festschrift for Oswald Szemerényi, 679–90. Amsterdam: Benjamins.

———. 1980. Creolization processes and diachronic linguistics. In A. Valdman and A. Highfield (eds.), Theoretical orientations in creole studies, 185–202. New York: Academic Press.

———. 1982a. Rural versus urban multilingualism in Tanzania: An outline. International Journal of the Sociology of Language 34:167–81.

———. 1982b. Sociolinguistically oriented language surveys: Reflections of the survey of language use and language teaching in Eastern Africa. Language in Society 11(2):265–83.

———. 1983a. Creolization and language change. In E. Wolford and W. Washabaugh (eds.), The social context of creolization, 126–36. Ann Arbor: Karoma.

———. 1983b. The linguistic situation in the western provinces of the Roman Empire. In H. Temporini and W. Haase (eds.), Aufstieg und Niedergang der römischen Welt: Geschichte und Kultur Roms im Spiegel der neueren Forschung, 509–53. Berlin: de Gruyter.

———. 1984. Standardization of Swahili. In C. Hagège and I. Fodor (eds.), Language reform: History and future, 53–77. Hamburg: Buske.

———. 1985. A study on the creole Shaba Swahili. In J. Maw and D. Parkin (eds.), Swahili language and society, 47–65. Vienna: Institut für Afrikanistik, Universität Wien.

———. 1988. A supplement to the study on the western provinces of the Roman Empire. Sociolinguistics 2:52–77.

———. 1989. Type of linguistic evidence for early contact: Indo-Europeans and non-Indo-Europeans. In T. Markey and J. Greppin (eds.), When worlds collide: Indo-Europeans and Pre-Indo-Europeans [The Bellagio papers], 267–89. Ann Arbor: Karoma.

———, P. C. Hill, and N. H. Kuhanga. 1980. The languages of Tanzania. Oxford: University Press for the International African Institute Series (Ford Foundation Language Surveys).

———, André Polomé, and Ali Abdullah. 1983. Language and religion in Tanzania. Orbis 30:42–67.

Porter, Doris. 1991. Language-culture types and their implications for vernacular literature use. In Gloria E. Kindell (ed.), Proceedings of the Summer Institute of Linguisics International Language Assessment Conference, Horsleys Green, 23–31 May 1989, 111–19. Dallas: Summer Institute of Linguistics.

Prator, Clifford H. 1950. Language teaching in the Philippines. Manila: U. S. Educational Foundation.

Prettol, Kenneth A. 1992. Toward a decision support tool for language planners: An expert system application. M.A. thesis. University of Texas at Arlington.

Pride, J. B. and Janet Holmes. 1972. Sociolinguistics. Baltimore: Penguin.

Prudent, Lambert-Félix. 1980. Diglossie ou continuum? Quelques concepts problématiques de la créolistique moderne appliqués à l'Archipel Caraïbe. Actes du Colloque organisé du 27 novembre au 2 décembre par le GRECO, Université de Rouen, Faculté des Lettres de Mont-Saint-Aignan, 583–94. In Bernard Gardin and Jean Baptiste Marcellesi (eds.), Sociolinguistique: Approches, théories, pratiques, 197–210. Paris: Publication of the University of France.

———. 1979. Du baragouin à la langue antillaise: Analyse historique et sociolinguistique du discours sur le créole martiniquais. Thèse de doctorat du troisième cycle, Université de Rouen. Paris: Editions Caribéennes.

———. 1980. Les processus de la minoration linguistique: Un coup d'oeil à la situation antillaise et à la créolistique. In Jean Baptiste Marcellesi (ed.), Sociolinguistique: Approches, théories, pratiques, 68–84. Paris: Publication of the University of France.

Quakenbush, J. Stephen. 1986. Language use and proficiency in a multilingual setting: A sociolinguistic survey of Agutaynen speakers in Palawan, Philippines. Ph.D. dissertation. Georgetown University.

Quemada, Bernard and John Ross. 1976. Le français dans le monde. Pour une sociolinguistique appliquée 121.

Radloff, Carla F. 1991. Sentence repetition testing for studies of community bilingualism. Summer Institute of Linguistics and the University of Texas at Arlington Publications in Linguistics 104. Dallas.

Rensch, Calvin R., Sandra J. Decker, and Daniel G. Hallberg. 1992. Languages of Kohistan. Sociolinguistic survey of Northern Pakistan 1. Islamabad: National Institutes of Pakistan Studies and Summer Institute of Linguistics.

———, Calinda E. Hallberg, and Clare F. O'Leary. 1992. Hindko and Gujari. Sociolinguistic survey of Northern Pakistan 3. Islamabad: National Institutes of Pakistan Studies and Summer Institute of Linguistics.

Rice, Frank A., ed. 1962. Study of the role of second languages: In Asia, Africa, and Latin America. Washington, D.C.: Center for Applied Linguistics of the Modern Language Association of America.

Richard-Zapella, Jeanine. 1991. Linguistique et materialisme. Cahiers de Linguistique Sociale 17.

Roberts, Janet. 1962. Sociocultural change and communication problems. In Frank A. Rice (ed.), Study of the role of second languages: In Asia, Africa, and Latin America, 105–23 Washington, D.C.: Center for Applied Linguistics.

Robinson, Clinton D. W. 1992. Language choice in rural development. International Museum of Cultures Publication 26. Dallas.

Rose, Edward. 1964. Small languages, vols. 1 and 2. Boulder, Colo.: Bureau of Sociological Research. Reports 14, 15.

Rubin, Joan. 1968. National bilingualism in Paraguay. Janua linguarum, Series practica 60. The Hague: Mouton.

—— and Björn Jernudd, eds. 1971. Can language be planned? Sociolinguistic theory and practice for developing nations. Honolulu: University Press of Hawaii.

—— Björn H. Jernudd, Jyotirindra Das Gupta, Charles A. Ferguson, and Joshua A. Fishman. 1977. Language planning processes: Contributions to the sociology of language 21. The Hague: Mouton.

—— and R. W. Shuy. 1972. Language planning: Current issues and research. Washington, D.C.: Georgetown University Press.

Ruhlen, Merritt. 1976. A guide to the languages of the world. Stanford: Language Universals Project, Stanford University Press.

Sadler, Victor and Ulrich Lins. 1991. Regardless of frontiers: A case study in linguistic persecution. In Samir K. Ghosh (ed.), Man, language, and society, 206–15 The Hague: Mouton.

Sandefur, John R. 1984. A language coming of age: Kriol of North Australia. M.A. thesis. University of Western Australia.

Sankoff, Gillian. 1969. Mutual intelligibility, bilingualism and linguistic boundaries. In International days of sociolinguistics, 839–48. Rome: Istituto Luigi Sturzo.

——. 1971. Language use in multilingual societies: Some structural approaches. In John B. Pride and Janet Holmes (eds.), Sociolinguistics, 31–51. Harmondsworth: Penguin.

Sapir, Edward. 1921. Language: An introduction to the study of speech. New York: Harcourt.

Savard, J. G. and R. Vigneault, eds. 1976. Multilingual political systems: Problems and solutions/Les états multilingues: problèmes et solutions. (Centre International de Recherche sur le Bilinguisme Publication A-9.) Québec: Laval University Press.

References

Schaechter, Mordkhe. 1982. Uriel Weinreich. Encyclopedia Judaica 16:405–6.
Schatzman, Leonard and Anselm Strauss. 1955. Social class and modes of communication. American Journal of Sociology 60:682–89.
Schooling, Stephen J. 1990. Language maintenance in Melanesia: Sociolinguistics and social networks in New Caledonia. Summer Instiute of Linguistics and the University of Texas at Arlington Publications in Linguistics 91. Dallas.
Schubert, Klaus and Dan Maxwell, eds. 1972. Interlinguistics: Aspects of the science of planned languages. Berlin: Mouton de Gruyter.
Scotton, Carol Myers. 1965. Some Swahili political words. Journal of Modern African Studies 3:527–42.
———. 1972. Choosing a lingua franca in an African capital. Monograph series in sociolinguistics. Edmonton: Linguistic Research, Inc.
———. 1976a. The role of norms and other factors in language choice in work situations in three African cities (Lagos, Kampala, Nairobi). In Rolf Kjolseth and Albert Verdoodt (eds.), Language and society, 201–32. Louvain: Editions Peeters.
———. 1976b. Strategies of neutrality: Language choice in uncertain situations. Language 52:919–41.
———. 1977. Bilingual strategies: The social function of codeswitching. International Journal of the Sociology of Language 13:5–20. (Also in Linguistics 193, with William Ury.)
———. 1978. Language in East Africa: Linguistic patterns and political ideologies. In Joshua A. Fishman (ed.), Advances in the study of societal multilingualism, 719–60. The Hague: Mouton.
———. 1982a. Learning lingua francas and socioeconomic integration: Evidence from Africa. In Richard L. Cooper and Bernard Barber (eds.), Language spread: Studies in diffusion and social change, 69–94. Washington, D.C.: Center for Applied Linguistics.
———. 1982b. The linguistic situation and language policy in Eastern Africa. In Robert B. Kaplan (ed.), Annual Review of Applied Linguistics, 8–20. Rowley, Mass.: Newbury.
———. 1982c. An urban-rural comparison of language use among the Luyia in Kenya. International Journal of the Sociology of Language 34:121–36.
———. 1983a. The negotiation of identities in conversation: A theory of markedness and code choice. International Journal of the Sociology of Language 44:115–36.
———. 1983b. 'Tongzhi' in Chinese conversational consequences of language change. In Language in Society 12:477–94. (with Zhu Wanjin. Translated into Chinese for Readings in Sociolinguistics.)

———. 1985. What the heck, sir? Style shifting and lexical colouring as features of powerful language. In Richard L. Street, Jr. and Joseph N. Cappella (eds.), Sequence and pattern in communicative behavior, 103–19. London: Arnold.

———. 1988a. Codeswitching and types of multilingual communities. In Peter Lowenberg (ed.), Georgetown University Round Table on Languages and Linguistics 1987, 61–82. Washington, D.C.: Georgetown University Press.

———. 1988b. Codeswitching as indexical of social negotiation. In Monica Heller (ed.), Codeswitching: Anthropological and sociolinguistic perspectives, 151–86. The Hague: Mouton de Gruyter.

———. 1988c. Patterns of bilingualism in East Africa. In Christina Bratt Paulston (ed.), International handbook of bilingualism and bilingual education, 203–24. Westport, Conn.: Greenwood.

———. 1988d. Self-enhancing codeswitching as interactional power. Language and Communication 8:139–211.

——— and John Okeju. 1973. Neighbors and lexical borrowings: A study of two Ateso dialects. Language 49:871–89.

Shapiro, Michael C. and Harold F. Schiffman. 1975. Language and Society in South Asia. Washington, D.C.: University Press. (Also 1981. Delhi: Motilal Banarsidass.)

Shell, Olive A., ed. 1988. Papers presented to the miniconference on vernacular literacy at Stanford, July 24–25, 1987. Notes on Literacy 54.

Showalter, Catherine J. 1991. Getting what you ask for: A study of sociolinguistic survey questionnaires. In Gloria E. Kindell (ed.), Proceedings of the Summer Institute of Linguisics International Language Assessment Conference, Horsleys Green, 23–31 May 1989, 203–22. Dallas: Summer Institute of Linguistics.

Showalter, Stuart D. 1991. Surveying sociolinguistic aspects of interethnic contact in rural Burkina Faso: An adaptive methodological approach. Ph.D. dissertation. Georgetown University.

Shuy, Roger W., ed. 1965. Social dialects and language learning. Champaign, Ill.: National Council of the Teachers of English.

———. 1971. Sociolinguistics, a cross-disciplinary perspective. Washington, D.C.: Center for applied Linguistics.

———. 1972. Sociolinguistics: Current trends and prospects. Georgetown University Monograph Series on Languages and Linguistics 25.

———. 1988. The social context of the study of the social context of language variation. In Thomas J. Walsh (ed.), Synchronic and diachronic approaches to linguistic variation and change, 293–309. Washington, D.C.: Georgetown University Press.

———. 1990. A brief history of American Sociolinguistics, 1949–1989. In Historigraphia Linguistica 17(1, 2):183–209. (Reprinted in this volume).

——— and Ralph W. Fasold. 1973. Language attitudes: Current trends and prospects. Washington, D.C.: Georgetown University Press.

Sibayan, Bonifacio P. 1967. Implementation of language policy. In Maxio Ramos, Jose V. Aguilar, and Bonifacio P. Sibayan (eds.), The determination and implementation of language policy, part III, 126–89. Quezon City: Alemar-Phoenix [Philippine Center for Language Studies Monograph No. 2].

———. 1971. Language policy, language engineering and literacy: Philippines. In Thomas A. Sebeok (ed.), Current trends in linguistics 8(2):1038–62. (Revised version in Joshua A. Fishman (ed.), Advances in language planning, 221–54. The Hague: Mouton.)

——— and Andrew B. Gonzalez, eds. 1991. Sociolinguistic studies in the Philippines. International Journal of the Sociology of Language 88.

Simons, Gary F. 1979. Language variation and limits to communication. Technical Report No. 3, NSF Grant No. BNS 76–006031. Department of Modern Languages and Linguistics, Cornell University; repub. 1983, Dallas: Summer Insitute of Linguistics.

Slobin, Dan I., ed. 1967. A field manual for cross-cultural study of the acquisition of communicative competence. Berkeley: Institute of Human Learning [now Institute of Cognitive Studies].

Smith, D. M. and Roger M. Shuy. 1972. Sociolinguistics in cross-cultural analysis. Washington, D.C.: Georgetown University Press.

Snow, Catherine and Charles A. Ferguson. 1977. Talking to children: Language input and acquisition. New York: Cambridge University Press.

Sorensen, Arthur P., Jr. 1967. Multilingualism in the northwest Amazon. American Anthropologist 69(6):670–82.

Soskin, W. F. and V. John. 1963. The study of spontaneous talk. In R. G. Barker (ed.), The stream of behavior. New York: Appleton.

Southworth, Franklin C. 1975. Sociolinguistic research in South India: Achievements and prospects. In S. Burton (ed.), Essays on South India. New Delhi: Vikas.

Sperber, Dan and Deirdre Wilson. 1986. Relevance: Communication and cognition. Oxford: Blackwell. (Reissued Cambridge: Harvard University Press; 1987, Precis of relevance: Communication, and cognition. Behavioral and Brain Sciences 10:697–710.)
Stoltzfus, Ronald Dean. 1974. Toward defining centers for indigenous literature programs: A problem of language communication. M.A. thesis. Cornell University.
Summer Institute of Linguistics. 1987. Second language oral proficiency evaluation (SLOPE). Notes on Linguistics 40:24–54.
———. 1992. Bibliography of the Summer Institute of Linguistics. Dallas: Summer Institute of Linguistics.
Sumpf, Joseph. 1968. Sociolinguistique. Langages 11.
Švejcer, A. D. and L. B. Nikol'skij. 1986. Introduction to Sociolinguistics. Amsterdam: Benjamins. (Translated from the Russian, published in 1978. Vvedenie v sociolingvistiku. Moscow: Vyssaja skola.)
Symoens, Edward. 1989. Bibliografio de disertacioj pri Esperanto kaj interlingvistiko/Dissertations sur l'espéranto et l'interlin- guistique/ Dissertations on Esperanto and Interlinguistics. Rotterdam: Universala Esperanto-Asocio.
Tabouret-Keller, Andrée. 1972. A contribution to the sociological study of language maintenance and language shift. In Joshua A. Fishman (ed.), Advances in the sociology of language 2, Selected studies and applications, 365–76. The Hague: Mouton.
———. 1976. Plurilinguisme: Revue des travaux français de 1945 à 1973. La Linguistique 11(2).
———, ed. 1982. Entre bilinguisme et diglossie: Du malaise des cloisonnements universitaires au malaise social. Linguistique 18:17–43.
Thibaut, John and Harold Kelley. 1959. The social psychology of groups. New York: Wiley.
Thiers, Jacques. 1989. Papier(s) d'identité. Albania: Levie.
Tokushuu. 1988. Sinpojiumu 'Shakai gengogaku no riron to hoohoo: Nihon to Oobei no apuroochi [Symposium 'Sociolinguistic theory and methods': Japanese and Western approaches]. Gengo kenkyuu 93:96–174.
Tonkin, Humphrey. 1968. Code or culture: The case of Esperanto. Era (University of Pennsylvania) 4(2):5–21.

———. 1983. World communications year and the new world information and communication order: Their significance for the teacher of foreign languages. In Humphrey Tonkin (ed.), World Communications Year 1983: Language and language learning, 11–40. (Report of a conference sponsored by the Center for Research and Documentation on World Language Problems and Esperantic Studies Foundation, New York, December 15, 1982.) New York: Center for Research and Documentation on World Language Problems.

———. 1983. Language and international communication. In Desmond Fisher and L. S. Harms (ed.), The right to communicate: A new human right, 185–95. Dublin: Boole Press.

———. 1984. A right to international communication? In George Gerbner and Marsha Siefert (eds.), World communications: A handbook, 69–79. New York: Longman.

Tournier, Maurice. 1978. Des tracts en mai. Champ libre. (Also 1978 repub. Fondation Nationale des Sciences Politique.)

Travaux. 1966. Travaux linguistique de Prague 2. Prague: Academia.

Tryon, D. T. and Malcolm Ross, eds. 1995. Comparative Austronesian dictionary: An introduction to Austronesian studies. Berlin; New York: Mouton de Gruyter

Uribe Villegas, Oscar. 1970. Sociolingüistica: Una introducción a su estudio. Mexico City: Universidad Nacional Autónoma de México, Instituto de Investigaciones Sociales.

Vachek, J. 1966. The linguistic school of Prague. Bloomington: Indiana University Press.

Verdoodt, Albert. 1974. Applied sociolinguistics. Heidelberg: Gross Verlag.

——— and Rolf Kjolseth. 1976. Language in sociology. (Institut de Linguistique de Louvain, Bibliotheque des Cahiers de l'Institut de Linguistique de Louvain #5.) Louvain: Editions Peeters.

Voegelin, Carl F. and Zellig S. Harris. 1951. Methods for determining intelligibility among dialects of natural languages. Proceedings of the American Philosophical Society 95:322–29.

——— and Florence M. Voegelin. 1964–1966. Languages of the world. Anthropological Linguistics 6:3–8:7.

——— and Florence M. Voegelin. 1977. Classification and index of the world's languages. New York: Elsevier.

Vološinov, see Bakhtine, Mikhail.

Wald, Paul and Gabriel Manessy. 1979. Bulletin du centre d'étude des plurilinguismes; 5 numéros parus. University of Nice.

Walker, Roland W. 1987. Towards a model for predicting the acceptance of vernacular literacy by minority-language groups. Ph.D. dissertation. University of California at Los Angeles.

Wallace, Anthony F. C. 1961. Culture and personality. New York: Random. (2nd ed. 1970.)

Ward, Robert. 1977. National needs for international education. Center for Strategic International Studies Monograph, Georgetown University.

Watters, John R. 1991. Three socioeconomic factors affecting the nature and development of language programs. In Gloria E. Kindell (ed.), Proceedings of the Summer Institute of Linguistics International Language Assessment Conference, Horsleys Green, 23–31 May 1989, 105–9. Dallas: Summer Institute of Linguistics.

Weber, David J., H. Andrew Black, and Stephen R. McConnell. 1988. AMPLE: A tool for exploring morphology. Occasonal Papers in Academic Computing 12. Dallas: Summer Institute of Linguistics.

———, Stephen R. McConnell, H. Andrew Black, and Alan Buseman. 1990. STAMP: A tool for dialect adaptation. Occasonal Papers in Academic Computing 15. Dallas: Summer Institute of Linguistics.

Weinreich, Uriel. 1944. Di velshishe shprakh in kamf far ir kiyem. Yivo-bleter 23:225–48.

———. 1950. College Yiddish. (Preface by Roman Jacobson) New York: Yiddish Scientific Institute for Jewish Research (5th rev. ed. 1971; 5th printing 1992).

———. 1951. Research problems in bilingualism, with special reference to Switzerland. Ph.D. dissertation. Columbia University. (Dissertation Abstracts 1952, 12:418–19.)

———. 1953a. Di shveyster romantshn arbetn farn kiyem fun zeyer shprakh. Bleter far yidsher dertsiyung 5:68–76.

———. 1953b. Languages in contact. New York: Linguistic Circle of New York. (8th printing 1974: The Hague: Mouton.)

———. 1953c. Review of J. B. Carroll, The study of language. Word 9:277–79.

———. 1953d. The Russification of Soviet minority languages. Problems of Communism 2:46–57.

———. 1957. Functional aspects of Indian bilingualism. Word 13:203–33.

———. 1960. Mid-century linguistics: Attainments and frustrations. Romance Linguistics 13:320–41.

———. 1966. Explorations in semantic theory. In Current Trends in Linguistics. The Hague: Mouton. 3:395–477. (Translated into German in 1979: Erkundungen zur Theorie der Semantik. Tubingen: Niemeyer; published as an English book in 1972: Explorations in Semantic Theory. The Hague: Mouton; and into Portuguese in 1977: Lucia M. P. Lobato, ed. A semântica na lingüística moderna o léxico. Rio de Janeiro: Francisco Alvez).

———. 1968. Modern English-Yiddish, Yiddish-English dictionary. New York: Yiddish Scientific Institute for Jewish Research. (4th printing 1990.)

———. 1980. On semantics (William Labov and Beatrice S. Weinreich, eds.). Philadelphia: University Press of Pennsylvania.

———. 1992. Language and culture atlas of Ashkenazic Jewry, vol. 1: Historical and theoretical foundations. ("Prepared and published under the aegis of an editorial collegium: Vera L. Bavisker, Marvin Herzog [editor in chief], Ulrike Kiefer, Robert Neuman, Wolfgang Putschke, Andrew Sunshine and Uriel Weinreich." Vol. 2, Research tools.) Tubingen: Niemeyer.

———, William Labov, and Mavis I. Herzog. 1968. Empirical foundations for a theory of language change. In W. P. Lehmann and Y. Malkiel (eds.), Directions for historical linguistics: A symposium, 95–195. Austin: University Press.

Wetherill, G. Barrie and Marie C. South. 1993. The use of regression and correlation in the assessment of speech repetition test trials. Second International Language Assessment Conference, Horsleys Green, England, June 2–9, 1993.

Whatmough, J. 1956. Language: A modern synthesis. New York: St. Martin's Press.

Whiteley, Wilfred H. 1969. Swahili, the rise of a national language. Studies in African History 3. London: Methuen.

Whorf, Benjamin Lee. 1956. Language, thought, and reality: Selected writings. Cambridge: MIT.

Wimbish, John S. 1989. WORDSURV: A program for analyzing language survey word lists. Occasonal Papers in Academic Computing 13. Dallas: Summer Institute of Linguistics.

Wolff, Hans. 1964. Intelligibility and inter-ethnic attitudes. In Dell Hymes (ed.), Language in culture and society: A reader in linguistics and anthropology, 440–45. New York: Harper and Row.

———. 1967. Language, ethnic identity and social change in southern Nigeria. Anthropological Linguistics 9:18–25.

Wolfram, Walt. 1969. A sociolinguistic description of Detroit Negro Speech. Washington, D.C.: Center for Applied Linguistics.
Wood, Richard E. 1979. A voluntary, non-territorial speech community. In William Francis Mackey and Jacob Ornstein (eds.), Sociolinguistic studies in language contact: Methods and cases, 433–50. The Hague: Mouton.
Zipf, G. K. 1949. Human behavior and the principle of least effort: An introduction to human ecology. Cambridge: Addison-Wesley.